T0408533

Call Me by
Your Name

Trajectories of Italian Cinema and Media

Series editor: Flavia Laviosa
Print ISSN 2632-487 | **Online ISSN** 2632-488

The book series Trajectories of Italian Cinema and Media intends to engage with diverse academic communities, build new conceptual frameworks and foster a globally focused and representative corpus of scholarship in Italian cinema and media studies. With the aim of exploring new critical and historical trajectories, this book series will trace the evidence of Italian cinema's international polysemy and polycentrism, define the extent of its inspirational force, examine other cinemas' artistic innovations resulting from their osmosis with the Italian film tradition, and foster comparative analyses of themes and genres between Italian and other world cinemas.

If you wish to propose a manuscript to be included in the series, please contact the series editor Flavia Laviosa (flaviosa@wellesley.edu).

In this series:

Fellini's Films and Commercials: From Postwar to Postmodern, by Frank Burke (2020)

Paolo Sorrentino's Cinema and Television, edited by Annachiara Mariani (2021)

Pasta, Pizza and Propaganda: A Political History of Italian Food TV, by Francesco Buscemi (2022)

The Many Meanings of Mina: Popular Music Stardom in Post-war Italy, by Rachel Haworth (2022)

Women's Work in Post-War Italy: In Oral History and Film, by Flora Derounian (2023)

Call Me by Your Name: *Perspectives on the Film*, edited by Edward Lamberti and Michael Williams (2024)

Call Me by Your Name

Perspectives on the Film

EDITED BY

Edward Lamberti and Michael Williams

Bristol, UK / Chicago, USA

First published in the UK in 2024 by
Intellect, The Mill, Parnall Road, Fishponds, Bristol, BS16 3JG, UK

First published in the USA in 2024 by
Intellect, The University of Chicago Press, 1427 E. 60th Street,
Chicago, IL 60637, USA

Copy editor: MPS Limited
Cover designer: Tanya Montefusco
Cover image: Croatian Apoxyomenos (detail), 4th century BC (original).
Credits: The Picture Art Collection / Alamy Stock Photo. | Water Background.
Credit: sbayram. Stock photo ID:155137107.
Production manager: Debora Nicosia
Typesetter: MPS Limited

Hardback ISBN 978-1-78938-942-5
ePDF ISBN 978-1-78938-944-9
ePUB ISBN 978-1-78938-943-2

To find out about all our publications, please visit our website.
There you can subscribe to our e-newsletter, browse or download our current
catalogue and buy any titles that are in print.

www.intellectbooks.com

This is a peer-reviewed publication.

Contents

List of Figures   vii

List of Tables   xi

Acknowledgements   xiii

Introduction: Somewhere in Northern Italy   1
Edward Lamberti and Michael Williams

PART I: STYLE   15

1. Temporary Paradise: Queer Space, Time and Pastoral Visions in *Call Me by Your Name*   17
   Adam Vaughan

2. 'But You Know, There Have Been Queer Characters from the Very First Film': *Call Me by Your Name* and the Long Shadow of James Ivory   34
   Claire Monk

3. 'Is It Better to Speak or Die?': Adaptation and Elio's Interiority   58
   Stuart Richards

4. Music as Narrator in *Call Me by Your Name*   76
   Kingsley Marshall

5. Sex Sounds: On Aural Explicitness in *Call Me by Your Name*   91
   Sarah Artt

6. *Call Me by Your Name* and the Ethics of Distance   110
   Edward Lamberti

PART II: THEMES   129

7. *Call Me by Your Name*, Chrononormativity and the (Queer?)   131
   Future of Italian Teen Film
   Daniel Paul

8. Plato to Elio: Ancient and Modern Sexualities in *Call Me by*   151
   Your Name
   Nikolai Endres

9. 'Daring You to Desire Them': Digital Classicism, Star Bodies   171
   and *Call Me by Your Name*
   Michael Williams

10. Call Me Bi Any Other Name: Anal Monstration, Formal   198
    Bisexualization, Gay Indigestion
    Jacob Engelberg

PART III: RECEPTION   225

11. *Call Me by Your Name* and Film Festivals   227
    Ruby Cheung

12. Tell Tim Chalamet to Tweet at Me: Situating Timothée   253
    Chalamet's Social Media Presence and Perceived (B)Romance
    with Armie Hammer
    Francesca Sobande

13. The Sexiest Risk-Taker? Armie Hammer, White Masculinity   270
    and *Call Me by Your Name*
    Jonathan A. Cannon

14. 'Finally, a Gay Movie without a Bad Vibe': Queer Nostalgia,   285
    Affection and Gender Identity in *Call Me by Your Name*
    Vinicius Ferreira, Victor Schlude and Gêsa Cavalcanti

Notes on Contributors   313
Index   319

Figures

1.1: An ecstatic retreat into nature: Elio (Timothée Chalamet) and 20
Oliver (Armie Hammer) explore their relationship in the
Bergamo Alps. Luca Guadagnino (dir.), *Call Me by Your Name*,
2017. Italy/France/USA/Brazil. © Frenesy, La Cinefacture.

1.2: The spectre of AIDS threatens to pierce Elio (Timothée Chalamet) 29
and Oliver's (Armie Hammer) rural idyll. Luca Guadagnino (dir.),
Call Me by Your Name, 2017. Italy/France/USA/Brazil. © Frenesy,
La Cinefacture.

2.1: *Maurice*: 'Happiness is its keynote.' Maurice (James Wilby) with Clive 38
(Hugh Grant) (top row); Maurice with Alec (Rupert Graves) (other rows).
James Ivory (dir.), *Maurice*, 1987. UK. © Maurice Productions Limited.

2.2: Problematic parallels – top: the most meme-tically cited romantic 42
parallel between Maurice (James Wilby) and Clive (Hugh Grant)
and Oliver (Armie Hammer) and Elio (Timothée Chalamet); below:
a more instructive parallel, as Clive resists Maurice's advances and
Elio mounts Oliver. James Ivory (dir.), *Maurice*, 1987. UK. © Maurice
Productions Limited; Luca Guadagnino (dir.), *Call Me by Your Name*,
2017. Italy/France/USA/Brazil. © Frenesy, La Cinefacture.

2.3: Ivory's queer prodigies: Francis (Anthony Roth Costanzo) vs. 46
Elio (Timothée Chalamet). James Ivory (dir.), *A Soldier's Daughter
Never Cries*, 1998. USA/UK/France. © Capitol Films, Merchant
Ivory Productions; Luca Guadagnino (dir.), *Call Me by Your Name*,
2017. Italy/France/USA/Brazil. © Frenesy, La Cinefacture.

3.1: Elio (Timothée Chalamet) realizes Oliver's absence and his body 59
betrays him. Luca Guadagnino (dir.), *Call Me by Your Name*, 2017.
Italy/France/USA/Brazil. © Frenesy, La Cinefacture.

3.2:   A moment of impatient rage (Timothée Chalamet as Elio and Armie   63
       Hammer as Oliver). Luca Guadagnino (dir.), *Call Me by Your Name*,
       2017. Italy/France/USA/Brazil. © Frenesy, La Cinefacture.

3.3:   Elio's (Timothée Chalamet) demeanour eases once at Monet's Berm.   68
       Luca Guadagnino (dir.), *Call Me by Your Name*, 2017. Italy/France/
       USA/Brazil. © Frenesy, La Cinefacture.

3.4:   The peach scene becomes a moment of vulnerability rather than   71
       unification (Timothée Chalamet as Elio and Armie Hammer as
       Oliver). Luca Guadagnino (dir.), *Call Me by Your Name*, 2017.
       Italy/France/USA/Brazil. © Frenesy, La Cinefacture.

4.1:   Elio (Timothée Chalamet) performs his own interpretation of   78
       a Bach piece for Oliver (Armie Hammer) on the piano. Luca
       Guadagnino (dir.), *Call Me by Your Name*, 2017. Italy/France/
       USA/Brazil. © Frenesy, La Cinefacture.

5.1:   Restless with desire: the sound of Elio's (Timothée Chalamet) body   96
       evokes feeling and touch and heightens the eroticizing gaze. Luca
       Guadagnino (dir.), *Call Me by Your Name*, 2017. Italy/France/
       USA/Brazil. © Frenesy, La Cinefacture.

5.2:   A flexing of thighs against groin. Luca Guadagnino (dir.), *Call Me by*   98
       Your Name, 2017. Italy/France/USA/Brazil. © Frenesy, La Cinefacture.

5.3:   The sound of mouth, tongue and wetness: Oliver (Armie   100
       Hammer) orally stimulates Elio (Timothée Chalamet). Luca
       Guadagnino (dir.), *Call Me by Your Name*, 2017. Italy/France/
       USA/Brazil. © Frenesy, La Cinefacture.

5.4:   The aural bottom: invoking and subverting the conventions   103
       of pornography. Luca Guadagnino (dir.), *Call Me by Your*
       Name, 2017. Italy/France/USA/Brazil. © Frenesy, La Cinefacture.

6.1:   'Call me by your name and I'll call you by mine': Oliver (Armie   116
       Hammer) and Elio (Timothée Chalamet) together but also separate
       from each other. Luca Guadagnino (dir.), *Call Me by Your Name*,
       2017. Italy/France/USA/Brazil. © Frenesy, La Cinefacture.

6.2:   Elio (Timothée Chalamet) and Oliver (Armie Hammer) ride into   120
       the distance and the magic of love's adventure sinks in. Luca
       Guadagnino (dir.), *Call Me by Your Name*, 2017. Italy/France/
       USA/Brazil. © Frenesy, La Cinefacture.

6.3: Elio (Timothée Chalamet) is wearing his rucksack when he first   123
      confesses his feelings to Oliver (Armie Hammer) and is wearing
      the same rucksack as he watches Oliver's train leaving the station.
      Luca Guadagnino (dir.), *Call Me by Your Name*, 2017. Italy/
      France/USA/Brazil. © Frenesy, La Cinefacture.

7.1: Oliver (Armie Hammer) and Elio (Timothée Chalamet) enjoy the   134
      dolce far niente way of life. Luca Guadagnino (dir.), *Call Me by Your
      Name*, 2017. Italy/France/USA/Brazil. © Frenesy, La Cinefacture.

7.2: Elio's (Timothée Chalamet) watch. Luca Guadagnino (dir.), *Call Me by*   138
      Your Name, 2017. Italy/France/USA/Brazil. © Frenesy, La Cinefacture.

8.1: Oliver (Armie Hammer) contemplates Elio's (Timothée Chalamet)   160
      peach. Luca Guadagnino (dir.), *Call Me by Your Name*, 2017.
      Italy/France/USA/Brazil. © Frenesy, La Cinefacture.

9.1: The bronze *Athlete* frames the introduction of Armie Hammer   174
      and Timothée Chalamet in the opening titles. Luca Guadagnino
      (dir.), *Call Me by Your Name*, 2017. Italy/France/USA/Brazil.
      © Frenesy, La Cinefacture.

9.2: The '*Farnese* Oliver' and '*Spinario* Elio': Oliver (Armie Hammer)   177
      stands *contrapposto* in the doorway as Elio (Timothée Chalamet)
      plays the piano; at the end of the scene Oliver is mirroring Elio's
      pose. Luca Guadagnino (dir.), *Call Me by Your Name*, 2017.
      Italy/France/USA/Brazil. © Frenesy, La Cinefacture.

9.3: Reaching out and touching: interchangeable views of the statue/   181
      Elio (Timothée Chalamet). Luca Guadagnino (dir.), *Call Me by Your
      Name*, 2017. Italy/France/USA/Brazil. © Frenesy, La Cinefacture.

9.4: Elio (Timothée Chalamet) in the final shot of *Call Me by Your   183
      Name*. Luca Guadagnino (dir.), *Call Me by Your Name*, 2017.
      Italy/France/USA/Brazil. © Frenesy, La Cinefacture; Troye Sivan
      in his 2013 YouTube video, 'Coming Out'.

9.5: Timothée Chalamet encounters his 'chalametinart' Instagram composite   186
      on *The Tonight Show Starring Jimmy Fallon* (NBC), 10 October 2018.

10.1: Elio (Timothée Chalamet) and Marzia (Esther Garrel): a   207
      (barely perceptible) moment not of idealized sexual union but of
      sweet sexual clumsiness. Luca Guadagnino (dir.), *Call Me by Your
      Name*, 2017. Italy/France/USA/Brazil. © Frenesy, La Cinefacture.

10.2:   Elio (Timothée Chalamet) gazing upon the embrace of Chiara   208
        (Victoire du Bois) and Oliver (Armie Hammer) the morning
        after the party. Luca Guadagnino (dir.), *Call Me by Your Name*,
        2017. Italy/France/USA/Brazil. © Frenesy, La Cinefacture.

10.3:   Marzia (Esther Garrel), Oliver (Armie Hammer) and Elio   209
        (Timothée Chalamet) touch in a moment equally caring and
        erotic. Luca Guadagnino (dir.), *Call Me by Your Name*, 2017.
        Italy/France/USA/Brazil. © Frenesy, La Cinefacture.

12.1:   Elio (Timothée Chalamet) and Oliver (Armie Hammer) lying   256
        down in the grass. Luca Guadagnino (dir.), *Call Me by Your
        Name*, 2017. Italy/France/USA/Brazil. © Frenesy, La Cinefacture.

12.2:   Elio (Timothée Chalamet) shaking a statue's hand which   258
        Oliver (Armie Hammer) is holding out to him. In the background
        is Lake Garda. Luca Guadagnino (dir.), *Call Me by Your Name*,
        2017. Italy/France/USA/Brazil. © Frenesy, La Cinefacture.

13.1:   The sexiest risk-taker? Armie Hammer with Timothée Chalamet   273
        on *The Ellen DeGeneres Show*, 2017.

13.2:   Armie Hammer as Billy Graham. Robby Benson (dir.), *Billy:*   276
        The Early Years, 2008. USA. © SOLEX/MATP Productions.

13.3:   Elio (Timothée Chalamet) and Oliver (Armie Hammer) meet   277
        for the first time. Luca Guadagnino (dir.), *Call Me by Your Name*,
        2017. Italy/France/USA/Brazil. © Frenesy, La Cinefacture.

14.1:   Lovers in the grass: James Wilby and Hugh Grant. James   294
        Ivory (dir.), *Maurice*, 1987. UK. © Maurice Productions
        Limited; Timothée Chalamet and Armie Hammer. Luca
        Guadagnino (dir.), *Call Me by Your Name*, 2017. Italy/France/
        USA/Brazil. © Frenesy, La Cinefacture.

14.2:   Video 1: Screen grab from Federico Devito's YouTube video   297
        'Assista: CALL ME BY YOUR NAME!', 2018.

14.3:   Video 2: Screen grab from Caio Braz's YouTube video   297
        'CALL ME BY YOUR NAME É O FILME MAIS LINDO
        QUE EXISTE', 2018.

14.4:   Video 3: Screen grab from Pink Popcorn's YouTube video 'ME   298
        CHAME PELO SEU NOME / O que achei / Pink Popcorn', 2018.

Tables

11.1:	*Call Me by Your Name* and its film festival screenings.	236
11.2:	FIAPF-accredited film festivals (2017 Edition) that screened *Call Me by Your Name* in 2017–18.	240
14.1:	Analysis universe.	296
14.2:	Examples of comments expressing the category Plot relevance.	300
14.3:	Further examples of comments expressing the category Plot relevance.	301
14.4:	Examples of comments expressing the category LGBTQIA+ approach.	302
14.5:	Examples of comments expressing the category Self-representation.	303

Acknowledgements

The seed for this collection was planted at the inspiring conference 'Straight to the Front Row: Investigating Contemporary Western Gay Male Cinema' held at the University of Northampton in 2019 where we both presented papers on *Call Me by Your Name*. Many thanks to the organizers, Connor Winterton and Anthony Stepniak, as well as the fantastic speakers at the event. We would very much like to thank all our chapter contributors, for all their work and for sticking with us during the COVID-19 pandemic. We are so grateful to have had the opportunity to collaborate with them and to include their writing in this collection. Thanks also to all the potential contributors whose work we were not able to include – we were overjoyed by the number of proposals and by the enthusiasm and affection they demonstrated for the film. Many thanks to Jelena Stanovnik, Flavia Laviosa, Debora Nicosia and their colleagues at Intellect Books for their unwavering support and guidance for the collection.

Michael would like to thank his colleagues in the Department of Film Studies and the Faculty of Arts and Humanities at the University of Southampton for supporting the editing of this collection through a period of research leave, as well as the attendees of the British Association of Film, Television and Screen Studies conference held at the University of Birmingham in 2019 for their valuable feedback on a version of his chapter in this book. Thanks also to his partner, David, for his support while he was tapping at the keyboard in another room.

Edward would like to thank his family and friends for their support. Special thanks to Richard Dyer, for keeping in touch on the book's progress from both nearby and afar, and to Edward Gallafent, for his thought-provoking comments on the film and for his encouragement.

Last but not least, thank you to André Aciman for writing the novel of *Call Me by Your Name*, and to Luca Guadagnino, James Ivory and all the cast and filmmakers who brought the romance of Elio and Oliver so vividly to the screen.

Introduction:
Somewhere in Northern Italy

Edward Lamberti and Michael Williams

Call Me by Your Name (2017), adapted for the screen by James Ivory from André Aciman's novel and directed by Luca Guadagnino, has been passionately received among audiences and critics ever since its release. A love story between 17-year-old Elio Perlman (Timothée Chalamet) and graduate student Oliver (Armie Hammer), the film presents a gay relationship in a romantic idyll seemingly untroubled by outside pressures, prejudices or tragedy. While this means it offers audiences welcome opportunities to swoon in front of an LGBTQ+ romance that equals classic heterosexual romances on screen, its relevance or political significance may not be immediately apparent. And yet *Call Me by Your Name* is infused with stylistic and thematic elements that can be read as speaking powerfully to questions of love, romance and sexual identity. This complex film rewards close attention.

The perspectives in this collection show *Call Me by Your Name* to be a multi-faceted film, a collaboration between major filmmaking talents, focused on a gay relationship but one that is also fluid in its sexuality. The collection presents a wide range of voices, to show how the film has struck a chord with audiences in many different ways, and how this predominantly Italian production has had an international impact. The contributors engage with well-established critiques of the film, but the overarching aim of their chapters is to offer perspectives that take our understanding of *Call Me by Your Name* in new directions.

Following the film's opening titles, a montage of ancient sculptures and modern ephemera accompanied by the lively pianos of John Adams' 'Hallelujah Junction – 1st Movement',[1] we find ourselves in Elio's bedroom as he gets dressed. Captions tell us that we have been taken back to 'Summer 1983' and, as Elio leans out of his window to gain his first view of Oliver, that we are 'Somewhere in northern Italy'. From those early moments, the film establishes a locale and yet also a romantically generalized, even mythic, approach to time and place, a non-specificity that is an aspect of the film's wide-reaching audience address. This collection, in considering *Call Me by Your Name* as a romance, as a gay, queer or LGBTQ+

text and as an Italian production, highlights the fluidity of these terms, and how that fluidity can help us understand the film's openness and freshness, its dramatization of what Sufjan Stevens sings of in one of the songs he wrote for the film, the 'mystery of love'.

A queer, Italian, transnational romance

Call Me by Your Name is directed by an Italian, produced with significant Italian financial resources, set in Italy and filmed in Italy with a predominantly Italian crew, and yet it has producers not just from Italy (Guadagnino and Marco Morabito) but also from Brazil (Rodrigo Teixeira), France (Emilie Georges) and the USA (James Ivory, Howard Rosenman and Peter Spears). It also has a cast speaking a mixture of English, French and Italian, and it is based on a novel by an Italian-American born and raised in Egypt. It is partly due to elements such as these that, for Rosalind Galt and Karl Schoonover, the film 'proclaims itself as transnational'.[2]

Mary Harrod, Mariana Liz and Alissa Timoshkina have argued more generally that theories of European national cinemas require a 'de-privileging of geocultural categories in favour of newly transnational forms of identity'.[3] Questions of Italian identity in relation to the film of *Call Me by Your Name* can benefit from this approach. Some critics have questioned not just the effectiveness of the film's Italian elements but also its treatment of Italy itself. Jonathan Romney, for example, notes that

> [d]espite his name, Elio comes from a family that's not Italian but a Jewish blend of American, Italian and French, in which speech is constantly slipping between English and the other two languages; strangely, too, he speaks French with Marzia, who's presumably Italian although she's played by a French actress, as is Oliver's makeshift squeeze Chiara [...]. Not only does the internationally cast film not remotely come across as an Italian movie, but it depicts its Italian characters in a cavalier or even mocking way.[4]

These elements may not preclude *Call Me by Your Name*'s being considered an authentic Italian film. Its deployment of multiple languages emphasizes the transnational but does not necessarily disrupt the portrait of this Italian milieu. Galt and Schoonover explain how, in discussing the film, they have opted primarily to use

> 'Italianicity' over 'Italianness', as the former evokes the Italian word *italianicità*, bringing with it a history of semiotically inflected cultural studies and discussions of what is now referred to as 'Brand Italy'. We understand Italianicity to be about discursive constructions of Italy, circulating both within and outside the nation.[5]

They say, further, that if it is

> an Italian film, one that performs Italianicity, it is nonetheless one that does not provide significant narrative space for Italian subjectivity to be staged through characters. Rather, [...] its Italianicity emerges through the film's setting, style, and how its narrative deploys historicity.[6]

Accordingly, *Call Me by Your Name* adds to a multi-faceted understanding of Italian film and Italian filmmaking in the twenty-first century.

This is echoed in how the director of *Call Me by Your Name*, Luca Guadagnino, has established himself as both an Italian filmmaker and an international filmmaker through his mixture of predominantly Italian-language films, such as *Melissa P.* (2005) and *Io sono l'amore* (*I Am Love*, 2009), and largely English-language works, including *A Bigger Splash* (2015), his 2018 remake of Dario Argento's renowned 1977 Italian horror film *Suspiria* and his road movie cannibal romance set in the United States and again featuring Timothée Chalamet, *Bones and All* (2022). Guadagnino, born in 1971, shares this dexterity with his Italian filmmaking contemporaries Matteo Garrone (*b*.1968) and Paolo Sorrentino (*b*.1970). Garrone's Italian-language films set within Italian cultural milieux – such as *Gomorra* (*Gomorrah*, 2008), *Reality* (2012), *Dogman* (2018) and *Pinocchio* (2019) – contrast with the internationalism of his English-language adaptation of a set of seventeenth-century tales by the Italian poet Giambattista Basile, *Tale of Tales* (2015), co-produced by British, French and Italian producers and starring, among others, British actor Toby Jones, Mexico's Salma Hayek, France's Vincent Cassel and the US's John C. Reilly. Sorrentino, too, has worked fluidly across films in Italian, such as *Il divo* (2008), *La grande bellezza* (*The Great Beauty*, 2013), *Loro* (2018) and *È stata la mano di Dio* (*The Hand of God*, 2021), and English-language works, including the films *This Must Be the Place* (2011) and *Youth* (2015). And in all of these, funding is not straightforwardly based in Italy, though Italian companies figure heavily.

Something that dissolves the borders between Italian and international productions further in the careers of many contemporary Italian directors is the blurring of the lines between the big and small screens. Major Italian filmmakers working for TV or heavily financed by TV broadcasting companies is nothing new, as evidenced by Roberto Rossellini's late-career history films such as *L'età di Cosimo de' Medici* (*The Age of the Medici*, 1973), Bernardo Bertolucci's *Strategia del ragno* (*The Spider's Stratagem*, 1970) and Marco Tullio Giordana's *La meglio gioventù* (*The Best of Youth*, 2003). But the internationalism of more recent productions stretches the definitions of Italian cultural production, such as Guadagnino's predominantly English-language series set in Italy, *We Are Who We Are* (2020), a co-production between Italian and US companies which achieved wide distribution, including on Sky Atlantic in Italy, HBO in the USA and the BBC in the UK; Sorrentino's TV dramas *The Young Pope* (2016) and *The New Pope* (2020), Italian-French-Spanish co-productions starring Jude Law and the saga *L'amica geniale* (*My Brilliant Friend*, 2018–23), adapted from Elena Ferrante's Neapolitan Quartet cycle of novels, created and directed by Saverio Costanzo and with other episodes directed by Alice Rohrwacher and Daniele Luchetti, all of whom are more usually associated with movies, and financed in Italy and the USA. This movement of directors between film and TV and between Italian productions and international co-productions makes ever more malleable the questions of identity that surround a work, how it fits into a country's output and into a global industry. Industrially and culturally, a director such as Guadagnino is Italian and also not just Italian, and is a film director and much more besides.

Call Me by Your Name was a resounding success on many levels: it made back approximately twelve times its budget at the global box office,[7] it received largely positive reviews, it was nominated for and won several major film awards and it achieved a pop-cultural success through the social-media-fuelled focus on its stars, especially Chalamet. The film's success – the splash it caused on first release and the popularity that endures – speaks to a wider appeal than is typically the case with gay-themed films, and chapters in this collection consider different ways of labelling *Call Me by Your Name*, as well as whether it might not be better to avoid labelling it altogether.

However one might refer to *Call Me by Your Name*, in terms of sexuality, national identity, genre or place in the culture, surely what's undeniable is that it is a romance – and one that has had positive effects far and wide. The book *Call Me by Your Name: How a Little Film Touched So Many Lives*, edited by Barb Mirell,[8] is compiled from contributions by fans of the film, who share personal stories that relate it to aspects of their own lives. The result is an emotional and impactful testament to how *Call Me by Your Name* inspires memories of loves won or lost, and thoughts of loves one hopes to have in the future. B. Ruby Rich, in her introduction to *New Queer Cinema*, writes that

> [a] desire to bear witness is still intense: the need to sit in an audience with others of one's kind for the shared experience of those stories and characters on the screen, marked by the unmistakable sensibility of a thousand kindred spirits holding their breath in the dark.[9]

Rich's comment on the shared experience of watching a queer film with a queer audience can apply to how audiences have enjoyed *Call Me by Your Name*. There are multiple audiences, countless viewers who pushed the film to its initial box-office success and who have kept its influence alive not just as an LGBTQ+ film but as a romance more generally. Those 'others of one's kind' might be anyone who wants to gather together before a romantic story such as this film offers.

Style, themes and reception

We are pleased to introduce the range of voices that provide the perspectives on *Call Me by Your Name* in this collection.

The first part of the book considers the film's style from a number of angles, including story, genre, performance, music, sound and camerawork. Adam Vaughan's chapter opens the collection by taking us into the film's 'temporary paradise', as he terms it, to explore the film as a queer pastoral text. The film's Arcadian setting, Vaughan notes, 'by virtue of its isolation, is thus a space for transgression, be that in terms of social class, gender or sexual identity'. Vaughan provides an overview of the pastoral tradition and locates key aspects of the approach to queer love in Guadagnino's film within it, including the significance of urban and rural spaces, borders and movements of retreat and return, focusing on specific sequences such as the trips to Lake Garda and the Bergamo Alps and their significance for expressing queerness. He then moves on to question how the film's apparently idyllic spaces relate to the oncoming AIDS crisis, which was already touching public consciousness at the time the film was set and which can, Vaughan argues, be glimpsed within the film itself.

Claire Monk shifts our attention towards cinematic history in locating the film within the career of *Call Me by Your Name*'s screenwriter James Ivory. As Monk explores, Ivory had been developing the project for ten years before the film's release in 2017, when his authorship also became a prominent part of the film's marketing and reception. Who can forget Ivory arriving at the Academy Awards, where he would take home the Oscar for Best Adapted Screenplay, wearing a shirt patterned with artwork depicting Chalamet's face in tribute to the shirt worn by Elio at the end of the film? Ivory's association as a director with the British heritage film, primarily through his collaboration with producer Ismail Merchant, is strong, and film fans remark on the intertextual connections between *Call Me by Your Name* and Ivory's still-influential 1987 adaptation of E. M. Forster's *Maurice*. Monk pushes her analysis well beyond the familiar realm of Ivory's heritage films, examining less well-known films that he directed such as *Slaves of New York* (1989) and finding a fascinating prototype for Elio in the gay teen Francis (Anthony Roth Costanzo) in *A Soldier's Daughter Never Cries* (1998). Monk thus situates *Call Me by Your Name* as a work of LGBTQ+ cinema within the long and impactful career of Ivory as a queer filmmaker.

Chalamet's performance as Elio was also prominent in *Call Me by Your Name*'s extraordinary critical reception, making Chalamet a star and garnering him an Academy Award nomination as Best Actor in a Leading Role, along with a BAFTA nomination and many other accolades. He was perhaps the most prominent individual, given the film's central focus on Elio, drawn from the first-person narrative of Aciman's novel. Stuart Richards' chapter is the first of several in this collection that examine different aspects of performance and stardom: his approach is to understand performance as a key aspect of adaptation and to consider how the novel's complex relationship between character and perspective is brought to the screen by, among others, Chalamet. Anyone who has read the novel before watching the film, and vice versa, is likely to have been struck by the ability of the filmmakers, and most visibly Chalamet, to bring what Richards terms the 'manic, obsessive and often conflicting inner dialogue' of Elio to the screen through a combination of subtle and complex performance and aesthetics. Rather than insisting on a model of fidelity in terms of the novel, however, Richards favours a post-structuralist approach to appreciate the 'quiet nuance of Chalamet's performance'.

The visual style of *Call Me by Your Name* rightly receives a great deal of attention in its critical and popular reception due to its vivid, and sometimes dare we say 'iconic', imagery, peaches and all. However, the success of the film's soundtrack, including early limited-edition blue, yellow and peach vinyl releases,[10] indicates that the film's sophisticated deployment of sound and carefully curated music tracks is equally significant to the film's production of meaning and the way it has engaged audiences worldwide. The next two chapters in the collection help us appreciate the film's use of sound.

Just as Richards explores how Chalamet's performance communicates Elio's interior thoughts, Kingsley Marshall in his chapter draws our attention to the way music is used in *Call Me by Your Name* as a 'complementary connotation' to bring us close to Elio and the wider narrative. Marshall demonstrates that 'each musical cue within the film offers a palimpsest of meaning for the audience'. While the idea of songwriter Sufjan Stevens playing the formal role of a narrator may have been abandoned, the presence of his songs alongside works by other composers nonetheless speaks volumes in terms of what they convey to the listener and viewer. As Marshall effectively demonstrates, it is a film that delights in form, but it is also a film 'about music and its ability to communicate place, motivation, and emotion'.

The distinctiveness of *Call Me by Your Name*'s aural landscape extends beyond music, however. In her chapter, Sarah Artt invites us to listen to the film's soundtrack as she argues that the 'aural explicitness' of the film presents a robust challenge to critics who have perhaps lazily conceptualized its representation of queer sex as somehow not explicit enough. Many contributors in this volume tackle this perception in their chapters, and on her part, Artt argues that contrary to the coy style described by those critics, if we closely attend to the film's sound design and learn from approaches to affect from 'body genres', we discover that the film 'deliberately evokes the affect of pornography in order to amplify the film's explicitness'. While acknowledging *Call Me by Your Name*'s status as a 'mainstream' film, Artt suggests, its sound design, enhancing the sounds of bodies moving against clothing, kissing and sex, takes us closer to the intimacy of its characters than is the case in many more visually explicit films.

Edward Lamberti develops this theme of the aesthetics of intimacy and distance in a philosophical direction. Lamberti applies Emmanuel Levinas's notion of proximity to Guadagnino's directorial style to explore 'how a sense of distance in *Call Me by Your Name* exists in productive ethical tension with the film's intimate portrayal of Elio and Oliver's romance'. Levinas argued that we can be near the Other but that we cannot know the Other, and that this inability to know helps found our ethical relation to the Other. Lamberti suggests that the film offers 'an experience of being close to Elio without understanding him', and that this means that Elio's developing relationship with Oliver is treated as the couple's own 'private business', hence numerous moments in the film that frame Elio and Oliver in ways that keep our desire for involvement at a distance. But, as Lamberti shows, the film involves us through its subtle structural elements, inspiring a more general sense of romance as authentic and private.

The second section of the collection focuses on some of the key themes of *Call Me by Your Name*. Daniel Paul's chapter discusses the film from the perspective of its being a welcome and positive queer development in the genre of the Italian teen film. Drawing from the concept of chrononormativity, Paul analyzes the film's use of narrative, motifs – such as Elio's checking the time on his watch at key moments – and soundtrack to argue that the film subverts heteronormative time and 'creates a space in which same-sex desire (and intimacy) can effectively ruminate and perhaps even thrive'. As well as the more inclusive representation of sexuality, Paul highlights how the positive relationship Elio enjoys with his father (Michael Stuhlbarg) offers a contrast with prior representations in Italian teen films. Paul argues that while *Call Me by Your Name* is a transnational production, its significance as an Italian film, and one that can be understood as being aimed at a young Italian audience, should not be forgotten.

Looking at the contemporary through the past, Nikolai Endres offers a detailed analysis of how the film draws upon ancient notions of homosexuality while adding much-needed nuance to our understanding of ancient Greek, as well as Roman, conceptions of sex between men. As much as the film draws on ancient representations of same-sex love, it also challenges them. Endres argues that Elio is hardly the passive youth, the *eromenos* of Platonic love, when he grabs Oliver's crotch in the meadow or masturbates for his own pleasure. Endres's reading of the film also directly addresses tensions in representation and reception, including what he sees as easy but uniformed attacks on the film by critics such as D. A. Miller[11] who use reductive notions of Greek homosexuality to frame the relationship of the older Oliver and younger Elio as sinister. Endres instead understands *Call Me by Your Name* to be a contemporary representation of queer love and sex that is both reciprocal and consensual.

The queer reception of classical constructions of male same-sex desire, and particularly as represented in sculpture, also provides the foundation of Michael Williams' chapter. Taking his cue from the design of *Call Me by Your Name*'s opening titles, with their photographs of ancient statues, Williams suggests that the titles provide a guide for viewing that frames both the relationship of Elio and Oliver and the imaginative fan works that continue to be produced online. The representation of the central romance of Elio and Oliver is richly palimpsestic, with juxtapositions and sometimes subtle notes in the performances of Chalamet and Hammer that invite the viewer to notice the classical associations that have been framed for us. Fostered by the film's marketing strategy, audiences were tacitly provided with iconic templates that shaped their reception, particularly when producing fanart responses to the film and its stars. Williams thus explores how the composite art shared on digital platforms offers carefully curated perspectives on the film, its characters, and classical reception.

Jacob Engelberg offers a different challenge to our understanding of the film's conceptions of sexuality, this time arguing that it is a 'fundamental anxiety around bisexuality' that has underscored the misgivings expressed by some critics about the film's not being 'gay enough'. Engelberg aims to turn some of these critical preconceptions around by exploring key phenomena. Firstly, rhyming with Sarah Artt's discussion of explicitness, he considers 'the cinematic monstration of certain sex acts' that are required to be seen to conform to convention – most specifically, anal sex. Then there is the transgressiveness of bisexuality itself on screen in its departure from the binary of gay/straight codes of signification, hence the anxiety about Elio's sex scene with Marzia, which here receives a fascinating new perspective, and Oliver's announcement of his engagement in the film's final sequence. As Engelberg proposes, '[a]nalysis of the roots of this discomfort not only reveals the ideological, identarian and intellectual limitations of certain queer methodologies but also uncovers the centrality of bisexuality to *Call Me by Your Name*'s cinematic project'.

The third section of the collection moves to examine the film's relationship to industry and audience in terms of reception. It begins with Ruby Cheung's wide-ranging study of *Call Me by Your Name*'s year-long tour of the international film festival circuit following its debut at the Sundance Film Festival in January 2017, taking in over 50 festivals along the way. Cheung builds on approaches from film festival studies using Guadagnino's film as a case study and provides tabulated data that illuminates the operation of the festival circuit and the film's performance within it. Cheung argues that the use of the festival circuit brought *Call Me by Your Name*, and Guadagnino himself, unprecedented 'global recognition' even though it had secured distribution with Sony Pictures Classics, along with smaller local companies, in advance of Sundance. She examines how the film used festivals to build its success but also examines the 'political-economic and sociocultural realities' that can challenge the performance of an LGBTQ+ film, particularly in non-Euro-American regions such as East Asia. Cheung thus argues that the film helped throw into sharp relief the hierarchies in a supposedly flat film distribution and exhibition system 'alternative to that of Hollywood'.

While press and audience attention was understandably drawn towards Chalamet as a rising, and very photogenic, young star playing the film's central character, the next two chapters explore aspects of not only Chalamet's stardom but also that of his co-star, Armie Hammer. As both Francesca Sobande and Jonathan A. Cannon detail, Hammer's public image took an unexpected turn during the development of this collection. In January 2021, multiple women came forward accusing Hammer of abuse, with one of the women also alleging rape. Hammer denied the allegations and, in mid 2023, the legal charges against him were dropped. The long-term impact on his career remains to be seen. Regardless of what turns the story may take going forward, Hammer's image has been changed by these events. In the reception of Hammer's only post-allegations release to date, *Death on the Nile* (Kenneth Branagh, 2022), for example, the 'Armie factor' was noted in *Rolling Stone* magazine's review as a key reason for the film's struggle at the box office, sounding 'a dissonant record-scratch' when viewing an ostensibly escapist film.[12] Sobande and Cannon each address the implications of the allegations on the reception of Hammer, and *Call Me by Your Name*, while connecting aspects of his ongoing persona to his career before and during Guadagnino's film, as well as his association with the still-rising stardom of Chalamet.

In her chapter, Francesca Sobande builds on her work on Chalamet as 'the internet's boyfriend'[13] and examines the contrasting uses of social media by Chalamet and Hammer and their performance of a bromance online and in public appearances. Chalamet has achieved what Sobande calls a 'hyper-visible' presence on social media that is inextricably entwined with his reception as Elio in *Call Me by Your Name*, despite his 'brevity and infrequency' in personally engaging with it. In contrast, and increasingly so, Hammer's social media presence is characterized by 'disengagement'. Sobande examines how the social media presence of both men continues to shape the reception of *Call Me by Your Name* while also highlighting how interventions in its reception, most notably Lil Nas X's 2021 hit song 'MONTERO (Call Me by Your Name)',[14] connected what is otherwise a film preoccupied with white masculinity to a new realm of 'Black gay, queer and femme experiences and aesthetics'.

Although given a new inflection following the allegations against Hammer, Jonathan A. Cannon asks whether risk-taking was a defining feature of the straight-identifying actor's persona on and off screen long before he took on the LGBTQ+ role of Oliver. Cannon looks closely at *Call Me by Your Name* and its promotion on shows such as *The Ellen DeGeneres Show* to explore the nature of the star discourse surrounding the film and the kind of conversations around masculinity and the display of the male body it permits. The chapter details how questions of class, privilege – conveyed in part by his voice – and whiteness are central to Hammer's image and sense of charm, as well as to his ability to bridge Hollywood and independent cinema. Cannon argues that the issues around masculinity associated with Hammer mean that it is essential that his contribution to the Elio–Oliver pairing should not be overlooked if we are to gain a balanced view of how the men's relationship is represented and received.

As several chapters make clear, *Call Me by Your Name* was an international critical and box-office success. It is only right that for the last contribution to the collection we look outside the European and North American context once more for Vinicius Ferreira, Victor Schlude and Gêsa Cavalcanti's discussion of the film's reception in Brazil. Their work focuses on the comments of YouTube review videos and user comments, which the chapter analyzes in terms of different groupings of sociocultural meanings. Examined in the context of the film's narrative and characters, these are used to explore aspects of LGBTQ+ identification and the phenomenon of queer nostalgia associated with the film's construction of a queer summer romance.

In *Call Me by Your Name: How a Little Film Touched So Many Lives*, one fan says, '*Call Me by Your Name* made me fall in love with film and life again'.[15] Elio and Oliver's summer romance draws on forms that may at first be familiar to us from culture, history and antiquity, but it does so in ways that create something new and renewing: a love story that proposes, gently, that romantic love can be positive, invigorating, life-changing. Our collection explores possibilities inherent in those propositions. André Aciman's generosity of heart with his novel finds its ideal counterpart in this film adaptation, a film that, B. Ruby Rich says, 'will be watched and shared by generations to come'.[16]

NOTES

1. John Adams, 'Hallelujah Junction – 1st Movement', track 1 on Various, *Call My by Your Name: Original Motion Picture Soundtrack*, Madison Gate Records/Masterworks/Sony Music Entertainment, 2017.

2. Rosalind Galt and Karl Schoonover, 'Untimely Desires, Historical Efflorescence, and Italy in *Call Me by Your Name*', *Italian Culture* 37, no. 1 (March 2019): 66, https://doi.org/10.1080/01614622.2019.1609220.

3. Mary Harrod, Mariana Liz and Alissa Timoshkina, 'The Europeanness of European Cinema: An Overview', in *The Europeanness of European Cinema: Identity, Meaning, Globalization*, ed. Mary Harrod, Mariana Liz and Alissa Timoshkina (London and New York: I. B. Tauris, 2015), 13.

4. Jonathan Romney, 'Film of the Week: *Call Me by Your Name*', *Film Comment*, 24 November 2017, https://www.filmcomment.com/blog/film-week-call-name/.

5. Galt and Schoonover, 'Untimely Desires': 78n1.

6. Galt and Schoonover: 67.

7. See '*Call Me by Your Name* (2017)', Box Office Mojo, accessed 13 April 2023, www.boxofficemojo.com.

8. Barb Mirell, ed., *Call Me by Your Name: How a Little Film Touched So Many Lives* (Philadelphia: Liberty Bell Publishers, 2018).

9. B. Ruby Rich, 'Introduction', in B. Ruby Rich, *New Queer Cinema: The Director's Cut* (Durham and London: Duke University Press, 2013), xxvii.

10. Keith Caulfield, 'How the Eclectic *Call Me by Your Name* Soundtrack Became a Surprise Vinyl Hit – Is Radio Next?', *Billboard*, 8 February 2018, https://www.billboard.com/music/music-news/call-me-by-your-name-soundtrack-vinyl-radio-8098824/.

11. D. A. Miller, 'Elio's Education', *Los Angeles Review of Books*, 19 February 2018, https://www.lareviewofbooks.org/article/elios-education/.

12. David Fear, '*Death on the Nile* and the Curious Case of the Accused-Cannibal Cancelled Movie Star', *Rolling Stone Magazine*, 10 February 2022, https://www.rollingstone.com/movies/movie-reviews/death-on-the-nile-review-armie-hammer-1294801/.

13. Francesca Sobande, 'The Internet's "Transnational" Boyfriend: Digital (Re)Presentations of Celebrity Men', *Feminist Media Studies* 21, no. 4 (2021): 539–55, https://doi.org/10.1080/14680777.2021.1900312.

14. Lil Nas X, 'MONTERO (Call Me by Your Name)', Columbia, 2021.

15. Entry by Noel Hahn in *Call Me by Your Name: How a Little Film Touched So Many Lives*, ed. Barb Mirell (Philadelphia: Liberty Bell Publishers, 2018), 97.

16. B. Ruby Rich, 'Sundance 2017: Of Snow and Anguish', *Film Quarterly* 70, no. 4 (Summer 2017): 106.

REFERENCES

Adams, John. 'Hallelujah Junction – 1st Movement.' Various, *Call My by Your Name: Original Motion Picture Soundtrack*, track 1. Madison Gate Records/Masterworks/Sony Music Entertainment, 2017.

Argento, Dario, dir. *Suspiria*. Seda Spettacoli, Produzioni Atlas Consorziate, 1977.

Bertolucci, Bernardo, dir. *Strategia del ragno* (*The Spider's Stratagem*, TV). RAI Radiotelevisione Italiana, Red Film, 1970.

Box Office Mojo. '*Call Me by Your Name* (2017).' Accessed 13 April 2023. www.boxoffice-mojo.com.

Branagh, Kenneth, dir. *Death on the Nile*. 20th Century Studios, Kinberg Genre, Scott Free Productions, 2022.

Caulfield, Keith. 'How the Eclectic *Call Me by Your Name* Soundtrack Became a Surprise Vinyl Hit – Is Radio Next?' *Billboard*, 8 February 2018. https://www.billboard.com/music/music-news/call-me-by-your-name-soundtrack-vinyl-radio-8098824/.

Costanzo, Saverio, creator. *L'amica geniale* (*My Brilliant Friend*, TV). Fandango, Wildside, The Apartment, 2018–23.

Fear, David. '*Death on the Nile* and the Curious Case of the Accused-Cannibal Cancelled Movie Star.' *Rolling Stone Magazine*, 10 February 2022. https://www.rollingstone.com/movies/movie-reviews/death-on-the-nile-review-armie-hammer-1294801/.

Galt, Rosalind, and Karl Schoonover. 'Untimely Desires, Historical Efflorescence, and Italy in *Call Me by Your Name*.' *Italian Culture* 37, no. 1 (March 2019): 64–81. https://doi.org/10.1080/01614622.2019.1609220.

Garrone, Matteo, dir. *Gomorra* (*Gomorrah*). Fandango, Rai Cinema, Sky, 2008.

Garrone, Matteo, dir. *Reality*. Fandango, Archimede, Le Pacte, Garance Capital, 2012.

Garrone, Matteo, dir. *Tale of Tales*. Archimede, Le Pacte, Rai Cinema, HanWay Films, 2015.

Garrone, Matteo, dir. *Dogman*. Archimede, Le Pacte, Rai Cinema, 2018.

Giordana, Marco Tullio, dir. *La meglio gioventù* (*The Best of Youth*). BiBi Film, Rai Fiction, 2003.

Guadagnino, Luca, dir. *Melissa P.* Bess Movie, Pentagrama Films, 2005.

Guadagnino, Luca, dir. *Io sono l'amore* (*I Am Love*). First Sun, Mikado Film, Rai Cinema, 2009.

Guadagnino, Luca, dir. *A Bigger Splash*. Frenesy Film Company, Cota Film, 2015.

Guadagnino, Luca, dir. *Call Me by Your Name*. Frenesy Film Company, La Cinefacture, RT Features, 2017.

Guadagnino, Luca, dir. *Suspiria*. Amazon Studios, K Period Media, Frenesy Film Company, 2018.

Guadagnino, Luca, dir. *We Are Who We Are* (TV). HBO, Sky Italia, Wildside, The Apartment, 2020.

Guadagnino, Luca, dir. *Bones and All*. Frenesy Film Company, Per Capita Productions, 2022.

Hahn, Noel. 'Untitled Entry.' In *Call Me by Your Name: How a Little Film Touched So Many Lives*, edited by Barb Mirell, 97. Philadelphia: Liberty Bell Publishers, 2018.

Harrod, Mary, Mariana Liz and Alissa Timoshkina. 'The Europeanness of European Cinema: An Overview.' In *The Europeanness of European Cinema: Identity, Meaning, Globalization*, edited by Mary Harrod, Mariana Liz and Alissa Timoshkina, 1–13. London and New York: I. B. Tauris, 2015.

Ivory, James, dir. *Maurice*. Merchant Ivory Productions, Cinecom Pictures, Channel 4, 1987.

Ivory, James, dir. *Slaves of New York*. TriStar Pictures, Gary Hendler, Merchant Ivory Productions, 1989.

Ivory, James, dir. *A Soldier's Daughter Never Cries*. Capitol Films, Merchant Ivory Productions, British Screen Productions, 1998.

Lil Nas Z. 'MONTERO (Call Me by Your Name).' Columbia, 2021.

Miller, D. A. 'Elio's Education.' *Los Angeles Review of Books*, 19 February 2018. https://www.lareviewofbooks.org/article/elios-education/.

Mirell, Barb, ed. *Call Me by Your Name: How a Little Film Touched So Many Lives*. Philadelphia: Liberty Bell Publishers, 2018.

Rich, B. Ruby. 'Introduction.' In *New Queer Cinema: The Director's Cut*, edited by B. Ruby Rich, xv–xxx. Durham and London: Duke University Press, 2013.

Rich, B. Ruby. 'Sundance 2017: Of Snow and Anguish.' *Film Quarterly* 70, no. 4 (Summer 2017): 99–108.

Romney, Jonathan. 'Film of the Week: *Call Me by Your Name*.' *Film Comment*, 24 November 2017. https://www.filmcomment.com/blog/film-week-call-name/.

Rossellini, Roberto, dir. *L'età di Cosimo de' Medici* (*The Age of the Medici*, TV). RAI Radiotelevisione Italiana, 1973.

Sobande, Francesca. 'The Internet's "Transnational" Boyfriend: Digital (Re)Presentations of Celebrity Men.' *Feminist Media Studies* 21, no. 4 (2021): 539–55. https://doi.org/10.1080/14680777.2021.1900312.

Sorrentino, Paolo, dir. *Il divo*. Indigo Film, Lucky Red, Parco Film, 2008.

Sorrentino, Paolo, dir. *This Must Be the Place*. Indigo Film, Lucky Red, Medusa Film, 2011.

Sorrentino, Paolo, dir. *La grande bellezza* (*The Great Beauty*). Indigo Film, Medusa Film, Babe Film, Pathé, 2013.

Sorrentino, Paolo, dir. *Youth*. Indigo Film, 2015.

Sorrentino, Paolo, dir. *The Young Pope* (TV). Wildside, Haut et Court, Mediapro, 2016.

Sorrentino, Paolo, dir. *Loro*. Indigo Film, Pathé, 2018.

Sorrentino, Paolo, dir. *The New Pope* (TV). The Apartment, Wildside, Haut et Court, Mediapro, 2020.

Sorrentino, Paolo, dir. *È stata la mano di Dio* (*The Hand of God*). The Apartment, Netflix, 2021.

PART I

STYLE

1

Temporary Paradise:
Queer Space, Time and Pastoral
Visions in *Call Me by Your Name*

Adam Vaughan

'Summer 1983. Somewhere in northern Italy.' So read the opening captions following the title sequence in *Call Me by Your Name* (2017), Luca Guadagnino's adaptation of the novel by André Aciman, which was first published in 2007. They appear over images of 17-year-old Elio Perlman (Timothée Chalamet) preparing his room for the arrival of his father's (Michael Stuhlbarg) latest doctoral student, Oliver (Armie Hammer), who will be spending the summer with the family at their villa, helping with research. Over the course of their time together, a mutual desire begins to grow. As such, the opening captions provide the viewer with the time and place in which the story of Elio and Oliver's romance occurs, albeit obliquely. We are not made aware of the specific date on which Oliver arrives, nor even what month. A train ticket from Rome to Milan is visible during the opening credits sequence and dated 8 July, but it is not clear to whom it belongs. Where is this 'somewhere'? The film provides us with clues later on – Oliver opening a bank account in the nearby town of Crema, a visit to an archaeological find at Lake Garda, and Elio and Oliver's trip to Bergamo – but at the beginning of the film, the geographical location is kept ambiguous. This initial imprecision, coupled with the subsequent stylistic devices and narrative details that emerge, invites a quasi-mythical reading of the film that largely centres on its pastoral resonances and images of Arcadia as a space in which queer love can occur.

This chapter begins by analyzing *Call Me by Your Name* as a queer pastoral text. It summarizes some of the pastoral tradition's main features, both stylistic and ideological, and identifies where we see examples in the film. These include an Arcadian setting, narrative movements of retreats and returns,[1] the carnivalesque and nostalgia for a lost Golden Age. With this in place, I consider the implications that viewing *Call Me by Your Name* as a pastoral text has for its representation of queer love. It asks questions such as where in the film is it safe to be queer and give in to gay desire? What attitudes are contained in the film towards the urban and the rural and what is the significance of this for queer ways of life? Is the film optimistic about the possibility of living as openly queer or does it provide a cautionary tale? To a large extent, this section deals with 'where' the film takes place. In the second section, I consider 'when' the story is set. The 1980s is a pivotal decade in gay history due to the AIDS crisis. I evaluate the extent to which the film engages with fears brought about by the so-called 'gay plague' and argue that due to the film's wider portrayal of temporality (pastoral's gaze upon the past, ancient statuary, and cinematic devices), Elio and Oliver's relationship is, increasingly, out of time.

Call Me by Your Name *as a queer pastoral text*

Pastoral began as a literary mode whose origins date back to the poetry of Theocritus in ancient Greece and Virgil in first-century BCE Rome. Throughout the course of its long history, pastoral has developed a set of consistent features and associations. By no means are these present in every example of pastoral; different cultures at different times have transformed them to suit their specific contexts and purposes. Yet they offer a useful starting point through which to explore *Call Me by Your Name*'s association with the pastoral tradition.

One of pastoral's fundamental features is its setting in Arcadia. This can be either a literal place called Arcadia or a location that is Arcadian because of its geographical features. Arcadia is a region in Greece located in the centre of the Peloponnese. In Virgil's *Eclogues* and the painting of Nicolas Poussin (*Et in Arcadia Ego* [1637–38]) and Jean-Antoine Watteau (*The Shepherds* [*c*.1717]), it is a place isolated from the rest of the world, surrounded by mountains, where people gather to frolic by lakes and in forests. According to literary scholar Terry Gifford, this makes it 'the perfect location for a poetic paradise, a literary construct of a past Golden Age in which to retreat by linguistic idealisation'.[2] Gifford reminds us that even if a text is set in Arcadia, it should not be seen as a 'real' place. Instead, it functions as a distancing device that allows for either an escapist retreat from or a critique of social reality through metaphor. At least in its earlier incarnations, pastoral usually centred on conversations between shepherds. Arcadia, by virtue of its isolation, is thus a space for transgression, be that in terms of social class, gender or sexual identity.[3]

There is no absolute Arcadia in *Call Me by Your Name*. However, we find its traces throughout the film. The Perlmans' villa has something of the Arcadian about it. It is a secluded estate surrounded by fruit orchards and expansive green spaces. Significant stretches of the film are given over to the portrayal of outside leisure time. Characters luxuriate in the sun, in the pool and play volleyball. They eat, drink and indulge in the pleasures that an Italian summer brings. For the most part, interiors are imagined as constraining. When giving Oliver a perfunctory tour of his old bedroom, Elio explains that the 'only way out' of his makeshift room next door is through the shared bathroom. An evening spent inside watching television and forced to play the piano is seen as torture if Elio's sulky reaction is any indication.

As Elio and Oliver's attraction grows, they are increasingly filmed outside of the Perlman villa and within more typically Arcadian spaces. It is the case that the film's focus on ancient statuary, and the role it plays in their relationship, connects Elio and Oliver to the ancient past from which pastoral and its concept of Arcadia emerged. In one pivotal sequence, which takes place at a dredging site at Lake Garda, the arm of a fourth-century BCE bronze statue of a male youth is used as an intermediary to bring them closer together. They are also often seen adopting the poses of statues throughout the film. For instance, earlier in the film, as Elio and Oliver lounge by the villa's pool, Oliver abruptly and playfully rolls over and falls into the water. As a startled Elio looks into the water, we see Oliver floating face down just below the surface. This foreshadows the sequence of the bronze statue's dredging. As it is raised, Mr Perlman (Stuhlbarg) explains that an associated version of the statue was melted down by one of the Farnese Popes and recast as a 'particularly voluptuous Venus'. With this information and with the name being spoken as the statue emerges from the depths resembling his pose in the pool earlier, here the film visualizes Oliver as a corporeal Venus, and a symbol of (queer) love, beauty and desire. In a fitting Arcadian gesture, Elio, Oliver and Mr Perlman celebrate the find by cavorting in the lake as the sun sets. (Michael Williams details the complex resonances artefacts from antiquity have in the film in his chapter for this collection.)

Other images of Arcadia include the secluded spot Elio leads Oliver to after he has confessed his feelings for the older man. Among green pastures winds a trickling stream that feeds a small pond. Elio informs Oliver that the freshwater comes from the Alpi Orobie. This reference to the Bergamo Alps anticipates the trip Oliver and Elio take towards the end of the film. It sees them venture further into nature and its Arcadian symbolism. A sense of the border crossing entailed in this movement is suggested by the camera's point-of-view shot attached to their coach as it ploughs along a bumpy mountain path into a dense forest. The next shot sees Elio and Oliver ecstatically running up a hill towards a waterfall in an image that captures the joy and freedom of the natural world that is fundamental to pastoral (Figure 1.1). The film revels in high art with characters often reading, discussing and performing works from philosophy, classical music and poetry. Elio

FIGURE 1.1: An ecstatic retreat into nature: Elio (Timothée Chalamet) and Oliver (Armie Hammer) explore their relationship in the Bergamo Alps. Luca Guadagnino (dir.), *Call Me by Your Name*, 2017. Italy/France/USA/Brazil. © Frenesy, La Cinefacture.

and Oliver's mountain trek can thus be interpreted as a further link to antiquity, specifically the mythical construction of Parnassus, home to the Muses.

These Arcadian sequences are significant for how the film expresses queerness. Writing about the film *Beautiful Thing* (Hettie MacDonald, 1996), David Shuttleton observes how the two main characters' embracing in the woods 'sentimentally signifies the "naturalness" of same-sex desire'.[4] Scenes of queer or non-queer sex linked to nature occur throughout *Call Me by Your Name*. Elio first has sex with his friend Marzia (Esther Garrel) outside on top of a grass lawn under the moonlight. Elio and Oliver share their first kiss at the teenager's secluded spot under a tree, after which Elio tenderly caresses a piece of grass across his lips before launching himself at Oliver once more. The morning after they have sex, the pair go swimming in a nearby lake. And the infamous peach masturbation sequence is a graphic merging of nature's bounty with sexual exploration. Because of its remoteness, Arcadia suggests a place where it is safe to be queer, explore same-sex desire and engage in what Byrne R. S. Fone calls homosexual rituals, such as sexual union and the exchanging of gifts.[5] The film's title alludes to one of these rituals and sees Elio and Oliver call each by their own names. It is a gesture that speaks to the intense feeling they have for one another after they have sex for the first time and, at the end of the film, a trigger that recalls their summer of love. In terms of gift-giving, Oliver bestows the shirt he wore the first day he arrived at the villa to

Elio towards the end of the film, with a note saying, 'For Oliver from Elio'. It acts as a reminder of Oliver for Elio to keep after he leaves, a further visual evocation of the all-encompassing nature of their relationship when Elio puts it on, and a link to their night together when they both use it to wipe semen from their bodies.

These stand as relatively safe spaces for Elio and Oliver to explore their relationship and sexualities partly due to their remoteness. Yet there are several spaces within the film that, if not directly dangerous for queer expression, are coded as being ambivalent and may or may not present difficulties for queer characters. The Perlman villa is, initially, one of these spaces. Despite being a site where family and friends converge to enjoy themselves, as Elio and Oliver learn of their mutual attraction, we question how Elio's parents will react should they find out. As if playing on this uncertainty, when Elio and Oliver are in the pool together and Oliver begins to tease and flirt with Elio, he turns to address Mrs Perlman (Amira Casar), who is somewhere out of shot and, unbeknownst to the spectator, has been there the entire time. A similar feeling of unease is felt by Elio and Oliver when they travel to rural towns. Oliver twice warns Elio that 'we can't talk about these things' when they stand in a town plaza and then, once they have had sex, 'I would kiss you if I could' after having escaped the town's prying eyes down a side alleyway. The implication is that these rural spaces are not safe for queer expression, which is made clear when the pair stop to ask for a drink from an elderly woman on the outskirts of town and notice a portrait of Benito Mussolini, '*Il Duce*', hanging proudly outside. 'That's Italy', Elio quips. These moments reflect the characters' fear that rural spaces represent more 'old-fashioned' values built on the traditional family and linked to a residual Fascist political system intolerant of sexual 'deviancy'. The film neither confirms nor contests Elio and Oliver's fears and therefore may be another example of queer 'metronormativity' that defines the city as a haven for queer folk to migrate to and escape the dangerous rural setting of their childhood.[6] Once Elio and Oliver are alone within natural settings, they are free to act on their feelings. However, the film also suggests that ambivalent spaces for queer expression can be altered, or newly created, to allow for gay desire.

Elio constructs such a space on the outskirts of the villa. It is a dilapidated outhouse that he uses to escape and explore his sexuality, first with Marzia, then the setting for the peach scene, and finally with Oliver. Notably, the first time that Elio and Oliver have sex occurs in Elio's old room in which Oliver is staying. The pair have arranged to meet at midnight and creep quietly into the room, appearing horrified when the door slams shut. All of this indicates that they remain unsure of whether they are allowed to engage in gay sex, or indeed any type of sex, within the villa. Significantly, Elio and his parents have just finished entertaining an older gay couple (one of whom is played by the source novel's author, Aciman). As Elio meets Oliver, they stand on a balcony looking down at Mr and Mrs Perlman saying goodbye to the couple. Queerness is thus figured as 'acceptable' and welcomed into this space and the gay couple possibly provides a glimpse of Elio and Oliver's potential future, even as Elio and his father have earlier poked fun at the pair, albeit in a light-hearted way. It is just as likely that Elio and Oliver's reluctance to make their feelings known to those at the villa is less to do with shame or fear of their queerness and more to do with Oliver risking insult to his hosts' hospitality and a general embarrassment on Elio's part. As they have sex, the camera slowly tracks away from the bed and rests on an image of trees outside, moving gently in the wind. It is a stylistic device that, on the one hand, could reveal the film's coyness about the (gay) sex act. On the other, and corresponding to a queer pastoral reading, it could stand as a further symbolic naturalizing of the gay sex act.

During my analysis of the film, I have already mentioned certain sequences that show Elio and Oliver in movements of retreat and return. According to Gifford, this is another crucial feature of pastoral's discourse. Retreat can operate at both the textual and extratextual level. In the former, characters move from one location to another to escape from something or somewhere. In the latter, the reader or viewer escapes from their present reality into an idealized world featured in the text that imagines an alternative way to live life. Whether purely escapist or critical of contemporary social reality, 'there must in some sense be a return from that location to a context in which the results of the journey are to be understood'.[7] On one level, the two main retreats and returns that occur in *Call Me by Your Name* – to the secluded spot where Elio and Oliver share their first kiss and to Bergamo before Oliver's departure – teach them more about their sexual identities and the possibilities for their relationship in the future.

In the first example, Elio and Oliver return to a dinner his parents are holding with an argumentative couple. The party look on perplexed as the visitors launch into a tirade that eventually rests upon contemporary Italian politics. Elio has a nosebleed at the table and rushes off to compose himself, with Oliver in tow. There are a variety of medical explanations for nosebleeds, among them allergies and high blood pressure, but the placement of this scene immediately after Elio and Oliver's first homosexual encounter and during a conversation about the realities of a shifting political landscape in Italy invites connections. Specifically, it could represent the potential dangers, prejudice and violence that awaits queers in 1980s Italy and countless nations around the world. Alongside this sociocultural reading, the scene depicts a marked change in how Elio and Oliver interact with each other, both before their first kiss and after, in that Oliver rushes into the villa after Elio to make sure he is okay. In a relatively short amount of screen time, the pair's relationship shifts from cool indifference (based on fear or reluctance to make their true feelings known to one another) to lust and then to care. The second retreat and return sees Oliver go back to his life in America and Elio return alone to the family villa. It is a sad moment for both of them. Yet rather than the end of summer and the potential end of their relationship (suggested when Oliver phones months later to inform the family that he is getting married), Elio's return sees his queer identity affirmed in a conversation with his father. Mr Perlman's lengthy monologue indicates that he knew about Elio and Oliver ('You two had a nice friendship [...] how special what you two had was [...]. What you two had, had everything and nothing to do with intelligence') and indicates that he came close to having a similar connection with someone in his youth. The film leaves ambiguous the gender of the person he's referring to, but he continues by encouraging Elio not to waste his youth by living with regret. And when Mr Perlman says, 'When you least expect it, nature has cunning ways of finding our weakest spot', once again there is a thematic link between one's nature – here meaning sexuality – and the natural scenes in which we have seen Elio and Oliver discovering their mutual attraction. From a feeling of intense sadness on his return from waving Oliver off at Clusone station, this scene provides Elio with an affirmation and a roadmap for how to live the rest of his life.

When we next see Elio, it is winter, and the family are preparing to celebrate Hanukkah. He seems to have taken his father's advice on board, dressed somewhere between a post-punk and a New Romantic with a beret, trench coat and black boots; he is expressing himself. For the attentive viewer, Elio's outfit transports us back to the streets of Bergamo when Elio and Oliver enjoyed a drunken night singing and dancing to 'Love My Way' by The Psychedelic Furs (which was heard earlier in the film at the town's disco). This sequence is an example of pastoral's carnivalesque. According to Mikhail Bakhtin, the carnivalesque comprises four categories. These are the free interaction and expression between people; the celebration of eccentric behaviours; carnivalistic *mésalliances* that allow for previously separated entities to combine; profanation, or the removal of strict rules associated with acceptability.[8] The sequence is imbued with an ethereal quality thanks to its night setting, nearly deserted streets and the characters' drunken antics. It is also a space for free expression where Elio and Oliver are able to enjoy their time together. Unlike the town plaza and alleyways earlier in the film, here the pair openly embrace, albeit under the cover of darkness. Elio and Oliver stumble upon three New Romantics who are listening to The Psychedelic Furs' song in their car and smoking. Oliver rushes to join their group and invites a woman to dance with him in the shadow of the town's church. As Elio watches on, he promptly vomits, contravening society's strict unspoken rules of behaviour by not being in full control of his body. Any concern for Elio's welfare is undercut by Oliver laughing before he comes over to make sure Elio is okay. The carnivalesque thus forms part of pastoral's function to offer social critique. In the Bergamo sequence, this means a space for alternative ways of behaving, where 'deviance' is embraced and celebrated.

Pastoral is often characterized as having a nostalgia for a lost or forgotten past that represents an ideal space and time. For some critics, this makes pastoral a deeply conservative form of writing that celebrates an escape from the troubles and traumas of the present into an idealized past. This is what Raymond Williams, writing about some English pastoral, describes as the 'habit of using the past, the "good old days", as a stick to beat the present'.[9] Other critics note that, within their escapes to Arcadia, pastoral texts can offer critiques of urban life. The fact that pastoral features an idyllic countryside paradise means that the reader/viewer, if they are a city-dweller, may have no choice but to contrast what they read and see with their humdrum and laborious lives. Of course, some writers might deliberately structure their work as an extended critique of social and political life in the city. By looking to a perfect past moment, these texts operate at an allegorical distance that allows room for the reader/viewer to appreciate what makes this time and place so desirable and what is missing from their current historical reality. For Gifford, this makes pastoral a discourse, adding that 'to the extent that pastoral represents an idealisation, it must also imply a better future conceived in the language of the present'.[10] In this view, far from being a regressive form, pastoral can sometimes act as a catalyst or provide a blueprint for social change.

What, if anything, is *Call Me by Your Name* nostalgic for? To twenty-first-century viewers, the film presents the iconography and paraphernalia of the 1980s through costume and soundtrack. The political present of summer 1983 saw Benedetto 'Bettino' Craxi become prime minister of Italy, the first from the Italian Socialist Party. Although the film references this shifting political landscape, it never takes precedence over the drama of Elio and Oliver's relationship. In the scene in which Elio reveals his feelings to Oliver, we glimpse a poster on a wall encouraging residents to vote in the election. At other times, Elio's parents watch a television sketch that pokes fun at Craxi, and the housemaids discuss his politics in the kitchen. But rather than focusing on the substance of their discussion, we watch Elio watching them at the periphery. When it seems as if the political events of the day will take a more central position in the story, the focus is returned to Elio and Oliver. We see this in the sequence mentioned earlier involving the bickering couple and Elio's nosebleed. Elio rushes off with Oliver following and they share a private moment. In the preceding scene, the pair have shared their first kiss and so this abrupt movement away from political conversation to enjoy their own company figuratively demonstrates the potential threat that queers like them could face. Rather than being nostalgic for an American-influenced 1980s culture or a period of political change in Italy, the film, I would argue, manifests a nostalgia for an even earlier moment. This is evident in its extensive use of classical music and, once again, classical statuary that can be seen as a gaze focusing on the past to ignore, or perhaps repress, events in the present.

The various sculptures from antiquity we see throughout the film, and the similar poses Elio and Oliver adopt as them, imply a nostalgic gaze to homosexuality in the Graeco-Roman ancient world. Although, to categorize same-sex relationships as 'homosexual' is to apply modern terminology to the classical world. Scholar David M. Halperin affirms that labels such as homosexuality and heterosexuality are 'relatively recent and highly culture-specific forms of erotic life – not the basic building-blocks of sexual identity for all human beings in all times and places, but peculiar and indeed exceptional ways of conceptualizing as well as *experiencing* sexual desire'.[11] In ancient Greece, this meant that sexual relations were not classified based on the gender of the participants. In other words, neither the coupling of a man and woman, nor the individuals themselves, were labelled as heterosexual. Two women having sex were not seen as homosexual. Rather, the relative actions of the individuals during sex were given prominence such that the penetrator was seen as male and the person penetrated as female. Pederasty, the relationship between an adolescent boy and an older man, was one of the most common forms of same-sex relationships in ancient Greece. It was considered a rite of passage for boys and young adults to be educated about the responsibilities they would soon be expected to fulfil as men, and it included a sexual component.[12] The ages of Elio and Oliver, and the physical appearance of Chalamet and Hammer who play them, suggest a similar dynamic in their relationship.

At the same time as adopting a view of sexuality from the ancient Graeco-Roman era, applying the work of John Champagne, who has written extensively on masculinity in Italian culture, reveals a context in which the film's queerness resonates within more recent historical times. Champagne's work does this by mapping the melodramatic form in Italian art, literature and film (which includes some mention of pastoral), for how it engages with the figure of the Italian male. Using the likes of painter Caravaggio, composer Giacomo Puccini and filmmaker Aurelio Grimaldi as examples, Champagne discusses how portrayals of masculinity through melodrama undercut any simplistic national and political ideal of the 'Italian man'.[13] Part of this project involves problematizing the strict male/female, heterosexual/homosexual binaries to allow for a spectrum of queerness, and this is apparent in *Call Me by Your Name*. Elio seems to equally enjoy his sexual activity with Marzia and with Oliver. There is only one moment in the film in which a relationship is labelled as 'gay' (by Mr Perlman to Elio referring to the older gay couple). For the most part, the film portrays an egalitarian approach to sexual identity at the same time as it suggests potential threats to some of these identities. It could be argued, therefore, that the film is providing a template for understanding the complexities of sexuality that builds upon an ancient paradigm projected into the 1980s and then to the contemporary moment when the film is viewed, a moment that increasingly understands sexuality as fluid. This is a construction of sexuality that does not categorize or prejudge but rather shows sexual desire in its multiple forms. It is therefore crucial that the camera moves away from Elio and Oliver's sexual act so that it does not assign reductive labels to their experience.

This is an idyllic representation of queer sexuality that nostalgically looks back into antiquity for a different way to imagine queerness in the present using the language of pastoral to organize a quasi-mythical narrative. (Nikolai Endres's chapter in this collection considers this angle.) However, the film is set in the historical reality of 1983. We are told as much at the start of the film and the *mise en scène* further consolidates this sense of place and time. This means that, despite protests to the contrary, the film operates within established understandings of sexuality that existed both at the time it is set and for those watching in the modern day. At first glance, that makes its omission of the AIDS crisis, which fully emerged in all its horror during the 1980s, somewhat perplexing. In the second section, I investigate the film's relationship to AIDS and the implications this has for the film's consideration of temporality.

Call Me by Your Name *and the AIDS crisis*

1981 is usually cited as the year in which the first case of HIV/AIDS was clinically diagnosed in America, although, as Randy Shilts maps in intricate detail, its origins predate this.[14] By 1983, when *Call Me by Your Name* takes place, the race to understand the causes of this new disease is continuing apace in America.[15] Gay Men's Health Crisis (GMHC) had been established the year before in New York City and becomes the first community-based AIDS organization in the country. The popular media are beginning to report on the disease, albeit cautiously, and later than local gay publications like the *New York Native* and the *San Francisco Sentinel*, which had published articles in May and June of 1981. In May 1982, the *New York Times* publishes a piece first mentioning 'GRID' or Gay-Related Immune Deficiency[16] and the *Los Angeles Times* releases the first front-page story on AIDS in the mainstream press, titled 'Mysterious Fever Now an Epidemic'.[17] It is in this year that the Center for Disease Control (CDC) first uses the term 'AIDS' along with the first case definition. In March of 1983, the CDC publishes an article noting that the majority of AIDS cases have been found in gay men and discusses how the disease is sexually transmitted through exposure to blood along with guidance about how to prevent transmission. In May, in its first front-page story on AIDS, the *New York Times* describes that 1,450 cases of AIDS have been reported and 558 people have died.[18] Concomitantly, Europe was reporting its own cases, although these too can trace their origins earlier than the 1980s. In the first half of 1983, there were two AIDS epidemics firmly entrenched on the continent. One had links to Central Africa and the other to gay men.[19] It is in this context that *Call Me by Your Name*'s narrative takes place, a historical world that was just beginning to wake up to the threat posed by the epidemic.

For the purposes of this section, the lived experience of AIDS has direct implications for time. In the 1980s, an AIDS diagnosis almost certainly meant death. Therefore, one's temporality is disrupted, the present moment acquires greater meaning and the future is cut short. This is what Jack Halberstam describes as 'a new emphasis on the here, the present, the now, and while the threat of no future hovers overhead like a storm cloud, the urgency of being also expands the potential of the moment'.[20] In this view, time may be running out, but it also adds an emphasis on subjectively prolonging the time that is left. For those queer subjects who already experience time differently, outside of what Elizabeth Freeman calls 'chrononormativity' as the process through which social structures bind subjects into uses of time that maximize productivity,[21] AIDS is but another factor that colours their temporal existence. In recent times, an HIV-positive diagnosis no longer means death. Commentators such as Tim Dean reflect on how this also impacts an individual's experience of time. From an inevitable death sentence, 'now it is a sentence whose terminus remains unknown and whose meaning therefore remains radically ambiguous'.[22] Dean comments on how the contemporary HIV-positive person's death is postponed with no definitive idea of when it will occur. Interestingly, he refers to the relief many people in the 1980s felt on discovering that they had seroconverted from being HIV negative to HIV positive. At a time of intense fear and anxiety on hearing of a new virus ripping through their community, this diagnosis provided some individuals certainty and an end to waiting. It also provided a clearer sense of how much time they had left to live their lives.

As we have already seen, *Call Me by Your Name* places Elio and Oliver's relationship apart from the major social, cultural and political concerns of the decade, such that they seem to inhabit a rural idyll in northern Italy which real-world events cannot reach. Guadagnino suggests as much when commenting on the decision to set the events of the film in 1983, four years earlier than Aciman's novel. He explains, 'I thought that '83 is the year – in Italy at least – where the '70s are killed, when everything that was great about the '70s is definitely shut down [...]. I think our characters in the movie are in a way untouched by the corruption of the '80s – in the U.S., Reagan, and in the UK, Thatcher.'[23] That said, the absence of any explicit mention of AIDS in a film about male same-sex love in the early 1980s remains curious, even as the director has since indicated that he may address the epidemic in subsequent films.[24] According to Aciman, an earlier draft of the film script included a scene in which Elio and his parents spoke about an unnamed disease spreading through the queer population, but Aciman asked for it to be removed so that audiences would be surprised by Professor Perlman's conversation with Elio at the end, where he suggests a certain knowledge of the nature of his son's relationship with Oliver.[25] Much like Guadagnino's terms above – the invocation of death and corruption – instead of overtly mentioning the AIDS epidemic, the film contains veiled references.[26]

Outwardly, *Call Me by Your Name* presents a paradise. The first half of this chapter has detailed the several connections the film makes to the pastoral tradition, particularly through Arcadian settings. The family's villa is almost always bathed in summer sunlight and is filled with glamorous people who lead lives of privilege. They are waited on by domestic servants who prepare copious amounts of food for the dinner table. It is also an intellectual haven for people to read classic literature, listen to and play classical music and engage in philosophical conversation. Yet beneath this idyllic exterior lies the possibility of something less desirable. Flies are an indicator of this potential threat to paradise. The buzz of insects is a consistent part of the film's diegetic soundtrack. However, there are points where they directly intrude upon the film's images. In one scene, we witness Oliver arriving back at the house in long shot from Elio's open window. This is followed by Elio laying on his bed, looking out of the window and beginning to play with himself. Through cutting between Elio beginning to masturbate and Oliver walking up the gravel path towards the front door, the film implies that Elio is thinking of Oliver. As Elio begins to touch himself, he is distracted by a fly that keeps buzzing near him. Without removing his hand from his shorts, he blows to try to remove the fly, which eventually flies away, settling on the duvet. In the final shot of the film, Elio sits facing the camera looking into a lit fireplace. He has just had a phone call from Oliver who has returned to America and is getting married. As Elio sits, a fly begins to crawl up his shirt and remains there for a long time. What are we to make of this? Surely if Guadagnino had found these insect interlopers too distracting, he would have cut and reshot the scene. In the first example, Elio's interaction with the fly complements the film's rather loose structure, which is full of incidental moments that contribute to a mundane reality in which the romance develops. But it could be argued that the flies take on a symbolic meaning. Flies have a relatively short life span that ranges from weeks to a few months. Elio and Oliver's romance takes place over a similarly short amount of time, meaning that the insects' appearances provide a metaphorical reminder that their and the pair's time is running out. However, taken together with other references in the film, I would argue that the flies should be understood as signifiers of decay linked to the spectre of AIDS.

Given the seemingly perfect location, it comes as a shock to see blood and wounding in the film. Oliver suffers a scrape from falling off his bike which happens off screen. The wound appears numerous times throughout the film. It is first seen when Elio and Oliver are going for a bike ride into town. Oliver raises his shirt to show Elio, who grimaces at the sight. It precedes the scene in which Elio reveals his feelings to Oliver in the town square. On the way back from town, Elio takes Oliver to his favourite spot, a secluded field near a stream, where they share their first kiss. Oliver stands up and again raises his shirt to look at the wound, which he thinks is starting to get infected (Figure 1.2). Finally, it is visible as the pair lie naked in bed after having sex for the first time. In other words, it is a motif that follows Elio and Oliver as they discover and act on their shared desire for one another. Once more, the focus on the scrape can be easily explained as part of the film's diegesis. Oliver uses it as an excuse to display his body to Elio at first, as a presentation that invites the teenager to gaze upon a desirable male form. However, the mention of it becoming infected after they kiss is less easily explained in these terms. The next scene involves Elio's nosebleed at the dinner table and therefore comes immediately after Oliver's mention of infection. Furthermore, this is not the only mention of illness. In the peach masturbation sequence, after Elio ejaculates into the fruit, Oliver knowingly licks the juice. Elio responds by saying, 'I'm sick, aren't I?' Elio uses the peach to explore his (homo)sexuality, so the fact that this reaction to the sharing of fluids is understood as an illness is significant.

FIGURE 1.2: The spectre of AIDS threatens to pierce Elio (Timothée Chalamet) and Oliver's (Armie Hammer) rural idyll. Luca Guadagnino (dir.), *Call Me by Your Name*, 2017. Italy/France/USA/Brazil. © Frenesy, La Cinefacture.

Two posters in Elio's room create a more direct link to the AIDS crisis. The first is a self-portrait of American photographer Robert Mapplethorpe. Mapplethorpe was famous for his confrontational works of gay men engaged in bondage, dominance, sadism and masochism (BDSM) practices. He died with AIDS in March 1989. The second poster is glimpsed as Elio and Oliver have sex. The camera pans past them revealing the year 1981 on a hand-drawn image of what appears to be the Swedish tennis player Björn Borg. This is the year generally attributed to the first clinically diagnosed case of AIDS in America.[27] Taken together, these subtle references, which could be interpreted as the spectre of AIDS that hangs over the film, threaten to pierce the space and time of Elio and Oliver's romantic utopia. For a contemporary spectator, it is difficult to separate the absence of AIDS in a story of homosexual love from a hindsight that has either lived, remembered or learned about the epidemic, so inextricably bound have the two become. As such, the time and place of our viewing intrudes upon the time and place of the film and may begin to fill gaps in its sociocultural contexts, or at least tease out the possibility that they were there in the film's *mise en scène* all along. If AIDS itself has a direct impact upon the person's temporal experience, as critics have noted, then its absence from *Call Me by Your Name* further queers the temporality of Elio and Oliver's experience, and our experience of time watching the film, in that it locates their love outside of 1980s sociocultural time at the same time as the film's references to Arcadia and the pastoral situate a relationship out-of-place.

Leo Marx considers pastoral to fall broadly into two categories. He labels these 'the pastoral of sentiment' and 'the pastoral of mind'.[28] To apply one of Gifford's features of pastoral, the former provides a 'retreat' to a literary construct that lacks the 'return' of the latter, where any insights for contemporary social reality can be processed. If we were to take issue with the lack of any direct reference to AIDS within the film, then we might well categorize *Call Me by Your Name* as a sentimental pastoral. However, I hope my analysis has shown that to understand *Call Me by Your Name* as a queer pastoral text is to acknowledge that it contains opportunities for us to peel back layers of representation. Doing this reveals, among other things, the film's application of pastoral conventions to construct safe spaces for queer subjectivity and, through a discourse that examines sexuality in the ancient world, a way to re-evaluate how we view queer sexuality, and human sexualities in general.

NOTES

1. See Terry Gifford, *Pastoral*, second edition (Abingdon and New York: Routledge, [1999] 2020), 2.

2. Gifford, 20–21.

3. Social and literary historian Rictor Norton catalogues pastoral literature's homosexual or homoerotic references from antiquity (including Aratus' love for a boy in *Idyll VII.* and a description of a kissing contest between boys in honour of Diocles in *Idyll XII.* by Theocritus) through to the European Renaissance period (such as Edmund Spenser's description of Fancy in *The Faerie Queene* [1589–96]). See Rictor Norton, 'An Era of Idylls', *The Homosexual Pastoral Tradition*, 20 June 2008, accessed 13 April 2023, http://rictornorton.co.uk/pastor01.htm.

4. See David Shuttleton, 'The Queer Politics of Gay Pastoral', in *De-Centring Sexualities: Politics and Representations Beyond the Metropolis*, eds. Richard Phillips, Diane Watt and David Shuttleton (London and New York: Routledge, 2000), 124.

5. See Byron R. S. Fone, 'This Other Eden: Arcadia and the Homosexual Imagination', in *Literary Visions of Homosexuality*, ed. Stuart Kellogg (New York: The Haworth Press, 1983), 14.

6. Scott Herring provides a counterpoint to the stereotype of the urban idyll in *Another Country: Queer Anti-Urbanism* (New York and London: New York University Press, 2010).

7. Gifford, *Pastoral*, 83.

8. Mikhail Bakhtin, *Problems of Dostoevsky's Poetics*, ed. and trans. Caryl Emerson (Minneapolis: University of Minnesota Press, 1984), 122–23, 130.

9. Raymond Williams, *The Country and the City* (Oxford: Oxford University Press, 1973), 12.

10. Gifford, *Pastoral*, 36.

11. David M. Halperin, *One Hundred Years of Homosexuality: And Other Essays on Greek Love* (Abingdon and New York: Routledge, 1990), 9.

12. Halperin, 9.

13. See John Champagne, *Italian Masculinity as Queer Melodrama* (New York: Palgrave Macmillan, 2015).

14. See Randy Shilts, *And the Band Played On: Politics, People and the AIDS Epidemic* (London: Souvenir Press, [1987] 2011), Kindle.

15. For a timeline of key events related to the AIDS epidemic in the United States, see HIV.gov, 'A Timeline of HIV and AIDS', accessed 13 April 2023, https://www.hiv.gov/hiv-basics/overview/history/hiv-and-aids-timeline.

16. Lawrence K. Altman, 'New Homosexual Disorder Worries Health Officials', *New York Times*, 11 May 1982, 1.

17. Harry Nelson, 'Mysterious Fever Now an Epidemic', *Los Angeles Times*, 31 May 1982, 1, 3, 20.

18. See Shilts, *And the Band*, 297.

19. See Shilts, 261.

20. Judith Halberstam, *In a Queer Time and Place: Transgender Bodies, Subcultural Lives* (New York and London: New York University Press, 2005), 2.

21. Elizabeth Freeman, *Time Binds: Queer Temporalities, Queer Histories* (Durham: Duke University Press, 2010), 3.

22. Tim Dean, 'Bareback Time', in *Queer Times, Queer Becomings*, ed. E. L. McCallum and Mikko Tuhkanen (New York: SUNY Press, 2011), 75–76.

23. Quoted in Stephen Garrett, 'Director Luca Guadagnino on Why *Call Me by Your Name* Is Making Everyone Cry', *Observer*, 13 October 2017, https://observer.com/2017/10/interview-luca-guadagnino-on-why-call-me-by-your-name-makes-people-cry/.

24. See Marc Malkin, '*Call Me by Your Name* Director Reveals Details of the Planned Sequel', *The Hollywood Reporter*, 25 January 2018, https://www.hollywoodreporter.com/rambling-reporter/call-me-by-your-name-director-reveals-details-planned-sequel-1077963.

25. Quoted in Mario Ximénez, 'André Aciman Discusses *Find Me* and His Shock Alternative Ending for Elio and Oliver', *Vogue*, 24 June 2020, https://www.vogue.co.uk/arts-and-life-style/article/andre-aciman-interview.

26. Spencer Kornhaber's article 'The Shadow Over *Call Me by Your Name*' in *The Atlantic* identifies some of the references the film makes to AIDS, including the presence of flies, blood and Oliver's wound. See Spencer Kornhaber, 'The Shadow Over *Call Me by Your Name*', *Atlantic*, 3 January 2018, https://www.theatlantic.com/entertainment/archive/2018/01/the-shadow-over-call-me-by-your-name/549269/.

27. See 'A Timeline of HIV and AIDS', https://www.hiv.gov/hiv-basics/overview/history/hiv-and-aids-timeline.

28. Leo Marx, *The Machine in the Garden: Technology and the Pastoral Ideal in America* (New York: Oxford University Press, 1964), 32.

REFERENCES

Altman, Lawrence K. 'New Homosexual Disorder Worries Health Officials.' *New York Times*, 11 May 1983.

Bakhtin, Mikhail. *Problems of Dostoevsky's Poetics*. Translated and edited by Caryl Emerson. Minneapolis: University of Minnesota Press, 1984.

Champagne, John. *Italian Masculinity as Queer Melodrama*. New York: Palgrave Macmillan, 2015.

Dean, Tim. 'Bareback Time.' In *Queer Times, Queer Becomings*, edited by E. L. McCallum and Mikko Tuhkanen, 75–100. New York: SUNY Press, 2011.

Fone, Byron R. S. 'This Other Eden: Arcadia and the Homosexual Imagination.' In *Literary Visions of Homosexuality*, edited by Stuart Kellogg, 13–34. New York: The Haworth Press, 1983.

Freeman, Elizabeth. *Time Binds: Queer Temporalities, Queer Histories*. Durham: Duke University Press, 2010.

Garrett, Stephen. 'Director Luca Guadagnino on Why *Call Me by Your Name* Is Making Everyone Cry.' *Observer*, 13 October 2017. https://observer.com/2017/10/interview-luca-guadagnino-on-why-call-me-by-your-name-makes-people-cry/.

Gifford, Terry. *Pastoral*. Second Edition. Abingdon and New York: Routledge, [1999] 2020.

Guadagnino, Luca, dir. *Call Me by Your Name*. Frenesy Film Company, La Cinefacture, RT Features, 2017.

Halberstam, Judith. *In a Queer Time and Place: Transgender Bodies, Subcultural Lives*. New York and London: New York University Press, 2005.

Halperin, David M. *One Hundred Years of Homosexuality: And Other Essays on Greek Love*. Abingdon and New York: Routledge, 1990.

Herring, Scott. *Another Country: Queer Anti-Urbanism*. New York and London: New York University Press, 2010.

HIV.gov. 'A Timeline of HIV and AIDS'. Accessed 13 April 2023. https://www.hiv.gov/hiv-basics/overview/history/hiv-and-aids-timeline.

Kornhaber, Spencer. 'The Shadow Over *Call Me by Your Name*.' *Atlantic*, 3 January 2018. https://www.theatlantic.com/entertainment/archive/2018/01/the-shadow-over-call-me-by-your-name/549269/.

MacDonald, Hettie, dir. *Beautiful Thing*. Channel Four Films, World Productions, 1996.

Malkin, Marc. '*Call Me by Your Name* Director Reveals Details of the Planned Sequel.' *The Hollywood Reporter*, 25 January 2018. https://www.hollywoodreporter.com/rambling-reporter/call-me-by-your-name-director-reveals-details-planned-sequel-1077963.

Marx, Leo. *The Machine in the Garden: Technology and the Pastoral Ideal in America*. New York: Oxford University Press, 1964.

Nelson, Harry. 'Mysterious Fever Now an Epidemic.' *Los Angeles Times*, 31 May 1982.

Norton, Rictor. 'An Era of Idylls.' *The Homosexual Pastoral Tradition*, 20 June 2008. Accessed 13 April 2023. http://rictornorton.co.uk/pastor01.htm.

Shilts, Randy. *And the Band Played On: Politics, People and the AIDS Epidemic*. London: Souvenir Press, [1987] 2011. Kindle.

Shuttleton, David. 'The Queer Politics of Gay Pastoral.' In *De-Centring Sexualities: Politics and Representations Beyond the Metropolis*, edited by Richard Phillips, Diane Watt and David Shuttleton, 123–44. London and New York: Routledge, 2000.

Williams, Raymond. *The Country and the City*. Oxford: Oxford University Press, 1973.

Ximénez, Mario. 'André Aciman Discusses *Find Me* and His Shock Alternative Ending for Elio and Oliver.' *Vogue*, 24 June 2020. https://www.vogue.co.uk/arts-and-lifestyle/article/andre-aciman-interview.

2

'But You Know, There Have Been Queer Characters from the Very First Film': *Call Me by Your Name* and the Long Shadow of James Ivory

Claire Monk

Ivory's authorship and the Merchant Ivory influence

The imprint of the veteran American independent gay director and (on fifteen prior films) screenwriter James Ivory on *Call Me by Your Name* (Luca Guadagnino, 2017) is fundamental: not merely as its 2017 Academy Award-winning credited screenwriter,[1] but via Ivory's intimate decade-long involvement in the project from 2007 onwards when Peter Spears and Howard Rosenman, Ivory's neighbours in upstate New York, first optioned the screen rights to Aciman's newly published novel, with Ivory on board as a producer. However, this imprint goes beyond Ivory's direct involvement: his sensibilities and oeuvre as a director – across six decades, 28 realized feature films, occasional TV projects and five documentaries – equally echo in *Call Me by Your Name*. So too (with limitations) does the unprecedented transcultural ensemble queerness of the five-decade Merchant Ivory Productions collaboration itself: a same-sex partnership (between Ivory, the adopted son of a Catholic US West Coast lumber-mill-owning family, and Indian-born Muslim producer Ismail Merchant) which, from 1961 until Merchant's unexpected death in 2005, was inseparably a way of filmmaking and a way of life, surrounded by a family of collaborators: most prominently, Merchant Ivory's twice-Academy Award-winning regular screenwriter and novelist Ruth Prawer Jhabvala and their soundtrack composer Richard Robbins.[2] Rather than presenting an adaptation study, this chapter's purpose is to explore Ivory's – and the collective Merchant Ivory – influence and legacy in *Call Me by Your Name* in these broader senses. Threading through this exploration, I argue that the Merchant Ivory collaboration itself is appropriately understood as *queer* – in view of its multifaceted pluralism in which personal, intimate and artistic relations were inseparable, and plural rather than binary – and demonstrate how the diffuse queerness, and the spectrum of queer characters and (thereby) precursors to *Call Me by Your Name* within Ivory's oeuvre, go significantly beyond 1987's *Maurice*.

Ivory was not, as he had hoped, permitted to co-direct *Call Me by Your Name*, nor (he reported) even present on Guadagnino's set.[3] Many elements in *Call Me by Your Name*'s cinematic realization nonetheless feel like an *emulation* of a Merchant Ivory film: the 'handwritten' opening credits superimposed on images of classical antiquities and art (and, specifically, classical male beauty); the naturalistic immersion in an ensemble, transnational, polylingual cast and caste of educated, cultured and privileged characters; a consummate commitment to beauty, locational, architectural and physical: Italy in summer, the sensuality of water, bodies and landscape; and the 'Ivory-esque' centring of a sprawling, architecturally striking house as the hub of the film's human interactions, polymorphous desires and erotic entanglements. From a realist perspective, the casual grandeur and scale of the Perlmans' summer home – the seventeenth-century Villa Albergoni in Moscazzano, Lombardy – and their small army of happy servants seem fantastical for a 1980s academic family. But this generous anachronism serves to powerfully establish the film's sense of a secluded, Edenic, summer idyll confined to a fixed place and time: 'Somewhere in northern Italy', 'Summer 1983'. *Call Me by Your Name*'s title-sequence design merely gestures towards Merchant Ivory's wider-ranging experimentation with witty, individuated and illustrated opening credits (which can be traced back as early as 1970's *Bombay Talkie*, in which the title card and opening credits are carried and positioned around the real streets of Mumbai as Bollywood-style billboard posters). However, its echoes of the ensemble casting and social dynamics of Ivory's films are more substantive. Literally and metaphorically, 'No Merchant-Ivory film is said to be complete without a big dinner party'[4] – a spirit of conviviality which the Perlmans' hospitality updates as late twentieth-century informal social dining – and in Ivory's films there is often queerness or unsanctioned desire at the table. As for the place of architecture, while it would be a cliché to claim that houses are 'characters' in Ivory's films, his fascination since childhood with architectural history and the detail of 'old structures'[5] and interiors – pursued further in his undergraduate studies at the University of Oregon School of Architecture and Allied Arts[6] – has sometimes inspired them. As the *New York Times* put it in a 1986 lifestyle profile, 'If the producer's [Merchant's] great hobby is food, Mr Ivory's is buildings and houses'[7] – including, from the mid 1970s onwards, the lengthy project of restoring and furnishing Merchant and Ivory's 1805 Greek Revival home at Claverack in the Hudson Valley. The parodically anthropological, allegorical *Savages* (1972), by common consent Ivory's strangest film (a fictitious semi-naked tribe, the Mud People, stumble across an abandoned, decaying Neo-Georgian mansion and are transformed, temporarily, into 1920s Jazz Age socialites/decadents), was inspired by Ivory stumbling across the house concerned, the abandoned Beechwood in Scarborough, New York state.[8] *Savages* stages one of the earliest Merchant Ivory screen dinner parties. There is female masculinity and male drag, camp Art Deco styling and absurdist performances. A framed portrait of a beautiful, androgynous young heir is lasciviously licked; Warhol superstar Ultra Violet performs a lesbian seduction in a car. Almost nothing here could be deemed straight.

The sections which follow consider Ivory's – and the Merchant Ivory – imprint on *Call Me by Your Name* through the lens of cinematic authorship and also textual and promotional strategies, in the distinctive context (carved out by Merchant Ivory and shared by Guadagnino) of queer filmmakers whose projects fuse low budgets, high artistic values and an intentional appeal to crossover (rather than compartmentalized gay male) audiences. My project, then, is to situate *Call Me by Your Name*'s twenty-first-century achievements and impact as LGBTQ cinema and same-sex romance with reference to Ivory's longer and wider film oeuvre – unified by its 'perfect fusion of style and subject' and 'absolute clarity of vision'[9] – and to Merchant Ivory's collaborative, representational and promotional practices as an independent queer filmmaking partnership. This goal is, however, complicated by the persistent peculiarities of reception around Merchant Ivory – with potential implications for how *Call Me by Your Name*'s relationship to the Ivory canon is interpreted and understood – which this chapter will therefore also seek to correctively address.

The critical erasure of 'queer Merchant Ivory' and the courage of Maurice (1987)

First, Merchant Ivory were for a long time widely and wilfully not even acknowledged as *gay* filmmakers – let alone *queer* filmmakers – particularly within the UK, in marked contrast with US media coverage[10] and the framing of their work by North American critics[11] since the release of *Maurice* in 1987. This erasure is countered by a body of more recent, transnational and postcolonial criticism which understands that 'sexuality and the impossibilities of desire' have long been themes of Ivory's films, along with an 'introspective tone [which has become] associated in contemporary feminist[12] and queer criticism with an emotionally charged staging of male sexuality that transgresses the bounds of heteronormativity'.[13] Following Merchant Ivory's breakthrough global critical, commercial and triple-Oscar success with *A Room with a View* (1985), adapted from the gay British author E. M. Forster's nominally straight 1908 novel, the critical denial of their gayness *or* queerness became closely aligned with their persistent framing as 'heritage' film-makers, both within UK academic anti-heritage-film criticism and beyond. Suzanne Speidel attributes the persistent 'journalistic and scholarly neglect' of the fact that Ivory and Merchant were 'a gay, long-term cohabiting couple' to this fact's inconvenience for the dominant 'hostile critical tendency to view Merchant Ivory films as celebrating the elite and bourgeois classes they depict', within a 'school of thought [...] which consistently reads costume drama [...] as ideologically conservative, regardless of the actual story and thematic content'.[14] In a further peculiarity, in the UK this erasure was often perpetuated by gay male critics: some closeted, others out and politicized (supporting Speidel's hypothesis).

In 1986, when 'we could probably have done anything we wanted',[15] Ivory and Merchant chose to follow *A Room with a View* by filming, as their twenty-fifth-anniversary production, Forster's affirmative gay novel *Maurice* (1971), first drafted by Forster in 1913–14 but self-suppressed during his lifetime.[16] In the mid 1980s, despite the wider vitality of gay male cinema, this quietly defiant decision was neither a safe nor a prestigious choice.

At that date, Forster's novel remained denigrated and its recuperation as a gay classic lay in the future (as testified by Jhabvala's refusal to adapt it and the resistance Merchant Ivory faced from Forster's literary executors at King's College Cambridge[17]). At the height of the HIV/AIDS crisis, amid anti-gay hysteria and real fear, Ivory honoured Forster's decree for *Maurice* that 'happiness is its keynote'[18] (Figure 2.1) and Forster's insistence on giving his bourgeois protagonist Maurice Hall (James Wilby) and Maurice's working-class second love Alec Scudder (Rupert Graves) a sexually fulfilled, optimistic happy ending.[19] In fact, at a time when '[g]ay romance onscreen [...] was rare. Happier endings were rarer still',[20] Ivory and his actors went further than Forster – and blurred cinematic categories – to deliver 'woozy, unadulterated romance, an intoxicating tuxedo-ripper' with both naturalistic male nudity and a 'Hollywood ending'[21] in the unprecedented form of a visceral real wet kiss between Maurice and Alec, shot in swooning ultra-close-up: 'the sort of thing that [...] just never happens' in films between male lovers.[22]

A further rarity is provided by *Maurice*'s joyous, positive treatment of the intersection of queer sexuality and class. Alec is a servant, the young under-gamekeeper to Maurice's chaste and disappointing landed-gentry first love Clive Durham (Hugh Grant) who, after three sexless years, spurns Maurice for a socially approved straight marriage to a sexually ignorant woman of his own class, Anne (Phoebe Nicholls), condemning Maurice to (it seems) permanent utter loneliness. Among Forster's many delicious ironies, Alec arrives as 'an importation' to the Durhams' country estate Penge (romanticized in the film to Pendersleigh, echoing Jane

FIGURE 2.1: *Maurice*: 'Happiness is its keynote.' Maurice (James Wilby) with Clive (Hugh Grant) (top row); Maurice with Alec (Rupert Graves) (other rows). James Ivory (dir.), *Maurice*, 1987. UK. © Maurice Productions Limited.

Austen's Pemberley), brought in by 'politics and Anne':[23] the twin conventionalities of Clive's straight marriage and his concurrent country-squire noblesse-oblige entry into Conservative politics. Alec is also ambitious, with plans to emigrate: not to the 'straight' Australia or Canada, but to Argentina, a less 'straight'-seeming destination also carrying connotations of colonialism and capitalism, which are referenced in the film. Alec is conceded even by Clive to be 'decidedly intelligent' – indeed, for his class, 'too smart to be straight';[24] and self-assured enough – about his own desires, and in his intuitions about Maurice – to take the initiative. Contrary to *Downton Abbey* stereotypes, the 1910s were a period of significant working-class empowerment and political consciousness in the UK, making Alec's intelligence and self-worth entirely credible for the time ('You called me Alec [...]. I'm as good as you';[25] 'I am not your servant, I will not be treated as your servant, and I don't care if the world knows it').[26] Within 72 story hours of Maurice's arrival at Penge/Pendersleigh for his reluctant first visit after Clive's marriage – the 'holiday' is actually a smokescreen for Maurice seeking a gay 'cure' via attempted hypnotism in London – Alec has climbed a ladder into the guest room and into Maurice's bed, rescuing him from years of sexual frustration[27] and a life of loneliness, and decisively causing Maurice's second hypnotism session to fail. As a working-class, sexual, self-assured historical queer British character, Alec is almost without precedent. The wider fragility of such representations in the twenty-first century can by indexed by their absence from *Call Me by Your Name*.

Ivory's *Maurice* achieved all this in the face of numerous adaptational and production challenges.[28] It then reached UK cinemas in November 1987, a month before the Thatcher government's notorious anti-gay legislation, Section 28 of the Local Government Act, was introduced to Parliament, with direct consequences for the film's continuing prospects (particularly in publicly subsidized venues beyond London) once Section 28 became law. Most poignantly, *Maurice*'s US gala premiere on 17 September 1987, held at the Paris Theatre in mid-Manhattan in aid of the Foundation for AIDS Research, was dedicated to the memory of *Maurice*'s publicist Steve Seifert, who had died of AIDS and whose memorial service had been held at the same cinema that morning.[29] The Paris, New York's pre-eminent arthouse, had long been pivotal to the release strategy for Merchant Ivory's films: *A Room with a View* had played there to packed houses for a year; *Maurice*'s Paris opening set a new box-office record. (Three decades later, in their footsteps, *Call Me by Your Name* played at the Paris from Thanksgiving Week 2017 until the first week of April 2018.) Yet *Maurice*'s full impact for its audiences would reveal itself over the coming decades and prove to be enduring, life-changing and inestimable:

> For many gay men coming of age in the eighties and nineties, *Maurice* was revelatory: a first glimpse, onscreen or anywhere, of what love between men could look like. One man recently told me that until *Maurice* he'd seen same-sex attraction only in *The Rocky Horror Picture Show*.[30]

The perversity of some gay critical responses to Ivory's *Maurice* in the face of all this is perhaps epitomized in Mark Finch and Richard Kwietniowski's 1988 essay 'Melodrama and *Maurice*', first published in the queer magazine *Square Peg* and subsequently in the journal *Screen*. Sidelining the film's validatory power, and rejecting its happy ending in favour of an arch reading which asserted that Maurice and Alec's union is an 'impossibility' and 'the happy homosexual [...] a contradiction in terms',[31] Finch (a pioneering promoter of LGBTQ cinema) and Kwietniowski (a gay filmmaker) insisted that *Maurice* is *not even a gay film*, expressly *because* it 'is, first and foremost, a "Merchant–Ivory" picture [...] secondly, a British-costume-drama [...] thirdly, a literary adaptation [...] [and therefore] fourthly, and only fourthly, about *le vice anglais*'.[32]

A further effect of the insistent pigeonholing of Merchant Ivory as makers of (indeed, synonymous with) 'English' heritage costume dramas on the basis of their 'big four' hits – *A Room with a View*, *Maurice*, *Howards End* (1992), all adapted from novels by E. M. Forster, followed by Jhabvala's adaptation of Kazuo Ishiguro's *The Remains of the Day* (1993) – has been to restrict public (and even academic) awareness of the full variety of their oeuvre: in particular, the cultural and geographical diversity of Ivory's films, his wide-ranging sources and subjects, and thereby the diffuse senses in which his films might be readable, however tentatively, as *queer*. While this shrinking of the perceived Merchant Ivory canon has been an act of wilful cultural amnesia, it is also exacerbated by the uneven availability of Ivory's films,[33] including some directly pertinent to a full, nuanced exploration of *Call Me by Your Name*'s relationship with a wider 'queer Ivory' canon – which, as I shall discuss, extends beyond *Maurice*. Equally pertinent to *Call Me by Your Name*, the same forces have served to reduce awareness of the nomadic, transcultural character of the Merchant Ivory project and its expression in Ivory's films via his – as well as Jhabvala's – sensibility as a conscious (plural) outsider and observer of (plural) outsider characters. Long before their 'heritage' hits, Merchant–Ivory–Jhabvala defined themselves as 'the wandering company', making films 'concerned with the meeting of cultures':[34] first in postcolonial modern India; from the 1970s, America, then continental Europe; only later England; and eventually Shanghai (the Ishiguro-scripted *The White Countess*, 2005) and Latin America (*The City of Your Final Destination*, 2009: Jhabvala's final adapted screenplay before her death and, to date, Ivory's last fiction feature as director). In a recent reappraisal of this oeuvre, the Delhi-based film scholars Nildeep Paul and Madhubanti De suggest that 'the many cultural intersections' between Merchant–Ivory–Jhabvala 'would come to bestow a narrative ambiguity to their films', coupled with 'an emotional charge entirely peculiar to them':[35] qualities which are equally suggestive for a consideration of where the queerness might lie.

Call Me by Your Name *and the mainstreaming of* Maurice: *problematic 'parallels'*

To return to 2017 and the reception of *Call Me by Your Name*, the restricted aware-ness of the breadth of Ivory's cinema generated a dominant assumption – abundantly reiterated across every stratum of discourse around *Call Me by Your Name*, from publicity and social media to cultural and film blogging and journalism – that *Call Me by Your Name*'s queer antecedents in Ivory's oeuvre consisted of just one film: *Maurice*. Ivory himself has been active in countering this impres-sion. Informally interviewed by the film blogger Nathaniel Rogers at the 2017 Middleburg Film Festival, Ivory fast countered Rogers' excited declaration – '*Call Me by Your Name* is your first queer film since *Maurice*!' – with: 'But you know, there have been queer characters from the very first film'.[36] Ivory has, moreover, expanded upon these earlier 'queer characters' in writing as well as in interviews.[37]

The discursive repositioning of *Maurice* from 2017 onwards as 'the turn-of-the-century *Call Me by Your Name* you need to see'[38] nonetheless served a cross-promotional function and signalled a new phase (though not the first) in *Maurice*'s progressive 'rediscovery'. More precisely, the rising excitement around *Call Me by Your Name* from its earliest 2017 festival screenings onwards coincided with the 4K digital restoration[39] and screenings of Ivory's *Maurice* for its thirtieth anni-versary, and thereby with *Maurice*'s elevation from (passionately loved, vitally important) cult film with a grassroots following to belated mainstream critical validation as an LGBTQ classic.[40] *Call Me by Your Name*'s rapturously received world premiere at the Sundance Film Festival on 22 January 2017 was followed by red-carpet crowds at the 67th Berlinale by 13 February. The *Maurice* restora-tion premiered at Berlin earlier the same evening, followed by a US premiere at the San Francisco International Film Festival in April, further festival screenings and a limited cinema re-release (initially in the USA and Taiwan), all coinciding with the build-up to Ivory's 2017 Academy Award nomination and win.

Throughout this period and beyond, a blitz of media and social-media attention began to focus on perceived 'parallels' between the two films. More often than not, however, the 'parallels' proposed were meme-tically repetitive – overwhelm-ingly based on the comparison of paired promotional stills or screen captures of the same few scenes – and superficial.[41] One 'parallel' was posted most repeti-tively of all: Elio (Timothée Chalamet) and Oliver's (Armie Hammer) cautious but mutual first kiss lying in the grass on their rural day out by bicycle (Scene 58: 'Ext. Country Road/Springs – Fontanili Gaverine – Day' in Ivory's shooting script), versus *Maurice*'s *rebuffed* attempt to kiss and get physical with the insist-ently chaste Clive, also in the grass, on their day of escape from Cambridge into the Fens by motorbike and sidecar.[42] Both scenes are pivotal in the trajectory of

Elio/Oliver's and Maurice/Clive's respective relationships – but with markedly different dynamics, implications and outcomes which the 'parallels' comparisons chose to ignore (Figure 2.2).

While these repetitive comparisons may have done viral promotional work for both films, their status as analysis of the affinities – or significant differences – between *Call Me by Your Name* and *Maurice* and the two films' same-sex erotic and love relationships was often unreliable and even misleading. Most problematically, much of the post-2017 'parallels' discourse has worked to reorientate understandings of *Maurice* away from both Forster's and Ivory's intentions (and also away from earlier, established understandings among audiences and fans) towards an elitist, classist appropriation which celebrates Maurice's – formative but ultimately failed – sexless first-love relationship with Clive[43] while ignoring Maurice's sexually fulfilled second love with the resourceful, wholehearted and incredibly sexy Alec.[44] (To the novel's and film's bitter end, Clive insists that 'the sole excuse for any relationship between two men is that it remain purely platonic' even after Maurice has broken the news that he and Alec are lovers.) In

FIGURE 2.2: Problematic parallels – top: the most meme-tically cited romantic parallel between Maurice (James Wilby) and Clive (Hugh Grant) and Oliver (Armie Hammer) and Elio (Timothée Chalamet); below: a more instructive parallel, as Clive resists Maurice's advances and Elio mounts Oliver. James Ivory (dir.), *Maurice*, 1987. UK. © Maurice Productions Limited; Luca Guadagnino (dir.), *Call Me by Your Name*, 2017. Italy/France/USA/Brazil. © Frenesy, La Cinefacture.

place of Maurice's struggles towards self-knowledge and a hard-won, radically uncompromising happiness (a journey activated and advanced but not completed by his love for Clive), this new appropriation wallows in – and prefers – queer tears and the agony of parting. The comments thread on one YouTube '*Maurice* X *Call Me by Your Name*' fanvid tellingly illustrates this trend.[45] One user asks 'why the fuck both of them have sad ending' – an impression fully cemented by the video itself, in which Maurice's story appears to end in tears and at Clive's wedding. (In reality, the two scenes concerned occur, respectively, 61 minutes and 74 minutes into Ivory's 140-minute film.) This erasure of the significantly different turn of events in the film's final hour just so happens to match the heavily censored cut of *Maurice*, which was reportedly released, belatedly, on DVD in Russia in 1997.[46] In reply to one YouTube user's question: 'Why is not [Alec] Scudder and Maurice :(' in the video, a second user replies simply: 'Because scudder never left maurice'.[47]

Call Me by Your Name *and the wider 'queer Ivory' canon*

Call Me by Your Name's relationship to Ivory's *Maurice* clearly presents scope for a range of more nuanced, considered and critical readings, in particular for readings which engage with the two films' significant differences in many vital respects: as queer narratives, politically and contextually. Such work might explore (not exhaustively) the political force and very high stakes of *Maurice*'s ending, absent from *Call Me by Your Name*'s; the opposed valuing of speech over silence in *Call Me by Your Name* and (ultimately) deeds over words in *Maurice*; the two films' differing approaches to representing queer sex (*Call Me by Your Name*'s much-criticized evasiveness, in contrast with *Maurice*'s relaxed, 'natural' approach to homoeroticism and full-frontal male nudity 30 years earlier); and the radically different place – or absence – of class difference, servants and any kind of social friction. Where the English class system and its obsolescence, class-based erotics and (for Forster more than Ivory) the subversive power of cross-class same-sex desire to topple the system are central in *Maurice*, *Call Me by Your Name*'s queer summer idyll rests on a frictionless, hegemonic, unquestioned social homogeneity. The 'real' characters – benign, loving, cultured, highly educated and (in Elio's case) prodigiously gifted – uniformly belong to an elite of intellectual equals; their servants serve solely to cocoon Elio and the Perlmans in a further layer of frictionless kindness.

In this section of the chapter, I look beyond *Maurice*, and beyond the 'heritage' mode, to expand upon *Call Me by Your Name*'s place and precursors within Ivory's wider, lesser-known field of work, via attention to three main examples: *Slaves of New York* (1989), *A Soldier's Daughter Never Cries* (1998) and *The City of Your Final Destination*: to date, Ivory's last feature film as director and his sole feature made and completed entirely after Merchant's death. All three are adaptations – from, respectively, the New York 'brat pack' writer Tama Janowitz's breakthrough collection of short stories (1986); Kaylie Jones's semi-autobiographical novel about growing up in Paris, then America, as the daughter of the American Second World War novelist James Jones (1990); and the gay US author Peter Cameron's PEN/Faulkner Award-nominated 2002 novel – but of a free kind in which the Merchant Ivory imprint and their own biographical inflections can be felt (most prominently in Ivory and Jhabvala's treatment, as credited joint screenwriters, of Jones's *A Soldier's Daughter*).

Example 1, the critically divisive *Slaves of New York*, is of interest as an at first glance wildly unlikely Merchant Ivory precursor to *Call Me by Your Name*'s early-1980s retro setting, styling and music references, but equally as an example of the diffuse and subtle queer sensibility which permeates Ivory's oeuvre even when filming what he here called 'a heterosexual story'.[48] Ivory's interest in filming Janowitz's stories began in the *Maurice* editing suite, where *Maurice*'s editor Katherine Wenning was reading them, but the resulting film's queer genealogy owes more to Andy Warhol, Janowitz's mentor and the previous rights-holder until the rights were acquired by Merchant. Unusually for Merchant Ivory, Janowitz self-adapted her own stories about a clutch of self-absorbed aspirant artists and creatives on the fringes of the 1980s downtown Manhattan art scene; the premise is that all – regardless of gender or sexual orientation – are 'slaves' to staying put in toxic or crumbling relationships to keep a roof over their heads. At the centre is Eleanor (Bernadette Peters), an unconfident hat designer stuck with the emotionally abusive Stash (Adam Coleman Howard), a comically narcissistic, dubiously talented artist who constantly puts her down. Robert Emmet Long describes *Slaves* as having 'a kind of freakish vitality and uniqueness' and being 'an absolutely unpredictable Ivory film [...] with unexpected shades of Andy Warhol',[49] including an experimental use of split screen detested by many 1980s critics. Although, Ivory wrote, 'we were criticised for not making it more queer',[50] the film has a gay following. The sympathetic-but-comic treatment of Eleanor's struggles recognizably fits a tradition of gay male appropriations of the woman's picture; in one of the standout sequences, a trio of black drag queens in red dresses sashay down the street at dawn to The Supremes' 'Love Is Like an Itching in My Heart' as Eleanor finally finds the courage to confront Stash about his infidelities. Eleanor's relationship may be straight, but the camera's gaze is not – one of Stash's few uses is that he spends time in Mickey Mouse boxer shorts complaining about flea bites. And, more quietly, nor is the dénouement, which suggests a growing bond between two of the more likeable and put-upon male characters, Sherman (Charles McCaughan) and Marley (Nick Corri), whose looks also recall Ivory's Maurice and Alec.

The film's wider attractions include a real Stephen Sprouse catwalk show (1987 collection; in February 1987, Warhol had been buried in a Sprouse suit), any number of post-punk NYC club and performance sequences and a killer soundtrack which (while miraculously sustaining the involvement of Richard Robbins) closes on Boy George's 'Girlfriend'. Yet *Slaves* also drew on Merchant Ivory's wider regular team of craft talent: *A Room with a View*'s cinematographer Tony Pierce-Roberts, *Maurice*'s editor Wenning and (in the first of her five Ivory credits) costume designer Carol Ramsey. In terms of '80s styling, it is no surprise that *Slaves of New York* is significantly more flamboyant than *Call Me by Your Name*. What does surprise is its invigoratingly high (even avant-garde) level of '80s music and style literacy in counterpoint to *Call Me by Your Name*'s '80s-of-discretion retro choices. In testimony to the authenticity of the latter, however, Oliver's preppy style (shirt, chino shorts and white sneakers) is recognizably close to the look Hugh Grant (and, with trousers, James Wilby) could be seen wearing in the real 1980s at the 1987 Venice Film Festival.

Example 2, 1998's *A Soldier's Daughter Never Cries*, anticipates the polylingual American expats-in-Europe milieu of *Call Me by Your Name*. But it does much more in its delicate but frank focus on the complexities of identity, the senses of belonging and not-belonging, that this raises for the teenage protagonist Channe Willis (Luisa Conlon as a child/Leelee Sobieski in her teens) and her adopted brother Benoît (Samuel Gruen/Jesse Bradford), renamed Billy by their parents Bill and Marcella (Kris Kristofferson as the James Jones writer figure, Barbara Hershey as his wife who works for the UN) to make him 'belong'. The narrative is set in the 1960s to 1970s; the parents are liberal and progressive; Channe 'belongs' when they live in France. But when Bill's declining health (Jones was a heavy drinker) prompts their return to the USA, things become bleak. Channe's ordinary teenage sexuality makes her an outsider in America, suddenly the butt of high-school misogyny and treated as a slut; Billy/Benoît is bullied for standing up for his sister and becomes withdrawn and depressed. This relatively little-seen Ivory film does something further: the Parisian (mostly French-language) segment introduces a captivating, prodigiously gifted – and here, effeminate – teenage precursor of Elio himself: the musically precocious, opera-loving, polylingual gay teen Francis Fortescue. Within the context of a notional 'queer Ivory' canon, it is no coincidence that Francis's role as Channe's gay best friend is the most joyous thing in the film (Figure 2.3).

Francis was played by the countertenor Anthony Roth Costanzo, 15 at the time of filming, and subsequently a superstar of the New York Metropolitan Opera. Francis's mother (Jane Birkin) is an English eccentric (there is a backstory about a transnational aristocratic long-gone father) who protectively adores her son and is also his accompanying pianist. In one of the film's most startling scenes, Francis is invited by the teacher at his and Channe's bilingual school to sing Mozart's 'Tell Me What Love Is' ('*Voi che sapete*') from *The Marriage of Figaro*, accompanied

FIGURE 2.3: Ivory's queer prodigies: Francis (Anthony Roth Costanzo) vs. Elio (Timothée Chalamet). James Ivory (dir.), *A Soldier's Daughter Never Cries*, 1998. USA/UK/France. © Capitol Films, Merchant Ivory Productions; Luca Guadagnino (dir.), *Call Me by Your Name*, 2017. Italy/France/USA/Brazil. © Frenesy, La Cinefacture.

on piano by his mother. Francis's nervousness and the anticipatory homophobic titters and whispers from the class are evident, and these initially continue when the soaringly high range of Francis's voice is heard, accompanied by his highly expressive hand gestures. But, as the editing crosscuts to Channe, we see her pride in her friend, then rapture, then eventually a wiped-away tear, and cutaways to the whole class reveal a mix of reactions: some kids still chatting, others confused, others enraptured. *A Soldier's Daughter Never Cries* is one of Ivory's named favourites among his own films, alongside the also autobiographically slanted *Mr. & Mrs. Bridge* (1990). Francis is Ivory's middle name and, Ivory writes, 'I based his character and style somewhat on myself at 15, though I was careful not to tell [Costanzo] so'.[51] The film's biographical detailing includes that Francis has a miniature theatre at his home, where he stages productions and practices costume and set design. Ivory's own father built him a miniature theatre where Ivory did more or less the same.

Example 3, *The City of Your Final Destination*, a subtle adaptation (by Jhabvala) of Peter Cameron's 2002 novel on the random nature of love and the mysterious meaning of home, and Ivory's last fiction feature as director, is instantly recognizable as a – perfectly good – Ivory film. Yet it was barely released beyond the festival circuit, and never released at all in the UK. This near erasure today looks even stranger because *The City of Your Final Destination* presents numerous points of comparison with *Call Me by Your Name* eight years later, and is even preferred to *Call Me by Your Name* by some audiences who have been able to see it.

The City of Your Final Destination is set in Uruguay and was shot in Argentina with a stellar transnational cast drawn from four continents, including Anthony Hopkins, Laura Linney, Charlotte Gainsbourg, Alexandra Maria Lara and Hiroyuki Sanada. An outsider, a young literature academic – here, an Iranian–American, Omar (Omar Metwally) – has won a grant to write the biography of the late Jules Gund, a Latin American writer of Jewish ancestry, but cannot proceed without the authorization of three people: Gund's widow (Linney), his significantly younger mistress (Gainsbourg) and his gay brother (Hopkins). Spurred on by his more focused and ambitious academic girlfriend Deirdre (Lara) (careers, tenure, and the funds for a home and future are at stake), Omar travels uninvited to Latin America to make his case. Gauche and unwelcome, the would-be biographer enters the home and lives of a complicated transnational literary/intellectual family (here, coexisting in conflict rather than *Call Me by Your Name*'s loving harmony) who inhabit an isolated, strikingly distinctive (but, here, eccentrically decayed) house and rural estate. Like *Call Me by Your Name*, *The City of Your Final Destination* hinges on the complex, shifting interpersonal relationships that ensue among an ensemble cast. More pronouncedly – and, at times, comically – than in *Call Me by Your Name*, there are rivalries and jealousies, incompatibilities rooted in clashing values, and unexpected love. And close to the film's centre, and providing its emotional and moral ballast, there is a model of what an enduring Elio and Oliver might possibly (in an alternative narrative) have grown into: an enduring, happy, ageing gay male relationship – here, between Jules's brother Adam (Hopkins) and his significantly younger Japanese lover Pete (Hiroyuki Sanada), now in his 40s. Many years earlier, Pete explains, Adam 'liked' him enough as a 15-year-old to rescue him from poverty; they are still together.

Towards a conclusion

Alongside these cinematic examples of the nature and richness of *Call Me by Your Name*'s antecedents in Ivory's oeuvre, in conclusion I want to look briefly beyond notions of purely textual affinity and authorship to propose that *Call Me by Your Name*'s remarkable impact owes a debt to a still-less-considered area of Merchant Ivory influence: the partnership's promotional strategies, driven by Merchant's marketing genius, and specifically the multi-faceted strategies adopted in the 1980s promotion of *Maurice*. In the hugely challenging 1980s climate in which *Maurice* was made and released, these strategies anticipated, understood and amplified *Maurice*'s appeal for unprecedentedly plural audiences – gay male, but also across the queer spectrum and beyond. Pitched from the outset as 'a film of immense power [...] that is romantic, moving, and a story of love and self-discovery for all audiences',[52] *Maurice* was a first in succeeding to be that without compromising its integrity, purpose and power as LGBTQ cinema. Asked by Benedict Nightingale of the *New York Times* whether 'so defiant a salute to homosexual passion [was] really to be welcomed during a spiraling AIDS crisis', Merchant replied that '[i]t would be wrong to turn our face from the homosexual community [...] and treat the subject as taboo'; Ivory said that '[I] didn't and couldn't see it as a reason for not making the film'.[53]

The intentionality of this hybrid vision and its distinctiveness within the terrain of 1980s gay male cinema are evident today when reading *Maurice*'s earliest trade press and set reports. Merchant told *Variety*: 'The film will be humorous and romantic';[54] 'It [...] will break away from the art-house mould to which such films are usually assigned';[55] 'It's done in a different way from other films about homosexuals – within the context of normal feelings as opposed to abnormal feelings'.[56] In the 1980s gay press, *Maurice* was promoted variously on the continuing relevance of its characters' dilemmas, the queer-history importance of Forster's novel and the promise of nudity – but it was also promoted lavishly in the high-end glossies, and in teenage girls' and young women's magazines. In August 1987, *Maurice* was presented as a marketing case study at the second Sundance Institute Annual Independent Producers Conference. In a 1987 profile of the Manhattan-based independent production and distribution company Cinecom, one of *Maurice*'s backers, Cinecom's youthful CEO Amir Malin, admitted that

> he was surprised to discover who the audience is for the film, a gay love story based on the E. M. Forster novel. 'It shattered the box office at the Paris Theater [sic] in New York City, but the largest segment of the audience is not gay. It's about 50/50, and we expected it to be more like 80/20. The lesson is, never second guess [sic] your audience.'[57]

These strategies provided the blueprint which *Call Me by Your Name* would adopt in its own crossover promotional and release strategy 30 years later (one might say right down to *Call Me by Your Name*'s Sundance premiere and months-long run at the Paris in NYC). As is sometimes said in post-2017 *Maurice* fan and social-media discourse, '*Maurice* ran so that *Call Me by Your Name* could walk' – in more respects than one.

NOTES

1. Ivory's 2017 Academy Award for Best Adapted Screenplay for *Call Me by Your Name* was one of 21 Best Adapted Screenplay award wins for the film, including from BAFTA, The

Writers Guild of America, the Alliance of Women Film Journalists and numerous international and regional US critics' awards. At 89, he became the oldest winner of a competitive Oscar in history, following three earlier Oscar nominations as Best Director (1986 for *A Room with a View*, 1992 for *Howards End* and 1993 for *The Remains of the Day*) and two earlier Best Adapted Screenplay Oscar wins for Merchant Ivory's regular screenwriter Ruth Prawer Jhabvala (for *A Room with a View* and *Howards End*).

2.   An extensive profile published in *New York* magazine as long ago as 1987, shortly after the US release of Ivory's *Maurice*, described producer Merchant and director Ivory as

> companions and partners – joined in a relationship that the great Indian actor Shashi Kapoor has called 'more than a marriage'. Around them, they've gathered a sort of moviemaking family […]. The group makes up one of the most unusual associations in the movie business.

Dinitia Smith, 'The Raj Duet: Riding High with Merchant and Ivory', *New York*, 5 October 1987, 58. Ivory and Merchant were first introduced in New York in 1961. They fast formed Merchant Ivory Productions, frequently credited as the world's first independent film production company, and by 1965 were living together, in a relationship which would endure until Merchant's 2005 death during surgery. Their collaboration and friendship with writer Ruth Prawer Jhabvala dates from their first feature, *The Householder* (1963), self-adapted by Jhabvala from her postcolonial modern Indian novel of the same title and starring Kapoor, then in his mid 20s. Jhabvala herself was a Jewish child refugee whose family had fled Nazi Germany and settled in England. In London, she met and married Cyrus Jhabvala, a Parsee Indian architect, and the pair settled in New Delhi, where Jhabvala remained until she relocated to New York in the mid 1970s. There, Robbins became music teacher to Jhabvala's youngest daughter and, from *The Europeans* (1979) to *The White Countess* (2005), the soundtrack composer/arranger for every Merchant Ivory film. Stephen Soucy's 2023 documentary *Merchant Ivory* makes public that, for a time, Robbins was also in an intimate relationship with Merchant. Also in the mid 1970s, Ivory and Merchant bought (and began the lengthy renovation of) their now-famous Greek Revival house at Claverack in upstate New York, where Ivory still lives. On 29 and 30 November 2017, Ivory's Instagram feed @mipfilms shared images of Timothée Chalamet as a guest at Claverack in 2015, including Chalamet reading through the *Call Me by Your Name* script.

3.   See Nathaniel Rogers, 'Interview: James Ivory on *Call Me by Your Name* and the Merchant Ivory Legacy', *The Film Experience*, 27 February 2018, http://thefilmexperience.net/blog/2018/2/27/interview-james-ivory-on-call-me-by-your-name-and-the-mercha.html.

4.   Robert Emmet Long, *The Films of Merchant Ivory* (London: Viking Penguin, 1992), 125.

5.   Joseph Giovannini, 'Merchant and Ivory's Country Retreat', *New York Times*, 3 April 1986, section C, 1, https://www.nytimes.com/1986/04/03/garden/merchant-and-ivory-s-country-retreat.html.

6. See Chelsea Fullmer, 'James Ivory '51', *Official University of Oregon Alumni Association News: Arts & Entertainment Edition*, May 2013, https://www.uoalumni.com/s/1540/uoaa/blank_archive.aspx?sid=1540&gid=3&pgid=1193.

7. Giovannini, 'Country Retreat'.

8. See Giovannini, 'Country Retreat'; Krista Madsen, 'Movies Made Here: *Savages* (1972)', patch.com, 30 August 2011, https://patch.com/new-york/tarrytown/movies-made-here-savages-1972; Robert Emmet Long, *James Ivory in Conversation: How Merchant Ivory Makes Its Movies* (Berkeley and Los Angeles: University of California Press, 2005), 118.

9. Janet Maslin, 'Foreword', in Long, *James Ivory in Conversation*, xi.

10. Indicatively, Smith, 'The Raj Duet'; John Stark, 'Partners and Friends for 26 Years, James Ivory and Ismail Merchant Film a Hotly Debated Gay Love Story', *People* 28, no. 17 (26 October 1987), http://www.people.com/people/archive/article/0,,20097439,00.html.

11. Indicatively, Andrew Sarris, 'Forster Care', *Village Voice*, 11 March 1986, 53; Stephen Harvey, 'Men in Love', *Village Voice*, 22 September 1987, 72; Rita Kempley, '*Maurice*', *Washington Post*, 2 October 1987, https://www.washingtonpost.com/wp-srv/style/longterm/movies/videos/mauricerkempley_a0ca53.htm; Thomas Waugh, 'Laws of Desire: *Maurice*, *Law of Desire*, and *Vera*', in *The Fruit Machine: Twenty Years of Writings on Queer Cinema* (Durham and London: Duke University Press, 2000), 187–94.

12. Including my own work since the 1990s. Paul and De specifically cite Claire Monk, 'The British "Heritage" Film and Its Critics', *Critical Survey* 7, no. 2 (1995): 116–24, https://www.jstor.org/stable/41555905.

13. Nildeep Paul and Madhubanti De, 'Merchant Ivory's India: Colonial Legacies and Expatriate Desires', *Sahapedia* (online), 24 May 2021, https://www.sahapedia.org/merchant-ivorys-india-colonial-legacies-and-expatriate-desires.

14. Suzanne Speidel, '"Scenes of Marvellous Variety": The Work-in-Progress Screenplays of *Maurice*', *Journal of Adaptation in Film & Performance* 7, no. 3 (2014): 310.

15. Quoted in Sarah Larson, 'James Ivory and the Making of a Historic Gay Love Story', *New Yorker*, 19 May 2017, https://www.newyorker.com/culture/persons-of-interest/james-ivory-and-the-making-of-a-historic-gay-love-story.

16. Forster hesitated to publish *Maurice* during his lifetime precisely because its happy, non-punitive, physically fulfilled ending laid the novel, and Forster, open to prosecution. After several decades as a privately circulated, periodically revised work, he finalized *Maurice* for posthumous publication in the late 1950s when he was almost 80 – following the 1957 publication of the Wolfenden Report, but some years before the 1967 Sexual Offences Act brought the partial decriminalization of male homosexual acts in the United Kingdom.

17. For a full account, see Claire Monk, '*Maurice* Without Ending: From Forster's Palimpsest to Fan-Text', in *Twenty-First Century Readings of E. M. Forster's* Maurice, ed. Emma Sutton and Tsung-Han Tsai (Liverpool: Liverpool University Press, 2020), 232–33.

18. E. M. Forster, 'Notes on *Maurice*' (1960), in *Maurice, The Abinger Edition of E. M. Forster*, Vol. 5, ed. Philip Gardner (London: André Deutsch, [1971] 1999), 216.

19. Ivory's original casting for *Maurice* would, further, have retroactively queered his *A Room with a View*. Ivory originally recast Julian Sands and Rupert Graves – *A Room*'s full-frontal skinny-dippers George Emerson and Freddy Honeychurch, the 'straight' romantic lead and the brother of his love interest Lucy Honeychurch (Helena Bonham Carter) – as Maurice and Alec. However, Sands dropped out of *Maurice* a month before shooting began and was replaced at short notice by Wilby.

20. Larson, 'James Ivory'.

21. Kempley, '*Maurice*'.

22. Quoted in Larson, 'James Ivory'. The real kiss – dubbed 'the face-eating scene' by some fans – was proposed by the actors themselves. Wilby and Graves 'struck an immediate friendship' on set – perhaps necessarily, as the kiss was shot within the first few days of *Maurice*'s autumn 1986 schedule – and have sustained a friendly rivalry ever since about which of them proposed it. Wilby quoted in Claire Monk, 'James Wilby in Conversation', in Blu-ray booklet, *Maurice* (London: BFI, [2017] 2019), Blu-ray Disc (4K Restoration), BFIB13304K: 13–14.

23. E. M. Forster, *Maurice, The Abinger Edition of E. M. Forster*, Vol. 5, ed. Philip Gardner (London: André Deutsch, [1971] 1999), 160.

24. Forster, *Maurice*, 178. While Forster's Clive uses the word 'straight' to mean 'honest', Forster himself would have been fully aware of the double meaning – particularly by the late 1950s when he finalized *Maurice* for publication – and intentional in invoking it. The manuscript history of *Maurice* shows Forster adjusting his use of the word 'queer' in later versions, signalling his apparent intentionality and authorial control in relation to such double meanings and perhaps also a dual address to knowing queer readers alongside a 'wider public'. Ivory and Kit Hesketh-Harvey's screenplay for *Maurice*, in contrast, removed these instances (in the film, Clive merely says 'he's a little too smart'), presumably on the assumption that Forster's uses of 'straight' and 'queer' were unwitting and likely to attract mockery from 1980s audiences.

25. Forster, *Maurice*, 195.

26. Forster, *Maurice*, 187.

27. 'They've taken that ladder away at last, I see, Sir', the film's all-knowing butler/valet Simcox (Patrick Godfrey) remarks to a bleary Maurice the morning after. One of Ivory's innovations in *Maurice* – made with Jhabvala's uncredited input – is the considerable enlargement of Simcox as a character and the decision to make the elderly manservant, subtextually, closet-queer. During the film's unfolding narrative, Simcox's queer knowledge (the servants have no illusions about Clive, or Maurice) serves as both veiled threat and fount of loaded innuendo. But he is ultimately also the enabler of Alec's seduction of Maurice, relaying suggestive messages which seep into Maurice's unconscious, then signing off for the night with a cattiness which exposes Alec's feelings for Maurice but

also tacitly endorses Alec's intentions ('An easy start tomorrow, with only Mr Hall's pleasure to wait upon').

28. See Claire Monk, '*Maurice* (1971) by E. M. Forster/*Maurice* (James Ivory, 1987)', in *Books to Film: Cinematic Adaptations of Literary Works*, Vol. 1, ed. Barry Keith Grant (Farmington Hills: Gale Cengage, 2017), 257–61; Monk, 'James Wilby'; Monk, '*Maurice* without Ending'.

29. Source: the programme for the 17 September 1987 memorial service in remembrance of Seifert and the brochure for *Maurice*'s US charity premiere on the evening of the same date are both held in the James Ivory Papers, University of Oregon Archives: Box 32, File 10 (accessed 24 May 2016) and Box 31, File 4 (accessed 19 May 2016), respectively.

30. Quoted in Larson, 'James Ivory'.

31. Mark Finch and Richard Kwietniowski, 'Melodrama and *Maurice*: Homo Is Where the Het Is', *Screen* 29, no. 3 (1988), 79.

32. Finch and Kwietniowski, 72.

33. In 2015, Ivory sold global distribution rights to the 'Merchant Ivory Library' to the US Cohen Media Group, comprising 21 features (of which only fourteen were directed by Ivory) and nine documentaries and shorts. However, the deal only covered films which Merchant Ivory owned entirely, not their features made with studio involvement, of which there are a significant number – by my calculation, thirteen directed by Ivory. The deal thus excludes all eight of Ivory's cinematic features as director since 1993, from *The Remains of the Day* through to *The City of Your Final Destination* (2009), as well as the earlier *The Guru* (1969), *The Wild Party* (1975), *A Room with a View* (1985), *Slaves of New York* (1989) and *Mr. & Mrs. Bridge* (1990). Among these studio films, two of Ivory's own favourites, both of exceptional autobiographical and queer interest, have vanished from distribution: *Mr. & Mrs. Bridge* (which starred Paul Newman and, Oscar-nominated, Joanne Woodward, and would be a recognized classic if it had been directed a few years later by Todd Haynes) and *A Soldier's Daughter Never Cries* (1998), discussed later in this chapter.

34. John Pym, *The Wandering Company: Twenty-One Years of Merchant Ivory Films* (London and New York: British Film Institute and Museum of Modern Art, 1983), cover copy.

35. Paul and De, 'India'.

36. Quoted in Rogers, 'Interview'.

37. See, for example, James Ivory, 'Introduction', in Blu-ray booklet, *Maurice* (London: BFI, [2017] 2019), Blu-ray Disc (4K Restoration), BFIB13304K: 1–3.

38. Claire Marie Healy, '*Maurice*: The Turn-of-the-Century *Call Me by Your Name* You Need to See', *AnotherMan*, 24 July 2018, https://www.anothermanmag.com/life-culture/10427/maurice-the-turn-of-the-century-call-me-by-your-name-you-need-to-see.

39. Funded and released by the Cohen Media Group: see Note 33.

40. For an account of the pre-2017 history of passionate audience/fan investments in Ivory's *Maurice*, its evolving visibility in twenty-first-century internet participatory culture, and the forms of fan productivity and crossover appropriation *Maurice* has inspired, see Claire

Monk, 'Heritage Film Audiences 2.0: Period Film Audiences and Online Fan Cultures', Participations: Journal of Audience & Reception Studies 8, no. 2 (2011): 431–77, http://www.participations.org/Volume%208/Issue%202/3h%20Monk.pdf; on the transnational dimension, see Claire Monk, 'From "English" Heritage to Transnational Audiences: Fan Perspectives and Practices and Why They Matter', in Screening European Heritage: Creating and Consuming History on Film, ed. Paul Cooke and Rob Stone (Basingstoke: Palgrave Macmillan, 2016), 209–34. The first, fragmentary, attempts to establish virtual fan communities around Maurice (novel and film) date from around 2004, the year in which Criterion first released the Merchant Ivory Collection two-disc DVD edition of the film, making Maurice's alternative opening sequence and many deleted scenes (vestiges of Ivory's non-linear, three-hour, shooting-script version) public for the first time.

41. For four examples of the 'parallels' genre, illustrating its meme-like similarities across professional media coverage and fan posts alike, see Healy, 'Maurice'; u/symbiandevotee, 'Just saw Maurice. Pretty much reminiscence [sic] of Call Me by Your Name', r/callmebyyourname Reddit, c.2018 ('4 years ago' at 25 April 2022), https://www.reddit.com/r/callmebyyourname/comments/8b10tm/just_saw_maurice_pretty_much_reminiscence_of_cmbyn/; Summer, 'Call Me by Your Name X Maurice [The Winter] Oliver&Elio + Maurice&Clive', YouTube, 3 February 2018, https://www.youtube.com/watch?v=I6XLu_mdx1g; hellish-cruelty, 'Cinematic Parallels: Maurice X Call Me by Your Name', 19 May 2021, https://hellish-cruelty.tumblr.com.

42. The version of this scene in Ivory's released Maurice is a departure from the shooting script.

43. The post-2017 pro-Clive reception turn would perplex most of Maurice's first- and second-generation gay male audiences, Ivory and Forster himself. In the estimation of the late London Evening Standard critic Alexander Walker: 'Clive, to put it bluntly, [is] a shit. […] [He] rats on his friends lest they land him in trouble, has a nervous breakdown, and finally decides to lead a social lie rather than face up to a sexual truth.' Alexander Walker, 'Of Flesh and Fashion', Evening Standard, 5 November 1987, 33. The Canadian gay critic and film scholar Thomas Waugh wrote, similarly, that 'Maurice had a profound impact on me: I never recovered from Hugh Grant having hurt Maurice so much and have not been able to stomach him to this day, star or martyr to lust or whatever'. Waugh, 'Laws of Desire', 187.

44. Even Ivory himself identified classism as the likely factor in any preference for Clive: 'unless one subscribes to English ideas about class, [how could it be that] Hugh Grant is acceptable, but the equally handsome and magnetic Rupert Graves is not?' (quoted in Long, James Ivory, 214). Among Maurice's first-generation male critics, of the three leads, both Walker and Waugh singled out Graves – as 'the best of the three actors' (Walker, 'Of Flesh', 33) and as destined for 'the summits of heartthrob-dom' (Waugh, 'Laws of Desire', 189).

45. Summer, 'Call Me'.

46. See Monk, 'From "English" Heritage', 228.

47. Summer, 'Call Me'.

48. Ivory, 'Introduction', 2.
49. Long, *James Ivory*, 184.
50. Ivory, 'Introduction', 2.
51. Ivory, 'Introduction', 3.
52. Criterion/Merchant Ivory. Cover copy, Merchant Ivory Collection DVD edition of *Maurice*. The Criterion Collection, 2004.
53. Benedict Nightingale, 'A Gay "Love Story"', *New York Times*, 13 September 1987, www.nytimes.com/1987/09/13/movies/a-gay-love-story.html.
54. Quoted in Anon, 'Merchant Ivory Pic Is First Ever Okayed for Cambridge Uni', *Variety*, 5 November 1986, 35.
55. Quoted in Tina McFarling, 'Merchant-Ivory's *Maurice* to Shoot with *Room* Star Sands', *Screen International*, 6 September 1986, 2.
56. Quoted in Victoria Radin, 'On the Set: *Maurice*', *Vogue* (USA) 177, no. 5 (May 1987), 62.
57. Quoted in Laurie Halpern Smith, 'Cinecom: East Indie: A Small New York Film Company Targets the Grownup Market', *Movieline*, 6 November 1987, 57.

REFERENCES

Anon. 'Merchant Ivory Pic Is First Ever Okayed for Cambridge Uni.' *Variety*, 5 November 1986: 35.

Criterion/Merchant Ivory. Cover copy, Merchant Ivory Collection DVD edition of *Maurice*. The Criterion Collection, 2004.

Fellowes, Julian, creator. *Downton Abbey* (TV). Carnival Film & Television, Masterpiece, 2010–15.

Finch, Mark, and Richard Kwietniowski. 'Melodrama and *Maurice*: Homo Is Where the Het Is', *Screen* 29, no. 3 (1988): 72–80.

Forster, E. M. *Maurice. The Abinger Edition of E. M. Forster*, Vol. 5, edited by Philip Gardner. London: André Deutsch, [1971] 1999.

Forster, E. M. 'Notes on *Maurice* [1960].' In *Maurice, by E. M. Forster. The Abinger Edition of E. M. Forster*, Vol. 5, edited by Philip Gardner, 215–20. London: André Deutsch, [1971] 1999.

Fullmer, Chelsea. 'James Ivory '51.' *Official University of Oregon Alumni Association News: Arts & Entertainment Edition*, May 2013. https://www.uoalumni.com/s/1540/uoaa/blank_archive.aspx?sid=1540&gid=3&pgid=1193.

Giovannini, Joseph. 'Merchant and Ivory's Country Retreat.' *New York Times*, 3 April 1986, Section C: 1. https://www.nytimes.com/1986/04/03/garden/merchant-and-ivory-s-country-retreat.html.

Guadagnino, Luca, dir. *Call Me by Your Name*. Frenesy Film Company, La Cinefacture, RT Features, 2017.

Halpern Smith, Laurie. 'Cinecom: East Indie: A Small New York Film Company Targets the Grownup Market.' *Movieline*, 6 November 1987: 56–57.

Harvey, Stephen. 'Men in Love.' *Village Voice*, 22 September 1987: 72.

Healy, Claire Marie. '*Maurice*: The Turn-of-the-Century *Call Me by Your Name* You Need to See.' *AnotherMan*, 24 July 2018. https://www.anothermanmag.com/life-culture/10427/maurice-the-turn-of-the-century-call-me-by-your-name-you-need-to-see.

hellish-cruelty. 'Cinematic Parallels: *Maurice X Call Me by Your Name*.' 19 May 2021. https://hellish-cruelty.tumblr.com.

Ivory, James, dir. *The Householder*. Merchant Ivory Productions, 1963.

Ivory, James, dir. *The Guru*. Twentieth Century Fox, Arcadia Films, Merchant Ivory Productions, 1969.

Ivory, James, dir. *Bombay Talkie*. Merchant Ivory Productions, 1970.

Ivory, James, dir. *Savages*. Angelika Films, Merchant Ivory Productions, 1972.

Ivory, James, dir. *The Wild Party*. American International Pictures, Merchant Ivory Productions, The Wild Party Production Company, 1975.

Ivory, James, dir. *The Europeans*. Merchant Ivory Productions, 1979.

Ivory, James, dir. *A Room with a View*. Goldcrest Films International, Merchant Ivory Productions, 1985.

Ivory, James, dir. *Maurice*. Merchant Ivory Productions, Cinecom Pictures, Channel 4, 1987.

Ivory, James, dir. *Slaves of New York*. TriStar Pictures, Gary Hendler, Merchant Ivory Productions, 1989.

Ivory, James, dir. *Mr. & Mrs. Bridge*. Miramax, Cineplex Odeon Films, Merchant Ivory/Robert Halmi, 1990.

Ivory, James, dir. *Howards End*. Merchant Ivory Productions, 1992.

Ivory, James, dir. *The Remains of the Day*. Columbia Pictures, Merchant Ivory Productions, 1993.

Ivory, James, dir. *A Soldier's Daughter Never Cries*. Capitol Films, Merchant Ivory Productions, British Screen Productions, 1998.

Ivory, James, dir. *The White Countess*. Merchant Ivory Productions, Sony Pictures Classics, Shanghai Film Group, 2005.

Ivory, James, dir. *The City of Your Final Destination*. Hyde Park International, Merchant Ivory, 2009.

Ivory, James. 'Introduction.' In Blu-ray booklet, *Maurice*. London: BFI, [2017] 2019. Blu-ray Disc (4K Restoration). BFIB1330: 1–3.

Kempley, Rita. '*Maurice*.' *Washington Post*, 2 October 1987. https://www.washingtonpost.com/wp-srv/style/longterm/movies/videos/mauricerkempley_a0ca53.htm.

Larson, Sarah. 'James Ivory and the Making of a Historic Gay Love Story.' *New Yorker*, 19 May 2017. https://www.newyorker.com/culture/persons-of-interest/james-ivory-and-the-making-of-a-historic-gay-love-story.

Long, Robert Emmet. *The Films of Merchant Ivory*. London: Viking Penguin, 1992.

Long, Robert Emmet. *James Ivory in Conversation: How Merchant Ivory Makes Its Movies*. Berkeley and Los Angeles: University of California Press, 2005.

Madsen, Krista. 'Movies Made Here: *Savages* (1972).' patch.com, 30 August 2011. https://patch.com/new-york/tarrytown/movies-made-here-savages-1972.

Maslin, Janet. 'Foreword.' In Robert Emmet Long, *James Ivory in Conversation: How Merchant Ivory Makes Its Movies*, ix–xi. Berkeley and Los Angeles: University of California Press, 2005.

McFarling, Tina. 'Merchant-Ivory's *Maurice* to Shoot with *Room* Star Sands.' *Screen International*, 6 September 1986: 2.

Monk, Claire. 'The British "Heritage" Film and Its Critics.' *Critical Survey* 7, no. 2 (1995): 116–24. https://www.jstor.org/stable/41555905.

Monk, Claire. '*Heritage Film Audiences* 2.0: Period Film Audiences and Online Fan Cultures.' *Participations: Journal of Audience & Reception Studies* 8, no. 2 (2011): 431–77. https://www.participations.org/08-02-24-monk.pdf.

Monk, Claire. 'From "English" Heritage to Transnational Audiences: Fan Perspectives and Practices and Why They Matter.' In *Screening European Heritage: Creating and Consuming History on Film*, edited by Paul Cooke and Rob Stone, 209–34. Basingstoke: Palgrave Macmillan, 2016.

Monk, Claire. '*Maurice* (1971) by E. M. Forster/*Maurice* (James Ivory, 1987).' In *Books to Film: Cinematic Adaptations of Literary Works*, Vol. I, edited by Barry Keith Grant, 257–61. Farmington Hills: Gale Cengage, 2017.

Monk, Claire. 'James Wilby in Conversation.' In Blu-ray booklet, *Maurice*. London: BFI, [2017] 2019. Blu-ray Disc (4K Restoration). BFIB1330: 12-23.

Monk, Claire. '*Maurice* without Ending: From Forster's Palimpsest to Fan-Text.' In *Twenty-First Century Readings of E. M. Forster's* Maurice, edited by Emma Sutton and Tsung-Han Tsai, 229–51. Liverpool: Liverpool University Press, 2020.

Nightingale, Benedict. 'A Gay "Love Story".' *New York Times*, 13 September 1987. www.nytimes.com/1987/09/13/movies/a-gay-love-story.html.

Paul, Nildeep, and Madhubanti De. 'Merchant Ivory's India: Colonial Legacies and Expatriate Desires.' *Sahapedia* (online), 24 May 2021. https://www.sahapedia.org/merchant-ivorys-india-colonial-legacies-and-expatriate-desires.

Pym, John. *The Wandering Company: Twenty-One Years of Merchant Ivory Films*. London and New York: British Film Institute and Museum of Modern Art, 1984.

Radin, Victoria. 'On the Set: *Maurice*.' *Vogue* (USA) 177, no. 5 (May 1987): 62 and 66.

Rogers, Nathaniel. 'Interview: James Ivory on *Call Me by Your Name* and the Merchant Ivory Legacy.' *The Film Experience*, 27 February 2018. http://thefilmexperience.net/blog/2018/2/27/interview-james-ivory-on-call-me-by-your-name-and-the-mercha.html.

Sarris, Andrew. 'Forster Care.' *Village Voice*, 11 March 1986: 53.

Sharman, Jim, dir. *The Rocky Horror Picture Show*. Twentieth Century Fox, Michael White Productions, 1975.

Smith, Dinitia. 'The Raj Duet: Riding High with Merchant and Ivory.' *New York*, 20, no. 39 (5 October 1987): 58–67.

Speidel, Suzanne. '"Scenes of Marvellous Variety": The Work-in-Progress Screenplays of *Maurice*.' *Journal of Adaptation in Film & Performance* 7, no. 3 (2014): 299–318.

Stark, John. 'Partners and Friends for 26 Years, James Ivory and Ismail Merchant Film a Hotly Debated Gay Love Story.' *People* 28, no. 17 (26 October 1987). http://www.people.com/people/archive/article/0,,20097439,00.html.

Summer. '*Call Me by Your Name X Maurice* [The Winter] Oliver&Elio + Maurice&Clive.' YouTube, 3 February 2018. https://www.youtube.com/watch?v=I6XLu_mdx1g.

u/symbiandevotee. 'Just saw *Maurice*. Pretty much reminiscence [sic] of *Call Me by Your Name*.' r/callmebyyourname Reddit, *c*.2018 ('4 years ago' at 25 April 2022). https://www.reddit.com/r/callmebyyourname/comments/8b10tm/just_saw_maurice_pretty_much_reminiscence_of_cmbyn/.

Walker, Alexander. 'Of Flesh and Fashion.' *Evening Standard*, 5 November 1987: 32–33.

Waugh, Thomas. 'Laws of Desire: *Maurice*, *Law of Desire*, and *Vera*.' In Waugh, *The Fruit Machine: Twenty Years of Writings on Queer Cinema*, 187–94. Durham, NC and London: Duke University Press, 2000.

3

'Is It Better to Speak or Die?':
Adaptation and Elio's Interiority

Stuart Richards

Film and literature each have their own devices for character development. These differences are particularly stark when considering the adaptation of Elio (Timothée Chalamet) from André Aciman's book to Luca Guadagnino's film. The arc is ultimately a 'coming-of-age' one, where Elio processes and embraces his feelings towards Oliver (Armie Hammer). *Call Me by Your Name* is a 1980s summer romance infused with passion, longing and the dreaded heartache that comes with the closing of Oliver's departure from the Perlman household. Elio is a deeply empathetic person. We see this with how close he is with both parents, who regularly display forms of non-verbal compassion. Yet when it comes to interactions with Oliver, Elio struggles to comprehend and express his desires. Aciman's book is driven by Elio's manic, obsessive and often conflicting inner dialogue. Timothée Chalamet's task, then, is a difficult one: he must convey these complex emotions not through voice-over or dialogue but largely through his non-verbal performance, often aided by other cinematic devices. In her essay on the film, Joanna Di Mattia writes:

> *Call Me by Your Name* is a film in which dialogue is used minimally for maximum effect – its most powerful moments contain few or no words at all. Many of these moments involve Annella, who often observes her son's interactions with Oliver or offers gentle encouragement.[1]

This is perhaps initially evident in an early scene as the family sits down to dinner. When it becomes clear that Oliver will not be joining them, Annella (Amira Casar) instructs Mafalda (Vanda Capriolo) to remove Oliver's plates from the table. 'Elio's body betrays him', writes Di Mattia.[2] For the briefest of moments, Elio's jocular temperament changes and he looks at his mother with an expression that's as if the wind is taken out of him. Chalamet looks up to the evening sky and takes a deep breath, willing the tears not to come. Often, Elio's non-verbal communication expresses more than his words ever do (Figure 3.1). Elio's first-person narration in Aciman's book appears to be adapted into a third-person narration. These moments in Chalamet's performance, however, speak to the narration being largely restricted to Elio's perspective and character development. He is both the agent and the psychological subject of the film's *syuzhet*, the plot's organization of broader story material. These moments in Chalamet's performance give insight akin to the interiority provided by the book. This is particularly evident for those with the foreknowledge of Aciman's book. Considering 'book Elio' and 'film Elio' as one and the same demonstrates the joy of experiencing an adapted text. This reading of Elio is granted a sense of interiority and a deeper appreciation of Chalamet's performance.

This analysis of Elio is an exploration of how performance, supported by other forms of cinematic grammar, is used to convey character development. Initially, this may seem to be yet another study on the matter of fidelity, i.e. how is the film different to the book? In answering that question, however, I intend to develop a reading that is post-structuralist in nature. How do new authors, each with their own forms of grammar, adapt Aciman's text? By analyzing the relationship between the book and the film, we can explore the quiet nuance of Chalamet's performance. The value of the adapted text – whether the film is any good – is not the focus of this study. Adaptation scholars have long argued against this value judgement of adapted texts. In 'Adaptation, or the Cinema as Digest', André Bazin argues against the 'faithfulness to a form' and advocates for a process of adaptation that seeks cinematic '*equivalence in meaning of the forms*'.[3] The greater meanings of a novel exist beyond the confines of surface 'style' and can, therefore, coexist with different formal equivalences: we need to consider 'book Elio' alongside 'film Elio'. In this chapter,

FIGURE 3.1: Elio (Timothée Chalamet) realizes Oliver's absence and his body betrays him. Luca Guadagnino (dir.), *Call Me by Your Name*, 2017. Italy/France/USA/Brazil. © Frenesy, La Cinefacture.

I argue that Chalamet's performance is appreciated further when viewed alongside Aciman's novel. For Catherine Grant, adaptation is a matter of reception, as screen texts require their audiences to 'recall the adapted work, or the cultural memory'.[4] Rather than most of the book's inner monologue being conveyed through dialogue, this is conveyed through performance, gesture and expression. If we are familiar with Elio's obsessive desire in the novel, we pay particular attention to Chalamet's minute changes in expression. As Elio looks up briefly as Oliver's plate and cutlery are removed, we see tears seemingly welling, glistening by the candlelight.

Adaptation of character

This analysis of *Call Me by Your Name* is shaped by Robert Stam's position that adaptation is a process of translation, where the story is decoded into a new medium. Stam's argument largely draws on Gérard Genette's work on textuality to argue that we should consider adaptation as a dialogue, with transtextuality being 'all that which puts one text in relation, whether manifest or secret, with other texts'.[5] Adaptation is then a form of transtextual dialogism between the literary and the screen. By considering book Elio and film Elio as one and the same, we can 'put them in dialogue' and consider the interiority of Chalamet's performance. If we were to consider key movements, gestures and expressions as signs of a larger text, they allow for a deeper reading of Elio's characterization. This dialogue allows us to consider Chalamet's achievements further. Adaptations, according to Stam, are an 'ongoing whirl of intertextual references and transformation, of texts generating other texts in an endless process of recycling, transformation, transmutation, with no clear point of origin'.[6] This will become clearer in my analysis of Chalamet's performance, where the film clearly draws on star power beyond Aciman's work. As Stam argues, screen adaptations are 'mediated by a series of filters – studio style, ideological fashion, political constraints, auteurist predilections, charismatic stars, economic advantage, evolving technology'.[7] As such, the film of *Call Me by Your Name* is a new text that simultaneously reminds the viewer of Aciman's original writing.

There is pleasure in viewing an adapted text through the identification of repetition; they are 'second without being secondary'.[8] The knowing reader or viewer enjoys the intellectual pleasure of intertextuality, in seeing various nods to Oliver as being Elio's Adonis, the emphasis on Oliver's 'Later', other allusions to a Graeco-Roman aesthetic or Elio's mother drawing their attention to the story of the shy knight. We can also appreciate the power of these minute moments in Chalamet's performance. This brief emotional moment from Elio at the dinner table is a powerful moment and an early indicator of his obsession. This is particularly evident for those who have read Aciman's novel. On one level, identifying these connections

can be nothing more than appreciation; on another, they can strengthen the transtextual relationship between the source novel and the film.

In his analysis of the construction of characters in film, Richard Dyer argues
that we gather information on the character through multiple sources. Audience foreknowledge, names, objective correlatives, i.e. 'physical correlatives to
symbolize mental states', the speech of the character in question and of those
around them, and *mise en scène* all shape our interpretation.[9] Without this foreknowledge, audiences can still enjoy, and be moved by, the relationship dynamics
of Elio and Oliver. These connections to the source text, however, allow for deeper
reading of film Elio. These signs will be my guide as I examine Chalamet's quiet
performance in light of Elio's manic nature in Aciman's book. This foreknowledge
of Elio's characterization in Aciman's book is pivotal to how we read Chalamet's
performance. In his 1976 book *The World in a Frame*, Leo Braudy distinguishes
between characterization in film and those from literature and theatre. While
he clarifies that the distinctions outlined are 'not absolute points but on a slip-
pery continuum',[10] for Braudy, one key difference is that of interiority, which is
often used to justify the superiority of literature over film. Literature, more often
than not, gives us insight into feelings, motivations and the psyche of characters,
whereas 'films are obsessed with the human face, yet constantly collide with its
final inscrutableness'.[11] There are of course many examples that provide a sense
of interiority through, say, the use of voice-over. Examples of films that use voice-
over very well in this regard include *Badlands* (Terrence Malick, 1973), *Kiss Kiss
Bang Bang* (Shane Black, 2005) and *Clueless* (Amy Heckerling, 1995). These are
all films that provide a sense of interiority to their leading characters. Even so,
Braudy argues that film characterization depends upon a lack of knowledge, as
opposed to literary characters that provide a sense of interiority.

Film Elio is thusly more elusive than book Elio. What follows is a look at a
series of pivotal moments from Elio's character arc. I assess how they are presented
in the book and offer an analysis of how they differ in the film. Coupled with other
cinematic signs, the quietness of Chalamet's performance allows for an expression
of character interiority. This analysis demonstrates the richness of transtextual
character development: that the reading of this character is polysemic in nature,
depending on your foreknowledge at the outset of the film.

The swoon

The moment in which Elio swoons is one of the first moments where reading
Chalamet's performance as an adaptive one allows for a greater appreciation of
the film. Elio's obsession becomes clearer when we are prevalent to the interiority

provided by the book. In the first chapter, 'If Not Later, When?', Aciman demonstrates Elio as being attuned to how Oliver presents himself, particularly in regard to his use of the word 'later'. It's in these early moments of the book that Elio's intense sexual obsession with Oliver begins. Aciman's writing describes this intensity like a confounding fire that signifies a multitude of emotions, from fear to a paralyzing panic, a yearning for Oliver to knock on his door and, above all else, for these emotions to be wrong. When they are playing volleyball and drinking lemonade in the sun, Oliver puts his arm around Elio in an amicable 'hug-massage'.[12] Any longer and Elio would have involuntarily swooned, 'like one of those tiny wooden toys whose gimp-legged body collapses as soon as the mainsprings are touched'.[13] This startling response, Elio realizes, is like when 'virgins are touched for the first time by the person they desire'.[14] Oliver continues and gets Marzia (Esther Garrel) to feel the knots in Elio's shoulder. Elio's following assessment of his response is indicative of his inability to communicate because he 'doesn't know how to speak in code'; he doesn't know 'how to speak at all'.[15] Elio's despair at his resulting silence gives off an air of impatient rage. Elio doesn't consider how Oliver would have perceived his actions. What follows in the subsequent paragraphs of this passage is a neurotic questioning over why he, for the briefest of moments, fell back into Oliver's grip and swooned. It's a ping pong match of conflicting thoughts, which reiterates this confounding fire of conflicting emotions; he is bothered by Oliver, yet has these intense sexual urges that he can't describe.

The adapted scene provides an interesting shift in perspective. The sound and *mise en scène* emphasize the leisurely nature of this world. Youths relax on the lawn watching the volleyball match. The buzz of cicadas dominates the soundscape. A panning shot captures Elio walking into the space staring intently at Oliver. In an inference to Elio's perspective, the scene cuts to a long shot of the group playing volleyball. The panning shot returns with Elio walking back from the table with fruit, a motif of desire that will return in the infamous peach scene. Oliver bursts into the frame wearing tight green shorts and grabs a water bottle from Elio. We quickly cut to a medium close-up from behind Elio. Oliver drinks with his right hand as he lays his left hand on Elio's shoulder. Elio's expression immediately shifts. For a brief second, Elio's eyes drop to Oliver's arm, the only part of Oliver in frame during this brief moment. As Elio pulls away, the camera cuts again, now positioned in front of Elio (Figure 3.2). Here, Elio looks onwards, indicating that he is trying to focus on the volleyball. Oliver enters the screen once again from the left and gives Elio another shoulder massage.

Elio appears nonplussed, almost annoyed. Elio looks down at his feet and breathes deeply. When Oliver says, 'You're too stressed. You just have to relax a little bit', Elio jerks back around quickly. 'I am relaxing.' This exchange is the moment of 'impatient rage' from Elio's inner monologue. For a brief moment, though, he looks down at his feet again and breathes deeply. Elio's expression returns to being

FIGURE 3.2: A moment of impatient rage (Timothée Chalamet as Elio and Armie Hammer as Oliver). Luca Guadagnino (dir.), *Call Me by Your Name*, 2017. Italy/France/USA/Brazil. © Frenesy, La Cinefacture.

blank. When Marzia repeats the line of Elio needing to relax, Elio's face winces, as if in total confusion. Elio walks off focusing on the direction that Oliver ran off in (with the quick 'Later!' of course) with Elio's expression being deep in thought. Processing this confusion, he passes Annella and Mafalda as they set the table.

Chalamet's expression here is sullen, uncomfortable and perhaps, to be more apt, exuding 'impatient rage'. This is the effect that Elio wishes wasn't conveyed in his internal monologue in Aciman's book. Watching this scene in isolation from the book, one would be forgiven for reading Elio as wary of Oliver. Viewed in isolation, this scene does not appear to contain any swoon at all; rather there is just impatient rage. Interpreting Elio's character development with the book in mind, however, can allow for a deeper appreciation of this scene. When we view this as an adapted performance, *the swoon becomes possible*. Both readings are valid interpretation as adaptations shouldn't be wholly prescribed by the original. The impatient rage can co-exist with the swoon. This translation of this 'essence' of the mania in the book, to draw on Bazin, is highlighted by Aciman in an interview with *Entertainment Weekly*:

> After the shoulder rub, Chalamet whittles paragraphs of obsessive dialogue down to a single, longing, anguished glance. The film is still near-exclusively told from his perspective, only without voiceover. It's still completely immersive in the touches, the stares, the smells – in everything we see.[16]

The scene ends with a quick cut to Elio shaving later that evening. 'M.A.Y. in the Backyard' by Ryuichi Sakamoto plays non-diegetically. Elio wipes the shaving cream off his face and stares pensively into the mirror. Here there are interesting signs to consider. The shot of the face alone is still, the expression of his face appears deep in thought; it's telling that this shot is coupled with the staccato notes of Sakamoto's score. My reading here is that this is a nod to Elio's manic, ping pong-like struggle as he tries to deduce his swoon during the shoulder rub. The mania from the book is indeed still present here in this sequence. It is, however, non-verbal and being conveyed through performance and sound.

The matter of characterization here recalls Braudy's aforementioned argument on interiority. Aciman's book relies on the inner monologue, while Chalamet's performance of Elio in Guadagnino's film draws upon other forms of cinematic grammar that are largely non-verbal. Aciman's book is largely a manic internal monologue from Elio's perspective as he falls in love with Oliver. This obsessive narration is ultimately replaced with wordlessness. The essence of the novel's thematic core is respected here, yet Guadagnino's direction and Ivory's screenplay use silence resulting in an enigmatic performance from Chalamet. In Aciman's novel, longing permeates throughout Elio's memory. This feverish account cycles through modes of confusion as he navigates his intense crush on Oliver. The account is so maddening that it really wouldn't work without the bliss of the northern Italian summer. In writing about the adaptation for *Vanity Fair*, Aciman acknowledges how the cinematic form results in a new way to express Elio's development:

> For me, the message was clear: film cuts and trims with savage brevity, where a shrug or an intercepted glance or a nervous pause between two words can lay bare the heart in ways written prose is far more nuanced and needs more time and space on the page. But the thing is, I couldn't write silence. I couldn't measure pauses and breaths and the most elusive yet expressive body language.[17]

This theme of 'is it better to speak or die?' permeates throughout Elio's longing for Oliver, informing Chalamet's performance.

The piazzetta *and Monet's Berm*

During their conversations at the *piazzetta* and Monet's Berm, Elio's confession of his feelings for Oliver is indicative of the differences in restriction of knowledge when comparing the two texts. According to David Bordwell, a 'film's narration can be more or less knowledgeable about the fabula it represents'.[18] The range and depth of information is situated from Elio's perspective. This scene provides a further shift in the film that lets us deeper into Oliver's perspective. In this passage that leads up to the two kissing in Monet's Berm, Elio's inner dialogue expresses his confusion. His obsession with Oliver leads him to blur the line between *having* Oliver and *being* him. This is where Elio begins to see himself in his love interest. In the opening moments of this chapter, the two discuss the fable of the princess and the knight, as told to them by Annella. In this story, the knight doesn't know whether to speak or to die. Oliver's response of 'Figures' upon hearing that the knight fudges his choice indicates that Elio should avoid the same mistake.

Elio's musings on this fable build towards his disclosure of his feelings for Oliver in the *piazzetta*. A central focus of their discussion is the war memorial, which functions as a marker of memory and sorrow, something that Elio reflects upon as he wonders if generations to follow will remember the momentous occasion that's taking place. Aciman's book provides this interior perspective of struggling to read Oliver's response. Elio's potential grief at getting rejected is likened here to the trauma felt by those who survived the battle at Piave River in the First World War. Following Elio's cryptic statement that while he knows a lot, he doesn't know anything about the things that matter, Oliver rebuffs him saying that they shouldn't talk about these matters. The two men cycle off to what the book labels 'Monet's Berm', a charming watering hole that supposedly inspired the Impressionist painter. Here, Elio gives an 'all-knowing, I-dare-you-to-kiss-me'[19] gaze and Oliver confesses his feelings and that they both must learn to control their yearnings. Nevertheless, the two men kiss, which Elio wishes to lose himself in.

In the film, this scene at the *piazzetta* conveys the tension felt by Elio. A long take captures the unease as the two men discuss the matter obtusely. For the most part, the two are captured by a long shot, framed by the antiquity of the town square. The distance between them and the camera speaks to the coldness between them. To draw on Bazin,[20] the use of deep space and the long take has the appearance of linking the cinematic image with reality, offering a sense of truth with spatial and temporal relations. According to Bazin, this offers the sense of objectivity before the filmmaker manipulates time and space with editing. This Bazinian approach argues that such 'realist' films 'not only provide an experience of the world of a film that replicates our habitual way of being in the world; they employ styles that emphasize it'.[21] Writing on Bazin and the long take, Mark Le Fanu argues that

> [i]n the epoch of MTV and of the 'quick thrills' associated with the 'event movie', we no longer, it could be claimed, have the patience to look – that is, to linger, to explore, to risk boredom in the search of epiphany – that not so long ago was part and parcel of serious cinemagoing experience.[22]

This presence of real time allows for a deeper sense of truth to the cinematic image. While the pace set by the editing throughout the film is languid, this shot length conveys the tension felt from Elio's perspective. We wait in anticipation *with* Elio *for* Oliver. Writing on the long takes in Alfonso Cuarón's *Children of Men* (2006), James Udden argues that many contemporary filmmakers reinforce these assumptions about the long take because they have a '*use-value*'.[23] As such, it isn't necessarily a matter of whether or not perception of truth is objectively captured here. This long take adds a weight of significance to this moment, as does the closing shot of the film. Perhaps the emergence of truth will occur or Elio in this moment is more real than what we have seen previously.

Sounds shape the tone of the scene while Oliver controls the space and action. Birds and cicadas sound in the background. Oliver enters the building to buy cigarettes while Elio waits for him obediently. André Laplante's '*Un Barque sur l'océan*' ('A Boat on the Ocean') from Maurice Ravel's *Miroirs* begins to stir non-diegetically, whose melody resembles that of a movement of the ocean surface. Elio's heart is aflutter like the rousing ocean. While Guadagnino toyed with the idea of having an omniscient narrator, something that Aciman vetoed, he opted for music to narrate key moments, particularly that of Sufjan Stevens.[24] This is perhaps a nod to the discussion between the two in the novel of Percy Shelley having drowned. Before he was cremated on the shore, Mary Shelley cut out his heart and kept it for many years – 'Cor Cordium, Heart of Hearts'.[25] This line is repeated in the closing moments of the book when Elio notices a postcard of Monet's Berm in Oliver's office with the inscription 'Cor Cordium' on the back. This speaks to the constant presence of them in each other's lives, even after they part. This score functions as a motif for their constant desire for the other.

Chalamet's movements respond to those of Hammer. As Oliver exits the building, he commands the space again. He walks over to Elio, offers him a cigarette and lights it for him. They walk to the centre of the *piazzetta*, Oliver in the lead. As Elio details key facts about the Battle of Piave:

> OLIVER: Is there anything you don't know?
> ELIO: I know nothing, Oliver.

They stop, either side of the monument, and look at each other in a beat of silence. Elio knows nothing of the things that matter.

> OLIVER: What things that matter?
> ELIO: You know what things.

The conversation is stunted, which is indicative of Elio's inability to communicate; this is a trope that Di Mattia identifies in her reading of the film:

> His communication skills are under-developed. When Elio finally tells Oliver how he feels about him on the morning when they circle the Battle of Piave monument in town, he does it obliquely. Even after they have slept together, he fumbles, unable to clearly articulate what he feels or what he wants.[26]

Oliver continues to move along the other side as the camera tracks him. When he is on the other side of Elio, the camera stops, he asks 'Why are you telling me this?'

ELIO: 'Cause I thought you should know.
OLIVER: Because you thought I should know?

ELIO *(to* OLIVER*)*: 'Cause I wanted you to know? *(To himself)* 'Cause I wanted you to know. 'Cause I wanted you to know.

The conversation in the *piazzetta* is repetitive and uncertain. Elio in the film, much like in the book, is unable to articulate how he feels about Oliver. The book's interior monologue provides an extensive internal exploration of these complex feelings. For much of this scene, Elio's back is turned to us. We can't see his expression. The interiority of the book has been restricted in the film. Elio begins to move to the right and Oliver disappears behind the monument. The camera looks up at the sculpted soldier at the top of the monument and then lowers again back to Elio. Laplante's '*Un Barque sur l'océan*' briefly stirs again. The two men join up on the other side and both are in profile as they continue their abstruse conversation – 'Are you saying what I think you are saying?' Oliver asks. As Oliver leaves to pick up his typed manuscript, Elio confirms that he isn't going anywhere. It's spoken to Oliver but it could almost be said to himself. He strolls to the right as the camera tracks him. Tourists arrive at the *piazzetta* behind him, his and Oliver's space increasingly less private. Laplante stirs yet again as Elio and the camera tilt upwards. The camera is positioned behind Elio, as we see Oliver exiting the building, angrily riffling through his mixed-up pages. The long take tracks forward entering a mid shot as Elio states 'I shouldn't have said anything'. This is the clearest angle so far that we have of his face even though his glasses still hide his eyes and the direction of his gaze.

The following section refers to the continuation of this sequence after the two characters have moved onto Monet's Berm. This watering hole is a place that is symbolic of Elio's inner sanctum, where he reveals his true self. It's the place he comes to read and be alone. Here, Elio invites Oliver to discover a deeper part of his psyche. Upon arrival, Elio enters the water and removes his glasses. He walks towards the camera into a mid close-up and lets Oliver know that this is his spot – 'It's all mine', he says. He is out of focus, though; the camera wants us to focus on Oliver's reaction. The camera cuts to parts of their bodies as the conversation continues: Oliver's back as he stretches, his hands and legs as he splashes water on his face. We return to a long mid shot of the two. 'Are you really that afraid of what I think?' asks Oliver. Elio does not reply. He just steps towards Oliver and looks at him – giving the 'all-knowing-I-dare-you-to-kiss-me' gaze. He grins, which makes Oliver laugh. The two continue to play in the water until a sharp cut sees them lying on the grass. This sharp cut increases the tension, as we wait for their inevitable kiss. Oliver traces his finger around Elio's lips. Elio sits up and the two finally kiss. Oliver pulls away – 'Better now?' Elio kisses again only for Oliver to pull away. We have a mid shot again of the two. Elio cups his hand on Oliver's crotch. He cheekily grins – 'Am I offending you?' he asks.

This sequence at Monet's Berm is notable due to the initial ambiguity of Elio's state. Without the interiority of the book, his panic and obsession are elusive. This is even more so due to the fact that, during the earlier *piazzetta* scene, the camera largely hides Chalamet's expression. The only clear body language we get is his stunted speech and cautious body posture. Now that they are at Monet's Berm, Elio is easier to read now that he has entered the water (Figure 3.3). In the *piazzetta*, he looks down at the

FIGURE 3.3: Elio's (Timothée Chalamet) demeanour eases once at Monet's Berm. Luca Guadagnino (dir.), *Call Me by Your Name*, 2017. Italy/France/USA/Brazil. © Frenesy, La Cinefacture.

ground when not looking at Hammer, leans over the railing, and tends to respond to Hammer's movements. When they move to Monet's Berm, Chalamet jovially runs to the water. When he takes off his glasses, Chalamet's smile is bathed in sunlight, visible for the camera. Chalamet's posture is straighter, and he looks up into the distance more. This scene in Monet's Berm is a notable transition for Elio's characterization.

The peach

The peach scene deepens the relationship between Elio and Oliver. Here, Elio famously ejaculates into a peach, which is discovered by Oliver. There are notable differences here between the book and the film. In the novel, Elio blissfully rests in bed, naked, sprawled out. He rips out the pit, so the fruit looks like a human orifice, be it a vagina or an anus. He masturbates into it, picturing it to be anyone from Marzia to Oliver, or perhaps even a character from Ovid. When Oliver enters an unknown amount of time later and awakens Elio, he dips his finger into the peach, licks the contents upon his finger and eats the peach. This shocks Elio, not because of the outrageousness of the scene but because he couldn't imagine Oliver being this generous. He tries to grab the peach off Oliver – 'you don't have to do this'.[27] For Oliver, this is the essence of Elio and everything that has brought him into being:

> Just think of the number of people who've come before you – you, your grandfather, your great-great-grandfather, and all the skipped generations of Elios before you, and those from places far away, all squeezed into this trickle that makes you who you are. Now may I taste it?[28]

They are now symbolically a part of each other; Elio will forever be in Oliver's bodily system. This moment further unifies the two into one being. Elio and Oliver's union blurs the boundaries between self and other; as Oliver says after their first sexual encounter, 'Call me by your name and I'll call you by mine'. Beyond eating the other's cum, they swap clothes, spit and, yes, each other's name. Elio even licks Oliver's eyeballs. During their venture to Rome, they defecate together. This speaks to the influence of Aristophanes' speech on the origin of love in Plato's *Symposium* through Aciman's novel, which many would be familiar with from the song 'Origin of Love' in *Hedwig and the Angry Inch*.[29] In this tale, we were originally joined with our other half until Zeus, feeling threatened, split us down the middle and separated us into two separate beings. Now, our desire for love is for this other half so we can be whole again. This desire for wholeness, being one and the same with our 'other', is what Aristophanes calls love. This making of one heals the 'wound of human nature'.[30] It's perhaps this element that moves

Elio so much during this moment, that he is becoming closer to being unified with his other half and healing this heartache: 'I was crying because no stranger had ever been so kind or gone so far for me'.[31]

Oliver in the film, however, does not eat the peach. He merely uses his finger to lick a small amount of the contents of the peach. For Aciman, this is enough to convey these themes:

> In the book, Oliver eats the peach. And he says, 'Because I want every part of you. If you are going to die, I want part of you to stay with me, in my system.' And that's the way I'm going to do it […]. In the film he just puts his finger [in] and almost licks it. And that is good enough for cinema. We don't need to see more […]. It is absolutely superlative. It is one of the most moving moments in the film.[32]

The vulnerable nature of Elio is the emphasis of this scene. As the radio plays an Italian song in the background, a high mid shot looks down on Elio as he handles the peach. The afternoon sun pours in through the window creating high-contrast shadows across his topless body. We then cut to a close-up of his fingers caressing the peach. The sound of his fingers piercing the fruit emphasizes the moisture and tactility of the moment. Elio breathes heavily off-camera. We return to the original shot, looking down at him. Juice pours onto his chest as he removes the pip and sucks it. The piercing of the fruit and sucking of the stone dominate the radio. He looks up to the ceiling, a notably similar movement to when Oliver did not appear at dinner. He pauses and breathes deeply before rubbing the fruit down his chest to his groin. The camera tracks down and up again as he orgasms. 'Fuck' as he looks down at the result, an indication of shame over his actions. He rolls over to sleep.

There is a sharp cut. The lighting in the room has changed to an increasingly dimmed room. The song on the radio has ended. To return to Dyer's work on characterization, these are all signs that portray Elio as being in an exposed posiion. Oliver enters the room and takes his top off. A long shot captures both men embracing on the bed as Oliver, with his back to us, briefly gives Elio oral sex, thus tasting the peachy remnants. Elio sits up and his face enters a stream of light. He pensively looks down. 'What did you do?' Oliver asks. 'Nothing', Elio replies. His face returns to darkness. The camera then cuts to the other side of them now, a mid shot of the two topless men, hard lighting once again streamed across their upper bodies. Elio looks over at the peach and Oliver laughs. 'Oh, I see, you have moved onto the plant kingdom already?' While the conversation continues in a similar fashion to the book, film Elio does not, however, say 'You don't have to do this'. Chalamet's expression turns to anger, as he demands 'Why are you doing this to me?' Rather than being an act of unification, perhaps this initial reaction is more of shock at Oliver seeming to mock Elio. Elio cries into Oliver's shoulder

FIGURE 3.4: The peach scene becomes a moment of vulnerability rather than unification (Timothée Chalamet as Elio and Armie Hammer as Oliver). Luca Guadagnino (dir.), *Call Me by Your Name*, 2017. Italy/France/USA/Brazil. © Frenesy, La Cinefacture.

briefly and lifts his head up and wipes his face and apologizes. Oliver holds Elio's face, and they kiss. 'I don't want you to go', Elio cries (Figure 3.4). The scene then dissolves into the evening, to a discussion on the time they have wasted.

The foremost evocation of this scene is that of vulnerability rather than that of unification. By refraining from eating the peach, the Aristophean approach to love is limited. The divergence here demonstrates the two different reading positions of an adapted text. For those who have not read the book, this scene focuses on the deepening connection between the two men, where Elio is open with his desires. The famous peach scene carries further significance from the book, however, as it is a major step in the unification of the two men, where there is a physiological merging of the two. As such, if we view this as an adaptation, and recall this significance, the fusion of their desires is emphasized. This is not a gross-out scene involving a peach; it's a noteworthy moment in this relationship arc.

Final shot, final thoughts

Following the close of summer, the character arc of Elio continues to diverge. In Aciman's book, Elio spends the next few years and decades revisiting his love for

Oliver. He visits the American university that Oliver is now lecturing at and the two get a drink to discuss their parallel lives, indulging in both the real and fantasy. In the closing passage, Oliver visits Elio at his family home in northern Italy, now twenty years after their romance. Elio's father has died, and he wonders if Oliver remembers everything – 'If you remember everything, I wanted to say, and if you are really like me'.[33] The sorrow of the epilogue draws upon the Aristophean wound of human nature. Elio feels as though Oliver is his 'other half' and continues to be incomplete without him. In Guadagnino's film, however, the final scene takes place at Hanukkah in the dead of winter. The family is sitting down to dinner and receives a call from Oliver, who tells them he is engaged to be married. Elio calls Oliver by his name and Oliver returns the gesture, saying he remembers everything. After the call, Elio sits by the fire and cries, recalling the summer he had with Oliver. One sustained close-up captures Chalamet as the film's credits scroll across the screen.

Labelled by Guadagnino as the film's narrator, Sufjan Stevens' closing song 'Visions of Gideon' plays as a lament for the film's closure. Gideon recalls the ancient Prophet in the Book of Joshua, who was sent visions from God, ordering him to lead a military mission. A doubtful man, he repeatedly questions whether the visions were in fact real. Sufjan Stevens' song likens Elio's romance with Oliver to these 'Visions of Gideon'. Elio doubts himself while, to him, Oliver is a God-like creature. Now that their romance has come to an end, Elio doubts whether these God-like visions, i.e. memories with Oliver, were in fact real. Coupled with Chalamet's performance, this represents Elio replaying the memories of their relationship and how vivid the memories are to him still. He stares into the fireplace, bites his lips, presses them together. He momentarily wipes the tears from his eyes. This moment recalls the advice of his father, which perhaps rings through this ending in its difference to the book – 'To feel nothing so as not to feel anything – what a waste!'[34] The camera doesn't cut away. As Elio embraces his feelings of love and sadness, we too end on this deeply intimate shot. In these closing moments, Elio embraces his sadness and briefly smiles, thinking fondly of his time with Oliver. Ultimately, the character arc of Elio in the film concludes on a hopeful note, that while our hearts may get broken, we can still take succour in the joy of our past romances and continue on having grown from the connections, still whole and not fundamentally broken like in the Aristophean model of love. In the book, however, it is a notably devastating conclusion that Elio never really gets over Oliver and remains incomplete without him.

In considering the character arc of Elio, it's important that we see Timothée Chalamet's performance as a form of adaptation. There are several elements that work with Chalamet to express this interiority. There is no need for an omnipresent narrator, as his performance, supported by Guadagnino's cinematic grammar, reveals Elio's interiority for us to embrace. While this interiority is evident for those not having read the book, foreknowledge of 'book Elio' does grant a deeper appreciation of the film's achievements. In this exploration of book Elio and film Elio, I have examined several moments that are key to characterization. Some moments, such as the swoon and the first kiss at Monet's Berm, demonstrate how transtextual foreknowledge of the book allows for a deeper insight into the performance of an adapted character. Other moments, such as the peach scene, speak to how the adapted work can meaningfully diverge from its source. Regardless of what we bring to this film, the essence of Elio's obsession remains in this new medium for us to devour.

NOTES

1. Joanna Di Mattia, 'Beating Hearts: Compassion and Self-Discovery in *Call Me by Your Name*', *Screen Education* 91 (2018): 14.
2. Di Mattia, 14.
3. André Bazin, 'Adaptation, or the Cinema as Digest', trans. Alain Piette and Bert Cardullo, in *Film Adaptation*, ed. James Naremore (New Brunswick: Rutgers University Press, [original language publication: 1948] 2000), 20, original emphasis.
4. Catherine Grant, 'Recognizing *Billy Budd* in *Beau Travail*: Epistemology and Hermeneutics of an Auteurist "Free" Adaptation', *Screen* 34, no. 1 (Spring 2002): 57.
5. Robert Stam, 'Beyond Fidelity: The Dialogues of Adaptation', in *Film Adaptation*, ed. James Naremore (New Brunswick: Rutgers University Press, 2000), 65.
6. Stam, 66.
7. Stam, 68–69.
8. Linda Hutcheon, *A Theory of Adaptation* (New York: Routledge, 2006), 9.
9. Richard Dyer, *Heavenly Bodies: Film Stars and Society* (New York and London: Routledge, 1986), 112.
10. Leo Braudy, *The World in a Frame: What We See in Films* (Chicago and London: University of Chicago Press, 1976), 424.
11. Braudy, 187.
12. André Aciman, *Call Me by Your Name* (New York: Farrar, Straus and Giroux, 2007), 16.
13. Aciman, 16.
14. Aciman, 16.
15. Aciman, 17.
16. Quoted in David Canfield, 'Why *Call Me by Your Name* Is a Brilliant, Essential Adaptation', *Entertainment Weekly*, 29 November 2017, https://ew.com/books/2017/11/29/call-me-by-your-name-movie-book-comparison/.
17. Quoted in Canfield, 'Why *Call Me*'.
18. David Bordwell, *Narration in the Fiction Film* (Madison: The University of Wisconsin Press, 1985), 57.

19. Aciman, *Call Me*, 78.
20. A key text is André Bazin, *What Is Cinema? Vol. 1 & 2*, trans. and ed. Hugh Gray (Berkeley: University of California Press, 1967–71).
21. Daniel Morgan, 'Rethinking Bazin: Ontology and Realist Aesthetics', *Critical Inquiry* 32, no. 3 (2006): 457.
22. Mark Le Fanu, 'Metaphysics of the "Long Take": Some Post-Bazinian Reflections', *P.O.V.: A Danish Journal of Film Studies* 4 (December 1997), http://pov.imv.au.dk/Issue_04/section_1/artclA.html.
23. James Udden, 'Child of the Long Take: Alfonso Cuarón's Film Aesthetics in the Shadow of Globalization', *Style* 43, no. 1, 'Film and Globalization' (2009): 35, original emphasis.
24. See Keith Caulfield, 'How Sufjan Stevens' Music Became a "Sort of Narrator" for *Call Me by Your Name*', *Billboard*, 11 January 2018, https://www.billboard.com/music/music-news/sufjan-stevens-call-me-by-your-name-music-luca-guadagnino-interview-8093818/; Joe Utichi, 'Sufjan Stevens Nearly Played the Narrator in Luca Guadagnino's *Call Me by Your Name*', *Deadline*, 13 December 2017, https://deadline.com/2017/12/call-me-by-your-name-sufjan-stevens-luca-guadagnino-musicinterview-1202225747/.
25. Aciman, *Call Me*, 71.
26. Di Mattia, 'Beating Hearts', 10.
27. Aciman, *Call Me*, 149.
28. Aciman, 148.
29. The musical *Hedwig and the Angry Inch*, first staged in 1998, has songs by Stephen Trask and a book by John Cameron Mitchell.
30. Plato, *Symposium*, trans. Alexander Nehamas and Paul Woodruff (Indianapolis: Hackett, [*c.*385–70 BCE] 1989), 27.
31. Aciman, *Call Me*, 149.
32. TIFF Originals, '*Call Me by Your Name*'s Peach Scene: Book vs Film', YouTube, 27 February 2018, https://www.youtube.com/watch?v=6BOgQlS9Uto&feature=emb_title&ab_channel=TIFFOriginals.
33. Aciman, *Call Me*, 248.
34. Aciman, 224.

REFERENCES

Aciman, André. *Call Me by Your Name*. New York: Farrar, Straus and Giroux, 2007.

Bazin, André. *What Is Cinema?* Vol. 1 & 2. Translated and edited by Hugh Gray. Berkeley: University of California Press, 1967–71.

Bazin, André. 'Adaptation, or the Cinema as Digest.' In *Film Adaptation*. Translated by Alain Piette and Bert Cardullo and edited by James Naremore, 19–27. New Brunswick: Rutgers University Press, [original language publication: 1948] 2000.

Black, Shane, dir. *Kiss Kiss Bang Bang*. Warner Bros., Silver Pictures, 2005.

Bordwell, David. *Narration in the Fiction Film*. Madison: The University of Wisconsin Press, 1985.

Braudy, Leo. *The World in a Frame: What We See in Films*. Chicago and London: University of Chicago Press, 1976.

Canfield, David. 'Why *Call Me by Your Name* Is a Brilliant, Essential Adaptation.' *Entertainment Weekly*, 29 November 2017. https://ew.com/books/2017/11/29/call-me-by-your-name-movie-book-comparison/.

Caulfield, Keith. 'How Sufjan Stevens' Music Became a "Sort of Narrator" for *Call Me by Your Name*.' *Billboard*, 11 January 2018. https://www.billboard.com/music/music-news/sufjan-stevens-call-me-by-your-name-music-luca-guadagnino-interview-8093818/.

Cuarón, Alfonso, dir. *Children of Men*. Universal Pictures, Strike Entertainment, Hit and Run Productions, 2006.

Di Mattia, Joanna. 'Beating Hearts: Compassion and Self-Discovery in *Call Me by Your Name*.' *Screen Education* 91, October 2018: 8–15.

Dyer, Richard. *Heavenly Bodies: Film Stars and Society*. New York and London: Routledge, 1986.

Grant, Catherine. 'Recognizing *Billy Budd* in *Beau Travail*: Epistemology and Hermeneutics of an Auteurist "Free" Adaptation.' *Screen* 34, no. 1 (Spring 2002): 57–73.

Guadagnino, Luca, dir. *Call Me by Your Name*. Frenesy Film Company, La Cinefacture, RT Features, 2017.

Heckerling, Amy, dir. *Clueless*. Paramount Pictures, 1995.

Hutcheon, Linda. *A Theory of Adaptation*. New York: Routledge, 2006.

Le Fanu, Mark. 'Metaphysics of the "Long Take": Some Post-Bazinian Reflections.' *P.O.V.: A Danish Journal of Film Studies* 4 December 1997. http://pov.imv.au.dk/Issue_04/section_1/artclA.html.

Malick, Terrence, dir. *Badlands*. Warner Bros., Pressman Williams, Jill Jakes Production, 1973.

Morgan, Daniel. 'Rethinking Bazin: Ontology and Realist Aesthetics.' *Critical Inquiry* 32, no. 3 (2006): 443–81.

Plato. *Symposium*. Translated by Alexander Nehamas and Paul Woodruff. Indianapolis: Hackett, [c.385-370 BCE] 1989.

Sakamoto, Ryuichi. 'M.A.Y. in the Backyard.' In Various, *Call My by Your Name: Original Motion Picture Soundtrack*. Madison Gate Records/Masterworks/Sony Music Entertainment, 2017.

Stam, Robert. 'Beyond Fidelity: The Dialogues of Adaptation.' In *Film Adaptation*, edited by James Naremore, 54–76. New Brunswick: Rutgers University Press, 2000.

TIFF Originals. '*Call Me by Your Name*'s Peach Scene: Book vs Film.' YouTube, 27 February 2018. https://www.youtube.com/watch?v=6BOgQlS9Uto&feature=emb_title&ab_channel=TIFFOriginals.

Udden, James. 'Child of the Long Take: Alfonso Cuaron's Film Aesthetics in the Shadow of Globalization.' *Style* 43, no. 1, 'Film and Globalization' (Spring 2009): 26–44.

Utichi, Joe. 'Sufjan Stevens Nearly Played the Narrator in Luca Guadagnino's *Call Me by Your Name*.' *Deadline*, 13 December 2017. https://deadline.com/2017/12/call-me-by-your-name-sufjan-stevens-luca-guadagnino-musicinterview-1202225747/.

4

Music as Narrator in *Call Me by Your Name*

Kingsley Marshall

This chapter examines the significance of music as a carrier of expositional information within the 2017 feature film *Call Me by Your Name* and how it is used to distinguish different narrative spaces for the audience – of the moment depicted or of recalling memories of the past – and how music provides the subtext for the emotions of, and relationships between, the central characters Elio and Oliver. Adapted by James Ivory from a novel by André Aciman, the film tells the story of the arrival of 24-year-old American doctoral student Oliver, played by Armie Hammer, at the home of the 17-year-old Elio Perlman, played by Timothée Chalamet. Elio is the son of a professor (Michael Stuhlbarg) who arranges for one of his students to stay with his family in their Italian holiday home each summer – an annual tradition that requires Elio to give up his room for this academic houseguest. As the film progresses, Elio's feelings for Oliver develop and the two embark on a summer affair.

In interviews at the time of the film's release, the director Luca Guadagnino acknowledged the significance of music in articulating the subjective experience of his film's protagonists as their relationship develops over the course of an Italian summer in 1983, explaining to Anne Thompson that music could be 'less heavy, less present, and more enveloping than a voice and text'.[1] Unusually, a large amount of narrative information is communicated through the deployment of the original score and existing music often written into – and foregrounded in – scenes. Elio's relationship to music is made explicit through the Talking Heads T-shirt he wears and also in his performances, and consideration, of music, where he is shown listening to or transcribing music, or playing guitar and the piano. As the film's music supervisor Robin Urdang notes: 'The music is a layer of the film that's telling a story',[2] this layered approach ultimately acknowledged by an Academy Award nomination for Best Original Song for Sufjan Stevens' 'Mystery of Love', which accompanies a central montage within the film.

The piano as motif

Embedded as a motif within the film, the piano as an instrument serves a psychological, in addition to a representative, function – a cipher of the lead character Elio's desire to interpret, perform and touch. Guadagnino had used piano music prominently in the preceding films of what the director has retrospectively described as his 'trilogy of desire',[3] *Call Me by Your Name* forming the third of this series, following the earlier *Io sono l'amore* (*I Am Love*, 2009) and *A Bigger Splash* (2015). Nine pre-existing compositions by American composer John Adams pepper the first film of the trilogy, with both the director and the film's producer Tilda Swinton having reportedly spent ten years pursuing Adams to secure his involvement.[4] The director described at the time this music as having influenced how the script had been written. He stated that Adams' music was 'a crucial emotional anchor' and that he had played the composer's music on set as motivation in some of the scenes.[5]

It is the first movement of Adams' 'Hallelujah Junction' that accompanies the opening credits of *Call Me by Your Name*[6] – serving as a peritextual connection with the first film in the trilogy, in addition to establishing immediately the significance of the piano to this specific film. This establishment of the piano at the audience's first encounter with the film situates it in a story in which the instrument is prominent and has a significance throughout the film, both in terms of the use of music inside and outside of the filmic world but also more directly within the story itself, the piano representing Elio's preoccupation with music and musicianship. Significantly, and more obliquely, 'Hallelujah Junction' was written for, and is performed by, two pianos. In the cue, melodic phrases shift back and forth between these two pianos – what Adams has described as a 'phased sequence'[7] in which the repetition of phrases between the instruments echoes and repeats, presenting as a mirroring of both Elio and Oliver's developing relationship and Elio's struggle to communicate.

The use of the piano is further reinforced through the use of the music of Japanese pianist and composer Ryuichi Sakamoto, whose spiky 'M.A.Y. in the Backyard' accompanies a sequence where Elio and Oliver make their first excursion into the local town and makes a second appearance in a later scene during which Elio shaves and dresses for dinner. Unlike Adams' music, Sakamoto's cue – originally released in 1984 – is broadly contemporary to the early '80s setting, made explicit in an introductory on-screen title card announcing the period as 'Summer 1983'. These selections, explained Chalamet, originated from Guadagnino's own life experience, the actor stating that

> the book is set in '88 and he [the director] changed it to '83 because he said that was the year in your life you can hear music from. [These are] all songs from Luca's youth, what it was like for him in Italy in the '80s.[8]

The significance of the piano is made most explicit by Elio's skill as a pianist within the story. In a scene in which Oliver asks Elio to play a piece he has been strumming on the guitar in the garden, Elio invites him into the house, where he performs his own interpretation of a Bach piece for Oliver on the piano (Figure 4.1). Urdang has suggested that the director had wanted to record this music on set, explaining that the actor 'Timothée [Chalamet] took piano lessons and guitar lessons' in order to play this himself within the film, rather than miming.[9] Ivan Raykoff notes the significance of this element of Chalamet's performance as Elio, suggesting that this use of music in the film serves to heighten its 'visual vocabulary with a palpable tactility of sound', where the film makes extensive use of close-up shots of hands, feet and skin – all accentuating the significance of the body in the story.[10] In the next scene, as Elio writes in a diary, a second Bach piano piece – '*Wachet auf, ruft uns die Stimme*' – is played non-diegetically. This is foregrounded in the audio mix and shifts to diegetic, filmic music in the next scene as we come to understand it is a piece that Elio is transcribing from his Walkman as he sits in the villa's garden. This situates Elio at the centre of the story, where often his personal listening choices drive the film and dominate the spaces he occupies.

Later, an extract from John Adams's 'Phrygian Gates' (1977–78) plays as Oliver's supervisor – and Elio's father – Samuel Perlman makes an archaeological find at Lake Garda. The cue plays again later when Elio invites himself along with

FIGURE 4.1: Elio (Timothée Chalamet) performs his own interpretation of a Bach piece for Oliver (Armie Hammer) on the piano. Luca Guadagnino (dir.), *Call Me by Your Name*, 2017. Italy/France/USA/Brazil. © Frenesy, La Cinefacture.

Oliver into the local town and Elio takes him to a small lake, where they kiss for the first time. In this instance and earlier, the piano signifies discovery: in Oliver's initial arrival at the villa, during these sequences of the archaeological find and latterly in the consummation of love between these two principal characters. As with 'Hallelujah Junction', this piece of Adams' draws from minimalism – making use of a limited palette of musical ideas that are repeated and built upon – and serialism, a break from traditional modes of composing that saw a shift in the twentieth century of ways in which music was organized and favoured experimentalism over long-established systems of tonality. As in the previous Adams cue, 'Phrygian Gates' speaks to dualism. The music modulates between the Phrygian and Lydian modes, which come together and drift apart over the course of the piece and have a different feel to major and minor musical scales in that they do not resolve to an expected tonic, the melodic and harmonic focus of a piece of music in conventional major or minor scales. Adams has referred to the piece as his 'opus one', an artistic work that could be considered the start of a career, and explained that his intent in the piece was to move between two musical ideas 'abruptly and without warning'[11] – a choice echoed in Elio's struggle with his identity. The composer described the Phrygian mode as 'very nervous and unstable' and the Lydian as in opposition to this, 'stable and yet ecstatic, used in a lot of New Age music, which is supposed to induce bliss and ecstasy'[12] – again, both descriptions that characterize the combative initial encounters between Elio and Oliver. These explicit and contextual points also serve to mirror Elio's discovery of his sexuality and the search for self that he finds – in part – through his developing relationship with Oliver.

Following this kiss, the first of three cues from the songwriter Sufjan Stevens soundtracks a dream-like montage where a remix of a pre-existing track 'Futile Devices' is played through in its entirety, as a non-diegetic device. The sequence appears at the midpoint of the film and takes place at the end of a day when another academic couple has visited the Perlmans' villa, and Oliver has left the family to explore the area on his own, leaving Elio with his friends Marzia (Esther Garrel) and Chiara (Victoire du Bois), and then alone. The montage begins with Elio sat outside on the *terrazza*; the colours are bleached out initially and the sequence overtly appears to be shot on celluloid, a device typically used in film to present as memory or recollection, before shifting back to the crisper images more familiar from earlier in the film. Elio ruminates on his day, first outside the house and then at his desk in his room. When he hears Oliver return, Elio leaps into his own bed and pretends to be asleep. The music in the sequence is connected to the previous music through its piano introduction, but it is Stevens's lyrics that throw light on Elio's feelings. Although not a direct break in the action, the combination of the celluloid film form and foregrounding the song in the sound mix privileges Stevens' music over and above other diegetic and non-diegetic cues in the soundtrack. Allowing it to play through is a stark and deliberate device, drawing attention to the lyrics that actualize Elio's thoughts – of his feeling of safety in Oliver's company, of his love for him and of his difficulty in articulating this in words. As Stevens explains, the director 'was entranced from the very beginning with the idea of using that song. I think it's just serendipity that the nature and content of the material fits so well into the film. It was a lucky accident.'[13]

This technique is deployed more subtly in other places. In a sequence where Elio's mother Annella (Amira Casar) reads to her son a tale from the *Heptaméron*, a series of stories by Marguerite de Navarre (1558), she is accompanied by a turntable softly playing a piano rendition of Ravel's 'Le Jardin féerique'. The story she selects is of the knight Amador who is uncertain of speaking of his love for a high-born princess and asks her whether it is better to 'speak or die', not knowing whether his feelings are reciprocated. Zora van Harten recognizes that this musical cue serves to mirror the fairy tale being read, in that Ravel's piece forms the final part of his *Ma Mère l'Oye* collection that accounts for the waking of sleeping beauty by a prince's kiss. She observes that Ravel's piece and the manner with which these musical and literary renditions operate work in parallel to Elio's sexual awakening as his relationship with Oliver develops.[14]

This complementary connotation of the music, with that made explicit by dialogue or action denoted on the screen, is a consistent theme in *Call Me by Your Name* and called upon repeatedly to throw light on Elio's inner feelings. The sophistication extends beyond the direct address of each text, however, with each cultural device having its own multi-layered meaning. De Navarre's book is in fact an anthology of interrelated stories, each individually narrated and providing differing interpretations of recalled events – an extratextual suggestion that the events of the film are being recounted by Elio as a memory of the past. Themes of dualism and duality are also evident in this choice of music for the scene. Ravel's piece was written as a piano duet for – and indeed dedicated to – his friend's children, with Ravel later acknowledging the manner with which two contrasting elements are interwoven in the suite. Emily Kilpatrick notes that both the fairy tale genre and Ravel's musical response form 'determinable patterns of action and reaction, clearly defined structures and a characteristic directness and simplicity of expression'.[15]

The use of music – particularly at the piano – as the manner with which Elio can most clearly communicate and connect with Oliver is expressed in the film's source material by Elio but made much more explicit in the film, where music effectively replaces Elio's inner monologue of the novel. Guadagnino acknowledges his use of the piano as a device to replace the interior thoughts of the book, stating that: 'in *Call Me by Your Name*, we have extensive usage of piano because those notes, in a way, are the interior and exterior dialogue between Elio and himself, and Elio and Oliver'.[16] Elio's various turns at the piano indicate play and performance – a place to improvise and try out ideas, to communicate and extend his understanding of music, while simultaneously serving as a site of resistance to tradition, and what has gone before. Elio unpicks the music he plays, transcribing and rewriting in his own voice. When he performs at the piano for Oliver, Elio displays an agency outside of his parents' understanding of his identity. This understanding of music, however, only demonstrates Elio's frustration in expressing other parts of his identity, including his sexuality. In a scene when the two men cycle to the local town and Oliver commends Elio's knowledge of the area's history, Elio responds by saying how little he knows 'about the things that matter' – his first, if coded and clumsy, spoken expression of his true feelings for the older man. This moment marks a turning point in the story and is followed by Elio taking Oliver to the isolated spring water lake for a scene in which their first physical expression of love takes place: their first kiss.

In contrast with this complex and multi-layered use of non-diegetic music, and the manner with which Elio's musical performance exists inside and outside of the filmic world, the use of pre-existing source music is much more conventional and literal in its use, typically acting in service of situating or reinforcing the film's period. The Psychedelic Furs' 'Love My Way' is prominent in two key sequences, and a mixture of 1980s pop drawn from Italian radio playlists of the time is woven into the fabric of the narrative. This sense of the contemporary is reinforced in much of the diegetic music within the film. Bandolero's 'Paris Latino' and Joe Esposito's 'Lady, Lady, Lady' – both released in 1983 – and the aforementioned Psychedelic Furs cue, released a year earlier, are all played by DJs at a party where Elio watches Oliver lose himself in the music and subsequently joins his friend on the dance floor.

Music as a cypher for feeling

Irina Melnikova has described Guadagnino's films as 'multimedial cinematic texts',[17] noting the manner with which the director makes use of music that relates to itself, in addition to the intertextual and transtextual significance of music in the construction of self for characters across all three films of his 'desire' trilogy. Melnikova addresses the significance of nostalgia in all three films – for a place, a time, and the relationships that occurred in the past and recounted through memory – but also in the manner with which memory attempts to 'resurrect the past'.[18] She adds that this closing film of the trilogy – *Call Me by Your Name* – is most clearly in a hypertextual dialogue with the preceding works in addition to its many other referents.[19] She highlights the significance of the richness of *hearing*, as opposed to *listening*, to the music in the film, specifically in Elio's performances, but also how this can be extended to an understanding of not just the references themselves as they are denoted in the film but their wider contextual connotations.[20]

As an example, in Elio's first piano performance of the film following a family dinner he plays Erik Satie's 'Sonatine bureaucratique'. Elio's performance is energetic, but appears to be made without much feeling. The scene cuts abruptly after only a few bars. A non-diegetic version of the same cue plays a little later, as Elio watches Oliver swim lengths of the villa's pool. The cue is one of Satie's humoristic pieces completed in 1917, a collage of existing musical components by other composers and part of a body of work that parodied existing compositions. In these works, Satie, much like Adams' use of seriality in his music 60 years later, uses repetition and structural reframing of phrases to create entirely new works. The work serves as a critique and expresses an interest in the idea of simultaneity – the relationship between two events, occurring in the same time and space, but altered by their frame of reference.[21] The selection of this cue – which appears for a few short seconds in the film – sets up an idea that is referred to repeatedly, and is explicitly addressed in the following scene. The next day, Elio takes to the piano after Oliver asks him to replay a piece by Bach – 'Postillon's Aria', from 'Capriccio on the Departure of a Beloved Brother' – that he had heard Elio playing on the guitar in the garden. As the two men relocate to the piano inside the house, Elio plays the piece very differently. When challenged by Oliver, Elio explains his own variations: 'I played it the way Liszt would have played it if he had played Bach's version'. In a second rendition he explains, 'I played it the way Busoni would have played it if he had altered Liszt's version'. His third performance responds to Oliver's requests to play the piece as Bach had intended, and Elio tells Oliver when he finishes that Bach had dedicated the piece to his brother. The intertextuality of the Satie piece requires existing knowledge, but its significance is made explicit through this later dialogue of Elio's, in the same way that Elio's explanation informs the audience of the significance of his confused feelings – whether of friendship, rather than desire – towards Oliver. In these performances and through his musical knowledge, Elio demonstrates his agency – of the paths ahead of him, and how he will play future events through in his mind. He is presented as a rewriter of the music, transcribing and reinterpreting each piece in an attempt to better understand it, and Elio writes his thoughts and replays events in his memory in much the same way – an attempt to find his true feelings and, ultimately, his identity.

This scene, early in the film, sets the stall for Elio's character – unsure of what he likes and desires, able to perform different roles in reaction to an audience and driven by a desire for knowledge and understanding work through playing and replaying, altering his interpretations in order to subject a text – and himself – to a thorough examination through these different lenses. In doing so, each musical cue within the film offers a palimpsest of meaning for the audience and each signposts a richness of the film text that rewards the audience that extends their thinking beyond the literal to be prepared to contextualize the significance of each cue through the prism of Elio's feelings, and the story as a whole.

The mystery of love: Sufjan Stevens' contribution

André Aciman's original novel, which forms the source material for James Ivory's script, makes use of Elio as a first-person narrator, articulating his thoughts and feelings in his account of his summer with Oliver. The songwriter Sufjan Stevens was initially asked to contribute to a version of this narration as a voice-over for the film, as an older Elio reminiscing on his experience of that summer's events. Guadagnino first contacted Stevens in 2016, when the musician was on tour for the *Carrie & Lowell* album. Guadagnino sent the songwriter Aciman's novel and subsequently the script. Stevens recalls that in this initial material,

> They had retained the monologue from the older Elio, and he initially asked me to be the voice of the older Elio; to contribute that voiceover. He also asked if I wanted to appear in the movie as a bard, performing the song, almost as a break in the narrative. I got back to him and I said, 'I think this voiceover is a mistake, and I think the interruption of me singing the song is a mistake'. I think he was just thinking out loud. I don't know if he was really committed to the idea. So I said, 'I'll write you some songs, but that's all I think you need from me'. And he agreed.[22]

Stevens elaborates on this initial idea that the break in the narrative was intended to provide respite from the film's intensity: 'There would just be a scene of me playing the song, almost like an intermission. The whole thing sounded a bit like the singer-songwriter who's in "The Life Aquatic".'[23] As the project developed, though this role of the narrator was central within Aciman's source material for the film, this idea was eventually abandoned by the filmmakers altogether. Instead, the script developed into the more implicit framing of memory in the final film where the focus shifts from the past-tense storytelling of the novel, where an older Elio recounts his experience two decades after the events of his summer with Oliver, to a screen version that instead occurs entirely contemporary to the characters and a far greater subtlety to the notion of this account being recalled by Elio.

The novel's coda, where Elio returns to the house twenty years after the events that had taken place that summer, was also refined and compressed in the film through an ending that instead takes place the following winter where Oliver's departure is still a fresh wound for Elio. Guadagnino explains this approach:

> It's my task, in order to be faithful to the novel, to betray the novel. When you translate any kind of text into a visual storyline, a cinema scene, you have to make sure you don't get crushed and overwhelmed by the weight of the source material.[24]

This narrative distinctiveness is balanced primarily by the cinematic deployment of music to articulate for the audience Elio's feelings and inner thoughts – rather than the direct voice-over originally suggested to, and described by, Stevens.

This solution of using music as a multi-layered narration of sorts, Guadagnino states, allowed the director to

> work on a contribution from the standpoint of music that could give the film a precise identity that was going to go beyond the philologic aspect of the '80s and the commentary music of the classical music. And that's why I was seeking a voice to add itself to the voices of the film – played by the actors playing the characters – and that's when I thought of Sufjan Stevens.[25]

Guadagnino explained,

> In a way the narrator became Sufjan Stevens with his new songs, made contemporary, about our story, which is back. We wanted a sort of narrator that could make justice of the book, of the film, drawn from the narrative of Elio.[26]

Stevens elaborates on this shift in thinking as the project developed: 'Luca designed this project around a more general aesthetic affiliation with me and my music, and what it means to him. He wasn't just thinking about specific content, he was thinking about all of my songs.'[27]

Ultimately then, Stevens' contributions came not through voice-over but as a songwriter, writing two original songs in response to the script that he was able to deliver to the director before principal photography. Stevens describes that:

> When I wrote them I hadn't seen any footage, so I wasn't sure how he was going to use them at all. I just handed them over and had to trust that he would know what to do. And, of course, having seen all his films, and how masterful he is with music, there was no question in my mind he would be responsible about it.[28]

These two songs – 'Mystery of Love' and 'Visions of Gideon' – play, respectively, as Elio and Oliver travel to the city of Bergamo prior to Oliver's departure back to the USA and poignantly over the closing titles.

In the Bergamo montage, 'Mystery of Love' provides the soundtrack of a sequence that begins with the two men boarding a bus and taking a hiking trip through a mountain scene – the first time that Elio and Oliver are able to escape Elio's family and the clandestine nature of their physical relationship back at the villa. With no other sound in the first part of the sequence and dialogue placed in the distant background of the hiking scene, the music cue is foregrounded here, and dominates the film – Stevens' lyrics foregrounding Oliver's departure – 'cursed by the love that I received'. The music ends abruptly as the men arrive at their hotel in Bergamo. In a call back to the earlier party scene as they explore the city that same night, the two men chance across a group of young men and a woman playing The Psychedelic Furs' 'Love My Way' from the radio of their car. In a direct echo of the previous use of this musical cue, Oliver initially dances with the woman, before dancing on his own. Again Elio watches his friend dancing though he himself doesn't dance at all this time, and is physically sick at the climax of the song. This use of the musical cue as a prompt to show the significance of when Elio had first fallen for Oliver again serves to foreground Elio's thoughts and memories and brings both Stevens' lyrics – and those of The Psychedelic Furs – to bear. It is in this scene that Elio comes to realize that their time together in Bergamo marks the beginning of the end of his relationship with Oliver. Again it is the deployment of music that narrativizes Elio's feelings in the film – the same moment expressed in the book through an expositional monologue between Elio and his father.

In the closing scene of the film, 'Visions of Gideon' plays in a sequence that takes place a few months after Oliver's return to the USA. It is a winter's day, snow falls outside the windows, and Oliver has called the villa to tell Elio that he is engaged to be married. After the call, Elio enters an empty dining room where the table is set for the family's Hanukkah dinner. He wears a Walkman, but the scene is silent other than the crackle of an open fire and the sound of his footsteps on the wooden floor. He removes his Walkman and crouches by the fire. The camera is locked, with Elio appearing in close up on the right hand side of the frame. As he looks into the fire, he cries and the first notes of Stevens' song start to play. The cue begins with the piano, the lyrics directly expressing Elio's thoughts. The title crawl begins, and his family enters the room, but Elio remains oblivious to them. As his tears turn to a smile, and his mother calls his name, Elio looks directly into the camera before he turns in response to his mother's voice. Guadagnino explains, 'we immediately felt that "Visions of Gideon" was the perfect song for this moment in which Elio thinks of his life. When we shot the scene, I put the earbud in Timothée's ear and played the song for him.'[29]

As with the earlier deployment of 'Futile Devices' in the montage sequence, Stevens' cues are distinguished from much of the other music in the film – whether source music or diegetic– by being entirely foregrounded in the sound mix where each of the three pieces of his music play through with little or no interruption by dialogue or sound effects. The narrative impact is further accentuated through the deployment of an enhanced environmental sound design in these scenes, extending the sense of these moments as significant, subjective, and centred entirely on Elio's experience.

Conclusion

Call Me by Your Name is a film not only about music and its ability to communicate place, motivation and emotion but also one that delights in using film form – communicating endless subtext through its *mise en bande*, the interaction of sonic components on the soundtrack. It rewards a metatextual study of its musical choices and their deployment, where diving into these palimpsests of meaning offers an enriched experience both as a viewer and as a listener. The film is a celebration of the abstraction of music as feeling, as desire, and of its shapeshifting ability to imbue identity through its reception, endless reinterpretation and performance.

The film throws down a gauntlet which challenges filmmakers who do not take such care in the provision of depths of meaning in their use of existing source music or commissioned score and songwriting, instead reliant on tried and tested techniques such as the expositional voice-over, or dialogue that doggedly explains the interior motivations of characters.

André Aciman's source material lends itself to the creative approach from the filmmakers in their adaptation, but Guadagnino and his team make bold choices in their selection and use of music both within the diegesis and outside of it. The result to these approaches to both expositional information and clues as to the motivations of its central characters presents a lesson in sophisticated approaches to music supervision and editing.

NOTES
1. Quoted in Anne Thompson, '*Call Me by Your Name* Could Land (at Least) Seven Oscar Nominations: Here's Why', *IndieWire*, 27 November 2017, https://www.indiewire.com/2017/11/call-me-by-your-name-oscars-luca-guadagnino-1201900981/.
2. Quoted in Andre-Naquian Wheeler, 'The *Call Me by Your Name* Soundtrack Is Its Own Queer Love Story', *i-D*, 18 December 2017, https://i-d.vice.com/en_uk/article/9knwzv/the-call-me-by-your-name-soundtrack-is-its-own-queer-love-story.

3. Quoted in Tomris Laffly, 'Sensual Summer: Luca Guadagnino's *Call Me by Your Name* Captures the Chemistry of Attraction', *Film Journal International*, 17 November 2017, http://fj.webedia.us/features/sensual-summer-luca-guadagninos-call-me-your-name-captures-chemistry-attraction.

4. See Fiona Maddocks, 'John Adams: *I Am Love* soundtrack', *The Observer*, 13 July 2010, https://www.theguardian.com/music/2010/jul/13/adams-i-am-love-cd-review.

5. See David Ng, 'John Adams Lends His Music to *I Am Love*, Starring Tilda Swinton', *Washington Post*, 18 June 2010, https://latimesblogs.latimes.com/culturemonster/2010/06/john-adams-lends-his-music-to-i-am-love-starring-tilda-swinton.html.

6. John Adams, 'Hallelujah Junction – 1st Movement', track 1 on Various, *Call My by Your Name: Original Motion Picture Soundtrack*, Madison Gate Records/Masterworks/Sony Music Entertainment, 2017.

7. John Adams, 'Hallelujah Junction, for Two Pianos', *Hollywood Bowl*, n.d., accessed 13 April 2023, https://www.hollywoodbowl.com/musicdb/pieces/1915/hallelujah-junction-for-two-pianos.

8. Quoted in Frank Ocean, 'Throwback Thursday: Frank Ocean Interviews Timothée Chalamet in *VMAN39*', *VMAN* 39, 16 April 2020, https://vman.com/article/timothee-chalamet-frank-ocean/.

9. Quoted in Wheeler, 'The *Call Me by Your Name* Soundtrack'.

10. Ivan Raykoff, 'Music and Touch in *Call Me by Your Name*', *OUPBlog*, Oxford University Press, 23 January 2018, https://blog.oup.com/2018/01/music-touch-call-me-by-your-name/.

11. John Adams, 'Phrygian Gates and China Gates', *Earbox – John Adams*, 2016–2018, n.d., accessed 13 April 2023, https://www.earbox.com/phrygian-gates-china-gates/.

12. Quoted in Edward Strickland, *American Composers: Dialogues on Contemporary Music* (Bloomington: Indiana University Press, 1991), 184.

13. Quoted in Joe Utichi, 'Sufjan Stevens Nearly Played the Narrator in Luca Guadagnino's *Call Me by Your Name*', *Deadline*, 13 December 2017, https://deadline.com/2017/12/call-me-by-your-name-sufjan-stevens-luca-guadagnino-musicinterview-1202225747/.

14. See Z. S. van Harten, 'Call Me Queer: Queer Theory and the Soundtrack of *Call Me by Your Name*', Bachelor thesis, University of Utrecht, 2018, http://dspace.library.uu.nl/bitstream/handle/1874/371071/ZoravanHarten-Eindwerkstuk%20.pdf?sequence=2&isAllowed=y.

15. Emily Kilpatrick, '"Therein Lies a Tale": Musical and Literary Structure in Ravel's *Ma Mère l'Oye*', *Context: Journal of Music Research* 34 (January 2009): 83.

16. Quoted in Matthew Schnipper, 'Luca Guadagnino on the Music of His Movies, and Why He Had to Have Sufjan Stevens for *Call Me by Your Name*', *Pitchfork*, 23 January 2018, https://pitchfork.com/thepitch/luca-guadagnino-interview-call-me-by-your-name-sufjan-stevens-music-of-his-movies/.

17. Irina Melnikova, 'Nostalgia, Adaptation, and (Textual) Identity: Luca Guadagnino's "Desire Trilogy"', *Adaptation* 13, no. 3 (December 2020): 379.

18. Melnikova, 379.

19. See, for example, Melnikova, 379–84.
20. Melnikova, 385–86.
21. See Belva Jean Hare, 'The Uses and Aesthetics of Musical Borrowing in Erik Satie's Humoristic Piano Suites, 1913–1917', PhD thesis, University of Texas at Austin, 2005, https://repositories.lib.utexas.edu/bitstream/handle/2152/2441/hareb78915.pdf?msclkid=2416b-d55ced611ecb437391cafc4e7ef.
22. Quoted in Utichi, 'Sufjan Stevens'.
23. Quoted in Tim Greiving, 'Sufjan Stevens Captured the Essence of *Call Me by Your Name* Before He Even Saw the Film', *Los Angeles Times*, 20 February 2018, https://www.latimes.com/entertainment/envelope/la-en-mn-sufjan-stevens-20180219-story.html.
24. Quoted in Pamela Hutchinson, 'My Summer of Love', *Sight and Sound* 27, no. 11 (November 2017): 34.
25. Quoted in Keith Caulfield, 'How Sufjan Stevens' Music Became a "Sort of Narrator" for *Call Me by Your Name*', *Billboard*, 1 October 2018, https://www.billboard.com/music/music-news/sufjan-stevens-call-me-by-your-name-music-luca-guadagnino-interview-8093818/.
26. Quoted in Joshua Encinias, '*Call Me by Your Name* Team on Romance, Sufjan Stevens, Maurice Pialat, and Sequel Potential', *The Film Stage*, 11 October 2017, https://thefilm-stage.com/call-me-by-your-name-team-on-romance-sufjan-stevens-maurice-pialat-and-sequel-potential/.
27. Quoted in Greiving, 'Captured the Essence'.
28. Quoted in Utichi, 'Sufjan Stevens'.
29. Quoted in Schnipper, 'Luca Guadagnino'.

REFERENCES

Adams, John. 'Hallelujah Junction – 1st Movement.' Various, *Call My by Your Name: Original Motion Picture Soundtrack*, track 1. Madison Gate Records/Masterworks/Sony Music Entertainment, 2017.

Adams, John. 'Hallelujah Junction, for Two Pianos.' *Hollywood Bowl*, n.d. Accessed 13 April 2023. https://www.hollywoodbowl.com/musicdb/pieces/1915/hallelujah-junction-for-two-pianos.

Adams, John. 'Phrygian Gates and China Gates.' *Earbox – John Adams*, 2016–2018, n.d. Accessed 13 April 2023. https://www.earbox.com/phrygian-gates-china-gates/.

Bandolero. 'Paris Latino.' Various, *Call My by Your Name: Original Motion Picture Soundtrack*, track 4 Madison Gate Records/Masterworks/Sony Music Entertainment, 2017.

Caulfield, Keith. 'How Sufjan Stevens' Music Became a "Sort of Narrator" for *Call Me by Your Name*.' *Billboard*, 1 October 2018. https://www.billboard.com/music/music-news/sufjan-stevens-call-me-by-your-name-music-luca-guadagnino-interview-8093818/.

Di Mattia, Joanna. 'Some Thoughts on the Erotic Aesthetic in Luca Guadagnino's "Desire Trilogy".' *Senses of Cinema* 86 (2018). https://www.sensesofcinema.com/2018/feature-articles/luca-guadagninos-desiretrilogy/.

Encinias, Joshua. '*Call Me by Your Name* Team on Romance, Sufjan Stevens, Maurice Pialat, and Sequel Potential.' *The Film Stage*, 11 October 2017. https://thefilmstage.com/call-me-by-your-name-team-on-romance-sufjan-stevens-maurice-pialat-and-sequel-potential/.

Esposito, Joe, and Giorgio Moroder. 'Lady, Lady, Lady.' In Various, *Call My by Your Name: Original Motion Picture Soundtrack*. Madison Gate Records/Masterworks/Sony Music Entertainment, 2017.

Greiving, Tim. 'Sufjan Stevens Captured the Essence of *Call Me by Your Name* Before He Even Saw the Film.' *Los Angeles Times*, 20 February 2018. https://www.latimes.com/entertainment/envelope/la-en-mn-Sufjan-stevens-20180219-story.html.

Guadagnino, Luca, dir. *Io sono l'amore* (*I Am Love*). First Sun, Mikado Film, Rai Cinema, 2009.

Guadagnino, Luca, dir. *A Bigger Splash*. Frenesy Film Company, Cota Film, 2015.

Guadagnino, Luca, dir. *Call Me by Your Name*. Frenesy Film Company, La Cinefacture, RT Features, 2017.

Hare, Belva Jean. 'The Uses and Aesthetics of Musical Borrowing in Erik Satie's Humoristic Piano Suites, 1913–1917.' PhD thesis, University of Texas at Austin, 2005. https://repositories.lib.utexas.edu/bitstream/handle/2152/2441/hareb78915.pdf?msclkid=2416bd55ced611ecb437391cafc4e7ef.

Hutchinson, Pamela. 'My Summer of Love.' *Sight and Sound* 27, no. 11 (November 2017): 32–35.

Ivory, James. *Call Me by Your Name* (screenplay). Sony Pictures Classics, 2017. https://sony-classics.com/awards-information/screenplays/callmebyyourname_screenplay-20171206.pdf.

Kilpatrick, Emily. '"Therein Lies a Tale": Musical and Literary Structure in Ravel's *Ma Mère l'Oye*.' *Context: Journal of Music Research* 34 (January 2009): 81–98.

Laffly, Tomris. 'Sensual Summer: Luca Guadagnino's *Call Me by Your Name* Captures the Chemistry of Attraction.' *Film Journal International*, 17 November 2017. http://fj.webedia.us/features/sensual-summer-luca-guadagninos-call-me-your-name-captures-chemistry-attraction.

Maddocks, Fiona. 'John Adams: *I Am Love* Soundtrack.' *The Observer*, 13 July 2010. https://www.theguardian.com/music/2010/jul/13/adams-i-am-love-cd-review.

Melnikova, Irina. 'Nostalgia, Adaptation, and (Textual) Identity: Luca Guadagnino's "Desire Trilogy".' *Adaptation* 13, Issue 3 (December 2020): 378–96.

Ng, David. 'John Adams Lends His Music to *I Am Love*, Starring Tilda Swinton.' *Washington Post*, 18 June 2010. https://latimesblogs.latimes.com/culturemonster/2010/06/john-adams-lends-his-music-to-i-am-love-starring-tilda-swinton.html.

Ocean, Frank. 'Throwback Thursday: Frank Ocean Interviews Timothée Chalamet in *VMAN39*.' *VMAN* 39 (16 April 2020). https://vman.com/article/timothee-chalamet-frank-ocean/.

Psychedelic Furs, The. 'Love My Way.' In Various, *Call My by Your Name: Original Motion Picture Soundtrack*. Madison Gate Records/Masterworks/Sony Music Entertainment, 2017.

Raykoff. Ivan. 'Music and Touch in *Call Me by Your Name*.' OUPBlog, Oxford University Press, 23 January 2018. https://blog.oup.com/2018/01/music-touch-call-me-by-your-name/.

Sakamoto, Ryuichi. 'M.A.Y. in the Backyard.' In Various, *Call My by Your Name: Original Motion Picture Soundtrack*. Madison Gate Records/Masterworks/Sony Music Entertainment, 2017.

Satie, Erik. 'Sonatine bureaucratique.' In Various, *Call My by Your Name: Original Motion Picture Soundtrack*. Madison Gate Records/Masterworks/Sony Music Entertainment, 2017.

Schnipper, Matthew. 'Luca Guadagnino on the Music of His Movies, and Why He Had to Have Sufjan Stevens for *Call Me by Your Name*.' In *Pitchfork*, 23 January 2018. https://pitchfork.com/thepitch/luca-guadagnino-interview-call-me-by-your-name-sufjan-stevens-music-of-his-movies/.

Stevens, Sufjan. 'Futile Devices (Doveman Remix).' In Various, *Call My by Your Name: Original Motion Picture Soundtrack*. Madison Gate Records/Masterworks/Sony Music Entertainment, 2017.

Stevens, Sufjan. 'Mystery of Love.' In Various, *Call My by Your Name: Original Motion Picture Soundtrack*. Madison Gate Records/Masterworks/Sony Music Entertainment, 2017.

Stevens, Sufjan. 'Visions of Gideon.' In Various, *Call My by Your Name: Original Motion Picture Soundtrack*. Madison Gate Records/Masterworks/Sony Music Entertainment, 2017.

Strickland, Edward. *American Composers: Dialogues on Contemporary Music*. Bloomington: Indiana University Press, 1991.

Thompson, Anne. '*Call Me by Your Name* Could Land (at Least) Seven Oscar Nominations: Here's Why.' *IndieWire*, 27 November 2017. https://www.indiewire.com/2017/11/call-me-by-your-name-oscars-luca-guadagnino-1201900981/.

Utichi, Joe. 'Sufjan Stevens Nearly Played the Narrator in Luca Guadagnino's *Call Me by Your Name*.' *Deadline*, 13 December 2017. https://deadline.com/2017/12/call-me-by-your-name-sufjan-stevens-luca-guadagnino-musicinterview-1202225747/.

van Harten, Z. S. 'Call Me Queer: Queer Theory and the Soundtrack of *Call Me by Your Name*.' Bachelor thesis, *University of Utrecht*, 2018. http://dspace.library.uu.nl/bitstream/handle/1874/371071/ZoravanHarten-Eindwerkstuk%20.pdf?sequence=2&isAllowed=y.

Wheeler, André-Naquian. 'The *Call Me by Your Name* Soundtrack Is Its Own Queer Love Story.' *i-D*, 18 December 2017. i-d.vice.com/en_au/article/9knwzv/the-call-me-by-your-name-soundtrack-is-its-own-queer-love-story.

5

Sex Sounds:
On Aural Explicitness in
Call Me by Your Name

Sarah Artt

On its reception, *Call Me by Your Name* (Luca Guadagnino, 2017) remained insufficiently explicit for some critics,[1] who lamented instances such as the pan shot that takes us away from Elio (Timothée Chalamet) and Oliver (Armie Hammer) in bed together:

> Once the two lovers begin having sex for the first time, however, the camera coyly drifts over to an open window, their early coital moans gentle in the background – the kind of tasteful dodge that practically nods to Code-era Hollywood.[2]

This response is certainly understandable and recalls a similar rallying cry from Rose Troche's 1994 film *Go Fish*: 'What would you rather our collective lesbian image be? Hot, passionate, say-yes-to-sex dykes or touchy-feely, soft-focus sisters of the woodlands?' Guadagnino, in making a mainstream, high-profile adaptation, has, in the eyes of some critics, opted for the 'touchy-feely soft-focus' route. However, I would like to suggest that the film locates its explicitness in its sound design. This clever strategy is used to clearly convey actions which are not shown directly on screen. The film is filled with the sound of clothing slipping on and off of bodies and with the sound of bodies in contact. In the scenes in which Oliver fellates Elio, there is audible sound design that articulates the action taking place. Drawing on work that discusses the importance of sound, audio design[3] and affect, I would like to counter the suggestion that *Call Me by Your Name* is overtly coy in its display of sex. By attending to the details of the film's sound design we can see that it deliberately evokes the affect of pornography in order to amplify the film's explicitness.

A case for the attentive listener

Lucy Fife Donaldson, in work which incorporates the study of both sound design practice and affect studies, points out that

> the ability to feel sound through our bodies has been expanded through sound technologies – such as Dolby Digital – which work to create an increasingly dense relationship between body and sound [...][.] [S]uch technologies intensify the extent to which feeling and listening are entangled.[4]

This deliberate entanglement is available for deeper appreciation and analysis by the attentive listener, who is attuned to the possibilities of how sound can act on the body. This is particularly evident in the case of *Call Me by Your Name*, where luxurious, detailed sound design is deployed as a way of creating an explicit aural landscape. Sharif Mowlabocus and Andy Medhurst note the importance of sound in relation to pornography:

> [W]here references to the pornographic are made in popular culture, or within every-day discourse (often as a point of humour), it is regularly through sound and most commonly through music that we refer to the explicitly sexual, the performatively sexual and the knowingly sexual.[5]

While this observation remains valid, it also registers as distinctly puritanical, as if to make any kind of visual reference to pornography already a transgression. It's therefore interesting to note that the route to explicitness undertaken by *Call Me by Your Name* is via its sound design, rather than through the visual proof of arousal so often demanded of people with penises in visual pornography: the erection. Discussions of sound design rather than music have tended to be comparatively rare in Film Studies until recently. Yet, there have been earlier advocates for what I am calling the attentive listener. Jack Halberstam writes about the relationship between sound and fear for women in horror cinema:

> [F]ear can also be produced from a sound: a click, a shutter (shudder?), 'knocking'. Productive fear, therefore, circulates through the power of the gaze but also through the power of directed listening. Within the structure of the horror film, furthermore, it is very often sound rather than sight that produces tension for the female viewer – soundtracks, for example, match and produce expected somatic responses to the images on the screen. [...] Very often the music transforms a spectator into a listener and then makes listening a part of the identifications between audience and victim or audience and slasher.[6]

If horror cinema can be experienced through this listening connection between audience and on-screen figures, then why not other kinds of cinema? Linda Williams in her landmark essay 'Film Bodies: Gender, Genre, Excess' argues for horror, pornography and melodrama as 'body genres' and I would like to argue that *Call Me by Your Name* is attempting to make use of the strategies that have long been at work in body genres, namely their strategies for evoking a bodily response from the viewer. While Halberstam comments on music in horror, he also notes the closeness of sound and bodily reaction in this phrase: 'shutter (shudder?)'. I think that *Call Me by Your Name* wants us to shiver, in the best sense. This aligns with the work of Donaldson and others, who argue for 'sound as a key agent in a blurring of the boundaries between audience and film'.[7] This blurring of boundaries using sound is deliberate and it is ripe for further investigation, particularly in a film like *Call Me by Your Name*.

Between men

There are recent precedents for taking a more visually explicit approach to portraying on-screen sex between men in films which are not deemed to be pornography. *L'Inconnu du lac* (*Stranger by the Lake*, Alain Guiraudie, 2013), a thriller set at a local cruising spot, displays explicit, condomless blow jobs and hand jobs (performed by body doubles for the lead actors) but the film does not display the same level of attention accorded to the sounds of sex and bodies as we find in *Call Me by Your Name*. First, the sex in *Stranger by the Lake* takes place out of doors, with actors who are completely naked, and the soundscape is dominated by the sound of the landscape (wind in the trees, or the hum of insects). In addition to the challenges of recording the synchronous sound of bodies in this setting, we might also consider that there is no particular need to attend to designing in the more subtle sounds of sex here, because the sex acts are completely visible to the viewer. Even when sex is simulated by the two named lead actors, it is still clear what is taking place because of the dialogue ('I want you to fuck me') and because of how they are positioned (when they have anal sex, for instance).[8] In a similar vein, *Théo et Hugo dans le même bateau* (*Theo and Hugo*, Olivier Ducastel and Jacques Martineau, 2016) opens its queer romance with an extended orgy scene in a Paris sex club, refusing to treat explicit, unsimulated sex as belonging solely to the realm of pornography.[9] In spite of these precedents, it is not entirely surprising that *Call Me by Your Name* did not undertake the approach of either *Stranger by the Lake* or *Theo and Hugo*. *Call Me by Your Name* is a film that was clearly positioned within Hollywood through its star lead actors and Oscar nominations and was therefore negotiating an industry that has long been both more conservative and more invested in heavily coding any kind of queer content. With this conservatism in mind, we might also consider the ways in which moving-image pornography sometimes demotes dialogue in favour of particular kinds of vocal and bodily performances, namely moans, grunts, undulations and other seemingly involuntary responses that evoke authentic desire and pleasure. *Call Me by Your Name* favours an approach that makes use of sensuously detailed sound design and the visual portrayal of longing, alongside well-chosen dialogue, which offers the opportunity to create a successful, mainstream adaptation from André Aciman's far more explicit novel.

The history of touches

Joanna Di Mattia, in contrast to some of the other critical responses mentioned, comments that 'Guadagnino is a master sensualist, crafting images we imagine we can taste, touch, and smell'.[10] But, sound also plays a crucial role here; as Fife Donaldson reminds us, 'Sound marks out and enlarges space onscreen and beyond, playing an important part in describing the feel of space and movement'.[11] The sound of touches in *Call Me by Your Name* is immediately discernible. Listening with or without headphones, we can hear a range of intimate sounds that not only place us inside the room with characters but puts us next to their bodies as they move. Subtle sounds are made audible even to the viewer who may not be listening all that attentively: Elio's pencil as it moves across paper when he transcribes music or writes to Oliver; Oliver breathing as he sleeps off jet lag. For the attentive viewer/listener, there are even greater layers to be discovered: descending for breakfast on his first day at the villa, Oliver runs his hand over part of the wall as he descends the staircase and we can hear the sound of his hand brushing against the texture of the wall. The film is particularly notable for its emphasis of the sound of clothing against skin, especially when clothing is being removed. But the auditory top notes here are firmly located in the sound of objects that squish: the squelch of egg, fruit and flesh. This places *Call Me by Your Name* as a film informed by the history and conventions of body genres, especially pornography. When it comes to porn, horror and melodrama, Williams notes, 'What seems to bracket these particular genres from others is an apparent lack of esthetic distance, a sense of over-involvement in sensation and emotion'.[12] This is precisely the strategy at work in *Call Me by Your Name*, where sound works to deliberately eliminate the distance between the spectator and the bodies on screen and elicits spectatorial involvement.

The egg

When Oliver inexpertly cracks open his soft-boiled egg, we see this shot in close-up and the sound is lusciously oozy and sharp. This is immediately followed by Elio's revelation that he and Marzia (Esther Garrel) nearly had sex last night. While the egg may register as a joke about Elio's bungled seduction of Marzia, the egg also feels decadent, suitable to the ooze of sweat, saliva and semen that is percolating beneath the surface of Elio and Oliver's interactions. Here, the film establishes its excessive auditory tone, and its intention to more or less crawl inside the listener's ear. The uncontainable egg connotes the expansive qualities of desire present here: Elio's desire for Marzia and Oliver, and Oliver's polymorphous appreciation for his surroundings.

In spite of its lush, romantic piano score and songs by the now ubiquitous Sufjan Stevens, quiet and silence also form a strong component of *Call Me by Your Name*'s soundscape. Silence in the sense of the absence of dialogue allows for what Cynthia Baron and Sharon Marie Carnicke identify as 'intensities', memorable emotions or 'moments in cinema where performance details are crucial [...] with the depth and intensity of the character's feelings conveyed largely by [the actor's] selection and combination of physical gestures'.[13] *Call Me by Your Name* is also built on intensities. If we consider the lead up to the first kiss between the lovers we can see these intensities at work in Elio's longing gazes, through shots that eroticize the bodies of both men and, crucially, through the sounds their bodies make in clothing. In order for these intensities to occur, this requires physical gestures from the actors, and a detailed approach to audio design that further emphasizes the impact of those gestures. Oliver, in particular, deliberately and unselfconsciously displays himself to Elio. Elio, who is less experienced and potentially unskilled in the ways of cruising,[14] looks at Oliver but cannot quite work out how to act right away. This is particularly evident in the space of their shared bathroom and interconnected bedrooms, where the propensity for nonchalant glimpses of nudity is to be expected. The lingering shots of Oliver's discarded clothing, particularly his wet swimming trunks left hanging in the shared bathroom, act as a visual code for Elio's building desire. In this way, the viewer/listener gains access to Elio's private world, watching him as he practices what it means to desire. Elio hasn't yet realized his own swoon-like affect, even when Oliver invites him to go swimming. Before the scene of the egg, we see Elio lying on his stomach across his bed. He is shirtless, in denim cut-offs, his bottom framed in medium shot as piano music drifts from the previous scene carrying over and mixing with the sound of Elio's body against the sheets as he turns over, sits up, shifting his weight on the bed as he changes position to write. This scene could just start with the extra-diegetic piano, without the sound of Elio's body against the bed. But, these additional sounds that accompany the choice of gestures are there to build up the importance of bodies, how they sound, and how they feel (in terms of both touch and emotion). This sequence in particular also firmly establishes Elio as a figure who is restless with desire and who is himself the object of an eroticizing gaze, though he is not yet aware of Oliver's desire for him (Figure 5.1).

Even when dialogue is used, silences and ellipses remain as spaces to be filled by gestures, as Di Mattia notes: '*Call Me by Your Name* is more concerned with mapping the erogenous zone that exists in the space between Elio and Oliver's bodies'.[15] Elio initiates the conversation in front of the monument to the Battle of Piave where he confesses his inexperience to Oliver and his desire to know more about 'the things that really matter'. Taking Oliver to the spring, 'his spot', we see Elio gaining in confidence as he initiates further physical intimacy by stepping closer to Oliver as they stand in the spring. In response, Oliver shifts his weight, and while he doesn't quite draw back from Elio, he doesn't immediately lean in either. This choice of gestures serves to maintain the tension between them – initially this tension is uncertainty about reciprocated desire, but at the spring this transforms into tension around how far this desire will take them. As Elio and Oliver are reclining in the grass, we hear birdsong and insects, and Elio wistfully comments, 'I love this, Oliver'.

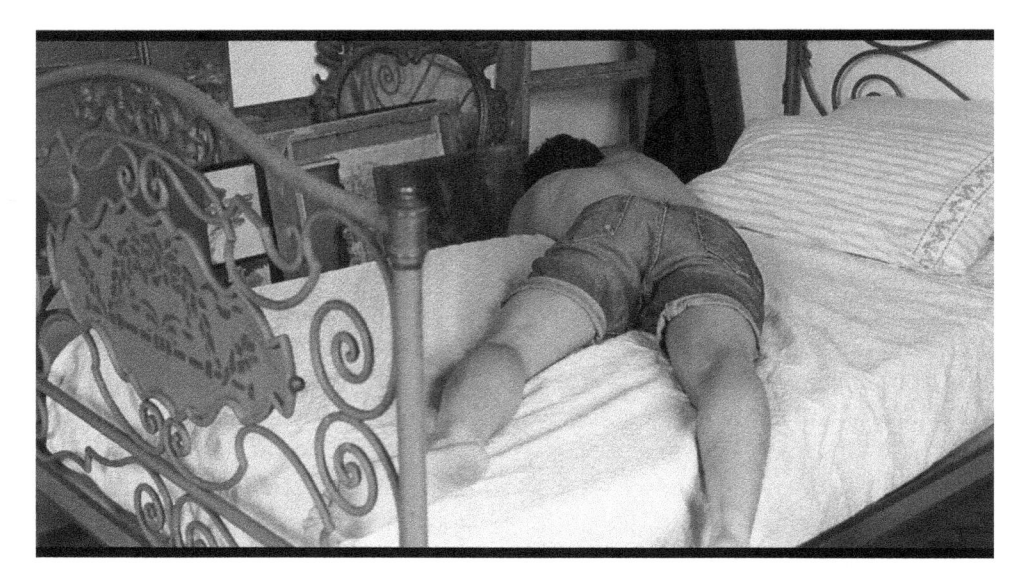

FIGURE 5.1: Restless with desire: the sound of Elio's (Timothée Chalamet) body evokes feeling and touch and heightens the eroticizing gaze. Luca Guadagnino (dir.), *Call Me by Your Name*, 2017. Italy/France/USA/Brazil. © Frenesy, La Cinefacture.

'What?'
'Everything.'
'Us, you mean?'
'Mmm, it's not bad, it's not bad.'

Only then does Oliver slowly turn his head, raising himself on his elbow, and lean over to touch Elio's mouth, tracing his lips. In response, Elio opens his mouth, and Oliver cups his chin. Elio sits up and it's then that they begin to kiss. We hear the sound of their lips meeting, but Oliver then gently pulls away, sucking in his breath and looking out to the horizon. Elio turns onto his stomach, an almost disappointed sigh escaping his lips at the disruption. 'Better now?' Oliver asks, before Elio initiates a second kiss, climbing on top of Oliver before being gently pushed back onto the grass as Oliver shakes his head and quietly says 'No, no, no, no'. While the gestures here are deliberate (no one has yet lost their head with desire), it's important to take note of the sound of their kisses: it is oversaturated, sticky, filled with breath and saliva. It is the sound of these kisses that evokes the body's involuntary responses. The enhancement of these sounds is deliberately implemented to make it sound like you are right next to them. The tranquillity of the setting for this heated moment forms a contrast with the urgency of the desires expressed, gesturing towards what we will hear more of later.

See you at midnight

The lovers' midnight assignation begins on the balcony, where Elio declares 'I'm nervous', amidst an audio mix of piano score, floor creaks and door sounds. This once again focuses the ear on the ways that bodies move through space, and does not rely solely on the emotional affect of a romantic musical score or on dialogue. Once the lovers enter the bedroom, all extra-diegetic music disappears and we can hear the sound of the night outside (insects, foliage in the breeze), the creak of floorboards, shared breath, and the sound of clothes being removed. This scene is perhaps surprisingly more dialogue-laden than expected, with Oliver explicitly asking Elio 'Can I kiss you?' and Elio's enthusiastic response 'Yes, please'. As Elio straddles Oliver on the bed, we can hear the sound of his T-shirt being pulled off. When Oliver removes his shorts, we hear the sound of his flapping belt buckle and the unzipping of his fly, as Elio looks up at him from the bed. As the camera pans away, in the moment that enraged many critics, we can hear breath, rustling fabric, soft moans and the edge of laughter. We are not treated to anything like the love scenes in Guadagnino's earlier films such as *Io sono l'amore* (*I Am Love*, 2009) or *A Bigger Splash* (2015). In *I Am Love*, Emma (Tilda Swinton) and Antonio

(Edoardo Gabbriellini) fuck on a deserted hillside, and this is depicted as a symphony of grass, insect noise, flesh, sweat and indeterminate fluids. In *A Bigger Splash*, Paul (Matthias Schoenaerts) performs cunnilingus on Maryanne (Swinton) until she orgasms. But in *Call Me by Your Name*, there is nothing like the same level of visual explicitness. But Guadagnino is not interested in a conventional love scene, nor is he interested in making straightforward pornography.[16] Instead, the film offers up a compelling combination of these two approaches, relying heavily on audio design to convey explicitness. Nowhere is this more evident than in the moments that follow Elio and Oliver's first fuck.

In the early morning light, a close-up shot frames the lovers' intertwined thighs. Here, a detail of performance is notable, where Oliver's thigh visibly flexes against Elio's groin (Figure 5.2). The shot of this gesture in particular, and what follows, suggests lovers who haven't wasted a second sleeping, they're just resting for a moment before continuing. After the upside-down shot of them kissing in bed, we cut to Elio and Oliver lying end to end, sideways across the bed. Oliver is clearly wiping semen off his chest before Elio does the same. There is a distinct shimmer and opacity to this fluid that makes it clearly legible as semen and not sweat, in spite of the scene's early morning light. The focus on the secretions of sex acknowledges the demands of pornography for 'proof' of arousal and orgasm, but couches it in the lush cinematography and romantic lighting beloved of both Hollywood and European art cinemas. These extended scenes of Elio and Oliver's nude, postcoital bodies in

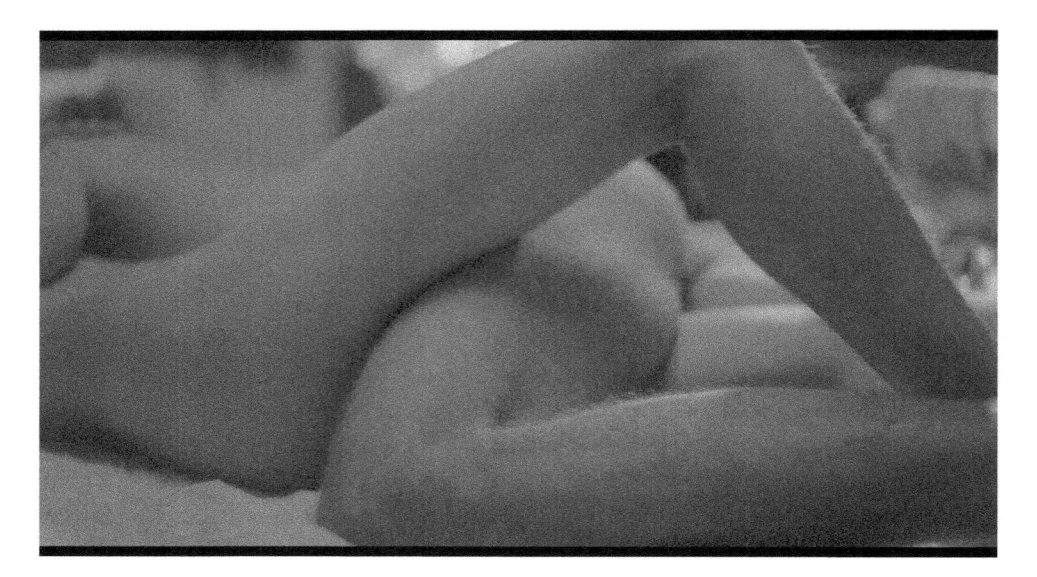

FIGURE 5.2: A flexing of thighs against groin. Luca Guadagnino (dir.), *Call Me by Your Name*, 2017. Italy/France/USA/Brazil. © Frenesy, La Cinefacture.

contact firmly establish what has taken place off screen, while remaining within the visual realm of presenting the male torso as an object of beauty to be appreciated, not unlike the bronze sculpture that has earlier been brought up from the bottom of Lake Garda. Just as Elio's father (Michael Stuhlbarg) describes these sculptures as 'daring you to desire them', Elio and Oliver have dared to desire each other.

C'mere

This scene of the aftermath of orgasm is shortly followed by a further explicit sex act, an instance of what Brody terms 'cannily framed sex'.[17] After they return from their early morning swim, Elio seems distant and Oliver is feeling insecure. In order to test the presence of desire, and perhaps drawing on what Adam Mars-Jones calls 'experience in the form that intoxicates',[18] Oliver initiates a further intimacy: the doorway blow job. 'Elio, c'mere. Take your trunks off', Elio obeys, and Oliver kneels. Elio holds Oliver's head, which is just visible at the bottom of the frame. As Oliver begins moving back and forth, Elio leans his forearms on the doorframe, we hear his intake of breath in anticipation and the sound of what is taking place is unmistakable: a wet, opening sound. The sound of fellatio: like chewing gum, saliva, flesh, wetness. After a few moments, Oliver laughs as he stands up, looking down at Elio's crotch: 'Well that's promising, you're hard again. Good', before closing the adjoining door. Oliver's facial expression here conveys elation, not quite believing he's been this bold. This declaration of proof of arousal, the arousal that dare not be shown on a mainstream screen, directly references the act of being hard, a physical state which is often one of the key markers of moving-image pornography.

This encounter is followed very shortly by what is certainly the story's most notorious scene: the peach. Elio in his attic hideaway is shown reading, listening to the radio and sucking on peach stones. We can hear him swallowing, wiping his mouth and digging his fingers into the peaches, as juices drip onto his flesh. In the aftermath of his realized desires for Oliver, Elio seems to exist in a heady dream of sensuality. The sequence is filled with sighs, the sound of his body against the mattress, and the thin sound of the mournful Italian song on the radio. The sequence captures the experience of eating a peach that is so ripe you can't so much bite into it as swallow its near-liquid flesh, an experience with a texture and taste that is almost too sweet, too messy. As Elio moves the split peach to his groin the sounds are slick, squelchy, reminiscent of the early soft egg yolk. His breathing quickens, 'Fuck', he exclaims, as he exhales and orgasms. He carefully places the peach on a nearby ledge, audibly and visibly wiping his hands on the sheet and his trunks. He turns over on the bed after this, a sense of release tinged with embarrassment, as he falls into an afternoon slumber. Elio's orgasm is marked out by the verbal exclamation, and the kind of bodily response narrative cinema tends to associate with the postcoital male body.

A short time later, Oliver appears in the doorway, smiling at the sight of Elio asleep. He enters, pulling off his shirt with an audible sound of fabric slipping against flesh, evoking the soundscape of the midnight bedroom. Elio awakes as Oliver kneels down and begins kissing Elio's chest and down his torso, repeating a gesture from their encounter in his bedroom. Elio raises his head slightly to watch what Oliver is doing to him. The sound of Elio's breathing remains audible as he spreads his legs a little wider, and Oliver uses both hands to caress him, an indication that additional stimulation of the testicles, perineum or anus may also be taking place, though blocked from view by Oliver's torso. As Oliver begins fellating Elio, we hear that distinct sound of opening one's mouth wide, the tongue placed to emphasize the wetness of the sound – audibly different from the sound of kissing (Figure 5.3). Oliver then pauses and looks up at Elio before continuing, then stopping again and asking 'What did you do?' 'Nothing', replies Elio before glancing guiltily over at the peach. The residue of the peach and semen is here acknowledged, because Oliver can taste it. Oliver laughs as he picks up the peach: 'Ah I see, you've moved onto the plant kingdom already. What's next? Minerals? I suppose you've already given

FIGURE 5.3: The sound of mouth, tongue and wetness: Oliver (Armie Hammer) orally stimulates Elio (Timothée Chalamet). Luca Guadagnino (dir.), *Call Me by Your Name*, 2017. Italy/France/USA/Brazil. © Frenesy, La Cinefacture.

up animals? You know that's me.' Elio, nervous and ashamed, shrinks away and asks, 'I'm sick, aren't I?' Oliver teases him further by holding the peach and admiring it with one hand, almost putting his finger inside. This imagery is clearly meant to stand in for other forms of penetrative pleasure that the mainstream screen is unused to seeing and still largely unwilling to show us. Oliver, in a display of radical acceptance, declares with a truly devastating sexiness, 'I wish everybody was as sick as you', putting his finger inside the peach and licking his finger even as Elio begs him 'Please don't do this!' before bursting into tears.

Aurality and orgasm

In their article 'Six Propositions on the Sonics of Pornography', Sharif Mowlabocus and Andy Medhurst observe the following conventions:

> Gay male pornography requires visual proof of sexual climax [...] where 'tops' are always expected to ejaculate, 'bottoms' are typically expected to maintain an orgasmic 'sound' throughout intercourse. The 'anal orgasm', like its vaginal sister, resists easy visual identification but remains identifiable (if not authenticated) via sonic registers. This is not to say that 'bottoms' do not ejaculate, but hierarchies of ejaculation are often present in gay male porn.[19]

In the aftermath of their night together, both Elio and Oliver are seen wiping ejaculate off their chests. This open display of the evidence of orgasms indicates that *Call Me by Your Name*, by displaying this 'visual proof' across both bodies, is not particularly interested in participating in these hierarchies of ejaculation. Equally, we might also consider the ways in which the physicality of the two characters and the actors who play them would function within these (now somewhat outdated) conventions of gay male porn. As the older, more muscular and more conventionally masculine of the pair, Oliver would at one time have been coded as the top, whereas Elio as the younger, more slender, androgynous one might have been coded as the bottom. Where Aciman's novel is clear about privileging Elio's agency and gaze, as well as the different kinds of penetrative sex Elio and Oliver have together, the film is much more ambiguous. While the film clearly portrays fellatio, it never ventures into the realm of anal sex. The peach (not unlike the ubiquitous emoji) is the closest the film gets to representing the anal. Mowlabocus and Medhurst comment on these conventions further, noting that

> [t]his splitting up of the 'visual top' and the 'aural bottom' is by no means mandatory in gay male porn, but where it does appear it often echoes older inscriptions of

gendered stereotypes regarding sex roles. In doing so it also (re)affirms the ongoing relegation of sound to the domain of the feminine. To repeat, the masculine orgasm is seen, the feminine orgasm is heard.[20]

This sets up an interesting dilemma when we consider the auditory landscape of the much-remarked-upon peach scene. Here, Elio is alone. This interlude takes place after he and Oliver have fucked for the first time. Since a mainstream film of this type would be unlikely to depict an erect, ejaculating penis, we are relegated to the 'domain of the feminine' in the depiction of Elio's autoerotic experimentation. We hear the sounds of the peach, and the squelch of its flesh. Chalamet's performance includes heavy breathing, and the utterance 'Fuck' to mark out the moment of orgasm as he is filmed in medium close-up, above the waistband of his shorts. As the younger man in the relationship, and playing on the contrast between Chalamet's slender androgyny (reverently described by one of my students as 'Elio's just a twink') versus Hammer's golden, gym-sculpted figure, Elio's orgasm is here rendered somewhere between those 'older inscriptions' and more contemporary conceptualizations of the fluidity of gender and the body. The orgasm is heard through the actor's bodily performance of breath and the word 'fuck', while the aftermath of this act is depicted via the discarded peach. Linda Williams notes that 'aurally, excess is marked by recourse not to the coded articulations of language but to inarticulate cries of pleasure in porn'.[21] In line with the film's unified approach to sensuous audio, this scene combines language with the aural excess of porn in its breath performance, and the soundscape of textures that evoke the sensations of touch and fleshly contact.

The convention of the 'aural bottom' of gay men's porn is maintained in the distinct sound that accompanies both instances of fellatio in *Call Me by Your Name*. While we are not allowed to see Hammer as Oliver open his mouth to perform this act, the distinct sound of a mouth opening as it makes contact with flesh is clearly discernible in the saturated soundscape. Sounds such as clothing against bare flesh, the ripping of zippers, and sighs are all enhanced to make them audible to the viewer/listener, to reinforce the intimacy of these scenes; it sounds as if you are in the room. This kind of approach to sound designing scenes of intimacy can also be seen in films such as Xavier Dolan's *Matthias & Maxime* (2019), where the climactic drunken kiss between the title characters is filled with the sound of lips, flesh, saliva and breath. The audio design is clearly intended as an intensification of the gestures that are being performed, gestures which are performed in such a way as to evoke spontaneous, instinctual bodily responses, and to implicate the spectator/listener. Williams suggests that there exists 'the perception that the body of the spectator is caught up in an almost involuntary mimicry of the emotion or sensation of the body on the screen'[22] and that this

FIGURE 5.4: The aural bottom: invoking and subverting the conventions of pornography. Luca Guadagnino (dir.), *Call Me by Your Name*, 2017. Italy/France/USA/Brazil. © Frenesy, La Cinefacture.

perception is part of the reason for the denigration of body genres. I would like to suggest that this is part of the reason we find films like *Call Me by Your Name* so compelling, as per Vivian Sobchack's observation, 'Movies provoke in us the "carnal thoughts" that ground and inform more conscious analysis'.[23] An implicated spectator/listener is potentially engaging in more conscious analysis, and in this case it is the soundscape that draws us in.

Even though the body parts most closely associated with pornography are not on screen in *Call Me by Your Name*, they can still be heard, listened for and therefore potentially felt by the spectator. But, the sounds of sex are not the only way in which *Call Me by Your Name* draws on the conventions of pornography. 'In gay porn, for instance, sexual "commands" are regularly issued in a manner that is highly gendered, privileging the active/penetrative partner.'[24] However, it should be noted that this convention has been increasingly disrupted in pornography and in everyday life, just as it is destabilized by the performances on offer in *Call Me by Your Name*. When Oliver orders Elio 'C'mere, take off your trunks', he occupies the role of the partner issuing a sexual command we might expect in porn, but equally in everyday life. While he is the 'active' partner verbally, he is also the one being penetrated as he fellates Elio in the bedroom doorway (Figure 5.4). Despite its setting in the early 1980s, *Call Me by Your Name* reflects a more fluid and versatile set of sexual practices and bodily expression, in line with the rise of terms like 'power bottom' and 'man pussy', as well as the growing presence of trans porn performers. Instead of maintaining outdated expectations, where we might expect fellatio to be received by the conventionally masculine Oliver, and given by the less conventionally masculine Elio, it is Oliver who kneels before Elio. This suggests that these pornographic conventions are acknowledged in the sex we see between men in *Call Me by Your Name*, but it also suggests that these are conventions that are falling by the wayside, acknowledging of a more fluid conception of bodies and sexuality, since both Elio and Oliver also display enthusiastic interest in intimate contact with women.

Ty Mitchell, in his article 'Boy Problems', writes about the challenges of navigating desire as a young gay man, as well as its depiction in films like *Call Me by Your Name*, a work he suggests attempts 'to affirm a shared adolescent experience of maturing through our sexual desires, not prior to them'.[25] This idea of maturing through desire forms an intriguing connection with a remark made by Susan Sontag in 'On the Pornographic Imagination'; she writes, 'Insofar as strong sexual feeling does involve an obsessive degree of attention, it encompasses experiences in which a person can feel he is losing his "self"'.[26] In *Call Me by Your Name*, the atmosphere of erotic swoon can be likened to this 'obsessive degree of attention'. Elio is obsessed with Oliver's clothes, the colour and texture of his skin, his smell. A key moment where this is evidenced is when we see Elio placing a pair of Oliver's shorts over his head, caressing the fabric and inhaling its scent, while he thrusts his hips into the mattress. The film displays this obsession in sumptuous detail in the worshipful shots accorded to the lovers' bodies, and the sounds these bodies make when they are in contact. Instead of losing himself, Elio experiences precisely what Mitchell articulates in his article, and what we as viewers are permitted to witness is the experience of maturing through desire. (The fact that Aciman's sequel novel is entitled *Find Me* is not lost on me.[27])

I would also argue that Oliver experiences a similar awakening, revelling in the ways he can touch and caress Elio, and how he is able to offer acceptance and understanding as well as pleasure. Sontag observes, 'Everyone has felt (at least in fantasy) the erotic glamour of physical cruelty and an erotic lure in things that are vile and repulsive. These phenomena form part of the genuine spectrum of sexuality.'[28] This provides another context for Elio's autoerotic experiments with the peach, and Oliver's declaration 'I wish everybody was as sick as you', which, in that moment, reclaims the idea of 'sick' as meaning someone who is open to sensation, to experiences, who is indeed interested in maturing through their desires, and exploring their own body's capabilities for sensation. Avgi Saketopoulou writes of being able to 'think the limit *with* pleasure',[29] and in many ways this is precisely what both Elio and Oliver seem to be offering each other – the opportunity to think and pursue bodily limit experiences through pleasure with each other.

On consent and self-knowledge

When Oliver repeats the phrase 'I know myself', it is often in relation to pleasures he initially denies: the further egg at breakfast, and deepening his intimacy with Elio after they have kissed. What these assertions demonstrate is that when it comes to his desires, Oliver does not yet know himself as well as he might think – he has not yet allowed himself to think with pleasure. As Katherine Angel observes, 'Self-knowledge is not a reliable feature of female sexuality, nor of sexuality in general; it is not a reliable feature of being a person'.[30] What happens to Oliver in *Call Me by Your Name* is what happens to Elio: what each character experiences is the process of maturing through one's desires, of letting things unfold in relation to another person. What the film portrays is the ambiguity of desire, and the ways in which we learn what we want only in relation to others. Angel argues further that 'Sex, and desire, compromise our sense of sovereignty, of knowing ourselves, and of being in control'.[31] This is what *Call Me by Your Name* offers us in its portrayal of the central queer relationship, and through the unexpected sensuousness of its sound design. The sound and texture of bodies, and their relationship to intimate surfaces such as skin and fabric, offers up the possibility of what body genres do in acting on the body, and provoking a response – these kinds of films can allow their audiences to think through pleasure. The auditory experience of the film can also compromise (and deepen) our sense of knowing ourselves.

What I have tried to do here is to make a case for examining and acknowledging the importance of the audio landscape in *Call Me by Your Name* as a technique for rendering explicitness in a non-visual manner and as a way of invoking bodily response. In spite of the film's absence of clear visual depictions of explicit sex acts between men, it nevertheless marks out kissing and fellatio as part of its sensuous soundscape, alongside the sound of clothing being removed. The film's unified approach to sensuous sound design establishes an atmosphere that encourages attentive listening, by drawing attention to bodily gestures of eating and disrobing, as well as the intimate touches performed by Elio and Oliver. The film's evocations of pornography, particularly in terms of bodily gestures and the performance of sex acts and orgasm, are a key part of the film's attempt to create a swoon-like affect. The question of whether this strategy sanitizes the film is, for me, still not fully resolved. Clearly films which are contemporaneous with *Call Me by Your Name*'s production have made different, more explicit choices when it comes to showing sex between men. However, since the advent of #MeToo, audiences are also more attuned to the conditions under which actors may be asked to perform intimate acts, and what types of performance and bodily display roles may require. Nevertheless, questions of desire, sex, pleasure and representation continue to matter. *Call Me by Your Name*'s audio design is certainly something more than subtext, and combined with the sensitive, vulnerable performances from Chalamet and Hammer, I would argue it is somewhere on the road to *Go Fish*'s 'hot, passionate, say-yes-to-sex'.

Acknowledgements

I am very grateful to the anonymous peer reviewers of this chapter for their attentive comments and for allowing me to deploy the term 'man pussy' in an academic context.

NOTES

1. See, for example, Richard Brody, 'The Empty, Sanitized Intimacy of *Call Me by Your Name*', *New Yorker*, 28 November 2017, https://www.newyorker.com/culture/richard-brody/the-empty-sanitized-intimacy-of-call-me-by-your-name; Guy Lodge, 'Why Is *Call Me by Your Name* So Coy About Gay Sex?', *The Guardian*, 23 November 2017, https://www.theguardian.com/film/2017/nov/23/call-me-by-your-name-gay-sex-oscars; Miz Cracker, 'Why Do Gays Keep Falling for *Call Me by Your Name*?', *Slate*, 28 November 2017, https://slate.com/human-interest/2017/11/call-me-by-your-name-is-not-a-gay-movie.html.

2. Lodge, 'Why Is'.

3. The Production Sound Mixer for *Call Me by Your Name* is Yves-Marie Omnes, who also worked with Guadagnino on *A Bigger Splash* (2015) and *Suspiria* (2018).

4. Lucy Fife Donaldson, 'Feeling and Filmmaking: The Design and Affect of Film Sound', *The New Soundtrack* 7, no. 1 (2017): 33–34.

5. Sharif Mowlabocus and Andy Medhurst, 'Six Propositions on the Sonics of Pornography', *Porn Studies* 4, no. 2 (2017): 212.

6. Jack Halberstam, *Skin Shows: Gothic Horror and the Technology of Monsters* (Durham and London: Duke University Press, 1995), 127.

7. Fife Donaldson, 'Feeling', 34.

8. *Stranger by the Lake* was well received at film festivals and was nominated for several Césars, though won only one (Most Promising Male Newcomer for Pierre Deladonchamps).

9. The film's lead actors are clearly visibly erect on screen, and in the film's final moments, Hugo (François Nambot) caresses Théo's (Geoffrey Couët) genitals in close-up.

10. Joanna Di Mattia, 'Some Thoughts on the Erotic Aesthetic in Luca Guadagnino's "Desire Trilogy"', *Senses of Cinema*, vol. 86 (2018), www.sensesofcinema.com/2018/feature-articles/luca-guadagninos-desiretrilogy/.

11. Fife Donaldson, 'Feeling', 32.

12. Linda Williams, 'Film Bodies: Gender, Genre, Excess', in *Feminist Film Theory: A Reader*, ed. Sue Thornham (Edinburgh: Edinburgh University Press, [1991] 1999), 271.

13. Cynthia Baron and Sharon Marie Carnicke, *Reframing Screen Performance* (Ann Arbor: University of Michigan Press, 2008), 77.

14. Jonathan Alexander comments on his own experience of being cruised by younger men:

> He flexed his taut buttocks, the fabric of his silver shorts perfectly cupping his glutes. Then another sideways glance, just to see if I'm looking. How could I not? He was clearly performing for me. And then he flipped over, supporting himself on his palms, his obvious erection filling the front of his shorts. [...] This is the challenge of cruising. What *did* he want, if anything? Or is the interest all in my own head? Certainly I was intrigued. Perhaps I'm not used to the protocols of cruising and don't know how to read the cues, and I am now *misreading* the cues, or reading *into* the cues, which aren't even cues at all.

See Jonathan Alexander, 'Being Cruised', *Los Angeles Review of Books*, 2 October 2018, https://lareviewofbooks.org/article/being-cruised/.

15. Di Mattia, 'Some Thoughts'.

16. In this sense, Guadagnino owes something to directors like Walerian Borowczyk and Radley Metzger, who favoured distinctive auteurist style alongside pornographic scenarios. In his film *Bones and All* (2022), there is a far more explicit queer sex scene, which is once more led by sound design. Lee (Chalamet) manually stimulates a lover (Jake Horowitz) in a corn field, while Maren (Taylor Russell) approaches from a distance, led by the sounds of sex, which include vocal utterances and the sound of flesh.

17. Brody, 'Sanitized Intimacy', 2017.

18. Adam Mars-Jones, *Box Hill: A Story of Low Self-Esteem* (London: Fitzcarraldo Editions, 2020), 12.

19. Mowlabocus and Medhurst, 'Six Propositions', 214.

20. Mowlabocus and Medhurst, 214.

21. Williams, 'Film Bodies', 270.

22. Williams, 270.

23. Vivian Sobchack, *Carnal Thoughts: Embodiment and Moving Image Culture* (Berkeley, Los Angeles and London: University of California Press, 2004), 60.

24. Mowlabocus and Medhurst, 'Six Propositions', 218.

25. Ty Mitchell, 'Boy Problems', *The New Inquiry*, 29 May 2019, https://thenewinquiry.com/boy-problems/.

26. Susan Sontag, 'The Pornographic Imagination', in Susan Sontag, *Styles of Radical Will*, (London: Penguin, [1966] 2009), 58.

27. André Aciman, *Find Me* (London: Faber & Faber, 2019).

28. Sontag, 'The Pornographic Imagination', 57.

29. Avgi Saketopoulou, 'To Suffer Pleasure: The Shattering of the Ego as the Psychic Labor of Perverse Sexuality', *Studies in Gender and Sexuality* 15 (2014): 260.

30. Katherine Angel, *Tomorrow Sex Will Be Good Again* (London: Verso, 2021), 40.

31. Angel, 102.

REFERENCES

Aciman, André. *Find Me*. London: Faber & Faber, 2019.

Angel, Katherine. *Tomorrow Sex Will Be Good Again*. London: Verso, 2021.

Alexander, Jonathan. 'Being Cruised', *Los Angeles Review of Books*, 2 October 2018. https://lareviewofbooks.org/article/being-cruised/.

Atherton Lin, Jeremy. *Gay Bar: Why We Went Out*. London: Granta, 2021.

Baron, Cynthia, and Sharon Marie Carnicke. *Reframing Screen Performance*. Ann Arbor: University of Michigan Press, 2008.

Brody, Richard. 'The Empty, Sanitized Intimacy of *Call Me by Your Name*', *New Yorker*, 28 November 2017. https://www.newyorker.com/culture/richard-brody/the-empty-sanitized-intimacy-of-call-me-by-your-name.

Di Mattia, Joanna. 'Some Thoughts on the Erotic Aesthetic in Luca Guadagnino's "Desire Trilogy"', *Senses of Cinema* 86 (2018). www.sensesofcinema.com/2018/feature-articles/luca-guadagninos-desiretrilogy/.

Dolan, Xavier, dir. *Matthias & Maxime*. Sons of Manual, Téléfilm Canada, Société de Développement des Entreprises Culturelles, 2019.

Ducastel, Oliver, and Jacques Martineau, dir. *Théo et Hugo dans le même bateau (Theo and Hugo)*. Ecce Films, Epicentre Films, 2016.

Fife Donaldson, Lucy. 'Feeling and Filmmaking: The Design and Affect of Film Sound', *The New Soundtrack* 7, no. 1 (2017): 31–46.

Guadagnino, Luca, dir. *Io sono l'amore (I Am Love)*. First Sun, Mikado Film, Rai Cinema, 2009.

Guadagnino, Luca, dir. *A Bigger Splash*. Frenesy Film Company, Cota Film, 2015.

Guadagnino, Luca, dir. *Call Me by Your Name*. Frenesy Film Company, La Cinefacture, RT Features, 2017.

Guadagnino, Luca, dir. *Bones and All*. Frenesy Film Company, Per Capita Productions, 2022.

Guiraudie, Alain, dir. *L'Inconnu du lac (Stranger by the Lake)*. Les Films du Worso, Arte France Cinéma, M141, Films de Force Majeure 2013.

Halberstam, Jack. *Skin Shows: Gothic Horror and the Technology of Monsters*. Durham and London: Duke University Press, 1995.

Lodge, Guy. 'Why Is *Call Me by Your Name* So Coy About Gay Sex?', *The Guardian*, 23 November 2017. https://www.theguardian.com/film/2017/nov/23/call-me-by-your-name-gay-sex-oscars.

Mars-Jones, Adam. *Box Hill: A Story of Low Self-Esteem*. London: Fitzcarraldo Editions, 2020.

Miz Cracker. 'Why Do Gays Keep Falling for *Call Me by Your Name*?', *Slate*, 28 November 2017. https://slate.com/human-interest/2017/11/call-me-by-your-name-is-not-a-gay-movie.html.

Miz, Cracker. 'Why Do Gays Keep Falling for *Call Me by Your Name?*', *Slate*, 28 November 2017. https://slate.com/human-interest/2017/11/call-me-by-your-name-is-not-a-gay-movie.html.

Mowlabocus, Sharif, and Andy Medhurst. 'Six Propositions on the Sonics of Pornography', *Porn Studies* 4, no. 2 (2017): 210–24.

Saketopoulou, Avgi. 'To Suffer Pleasure: The Shattering of the Ego as the Psychic Labor of Perverse Sexuality', *Studies in Gender and Sexuality* 15 (2014): 254–68.

Sobchack, Vivian. *Carnal Thoughts: Embodiment and Moving Image Culture*. Berkeley, Los Angeles and London: University of California Press, 2004.

Sontag, Susan. 'The Pornographic Imagination.' In *Styles of Radical Will*, by Susan Sontag, 35–73. London: Penguin, [1966] 2009.

Troche, Rose, dir. *Go Fish*. Can I Watch, Islet, KPVI, Killer Films, The Samuel Goldwyn Company, 1994.

Williams, Linda. 'Film Bodies: Gender, Genre, Excess.' In *Feminist Film Theory: A Reader*, edited by *Sue Thornham*, 267–81. Edinburgh: Edinburgh University Press, [1991] 1999.

6

Call Me by Your Name and the
Ethics of Distance

Edward Lamberti

Early on in the film of *Call Me by Your Name* (Luca Guadagnino, 2017), Elio (Timothée Chalamet) and Oliver (Armie Hammer) are hanging around in the swimming pool at the Perlmans' villa, and Oliver asks Elio what he is doing. Elio says, 'Reading my music', and when Oliver says, 'No you're not', Elio says, 'Thinking, then'. This dialogue exchange is shot with Elio in close-up and more or less in profile; we are looking at his right side; he is standing in the water and resting at the side of the pool, his elbows on the tiles that surround it. Oliver is in the middle distance behind him and swims over to him. Oliver asks, 'Yeah? About what?' Elio smiles: 'It's private' – it's as though he's flirting a bit, by self-consciously denying Oliver access to his feelings. His sunglasses don't help Oliver – or us – work out what's on his mind. Elio's presence is tangible, but although we're close to him, he's distant.

There are numerous moments like this in *Call Me by Your Name*, moments in which we are, in effect, hanging out with Elio but where he's distant from us. This chapter explores how a sense of distance in *Call Me by Your Name* exists in productive ethical tension with the film's intimate portrayal of Elio and Oliver's romance. The sense of distance expresses Elio's relationship with Oliver as something that is his own private business, even as the film's subtle use of film style and story structure invites us to connect with this story of desire.

Observing character behaviour

Director Luca Guadagnino, in an interview with Hillary Weston, has explained how he and cinematographer Sayombhu Mukdeeprom 'tried to have the medium be as unobtrusive as possible'[1] and so decided to shoot the whole film with one lens (a Cooke S4 35 mm lens, as the end credits tell us) because they didn't want technique to get in the way of the characters. Guadagnino explains that

> [a]ll the usual tools were no longer there, so my focus was not on how to frame the shot but on what happens in front of the camera. [...] Imagine if I could have zoomed in on one of Elio's expressions or had the ability to create depth of field. I would have used that film grammar to deliver what I wanted instead of just allowing the characters' behavior to unfold.[2]

Guadagnino is therefore seemingly not inclined to deploy many of the stylistic techniques available to him to convey character. The sense of 'hanging out' occurs not just because of the use of only one lens but also because Guadagnino and Mukdeeprom use the camera mostly with little or no movement. As such, in *Call Me by Your Name* the camera has the primary effect of offering a window into the world of the film, as per Weston's observation that '[l]ike Renoir, [Guadagnino makes] the camera almost invisible in *Call Me by Your Name*, and it creates a feeling of intimacy'.[3] Guadagnino is not looking to mobilize style to express Elio's thoughts and feelings except insofar as it gives Chalamet the space to perform Elio.

For some critics, this is somewhat ineffective. Kyle Turner says that 'the film's is almost a coldly respectful gaze. It's like being in a museum.'[4] Turner discusses this problem in terms of distance:

> The first half of *Call Me by Your Name* is *about* Elio training himself: how to recognize glances, how to look for meaning in a touch of the shoulder. Every intellectual gambit between Elio and Oliver is this little in-game, a performance in a secret language that's not supposed to be very recognizable to anyone else. But Guadagnino seems ambivalent about letting his audience in on that game, watching Elio try to find that intimacy and desire in intimation – from a distance, literally.[5]

As such, says Turner, 'rarely are we given the chance to get close enough to any surface to really unearth libidinous pleasures'.[6] Richard Brody goes further:

> Guadagnino can't be bothered to imagine [...] what they might actually talk about while sitting together alone. Scenes deliver some useful information to push the plot ahead and then cut out just as they get rolling, because Guadagnino displays no interest in the characters, only in the story.[7]

And yet it is not as though Guadagnino's style is inexpressive. The style does not have the formal rigour of, say, Éric Rohmer's style, his faith in master shots and two-shots of characters talking with each other, or that of Yasujirô Ozu, for whom a consistency and repetition of camera angles and lenses becomes part of a visual philosophy towards characters, actions and settings, and thus a stylistic hallmark of his work. But while *Call Me by Your Name* doesn't seem to have a visual philosophy in similarly overt ways, Guadagnino's stated aim of wanting not to get in the way of character behaviour is its own philosophy.

This philosophy creates, I believe, an ethics of character presentation – one that is reflected in the film's shot duration and overall pacing. Asbjørn Grønstad's work on the ethics of slow cinema includes observations applicable to *Call Me by Your Name*. Grønstad observes how 'slow cinema generates, across its very different films, a recognisable poetics that is observational, meditative and poetic'.[8] I am not suggesting that *Call Me by Your Name* should be considered an example of slow cinema, but 'observational, meditative and poetic' are adjectives that easily apply to the film – and, indeed, to Elio. Shot duration in slow cinema pointedly gives us time to contemplate what the image can tell us and is thus 'more amenable [than faster films] to the kind of transcendental, revelatory experience the film image [...] is capable of transmitting'.[9] We can relate this to the sense of our 'hanging out' with Elio: Mukdeeprom's camerawork and the pacing of Walter Fasano's editing provide us with many opportunities to observe Elio, to scrutinize his behaviour and to have what Grønstad identifies as a 'transcendental, revelatory experience'.

What might that experience reveal to us? *Call Me by Your Name* spends a lot of time showing us Elio doing things that Elio likes to do – reading; listening to, transcribing and playing music; swimming; hanging out with his family and friends; watching Oliver. But the more we observe Elio, the greater the puzzle becomes – not because the film seeks to characterize Elio as especially complicated or hard to understand, but because it *doesn't* seek to do so.

Elio, for all his intellectual inquisitiveness and musical prowess, is verbally rather inarticulate when it comes to his feelings. He and Oliver spend a lot of their time together trying *not* to reveal what they feel for each other. As Molly Haskell observes, '[t]he minutely observed vicissitudes of their duet of mutual approach and avoidance, set against a backdrop of picnics, dances, bicycle rides, and swims, form the essence of the drama'.[10] One reason for Elio's inarticulacy is that he doesn't know what Oliver feels for him. Another is that he doesn't know what he feels for Oliver. The feelings are beyond easy words. Something this may be conveying is that what Elio is feeling he's feeling for the first time.

One way the film performs this is by springing surprises on us that express the surprises Elio is navigating. An example is the scene in which Elio first confesses his feelings to Oliver. By this point – over 45 minutes into the film – we might be expecting something like this, but the film has held us so much in the moment, hanging out with Elio and Oliver, that when, all of a sudden, Elio blurts out his feelings as he and Oliver stand on opposite sides of the monument to the Battle of

Piave, the opportunity is upon us almost the way it's upon Elio. This suddenness of the opportunity for Elio accounts for the sheer weirdness of his words (taken almost verbatim from the novel),[11] aided by Chalamet's off-kilter delivery of them, and of the camera angle, a medium shot of Elio's back as he calls out his feelings to Oliver, who is in the distance on the other side of the monument. This part of the scene conveys a sense that Elio is unmoored from us, stranded in a middle distance, vulnerable and exposed: an Other.

In ethical proximity to Elio

In seeing our relationship with Elio in terms of otherness, I am thinking of the ethical philosophy of Emmanuel Levinas, and in particular his idea of proximity. For Levinas, a person exists in proximity to the Other, and this relationship 'cannot be resolved into "images" or exposed in a theme'.[12] This inability to 'resolve' the Other or to explain them in terms of a theme means that their 'otherness' is preserved. This is key to Levinas's claim that a person's ethical relationship with the Other is one of *not* knowing, of *not* understanding. Rather, there is an openness toward the Other, and this openness fosters responsibility: 'Proximity, difference which is non-indifference, is responsibility. It is a response without a question [.]'[13] This vitally important inability to understand the Other means that the subject doesn't judge the Other:

> Proximity does not resolve into the consciousness a being would have of another being that it would judge to be near inasmuch as the other would be under one's eyes or within one's reach, and inasmuch as it would be possible for one to take hold of that being, hold on to it or converse with it.[14]

Although we are 'hanging out' with Elio, he is beyond us, on the screen, impossible to 'hold on to' or 'converse with', impossible to possess. And as a subject – our main character, falling in love – he is not us. What the film provides is proximity: an experience of being close to Elio without understanding him.

Film Studies scholars have considered films from the point of view of Levinasian proximity. Robert Sinnerbrink, for example, speaking about the Dardenne brothers' *La Promesse* (*The Promise*, Luc and Jean-Pierre Dardenne, 1996), says that the film

> offers less a case of cinematic empathy than one of ethical proximity: a sense of responsiveness to the Other, acknowledging their alterity, without seeking to 'judge' those who reveal themselves, however opaquely, through their gestures and actions,

and without affording the viewer an unambiguous sense of moral allegiance that would risk subsuming the singularity of the Other under one's own conception of morality.[15]

A key aspect of this is how the film resists, on the whole, depicting its characters' points of view overtly: '*The Promise* eschews direct representation of characters' subjectivity in favour of an ethical proximity coupled with empathic distance'.[16] I would argue that we can detect a similar 'empathic distance' in the depiction of Elio in *Call Me by Your Name*. And for Kristin Lené Hole, writing about Claire Denis' film *J'ai pas sommeil* (*I Can't Sleep*, 1994) from a Levinasian perspective,

> the film refuses character psychologisation, leaving characters unknowable and opaque. [...] Denis constructs her narrative to reveal a fundamental being-with that resonates with Levinas's concept of the subject as constituted relationally via a call to ethical responsibility to the other.[17]

That Levinasian 'being-with' chimes with the sense of our 'hanging out' with Elio in *Call Me by Your Name*.

My response to Otherness is, for Levinas, the founding of my ethical self. Indeed, I am nothing without my ethical relationship with the Other: 'The community with him begins in my obligation to him'.[18] Colin Davis writes that Levinas's work on proximity seeks to convey 'exposure to alterity rather than exposition of it',[19] and we could say that the film is aiming for this in how it invites us to engage with Elio. And it simulates what it is like to hang out with someone for real, rather than via a movie screen. If the film doesn't present an Elio that an audience can 'understand', they are gently dissuaded from wanting to place Elio within their own understanding of how the world works. Instead, the film leaves Elio as enigmatic, unknowable – and thus, the relation the audience has with Elio is, naturally and before anything else, one of responsibility for otherness. It is ethical in a Levinasian sense.

The queerness of Levinasian proximity

Robin Podolsky notes how 'Levinas denounces the privileging of ontology (what is real) and epistemology (how we know what is real; what is true) in favour of ethics as first philosophy. For Levinas, the other person, the Other, resists any categorization.'[20] Thus, the Other is a person but not a category, an individual but not an identity. This lack of specificity is a touchstone of Levinas's ethics.

Levinas sometimes lapses. Podolsky points out how '[i]n most ways Levinas' approaches to gender, and to marriage, develop clearly from his approach to the human and to justice' but that '[t]he biggest problem with Levinas' work regarding gender is that he employs the term "the feminine" in ways that appear to violate his proscription against shunting human beings into categories'.[21] Podolsky surveys a number of critics of Levinas who consider this aspect of his philosophy to be a sexist lapse that undermines his ethics' championing of otherness without categorization. But Podolsky also refers to how Levinas's references to the feminine in his work need not point to a gender category but may instead point towards a quality of 'the feminine' that might apply across genders. Moments of gender interchangeability that Podolsky notes in Levinas's language speak to this.[22] And there is a queerness in Levinas's refusal of categorization, of totalization, of the unethical practice of labelling and compartmentalizing.

Haskell points to this gender slippage in *Call Me by Your Name* when she says that 'Elio is every teenager beset by raging hormones, every adolescent not yet formed, who alternates between longing and terror, flight or fight or fuck, in whom male and female sides still struggle for domination or truce'.[23] Guadagnino takes a similar approach in the presentation of the principal characters in his TV drama series *We Are Who We Are* (2020). The eight-part series follows Fraser (Jack Dylan Grazer) as he settles into the US army base in Italy that he has moved to with his colonel mother (Chloë Sevigny) and her partner (Alice Braga), and as he feels his way into new friendships and relationships. The title of the series is a statement of intent: we are who we are, not what people might label us as. In both *We Are Who We Are* and *Call Me by Your Name*, Guadagnino's direction commits to observing behaviour, so that we might experience characters without being prompted to judge them, and while moving as if naturally through the unfolding of time.

Grønstad's approach to the slowness of slow cinema leads him to consider the ethical implications of such an aesthetics, one that would seem to pull against the clarity and, indeed, storytelling drive that many films have habituated us to expect and recognize. Grønstad cites philosopher Jean-Luc Nancy's work on the films of Abbas Kiarostami. For Nancy, 'the loss of a world which makes sense is actually an improvement because a world without meaning, without signs, is exactly what it takes for the real to open itself up to us'.[24] A 'world without meaning, without signs' – this sounds very much in keeping with Levinas's resistance to categorization. In this regard, the directing style of *Call Me by Your Name* is perhaps suitably plain. Returning to Brody's critique of the film: when discussing the scene in which Elio and Oliver talk in the town centre after having slept together for the first time, he laments the stylistic choices again:

Adding a reverse angle or a broad pan shot on a setting is something that Guadagnino can't be bothered with, because it would subordinate the scene's narrow evocations to complexities that risk puncturing the mood just as surely as any substantive discussion might do.[25]

But are these 'narrow evocations' averse to complexity? The film is presenting Elio's behaviour and inviting us to hang out with it. Grønstad says of slow cinema that '[m]ood usually trumps action'.[26] The mood of *Call Me by Your Name* sustains, among other things, our proximity to Elio. It would be a shame to puncture it.

But if Elio is an Other to whom we are in proximity, he is also our protagonist, and therefore, our access point into this love story. The relationship between Elio and Oliver is one of unknowability, of Otherness, of proximity without understanding. This is the mystery of the heart: what Elio feels, what Oliver feels, the extent to which they come together emotionally and the extent to which they remain separate. Oliver's 'Call me by your name and I'll call you by mine' is an invitation to intimacy, but it is also a tacit admission that he and Elio need such actions to feel as though they are together, that they are essentially apart from each another. It brings Oliver and Elio closer to each other but it also preserves their own identities, through the saying of their own names (Figure 6.1). The morning

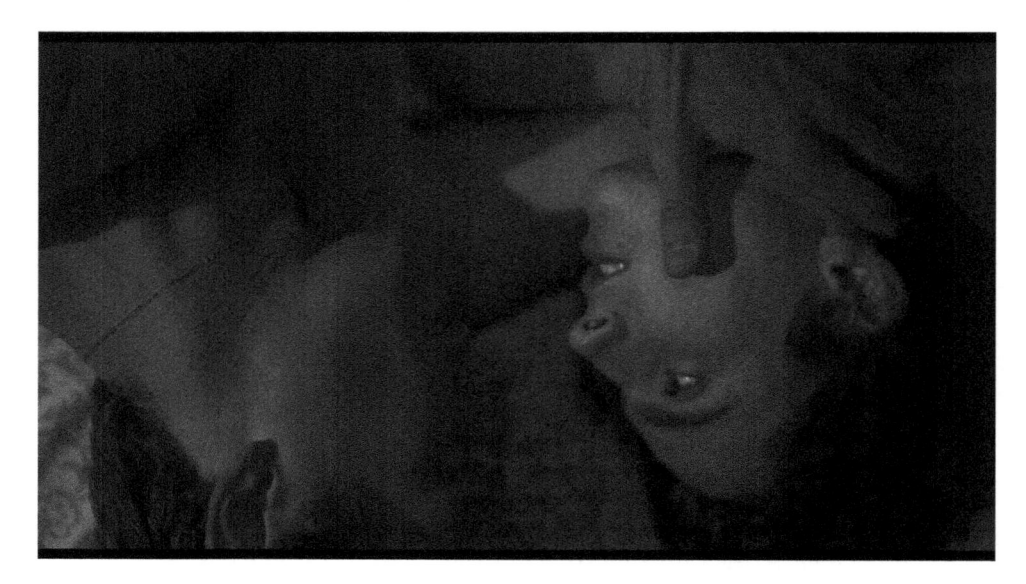

FIGURE 6.1: 'Call me by your name and I'll call you by mine': Oliver (Armie Hammer) and Elio (Timothée Chalamet) together but also separate from each other. Luca Guadagnino (dir.), *Call Me by Your Name*, 2017. Italy/France/USA/Brazil. © Frenesy, La Cinefacture.

after they have first slept together, Elio gets out of bed and Oliver looks at him with an expression of puzzled yearning. Elio's response, 'Let's go swimming', bewilders Oliver in its evasiveness, and at the watering hole, he says to Elio, 'Are you gonna hold what happened last night against me?' Elio's 'No' is an act of tender clarification. In other moments too, Elio and Oliver each find themselves suffering from a lack of clarification as to the other's feelings. Thus, it is not just that we are in proximity to Elio and Oliver; it is also that they are in proximity to each other. This makes the story more relatable to us.

Molly Haskell observes that

> where Aciman's novel unfolded in a heated burst of first-person recollection from the older Elio's point of view, the movie takes place in the present tense (though it's set in 1983), and widens the field of vision. Elio is still at the center, bored, flailing, given to fits of despair, but we are no longer cloistered within the sometimes suffocating hothouse of an acutely self-conscious adolescent mind.[27]

That wider field of vision takes us away from the first-person narration of the novel. Thus, we are experiencing events in proximity to Elio *and* we are able to stand back from them. Rather than just identifying with Elio and engaging with his point of view, we identify also, I think, with the film's presentation of the events, its subtly structured take on 'hanging out' with Elio and being in proximity with him.

The significance of the dissolves

As we think back through the film, we can see moments in which the story structure pierces the ambiance of this meanderingly love-struck summer in northern Italy. The dissolve – the visual transition formed of an image fading in onto an image fading out – is one way in which *Call Me by Your Name* structures the emotional trajectory of the romance. A dissolve is always a visual transition that draws attention to the moment *as* transition. The dissolves in *Call Me by Your Name* often come at moments when seemingly no significant development has occurred; it is the dissolve itself that invites us to consider how what we have just seen may count as significant. With the film's pacing generally giving the impression of time unfolding at an unhurried pace, the dissolves indicate impactful moments – many small, some larger – in the progress of the relationship between Elio and Oliver.

The film has fourteen dissolves. The first five occur in the first 45 minutes, then there are none in the next 40 minutes and then the remaining nine occur in the film's final third. This suggests that those impactful moments are gathering as the film nears its climax and dénouement. These moments of directedness, especially as they amass in the later stages of the film, emerge as shy admissions that Elio and Oliver's encounters are starting to amount to something of major significance to them, and perhaps especially to Elio.

Let's look at three of the dissolves here. The film's first dissolve comes at the end of the scene in which Mr Perlman (Michael Stuhlbarg) has posed the question about the etymology of the word 'apricot' and Oliver has answered comprehensively. Elio, watching on with amusement, says, 'He does this every year'; thus, Mr Perlman's question is revealed to be a test for Oliver as it has been for Mr Perlman's graduate students in previous summers. The scene ends on Oliver's face before dissolving through to the next scene, in which Elio and Oliver walk together in the town. The dissolve represents Oliver's true welcome into this intellectual family and means he is no longer a newcomer. Elio's fascination with Oliver can develop on a firmer footing.

The film's second dissolve comes in a moment when Elio is tossing and turning in bed at night, unable to sleep, after Oliver has been absent at dinner. The dissolve conveys the sense that Elio's fascination with Oliver is exerting its grip, causing him a troubled night. Elio might know the reason for his troubled night – or he might not – but the dissolve invites us to reflect on his behaviour, and how it expresses the physiological turmoil that Oliver has (benignly, unwittingly) visited upon him.

The film's dissolves, by being overt transitions, disrupt our experience of the passage of time. In a chapter on queer temporality in the movies, Karl Schoonover and Rosalind Galt note: 'Queers have problems with time. We can never seem to make it work for us, and we often appear outside of it, our milestones not recognized by the conventional intervals of heterotemporality.'[28] (Daniel Paul's chapter in this collection explores time in the film further, through the lens of chrononormativity.) The disruption of time is thus in itself queer: it keeps bodies from conforming to the strict tenets of socialized time, which, for Schoonover and Galt, is heteronormative. In Levinas, this points to another queerness, in proximity itself: 'The proximity does not enter into the common time of clocks, which makes meetings possible. It is a disturbance.'[29] Elio and Oliver's romance ticks to its own timeframe.

But of course that timeframe has to succumb to the end of summer. This is the significance of the eighth dissolve, which occurs once Elio, after crying in Oliver's arms, says 'I don't want you to go'. That dissolve is perhaps the pay-off to all the dissolves that have come before it in the film. This dissolve thrusts us into a future Elio doesn't want to get to, a future in which his and Oliver's time is running out and every moment becomes not just precious but vitally important to him.

Elio and Oliver's privacy in love

Something that is so romantic about *Call Me by Your Name* is the privacy it affords its central couple. Distance is key here, and it takes many forms in this film. One of these is the way in which, at several moments, the film expresses Elio and Oliver's relationship in terms of visual distance from the camera, and thus from us. At many crucial moments in Elio's relationship with Oliver, the connection they make occurs in the depths of the frame.

Early scenes establish this. When Elio first sees Oliver, it is from a vantage point: Elio is leaning out of his upstairs bedroom window down towards the front drive, where Oliver is getting out of a car and being greeted by Elio's parents. A minute later, in the narrative and in the film, Elio and Oliver meet for the first time. The camera observes Elio as he comes down the stairs and his mother, Annella (Amira Casar), collects him to take him into the study to introduce him to Oliver. The camera remains outside the doorway, observing Elio as he walks into the room, away from us and with his back to us, and shakes hands with Oliver, who is in the far distance and facing Elio (and us). A little later, when Elio and Oliver are hanging out at the pool and Elio refuses to tell Oliver what he is thinking, saying 'It's private', Oliver loses patience – playfully – and says 'I guess I'll go hang out with your mum'. He wades to the far edge of the pool, gets out and pads over towards Elio's mum off screen. Elio follows him, but the camera remains at the pool – observing as Elio walks away from it, again with his back to us, to join his mum and Oliver in the distance as they pick apricots from the tree. And another example of distance is when Elio and Oliver travel with Elio's father to Lake Garda to witness an ancient sculpture being brought to the surface of the water, a sequence that has begun with frostiness between Elio and Oliver: the trip ends with them having made up and swimming in the lake, and in extreme long shot we see them in the water as they call out each other's names.

In each case, Elio and Oliver bond away from the camera, away from us. It's less easy for us to hang out with Elio when he is not close to the camera. We observe these moments, and we understand their importance, but the film keeps detail at arm's length from us. These may be among the moments Kyle Turner is thinking of when he says, 'We sometimes see the way Elio looks, but for the most part, *when* he looks, and when Oliver looks back or doesn't look back, touches or doesn't touch? We're too far away, unfortunate voyeurs'.[30]

As Elio and Oliver's feelings for each other grow, there are moments in which the two of them escape together into the far distance, leaving us behind as they enter a private realm of happiness. After Elio has confessed his feelings to Oliver in front of the monument to the Battle of Piave, the ensuing scenes across that same afternoon see them riding their bikes towards the horizon three times. The first of these shots is especially lengthy, lasting 54 seconds. If this seems excessive on a first viewing, on a subsequent viewing it seems to herald the deepening of their romance: as they ride away into the distance, the magic of love's adventure sinks in, thanks to the shot's duration – perhaps one of Grønstad's 'transcendental, revelatory experiences' (Figure 6.2). Later, when Elio and Oliver go away together to Bergamo for a few days before Oliver heads home to the USA, we observe them climbing up a hill towards a waterfall as Sufjan Stevens' song 'Mystery of Love' plays on the soundtrack. As Elio and Oliver climb up the hill, their backs are to us as, again, they recede into the distance. These moments of closeness between Elio and Oliver express how they are harmonizing in their love for each other, not so much exploring their relationship as simply experiencing it. It's proximity – but private, between them.

These moments seem to run counter to what may be a tendency of the film romance, which is to bring us visually closer to the romantic couple. In *Call Me by Your Name*, the romance keeps us at a distance. It isn't our romance; Elio isn't us; we don't know the manoeuvres of his head or his heart. We can't enjoy the romance the way he is enjoying it. Nevertheless, these rhyming instances of visual distance that link together these key moments invite us into the romance in another way. They don't just evoke distance (from us) and intimacy (for Elio and Oliver); they also subtly structure the material, giving it dramatic shape even

FIGURE 6.2: Elio (Timothée Chalamet) and Oliver (Armie Hammer) ride into the distance and the magic of love's adventure sinks in. Luca Guadagnino (dir.), *Call Me by Your Name*, 2017. Italy/France/USA/Brazil. © Frenesy, La Cinefacture.

while we are 'hanging out' with the characters. And when Elio and Oliver part at the train station, the train carries Oliver away into the far distance and the camera, stationed behind Elio, observes Elio's back as he watches the departing train. Then the camera moves in gently towards Elio – bringing him closer to us, or perhaps simply closer to himself, as his beloved departs. The near distance is the site of heartache; the object of desire is in the far distance, and Elio is unable to join him in that distant place.

The sense of privacy between Elio and Oliver also contributes to a depiction of the difference between straight and same-sex romance – the one being the more 'acceptable', the other being, in this story, the more authentically felt. 'We almost had sex last night – Marzia and me', Elio says to his father over breakfast when talking about his friend Marzia (Esther Garrel), a young local woman with whom he enjoys a flirtatious friendship, and who wants more from Elio. Elio's line – explaining how close he came to having sex with Marzia the previous evening when they went for a late-night dip in the pond – speaks to more than just his awareness that Marzia likes him; it speaks to a wider sense of the possibilities of courtship between young men and young women. Elio's ability to bring up the subject so openly at the breakfast table shows how well-ingrained the sense of social ritual is for young heterosexual would-be lovers somewhere in northern Italy in the summer of 1983. This is in contrast to Elio's slowly emerging relationship with Oliver. When Elio meets up with Marzia in the town, it has the feeling of a 'date'. He brings her a gift (a book of poetry). He takes her hand. They look like a young courting couple. When they kiss, in a rather more private location (a doorway, geographically indistinct but clearly set apart from the most 'public' parts of the town), he moves his hips against her and she says 'You're so hard', indicating how turned on he is. And yet there is something overdetermined about Elio's courtship. It is not that he is hard; it is that he is trying too hard. Marzia seems to know this; she has said earlier, 'I think you're going to hurt me, and I don't want to be hurt'.

When, later, Elio and Marzia have sex in the attic, a sense of a courting ritual remains. Elio drags the dusty mattress away from the wall and lets it drop to the floor. He then somersaults onto it, as Marzia watches. Here, Elio assumes the conventional role of the young man in the relationship, doing daft tricks to impress the young woman. He courts her – not the other way round. But it will turn out that only Marzia's feelings are authentic. Elio's later rejection of her for Oliver is not necessarily the rejection of a straight romance for a gay one *per se* – it is the rejection of inauthentic desire for authentic desire. Elio hardly knows the one from the other himself. When he rejects Marzia, he does it passively. She has come to find him at the house; when she says she hasn't heard from him, his explanation is a weak one: he had to work, he had a lot to do. Then she asks the unavoidable question: 'I'm not your girl?' Elio just shrugs. He doesn't have the words. He doesn't want to hurt her, or himself, by saying the honest thing. But his action hurts her anyway. And he has perhaps already hurt himself, by taking up with Marzia and launching himself into the attempt. But then maybe he didn't know any better. Inauthentic desire can sometimes only become apparent when authentic desire turns up to claim its unassailable place in the heart.

This may help explain why, when Elio and Marzia have sex, the nudity is somewhat more explicit than it is in the sex scenes with Oliver. We see Marzia's breasts, as Elio tenderly touches them. We see side nudity of her middle as Elio descends between her legs to perform oral sex on her. And the scene is lit brightly. We could read this as a capitulation to a heteronormative emphasis on a straight coupling and on a crushingly conventional display of the female body on screen. But I see the scene rather as expressive of Elio's lack of satisfaction with Marzia. His relationship with her has a performative dimension in that it operates under the rules of conventionality[31] – he is trying out what being 'normal' feels like. The nudity in their sex scene emphasizes the societal expectation of his attempt to be with Marzia. Granted, the sex he has with Marzia takes place in private. But it is shadowed by the weight of public expectation (and approval) for what Elio and Marzia are doing, and as such it is a 'public' performance of heteronormativity.

By contrast, Elio's affair with Oliver is all private, shadowy, quiet and interior; it does not conform to convention and, as such, does not carry with it a self-conscious sense of ritual. This is why Elio's sex with Oliver occurs mostly off screen: it is private between them. It places it into our imaginations as the 'right' sex – not sex as overdetermined public performance but sex as intimate, private, and unknowable to outsiders. Once again, the visual strategy is one of distance from us. When Elio and Oliver start to kiss on the bed, the camera cannot depict them too much in the distance – the bedroom is small – and so the camera seeks to distance itself from them, hence the pan to the shot out of the window into the trees. Why should Elio and Oliver move away from us? It's their intimate moment – perhaps it's we who should be moving away.

Some critics have expressed disappointment – dismay, even – that the sex scene between Elio and Oliver is not more visually explicit. (Sarah Artt looks at this in her chapter in this collection.) I get that there is anxiety at a perceived compromise over the representation of gay sex on screen. After all, it's happened before in other films – too many times. But complaining that the sex scene between Elio and Oliver is not explicit enough is, to me, an odd stance to take if one is invested in Elio and Oliver as characters. The privacy speaks to unknowability. And, as we have seen, the unknowable evades categorization. In Levinasian terms, the privacy of Elio and Oliver's affair – its distance from us – is ethical in that the film keeps us from being able to know enough about the characters to obliterate their otherness, their uniqueness. Elio and Oliver's later meeting in the town centre is furtive, and therefore a contrast with the openness of Elio's time there with Marzia. This shows the relative degrees of perceived acceptability of a straight relationship and a same-sex relationship within the story's milieu. In seeking to preserve Elio and Oliver's otherness, the film wants to place them beyond judgement – and, therefore, ideally beyond the reach of persecution. It wants them to have the freedom to be together without interference from outside.

Answering moments

There are also numerous moments that seem to 'answer' previous moments, further structuring the story. For example, the rucksack Elio is wearing on his back when he first confesses his feelings to Oliver is present again on his back as he watches the train leaving the station with Oliver on it heading back to the United States (Figure 6.3). And when Elio returns home, he skips dinner – just as Oliver skipped dinner on the night he arrived at the Perlmans'. Another example is when Elio and Oliver are on their bike ride after Elio has confessed his feelings. They stop at a house where an elderly woman sits shelling peas, they ask her for a glass of water, and as she goes inside to fetch the glasses, Elio steals one of her peas. This moment links to a moment later: as Elio calls his mother, tearfully, to come and pick him up after Oliver's train has departed, Elio is on the left of the shot, and on the right, in the shadowy interior by the payphone, is an elderly woman. Does she represent a kind of natural order, the universe's comment on the start (the water, the peas) and end (the departing train) of happiness? We can't know if that's what Elio thinks, because there is no evidence that he notices the link. But it's there for us to consider. And there is one answering moment that Elio certainly

FIGURE 6.3: Elio (Timothée Chalamet) is wearing his rucksack when he first confesses his feelings to Oliver (Armie Hammer) and is wearing the same rucksack as he watches Oliver's train leaving the station. Luca Guadagnino (dir.), *Call Me by Your Name*, 2017. Italy/France/USA/Brazil. © Frenesy, La Cinefacture.

notices. When he and Oliver are in Bergamo, drunk and wandering through the city at night, they encounter two men and a woman hanging out with stereo, and the song it is playing is 'Love My Way' by The Psychedelic Furs. This is the song that Elio had earlier danced to, along with Oliver, at the local outdoor disco. Now, Oliver dances to it, and Elio sits to watch – and then vomits. His vomiting seems to convey his linking of the two moments, and the contrast between them – the happiness of the earlier moment and the sadness of this one, so near in time to Oliver's departure.

As with the moments of visual distance, these moments aren't *obviously* structural – for example, they are not emphasized through overt repetition of camera angles, editing patterns or *mise en scène*. But they are the pegs that hang the film on the clothes line, the better for it to waft in the summery northern Italian breeze.

There are also a few moments in *Call Me by Your Name* in which the texture of the image changes overtly. Five times, it goes out of focus: as Elio sits back while watching Oliver dance; when Elio is sitting under the tree one evening wondering where Oliver is; as the two of them kiss on the bed; when they kiss after Elio has vomited; and finally, as Oliver watches Elio sleeping in Bergamo. In the last of those moments, we also see a dream depicted in negative images: is this Oliver trying to imagine what Elio is dreaming about? And earlier, when Elio is sitting under the tree, there is an additional filmic effect: a flashing, a whitening-out to some extent, of the image. With these moments, the film has found another way of expressing how important it is that we are in proximity to Elio, too close to know what to think. Kristin Lené Hole says that

> [t]erms like 'knowing', 'cognition' and 'experience' are always associated with the ontological in Levinas, and with the realm of light, enlightenment, vision and totality. [...] For Levinas, ethics takes place in darkness, in the space of *not* knowing, *not* mastering, and being vulnerable and exposed to the call of the other.[32]

Levinas is sceptical of the visual. He believes the visual, and art in general, fixes things too definitively.[33] These brief moments in *Call Me by Your Name* depart from Guadagnino's camera philosophy of not using techniques beyond observing character behaviour. As obfuscations of the image, they have, I think, a Levinasian dimension of scepticism of the visual, and thus they enrich the film.

The film's final answering moment comes during the coda, set in the snow during Hanukkah, several months after Elio and Oliver's summer together. The sequence is preceded by the film's only fade to black (outside the opening and end credits), indicating a break from the main body of the film. The continuity is that it's Hanukkah; Elio and Oliver both have Jewish heritage, which they have bonded over during the course of the story. But when Oliver calls Elio to tell him that he may be getting married in the spring, it is horrible news that, for Elio and for us, comes out of nowhere, and seems to spell the end of Elio's hopes for an ongoing relationship with Oliver. The final, lengthy close-up of a sorrowful Elio sitting in front of the fire, accompanied by the words and music of Sufjan Stevens' song 'Visions of Gideon', makes for an emotionally harrowing conclusion. This final scene hurts not only because of the news Elio has just heard but because, as a contrast to the happiness of the shots of Elio and Oliver together in the depths of the frame, the film has trained us to see close-ups as sad moments.

There are two elements to this answering moment. We may not recall on a first viewing but we have heard some of 'Visions of Gideon' already in the film: its opening bars play on the soundtrack at the start of the bedroom sequence in which Elio and Oliver sleep together for the first time. We don't know at that stage what the music is – and we don't know we will encounter it again. And when 'Visions of Gideon' arrives in the final scene of the film, we perhaps don't recognize its opening as something we heard in the bedroom sequence. But the repetition acts as a kind of pay-off to an earlier foreshadowing: this is a relationship that was going to come to an end. Knowledge of that on subsequent viewings doesn't negate the beauty of the time Elio has spent with Oliver; indeed, it may enhance it.

Secondly, the lengthy duration of the shot takes us back to the single-take scene in which Elio confesses his feelings to Oliver. There, the duration spoke of nervous action proving momentous for Elio, as he took a bold step towards intimacy with the man with whom he was falling in love. Here, the duration is a similar test: we see Elio in a single take as he encounters another psychological threshold and, again, has to cross it alone.

He crosses it. And the duration of the shot enables us to grow accustomed to the hurt: it begins a process of healing. And it gives us time to contemplate the shot *as* an ending, not least as the film's end credits are on screen along with Chalamet's face. Elio is looking forward into the past – remembering his romance with Oliver, seeing it for the second time for the first time – and then he looks backwards into the present as his mother calls him to the dining table (calls him by his own name, a parental gesture that gives him renewed life, gives his identity back to him now that Oliver has moved on). And as the film fades out on that moment, it leaves us to look, on Elio's behalf, to the future.

Concluding remarks

In *Call Me by Your Name*, an ethics is found in the approach to the characters' otherness. It is in the combined proximity to and distance from Elio that audiences can respond to him without judgement. Kristin Lené Hole's comments on the work of *J'ai pas sommeil* can, again, stand also for *Call Me by Your Name*:

> By its invitation to encounter the other, the film itself offers an opportunity to view ethically and to develop an ethical sensibility that extends beyond the timeframe of the film. [...] The potential for this experience to alter the viewer herself reveals that we are fundamentally *with*; our subjectivities are the result of the ongoing process of encountering.[34]

Although we are able to follow Elio's relationship with Oliver, there are ways in which it remains at a distance from us – private and uncategorized. This is, I hope, an inspiring aspect of the film, encouraging audiences to believe that their own romantic relationships can be equally private, and equally free.

NOTES

1. Hillary Weston, 'Love My Way: A Conversation with Luca Guadagnino', *The Criterion Collection*, 19 December 2017, https://www.criterion.com/current/posts/5075-love-my-way-a-conversation-with-luca-guadagnino.
2. Weston, 'Love My Way'.
3. Weston, 'Love My Way'.
4. Kyle Turner, '*Call Me by Your Name* (2017 New York Film Festival Review)', *Paste*, 4 October 2017, https://www.pastemagazine.com/movies/call-me-by-your-name/call-me-by-your-name/.
5. Turner, '*Call Me*'.
6. Turner, '*Call Me*'.
7. Richard Brody, 'The Empty, Sanitized Intimacy of *Call Me by Your Name*', *New Yorker*, 28 November 2017, https://www.newyorker.com/culture/richard-brody/the-empty-sanitized-intimacy-of-call-me-by-your-name.
8. Asbjørn Grønstad, 'Slow Cinema and the Ethics of Duration', in *Slow Cinema*, ed. Tiago de Luca and Nuno Barradas Jorge (Edinburgh: Edinburgh University Press, 2015), 274.
9. Grønstad, 277.
10. Molly Haskell, '*Call Me by Your Name*', *Film Comment* 53, no. 6 (November–December 2017), 67.
11. André Aciman, *Call Me by Your Name* (London: Atlantic Books, [2007] 2009, 71–73.
12. Emmanuel Levinas, *Otherwise than Being or Beyond Essence*, trans. Alphonso Lingis (Pittsburgh: Duquesne University Press, [1981; original language publication: 1974] 2008), 100.
13. Levinas, *Otherwise than Being*, 139.
14. Levinas, *Otherwise than Being*, 83.

15. Robert Sinnerbrink, *Cinematic Ethics: Exploring Ethical Experience through Film* (Abingdon and New York: Routledge, 2016), 156.
16. Sinnerbrink, 160.
17. Kristin Lené Hole, *Towards a Feminist Cinematic Ethics: Claire Denis, Emmanuel Levinas and Jean-Luc Nancy* (Edinburgh: Edinburgh University Press, 2016), 86–87.
18. Levinas, *Otherwise than Being*, 87.
19. Colin Davis, *Levinas: An Introduction* (Cambridge and Malden: Polity Press, 1996), 56.
20. Robin Podolsky, *L'Aimé Qui Est l'Aimée*: Can Levinas' Beloved Be Queer?', in *European Judaism: A Journal for the New Europe*, Vol. 49, No. 2 (Autumn 2016): 51.
21. Podolsky, 57.
22. See especially Podolsky, 58–62.
23. Haskell, '*Call Me*', 68.
24. Grønstad, 'Slow Cinema', 278.
25. Brody, 'Sanitised Intimacy'.
26. Grønstad, 'Slow Cinema', 274.
27. Haskell, '*Call Me*', 67.
28. Karl Schoonover and Rosalind Galt, *Queer Cinema in the World* (Durham: Duke University Press, 2016), 286.
29. Levinas, *Otherwise than Being*, 89.
30. Turner, '*Call Me*'.
31. For an excellent discussion of conventionality within performativity, see Sandy Petrey, *Speech Acts and Literary Theory* (New York and London: Routledge, 1990), 153.
32. Hole, *Towards*, 146–47.
33. Levinas's 1948 essay 'Reality and Its Shadow' is a key text in this regard. See Emmanuel Levinas, 'Reality and Its Shadow', in Emmanuel Levinas, *Collected Philosophical Papers*, trans. Alphonso Lingis (Pittsburgh: Duquesne University Press, [1987; original language publication of essay: 1948]) 2006, 1–13.
34. Hole, *Towards*, 88.

REFERENCES

Aciman, André. *Call Me by Your Name*. London: Atlantic Books, [2007] 2009.

Brody, Richard. 'The Empty, Sanitized Intimacy of *Call Me by Your Name*.' *New Yorker*, 28 November 2017. https://www.newyorker.com/culture/richard-brody/the-empty-sanitized-intimacy-of-call-me-by-your-name.

Dardenne, Luc, and Jean-Pierre Dardenne, dir. *La Promesse (The Promise)*. Les Films du Fleuve, Touza Productions, Touza Films, Samsa Film, RTBF (Télévision belge), 1996.

Davis, Colin, *Levinas: An Introduction*. Cambridge and Malden: Polity Press, 1996.

Denis, Claire, dir. *J'ai pas sommeil (I Can't Sleep)*. Arena Films, Orsans, Les Films de Mindif, 1994.

Grønstad, Asbjørn. 'Slow Cinema and the Ethics of Duration.' In *Slow Cinema*, edited by Tiago de Luca and Nuno Barradas Jorge, 273–84. Edinburgh: Edinburgh University Press, 2015.

Guadagnino, Luca, dir. *Call Me by Your Name*. Frenesy Film Company, La Cinefacture, RT Features, 2017.

Guadagnino, Luca, dir. *We Are Who We Are* (TV). HBO, Sky Italia, Wildside, The Apartment, 2020.

Haskell, Molly. '*Call Me by Your Name*.' *Film Comment* 53, no. 6 (November–December 2017): 67–69.

Hole, Kristin Lené. *Towards a Feminist Cinematic Ethics: Claire Denis, Emmanuel Levinas and Jean-Luc Nancy*. Edinburgh: Edinburgh University Press, 2016.

Levinas, Emmanuel. 'Reality and Its Shadow.' In Emmanuel Levinas, *Collected Philosophical Papers*. Translated by Alphonso Lingis, 1–13. Pittsburgh: Duquesne University Press, [1987; original language publication of essay: 1948] 2006.

Levinas, Emmanuel. *Otherwise than Being or Beyond Essence*. Translated by Alphonso Lingis. Pittsburgh: Duquesne University Press, [1981; original language publication: 1974] 2008.

Petrey, Sandy. *Speech Acts and Literary Theory*. New York and London: Routledge, 1990.

Podolsky, Robin. '*L'Aimé Qui Est l'Aimée*: Can Levinas' Beloved Be Queer?' *European Judaism: A Journal for the New Europe* 49, no. 2 (Autumn 2016): 50–70.

Schoonover, Karl, and Rosalind Galt. *Queer Cinema in the World*. Durham: Duke University Press, 2016.

Sinnerbrink, Robert. *Cinematic Ethics: Exploring Ethical Experience through Film*. Abingdon and New York: Routledge, 2016.

Turner, Kyle. '*Call Me by Your Name* (2017 New York Film Festival Review).' *Paste*, 4 October 2017. https://www.pastemagazine.com/movies/call-me-by-your-name/call-me-by-your-name/.

Weston, Hillary. 'Love My Way: A Conversation with Luca Guadagnino.' *The Criterion Collection*, 19 December 2017. https://www.criterion.com/current/posts/5075-love-my-way-a-conversation-with-luca-guadagnino.

PART II

THEMES

7

Call Me by Your Name, Chrononormativity and the (Queer?) Future of Italian Teen Film

Daniel Paul

Upon its release in 2017, *Call Me by Your Name* – the third and final instalment in Luca Guadagnino's 'desire trilogy' – was readily accepted into the queer cinema canon. *Call Me by Your Name* centres around the summer romance between 17-year-old Elio Perlman (Timothée Chalamet) and Oliver (Armie Hammer), the 24-year-old graduate student and research assistant working with Elio's father (Michael Stuhlbarg) during the summer near Crema, a small town in northern Italy and Guadagnino's hometown. However, although *Call Me by Your Name* has been adopted into the corpus of gay or queer cinema by queer audience measures,[1] film critics remain puzzled at its reception as an inherently queer text. For example, Miz Cracker wonders:

> Why has *Call Me by Your Name* attained such an iconic 'gay' status when it is anything but? When its main characters seem almost aggressively isolated from gay culture or politics? When its precocious protagonist has to be reminded that it's gauche to make fun of people who are openly gay?[2]

Cracker concludes that '[t]he straightness is everywhere once you clear the lust from your eyes', pointing to extra-diegetic details such as the heterosexuality of novelist André Aciman and actors Chalamet and Hammer. D. A. Miller, in a similar vein, citing the film's somewhat graphic spectacle of Elio's heterosexual intercourse with Marzia (Esther Garrel), and its apparent avoidance of the depiction of gay sex between Elio and Oliver, argues that the film 'is not homosexual'.[3] If this is in fact the case, how and why, then, has a film so overtly straight become so iconic for the gay and queer community?

What is more, because *Call Me by Your Name* is a transnational production that, according to Guadagnino and some of the film's critics, has a universal appeal,[4] few recognize it as a specifically Italian product or aimed directly at an adolescent audience. Despite the film's central romance between two males, critics hailed *Call Me by Your Name* as a 'universal' love story, one which appeals to, according to Tim Gray, '[a]udiences of all sexual persuasions and ages'.[5] Nor does it appear that *Call Me by Your Name* is either an Italian film or a teen film, at least in the most basic sense: in spite of its setting, Italian is not the primary spoken language, and the main cast is made up of non-Italian actors, while the film's serious subject matter pushes it away from the genre of teen films and towards its more obvious classification as a serious, highbrow melodrama.[6]

In this chapter, I argue that *Call Me by Your Name* is a queer Italian teen film. I contend that *Call Me by Your Name* deftly subverts the structures of heteronormative time through its soundtrack and narrative and that, as a result, it represents a positive future for the representation of queer desire and for the genre of Italian teen film. To be clear, by labelling *Call Me by Your Name* a queer text, I mean first that the film questions and problematizes long-standing notions of normativity as being strictly heterosexual. I employ the term queer in this sense as a means of exploring how *Call Me by Your Name* confronts and subverts entrenched ideas regarding gender and sexuality. By demonstrating how the same-sex relationship between Elio and Oliver in *Call Me by Your Name* centralizes queerness and pushes against heteronormativity, I contend that the film creates a space in which same-sex desire (and intimacy) can effectively ruminate and perhaps even thrive. *Call Me by Your Name* thus functions as a site of negotiation for new narratives for queer Italian cinema.[7] Indeed, *Call Me by Your Name* differs from other Italian queer films, such as *Benzina* (*Gasoline*, Monica Stambrini, 2001), *Saturno contro* (*Saturn in Opposition*, Ferzan Özpetek, 2007) or *Né Giulietta né Romeo* (*A Little Lust*, Veronica Pivetti, 2015), in that those who experience same-sex desire or who engage in erotic encounters with those of the same-sex do not succumb to death, be it physical or social. Crucially, the film's transnationalism, which blurs linguistic, racial and, above all, national boundaries, lends itself to the film's queer project and allows for a possible new norm in queer representation.[8]

Call Me by Your Name: *A (queer) Italian teen film?*

Despite its Italian setting, *Call Me by Your Name*'s use of English as its primary language and cast of mainly non-Italian actors resist a simple classification of the film as Italian. However, to repurpose Miz Cracker, Italianness is everywhere once you clear the Anglophone from your eyes. Applying Michael Z. Newman's analysis of Italian-American kitchen guru Giada de Laurentiis's cooking show *Everyday Italian* to *Call Me by Your Name*, one can easily observe how Guadagnino's film provides its audience with 'a vision of good taste', high social standing, and seemingly unlimited time constraints, presenting as a result 'a model of how to live that [a viewer] might attain, but more likely merely aspire to'.[9] Shots of the luscious Italian landscape allow spectators to escape the mundane routine of their everyday social reality to 'a fantasy realm of sensual pleasures'[10] wherein the audience can vicariously indulge in an apparently 'more authentic and dignified'[11] way of life glimpsed in the Perlmans' lavish home and in Elio's spatial mobility and sexual freedom. This depiction of the Italian countryside as exotic and sumptuous led one reviewer to label the film 'a luxurious vacation movie'.[12] Each of these attributes is indeed emblematic of media representations of so-called *italianità*. Additionally, *Call Me by Your Name* received financial support from the Ministero dei Beni e delle Attività Culturali e del Turismo (MiBACT), and such funding imbues the film with an inherent cultural value and capital and helps situate it as an Italian product. On the one hand, then, by purchasing a ticket to see the film, viewers can participate in a type of virtual tourism, visiting Italy without ever leaving the comfort of their home(land); on the other hand, *Call Me by Your Name* allows spectators access, however brief, to a certain kind of Italian lifestyle that could be purchased or attained so long as one has the time and financial means to do so. In this way, the film promotes Italy and the Italian brand emblematized by Elio and Oliver's iconic *dolce far niente* way of life (Figure 7.1).[13] At the same time, however, it is important to note that *Everyday Italian* is directed at an Anglophone audience and focuses on an Italian-American, and that both it and *Call Me by Your Name* provide a commodified version of Italy that, under close scrutiny, exposes cracks in their perceived Italianness. Despite their best attempts, in other words, the vision of Italy that these two texts provide can be seen as potentially compromised.

As this caveat suggests, situating *Call Me by Your Name* as Italian is not without its flaws. After all, the film is, as previously mentioned, uniquely transnational, both in its production and in its address. Although characterizing the film as transnational complicates its designation as 'Italian', the two terms (i.e. 'Italian' and 'transnational') are not mutually exclusive. As Steven Rawle contends, 'transnational cinema does not replace thinking about national cinemas, but supplements it'.[14] In other words, *Call Me by Your Name* can and likely should be considered as representative of Italy and Italian cinema despite, or perhaps even because of, its transnationalism. I would argue, in fact, that it is precisely the film's transnational appeal which evidences its uniquely Italian style and setting.[15]

A straightforward designation of the film as a teen movie is likewise problematic. In her work on the genre, Catherine Driscoll identifies a number of tropes

FIGURE 7.1: Oliver (Armie Hammer) and Elio (Timothée Chalamet) enjoy the *dolce far niente* way of life. Luca Guadagnino (dir.), *Call Me by Your Name*, 2017. Italy/France/USA/Brazil. © Frenesy, La Cinefacture.

that are characteristic of teen movies including youthfulness of main protagonists; a focus on young heterosexual romance; intense peer relationships and conflicts; and coming-of-age plots dealing with virginity, graduation or the makeover.[16] *Call Me by Your Name* clearly adheres to some, though not all, of these conventions: despite Elio's heterosexual relationship with Marzia, for example, it is his homosexual relationship with Oliver that seems to shape his adolescence the most. Although Elio occasionally interacts with his peers, it is equally true that his most intense relationship is not with those of his age group but with the significantly older Oliver. These tensions notwithstanding, the film still centres around the coming-of-age experience of a teenager. Elio grapples with the difficulties of adolescence; he starts up a relationship with Marzia, even eventually having sex with her; he struggles with his sexual identity and his same-sex attraction and desire for Oliver; he engages sexually with Oliver, having his first homosexual experience; and Elio is significantly changed by this erotic encounter with Oliver such that it is precisely their relationship that pushes Elio into adulthood. Thus, inasmuch as *Call Me by Your Name* speaks to the adolescent condition and centralizes the adolescent Elio, it can be classified as a teen film, whether or not it was necessarily consumed by its ideal (adolescent) audience. And, as I suggest, it is the film's inability to be easily denoted as 'Italian' and as 'teen', that is, its inability to be compartmentalized, as it were, as *only* Italian or *only* directed at teens that allows for queer futurity, for Elio within the film and for the genre of Italian teen film.

With regard to a simplistic generic classification, the difficulty presented by this film reflects the tensions inherent in Elio's coming to terms with his own sexuality, at least to some extent. Elio's wrestle with his sexual identity and orientation personifies the confusion surrounding the film's ability to be considered as an Italian, teen or queer text. In truth, the film keeps all of these elements at play at any one time. Though I examine and emphasize the film's queer narrative, the dichotomy made clear through critics' consideration of *Call Me by Your Name* as *either* a universal love story *or* a queer one would seem to suggest that Elio is *either* straight *or* gay, whereas it seems possible, as we shall see, that he identifies, albeit in different parts of his life, as *both* straight *and* gay, a type of sexuality that has not traditionally been privileged in Italian cinema.[17] In its own right, then, *Call Me by Your Name* represents a queer fantasy wherein the acceptance and encouragement of Elio and Oliver's romance on behalf of their family and friends embodies director Luca Guadagnino's struggle for acceptance, as a gay man, by an Italian society which has historically tended to be both patriarchal and heteronormative. And it is precisely within this fantasy that queer desire is actually given a space for representation, wherein same-sex desire and queer sexuality can be centralized rather than marginalized. What a study of *Call Me by Your Name* reveals is that the Italian teen film may provide a safe space in which to explore non-normative sexualities and, by making such sexualities central, allow those who embody them a place within the Italian landscape, rather than condemnation to the margins or to death – be it physical or social.

Undermining chrononormative time: Call Me by Your Name*'s queer soundtrack*

In the following sections, I wish to demonstrate a variety of ways in which *Call Me by Your Name* embodies queerness. In particular, I draw attention to a number of seemingly insignificant details – the skipping of meals; the film's soundtrack; and the obsessive focus on Elio's watch – in order to show how these elements push against normative time and heteronormative practices. I conclude with a close analysis of the film's final sequence, Elio's longing and mournful stare into the fireplace which accompanies the closing credits. As previously mentioned, the film's acceptance of queerness may in fact provide a potential future for queer representation; indeed, I propose that a close textual examination lays bare its queer project.

In her book *Time Binds: Queer Temporalities, Queer Histories*, Elizabeth Freeman theorizes chrononormativity or chrononormative time as 'the use of time to organize individual human bodies toward maximum productivity', or, in the most basic sense, time as a guiding principle with regards to work and sexual reproduction through the heterosexual couple and/or marriage.[18] Halberstam likewise argues that queer time and queer spaces develop, in part, 'in opposition to the institutions of family, heterosexuality, and reproduction'.[19] *Call Me by Your Name* is particularly conscious of queer time and resists chrononormativity: for example, at several points Elio, Oliver or both skip out on family meals. Though it could easily go unnoticed, the fact that they often skip dinner – the meal which, due to the amount of preparation dedicated to it each day, is inherently linked to the domestic in Italian culture and cuisine – signals a resistance to heteronormative practices based around family and mealtime on the part of Elio and Oliver. Oliver's tendency to attend only part of meals, leaving the Perlmans with his signature 'Later', likewise suggests a purposeful non-conformity to accepted cultural norms regarding meals and, at the same time, evokes the melodramatic mode – by constantly delaying his being together with Elio and by recalling the 'too late' of melodrama.[20]

The film queers time in other ways as well: the at times dissonant, staccato soundtrack, for example, contributes to the feeling of time as disconnected and non-linear. In addition, a number of the songs – such as John Adams' 'Hallelujah Junction'[21] – make use of syncopation, the displacement of accents from strong beats to weak ones. In this way, the music plays with time, and does not readily adhere to commonly acceptable and aurally pleasing organizations of rhythm and metre. Although 'Hallelujah Junction' wasn't composed for *Call Me by Your Name*, it feels as if it were. In an interview about the piece, Adams explains that composing for two pianos allows him to 'write very similar material but interlock them slightly out of phase so it creates a kind of acoustical version of a digital delay'.[22] Thus, not only does Adams play with tempo and rhythm, but his transposition of the acoustic medium into a digital realm situates the piece as somehow queer in its own right. By blurring the boundary between the 'live' aspect of a piano performance and the 'recorded' aspect of the digital delay, 'Hallelujah Junction' pushes against established ideas and ideals relating to musical structure – beat, measure, rhythm – and aural pleasure. Like the pianos, Elio and Oliver's relationship is characterized early on as being 'slightly out of phase' in that they do not pick up on each other's signals and sexual advances.

The language which Adams uses to describe the movement and melodies of the pianos is itself rather sexually charged and could be construed as speaking to, at least to some degree, same-sex desire and intimacy. He points out that the music 'has its own resonance that only can happen when you have *two instruments playing almost the exact same material*'.[23] The homogeny of the instruments, or, in the case of *Call Me by Your Name*, the same-sexed bodies of Elio and Oliver, is what allows for the resonance to come through. What was fun about composing 'Hallelujah Junction', Adams explains, was its 'sense of *pulsation*' achieved through the two pianos 'working at the *same tempo*, with the *same material* and tossing [...] little motivic ideas back and forth' and then 'riffing', where one piano 'will stay down low while another one goes up high and jabbing back and forth'.[24] It is here where Adams' description seems at its most erotic, with the two bodies – the harmonies on each piano – moving at the same speed or tempo, intertwining in an instrumental topping and bottoming, a thrusting back and forth, and an eventual climax in orgasmic pulsations. In the song's final section, the constant shift of pulse between the two pianos creates an 'ambiguity [that] produces a kind of giddy uncertainty as the music pings back and forth in bright clusters'.[25] This *giddy uncertainty* exemplified in the soundtrack is made apparent within the narrative through Elio's relationship with Oliver, as Elio takes pleasure in getting to know Oliver, be it sexually or otherwise.

'Hallelujah Junction' accompanies the film's opening credits, playing over images of bronze statues that at once emphasize the concept of beauty – a topos of Guadagnino's cinematographic choices – and invoke Greek antiquity. This allusion to Greek history, considered in relation to the film's queer narrative, calls to mind the practice of pederasty which was, at least in that culture, 'not only tolerated but the object of considerable social esteem'.[26] Even in these initial moments, then, the film takes on – as I will show later on – a feeling of nostalgia, in this case for a society that accepted and even privileged male–male intimacy and desire. Although 'Hallelujah Junction' was not composed for *Call Me by Your Name*, it is impossible to ignore its importance as a potential marker of queerness within the film's diegesis.

Elio's watch: Disavowing chrononormative time

Call Me by Your Name further refuses to be constrained by, citing Freeman, '[s]chedules, calendars, time zones, and even wristwatches', instruments which perpetuate chrononormative time and reinforce the forward movement and linearity of time.[27] When Elio receives a note from Oliver setting up a midnight rendezvous, the narrative returns obsessively to time-checking: Elio immediately checks his watch after reading Oliver's note; Oliver grabs Elio's wrist and inquires after the time during lunch; Elio checks his watch while swimming with Marzia and when he takes her to the musty attic; he looks at it when the gay couple arrives for dinner; and Elio's father hands him the watch following his evening piano performance. Inasmuch as the watch is connected to the family's repetitive routines, primarily those associated with meals, the obsession with the device could be taken as evidence to support the insistence of normative time. I would argue, however, that although the timepiece is omnipresent throughout the day, it is, nonetheless, always connected to the potential liaison with Oliver at the midnight hour and, as such, is clearly laden with Elio's homoerotic desire. To the extent that the watch anticipates the homosexual encounter between Elio and Oliver even despite its apparent association with the heteronormative moments outlined above strongly suggests that it ultimately subverts linear time (Figure 7.2).

There is one instance where the watch subtly undermines the reinforcement of chrononormative time and that is when Elio removes the watch before engaging in heterosexual intercourse with Marzia in the attic. This moment is significant precisely because of Elio's fixation on the watch and what it ultimately stands in for, that is, the planned midnight meeting and the hoped-for erotic encounter with Oliver. After Elio and Marzia share a passionate kiss, Elio checks his watch. He does so again upon turning the radio on, this time taking a moment to contemplate it (and its significance?) before setting it down beside the mattress on which the two will eventually make love. The watch's placement in plain view beside the bed is important here as it allows Elio to look at it even while going down on Marzia. And, Elio's desire to gaze upon the watch whilst engaging in heterosexual intercourse undermines the significance and centrality of heterosexual sex. By drawing attention to this symbol of the queer relationship, particularly during this quintessentially heterosexual moment, *Call Me by Your Name* pushes against

FIGURE 7.2: Elio's (Timothée Chalamet) watch. Luca Guadagnino (dir.), *Call Me by Your Name*, 2017. Italy/France/USA/Brazil. © Frenesy, La Cinefacture.

chrononormative time and instates queer time – represented by Elio's obvious longing to be with Oliver – as central.

To further support this argument, it is equally important to note that, although the watch repetitively returns to the foreground, only once – when Oliver asks Elio the time after lunch – do we actually know what time it really is. In all the other instances, the watch's face is obscured from view. In this way, the watch acts as a foil to what is really important: the actual coming together of Elio and Oliver and sharing their first sexual encounter with each other. Once that coming together takes place, the obsessive return to the watch stops and Elio and Oliver freely navigate their relationship. They soon embark on a sort of honeymoon retreat in Bergamo with the support, even encouragement, of Elio's parents. This couples' retreat is characterized by a sense of timelessness, with the flowering mountainsides becoming a veritable *locus amoenus* wherein time slows and the bond between the two flourishes. In addition, despite the passing of time, marked by the change of season from summer to winter in the film's conclusion, Elio and Oliver immediately revert to calling each other by their own names while chatting on the phone. The facility with which the two slip back into this habit, and Oliver's remark that he 'remember[s] everything' about their brief relationship, lends weight to this timeless feeling.

Indeed, their falling back into their aestival ritual is inherently nostalgic, and this nostalgia is central to the queer fantasy which *Call Me by Your Name* proposes. In his book *Queer Nostalgia in Cinema and Pop Culture*, Gilad Padva draws attention to the word's roots – *nostos* meaning 'return home' and *algia* meaning 'longing' – in order to then define nostalgia as primarily 'a desire for a home that no longer exists or has never existed'.[28] Such a definition highlights the role of fantasy and its intrinsic relation to nostalgia. Padva further argues that, due to their alienation in and exile from their childhood homes, queer people often have little desire to return to the literal space of the home; instead, those of the LGBTQ community have nostalgic memories about certain times, years, and happy days of their childhood. This leads Padva to conclude that '*most of* [...] queer nostalgia is involved with temporal rather than [*spatial*] *narratives*'.[29] What is queer about queer nostalgia, then, is how it undermines linear and historical perceptions of time by collapsing the distance between past and present (and perhaps even future). If nothing else, this moment of queer nostalgia provides a means to momentarily delay progress towards Oliver's heteronormative future, and hence signals a temporary subversion of chrononormative time.

The queerness of queer nostalgia is certainly evidenced in *Call Me by Your Name*: while the film constructs a utopic queer fantasy through the positive reception of same-sex desire on the part of Elio's parents and community, the historical reality does not coincide with the film's progressive social milieu. The conversation between Elio and his father towards the end of the film therefore functions as a nostalgic look back to what life *should* have been like during the period of intense crisis and fear about HIV/AIDS. At the same time, it casts a hopeful glance forward to what life could be like, a fantasy that has the potential to become a future reality. By layering the past (the should have been) and the future (the could be) onto this present moment, the temporality of *Call Me by Your Name* becomes rather non-linear, bordering on palimpsestic, and thus engages again in Freeman's project of queer time.

Contemporary notions of nostalgia see a 'drastic loss of engagement with historical time'.[30] Within the context of *Call Me by Your Name*, this temporal disconnect – reminiscent of the way queer time functions in Freeman's formulation – makes the film's construction of nostalgia inherently queer, particularly in the way that it breaks down and subverts normative or historical time by collapsing the distance between the past and present, and, as is the case in *Call Me by Your Name*, by invoking the future. One means by which the film accomplishes this disengagement with historical time is through its elliptical structure, an extra-diegetic reflection of the way that memory works as often non-coherent moments or flashes of one's personal history. This lack of trackable temporality likewise lends itself to the sense of timelessness constructed by the film. While the film unfolds in the 1980s, it also feels as though it could also be unfolding right before our eyes. What is more, the film's setting 'somewhere in northern Italy' and the lack of specificity regarding the location further contribute to the film's implicit resistance against historical time, even in spite of the presence of some historical markers such as the monument to the Battle of Piave around which Elio's desire for Oliver first comes to light.

This vagueness encompassing *Call Me by Your Name* contributes to my consideration of the film as a utopic vision of 1980s Italy, a nostalgic fantasy of what those in the queer community of the time could only have wished for. Significantly, judgement about Elio's same-sex relationship with Oliver and fear about the 'homosexual threat' of HIV and AIDS are entirely absent from *Call Me by Your Name*. Not only do Elio's (heterosexual) parents support and encourage him to experiment with his same-sex attraction and his sexuality, but other members of the community, including his (ex) girlfriend Marzia, seem to encourage him as well.

A number of the film's critics have pointed out how Elio's parents – and above all, his father – are so openly accepting of his pursuit of Oliver.[31] I would argue that this acceptance, characterized by an unrealistic optimism, pushes the limits of the believable and, in this way, foregrounds queer fantasy and nostalgia. In his discussion of Mr Perlman's heart-to-heart with his son near the end of the film, for example, Peter Debruge observes that

[n]o matter how intellectually progressive the Perlman family is, no father has ever said something so open-minded and eloquent to his son, and yet, the film offers this conversation as a gift to audiences who might have desperately needed to hear it in their own lives.[32]

I would tend to agree with Debruge and I would add that the father's acceptance of his son's same-sex desire evidences the way the film functions as a queer fantasy which arises from having sympathetic and supportive parents. In reality, and as Debruge's comment suggests, no parent in 1980s Italy would encourage their child to meander outside the strict bounds of heteronormativity.[33] Thus, the lack of cultural disdain for Elio and Oliver's relationship, coupled with the absence of the threat of being infected with HIV, situates the film as a nostalgic contemplation of a problematic historical moment that functions as a type of melodramatic 'if only', a fantasy wish-fulfilment of what could have been: 'if only' I had parents like Elio's; 'if only' Italy had been so accepting.

'Is it a video?': Queer time and mourning

I now focus my analysis on the closing moments of the film, a sequence in which Elio's emotions following his break-up with Oliver are on raw display. The finale, which is composed of a single long take lasting three and a half minutes, centres on male suffering, but also offers a rather progressive outlook on same-sex desire. The resistance to chrononormative time is perhaps made most obvious when Elio gazes forlornly into the fireplace. In these moments, we glimpse his reaction to Oliver's marriage announcement, which took place a short time earlier. As Elio begins to cry, the scene unfolds in shallow focus, with Elio in the foreground in focus and the dining area behind him heavily out of focus. With Elio in sharp focus, the viewer is constrained to witness Elio's reactions as he manifests a variety of emotions and facial expressions, ranging from sadness and tears, to a knowing smirk, to what looks like a nostalgic remembrance of the joyful ecstasy of the summer. His suffering, as I have mentioned, remains on display at all times. On the one hand, the use of shallow focus during this sequence emphasizes male melodrama through the centrality of Elio's pain. On the other hand, the use of shallow focus also foregrounds queer time: while Elio's emotional reactions to his same-sex relationship with Oliver remain clearly in focus (queer time), the domestic tasks of preparing dinner and setting the table, representative of heteronormative time, are carried out off-screen or in the background where they are obscured and heavily out of focus.

Once again, memory and queer affect are central to the final sequence and to the possibility of queer futurity, both in Italian teen film and, possibly, elsewhere. The extra-diegetic soundtrack during Elio's mourning of love lost does much work in foregrounding the role of memory in the film and lends itself to the queer reading I have been furthering up to this point. The insistence in Sufjan Stevens' 'Visions of Gideon' of loving, touching and kissing, perhaps for the last time, situates Elio's gazing into the fire as a contemplation of the love that he once enjoyed but which is now no longer available to him. The refrain in the lyrics creates a sense of (religious) ecstasy – not unlike the 'llelujah' of John Adams' 'Hallelujah Junction' – and, as a result, draws attention to the joy of being wrapped up in something beautiful, such as his relationship with Oliver. The repetitive contemplation of life as a video, on the other hand, emphasizes the surreality of Elio's summer fling and raises the question of whether it was all a dream. Each lyric likewise evidences the realm of fantasy, whether it be found in a moment of rapture or on a screen. The homophony of the phrases in the lyrics can also be read as a linguistic marker of queerness, with the boundary between the two being blurred.

There is one final way in which Sufjan Stevens' contribution lends itself to the queer project of *Call Me by Your Name* and that is through the way in which it blurs the boundaries of time. As a song written expressly for the film, 'Visions of Gideon' is a contemporary piece of music; yet, the song's style and overall feel – its folky, nostalgic melodies – fit perfectly with the 1980s setting of the film. One reviewer even characterizes Stevens' singing as 'a soft breeze', an observation which calls to mind the summer setting of the film itself.[34] Thus, 'Visions of Gideon' invokes the present through its contemporary composition while at the same time conjuring up the past through its wistful, dreamy and warm refrains. In this way, the conflation of past and present in 'Visions of Gideon' which accompanies Elio's mourning his break-up with Oliver centralizes queer time and, as we will see, helps code that mourning as productive, opening up a space for Elio's queer desire and allowing for a queer future, one that, unlike many other queer films, does not end badly.

Elio's grief in these final moments evidences an attachment to the past that is productive in that it leaves open the potential for a queer future. Paired with the expressiveness of the soundtrack in this moment, the long take foregrounds Elio's emotions through his melancholic attachment to Oliver and his refusal to let go of the past and move on. Earlier on in the film, after returning from the brief 'honeymoon' in Bergamo with Oliver, Elio encounters his one-time girlfriend Marzia. Following a brief exchange between the two, Elio accepts Marzia's proposal to stay friends, with the caveat that it be 'for life'. This proviso closes off the possibility of a heterosexual future for Elio, at least one with Marzia.[35] At the same time, their interaction again foregrounds male melodrama: even though Marzia too is going through a break-up, from Elio nonetheless, her sadness and pain is pushed aside so that Elio's melancholia can be validated. Despite his tears, both in his interaction with Marzia and in the final scene of his melancholic grief, Elio evinces no sign of wanting to pick up where he left off with Marzia and integrate into a 'normal' heterosexual economy. Indeed, his nostalgic smile in the closing moments expresses a sense of relishing in the pain and suffering he has experienced post-break-up. By allowing Elio to dwell in his sadness at seeing his relationship with Oliver end and through his refusal to pair up with Marzia again, the film privileges queer affect.

A queer future for Italian teen film?

Although imbued with sorrow, the dénouement of *Call Me by Your Name* varies significantly from two other Italian queer coming-of-age films, namely *Né Giulietta né Romeo* and *Un bacio* (*One Kiss*, Ivan Cotroneo, 2016). In these films, same-sex attraction and desire have no future, at least in Italy.[36] In *Né Giulietta né Romeo*, Rocco Bordin's (Andrea Amato) love interest supposedly dies. Though Rocco subsequently sees the young man on the street, he appears ill, his face ghostly white, perhaps a visual allusion to the effects of the HIV/AIDS virus on the body. Although the two do seem to pair off at the end of the film, the final shot depicts them walking away from the camera, towards an arch, an image which suggests departure, marginalization and haunting. That the love interest has faked his own death also insinuates that he is victim to a social death, having to leave his old self behind in order to attempt to move on. The outcome of *Un bacio* is equally bleak as the one (ill-fated) kiss of the title leads to Lorenzo (Rimau Ritzberger Grillo) eventually being killed by his crush, Antonio (Leonardo Pazzagli). One could argue that the film technically has two endings, one being Lorenzo's funeral and Blu's (Valentina Romani) voice-over recounting how things could have been different; and the other, a more hopeful yet unlikely fantasy, which transports the viewer back to the moments leading up to the ill-fated caress between Antonio and Lorenzo. In this alternative flashback ending, Antonio simply confesses that he is not ready for a same-sex relationship and Lorenzo easily accepts this confession. Although the film ends with shots of Antonio, Lorenzo and Blu giddily playing in the river and embracing each other, the fact that Blu passes by the fantasy-projected trio on her scooter, with tears streaming down her face, suggests that the funeral for Lorenzo is indeed the sad and bitter end to the film. Thus, in both films, the message is clear: same-sex desire and homoeroticism result only in death.

D. A. Miller reads the final image of Elio mourning by the fire as a type of social death, referring to him as 'a ghost' embodying what 'gay coming of age [...] still amounts to'.[37] However, as I would counter, by departing from the macabre and negative finale posed by death, *Call Me by Your Name* provides a hopeful outlook for a queer future of Italian teen film, moving beyond the inevitable death – social or physical – that has come to be expected in queer Italian films like *Né Giulietta né Romeo* and *Un bacio*. I thus agree with Tim Gray's statement that *Call Me by Your Name* is radical in subtle ways: whereas other LGBTQ films such as *Brokeback Mountain* (Ang Lee, 2005), *Carol* (Todd Haynes, 2015) or *Moonlight* (Barry Jenkins, 2016) also have positive depictions of gay or same-sex-oriented characters, they are all 'tortured by their urges' (and, I would add, in the case of *Brokeback Mountain*, even killed for them);[38] Elio, on the other hand, is not. He is not condemned by his parents or by his community but is instead encouraged by them, his same-sex desire validated and praised.

Elio's positive relationship with his father marks an exception in Italian teen film as the absence of the father and the son's attempts to reconcile with that absence has been a hallmark of the genre (and of Italian cinema more broadly). This is not the case in *Call Me by Your Name*, where Elio's father is not only present and supportive of his son's relationship with Oliver, but potentially even a bit jealous of him. On the one hand, the father's presence is attributable to the fantasy aspect of *Call Me by Your Name*, that is, he is a projection of the ideal father of a son struggling with homosexual desires. On the other hand, the father's being there for his son may be a consequence of his heritage, that is, he is not an Italian.[39] Even in spite of this, the fact that he is indeed there for his son remains significant, especially for future iterations of Italian teen film. The same is true of the film's positive representation of same-sex desire. While many Italian teen films insist on the centrality of male–male bonds, few, if any (at least to my knowledge), allow the homosocial to spill over into the homosexual but rather actively stave off the homoerotic threat. Tim Gray points out that this positive representation of same-sex desire and queerness alone makes *Call Me by Your Name* an important text for gay cinema; he concludes, however, that 'it's more universal than that' in that '[a]udiences of all sexual persuasions and ages are relating to the film's emotional honesty and heart'.[40] Although I agree with Gray's observation to some extent, I also recognize that the film's apparent universality has the potential to detract from its radicalness: the act of labelling the film a universal love story effectively normalizes its queer narrative, reappropriating it for a heterosexual audience, even though being queer is still not considered 'normal', particularly within Italy's heteronormative context. Indeed, it is precisely this universalism – which at times covers up the subtle resistance to chrononormativity that lurks beneath the film's surface – that has caused critics like Miz Cracker, cited above, to wonder whether the film is queer or not. As I have sought to demonstrate here, the film resides firmly within a queer space, one in which heterosexual and same-sex desires are able to be explored, and which privileges Elio's attraction to Oliver over that towards

Marzia. The film's positive depiction of same-sex desire, coupled with its refusal to be easily classified as only Italian or as only a teen film, opens up new avenues for future Italian teen films to explore the adolescent condition.

NOTES

1. As of 22 April 2024, the film holds the #1 spot of 'Users' most loved films' ['*I film più amati (dagli utenti)*'] on cinemagay.it, www.cinemagay.it/film/ordinaper/i-piu-amati/desc/.

2. Miz Cracker, 'Why Do Gays Keep Falling for *Call Me by Your Name?*', *Slate*, 28 November 2017, https://slate.com/human-interest/2017/11/call-me-by-your-name-is-not-a-gay-movie.html.

3. D. A. Miller, 'Elio's Education', *Los Angeles Review of Books*, 19 February 2018, https://www.lareviewofbooks.org/article/elios-education/.

4. See Ashley Lee, 'Why Luca Guadagnino Didn't Include Gay Actors or Explicit Sex Scenes in *Call Me by Your Name*: (Q&A)', *The Hollywood Reporter*, 8 February 2017, https://www.hollywoodreporter.com/news/general-news/call-me-by-your-name-why-luca-guadagnino-left-gay-actors-explicit-sex-scenes-q-a-973256/.

5. Tim Gray, '*Call Me by Your Name*: A Global Effort to Create a Simple, Well-Told Tale', *Variety*, 8 November 2017, variety.com/2017/film/awards/call-me-by-your-name-global-effort-1202607919/.

6. As we may recall, the dictionary sense of 'melodrama', to cite Thomas Elsaesser, refers to 'a dramatic narrative in which musical accompaniment marks […] emotional effects'. See Thomas Elsaesser, 'Tales of Sound and Fury: Observations on the Family Melodrama', in *Imitations of Life: A Reader on Film & Television Melodrama*, ed. Marcia Landy (Detroit: Wayne State University Press, 1991), 74. Inasmuch as I engage at length with *Call Me by Your Name*'s soundtrack and the ways in which it heightens the sentimentality of the film and contributes to the film's queer project, I find 'melodrama' a more suitable designation than 'drama'.

7. For more on queer Italian cinema, see Derek Duncan, 'The Queerness of Italian Cinema', *A Companion to Italian Cinema*, ed. Frank Burke (Chichester and Malden: John Wiley & Sons, 2017), 467–83; Derek Duncan, 'The Geopolitics of Spectatorship and Screen Identification: What's Queer About Italian Cinema?', *The Italianist* 33, no. 2 (2013): 256–261; Sergio Rigoletto, 'Against the Teleological Presumption: Notes on Queer Visibility in Contemporary Italian Film', *The Italianist* 37, no. 2 (2017): 212–27.

8. Queer characters in recent Italian Netflix Original programs *Suburra: Blood on Rome* (Michele Placido, Andrea Molaioli, Giuseppe Capotondi, Piero Messina and Arnaldo Catinari, 2017–20), *Baby* (Andrea De Sica, Anna Negri and Letizia Lamartire, 2018–20), and *SKAM Italia* (Ludovico Bessegato and Anita Rivaroli, 2018–present) have fared significantly better, which would suggest that the small screen and the Netflix platform may provide a shift away from the negative representations of Italian cinematic production. For

a more positive reading of queer characters in film, see also Dom Holdaway's 'The Queer Potential of Mainstream Film', in *Queering Italian Media*, edited by Sole Anatrone and Julia Heim (New York: Lexington Books, 2020), 75–96.

9. Michael Z. Newman, '*Everyday Italian*: Cultivating Taste', in *How to Watch Television*, ed. Ethan Thompson and Jason Mittell (New York: New York University Press, 2013), 332.

10. Newman, 332.

11. Newman, 333.

12. David Sims, 'The Sumptuous Love Story of *Call Me by Your Name*', *Atlantic*, 29 November 2017, https://www.theatlantic.com/entertainment/archive/2017/11/call-me-by-your-name-review/546872/.

13. For more on nation branding, see Melissa Aronczyk's *Branding the Nation: The Global Business of National Identity* (New York: Oxford University Press, 2013).

14. Steven Rawle, *Transnational Cinema: An Introduction* (London: Palgrave Macmillan, 2018), 2. See also Elizabeth Ezra and Terry Rowden's introduction to their co-edited volume *Transnational Cinema: The Film Reader* (London and New York: Routledge, 2006), 1–12, as well as Andrew Higson's entry in that volume, 'The Limiting Imagination of National Cinema', 15–25.

15. For more on the Italianicity of *Call Me by Your Name*, see Rosalind Galt and Karl Schoonover, 'Untimely Desires, Historical Efflorescence, and Italy in *Call Me by Your Name*', *Italian Culture* 37, no. 1 (March 2019): 64–81, https://doi.org/10.1080/016146 22.2019.1609220.

16. Catherine Driscoll, *Teen Film: A Critical Introduction* (Oxford and New York: Berg, 2011), 2.

17. Though it is impossible to know for certain whether Elio identifies as bisexual, this kind of sexuality is relatively rare in Italian cinematic production. While Dom Holdaway notes a dearth of trans, asexual, intersex and nonbinary characters in contemporary mainstream Italian films, bisexual characters seem equally rare within the peninsula's cinematic landscape. For more on this topic, see Dom Holdaway's 'The Queer Potential of Mainstream Film', in *Queering Italian Media*, edited by Sole Anatrone and Julia Heim (New York: Lexington Books, 2020), 75–96.

18. Elizabeth Freeman, *Time Binds: Queer Temporalities, Queer Histories* (Durham: Duke University Press, 2010), 3.

19. Judith Halberstam, *In a Queer Time and Place: Transgender Bodies, Subcultural Lives* (New York and London: New York University Press, 2005), 1.

20. For more on delay and 'too late' in melodrama, see Steve Neale, 'Melodrama and Tears', *Screen* 27, no. 6 (1986): 11.

21. John Adams, 'Hallelujah Junction – 1st Movement', track 1 on Various, *Call Me by Your Name: Original Motion Picture Soundtrack*, Madison Gate Records/Masterworks/Sony Music Entertainment, 2017.

22. John Adams, 'John Adams on "Hallelujah Junction"', Vimeo, 4 September 2015, vimeo.com/138363828.

23. Adams, 'On Hallelujah Junction', emphasis added.

24. Adams, 'On Hallelujah Junction', emphasis added.

25. John Adams, 'Hallelujah Junction', *Earbox – John Adams*, 2016–18, n.d., accessed 13 April 2023, www.earbox.com/hallelujah-junction-solo-piano/, emphasis added.

26. Andrew Lear, 'Ancient Pederasty: An Introduction', in *A Companion to Greek and Roman Sexualities*, ed. Thomas K. Hubbard (Chichester: Blackwell Publishing Ltd., 2014), 106.

27. Freeman, *Time Binds*, 3.

28. Gilad Padva, *Queer Nostalgia in Cinema and Pop Culture* (New York: Palgrave Macmillan, 2014), 4.

29. Padva, 7, original emphasis.

30. Pickering, Michael, and Emily Keightley. 'The Modalities of Nostalgia', *Current Sociology* 54, no. 6 (2006), 924.

31. Spencer Kornhaber notes that, through the father's heartfelt monologue, 'forbidden love is made okay, even encouraged'. See Spencer Kornhaber, 'The Shadow Over *Call Me by Your Name*', *Atlantic*, 3 January 2018, https://www.theatlantic.com/entertainment/archive/2018/01/the-shadow-over-call-me-by-your-name/549269/. Stephen Garrett likewise draws attention to how Elio's parents 'seem so effortlessly tolerant and open-minded as they shift between speaking French, Italian, and English'. See Garrett, 'Director Luca Guadagnino on Why *Call Me by Your Name* Is Making Everyone Cry.' *Observer*, 13 October 2017. https://observer.com/2017/10/interview-lucaguadagnino-on-why-call-me-by-your-name-makes-people-cry/.

32. Peter Debruge, 'Film Review: *Call Me by Your Name*', *Variety*, 23 January 2017, https://variety.com/2017/film/reviews/call-me-by-your-name-review-1201966646.

33. The brutal murder of openly gay Italian film director Pier Paolo Pasolini, which occurred in 1975 (only a few years prior to the film's 1983 setting), comes to mind as an instance of the strictness of Italian heteronormativity. Though there is much speculation surrounding the motive for his murder, the fact that he was found with his testicles crushed would suggest his sexuality was targeted.

34. Andre-Naquian Wheeler, 'The *Call Me by Your Name* Soundtrack Is Its Own Queer Love Story', *i-D*, 18 December 2017, https://i-d.vice.com/en_uk/article/9knwzv/the-call-me-by-your-name-soundtrack-is-its-own-queer-love-story.

35. At the time of writing, the sequel to *Call Me by Your Name* has yet to enter production, but rumours suggest that Elio and Oliver won't get back together but instead pursue or remain in heterosexual relationships.

36. For an in-depth study of this concept, see Lee Edelman, *No Future: Queer Theory and the Death Drive* (Durham: Duke University Press, 2004).

37. Miller, 'Elio's Education'.

38. See Gray, '*Call Me*'.

39. For more on the figure of the (absent) father in Italian teen film, see Daniel Paul, 'Marking Their Territory: Male Adolescence Abroad in Recent Italian Teen Film', *California Italian Studies* 7, no. 1 (2017): 1–18.

40. Gray, '*Call Me*'.

REFERENCES

Adams, John. 'Hallelujah Junction – 1st Movement.' Various, *Call Me by Your Name: Original Motion Picture Soundtrack*, track 1. Madison Gate Records/Masterworks/Sony Music Entertainment, 2017.

Adams, John. 'Hallelujah Junction.' *Earbox – John Adams*, 2016–2018, n.d. Accessed 13 April 2023. www.earbox.com/hallelujah-junction-solo-piano/.

Aronczyk, Melissa. *Branding the Nation: The Global Business of National Identity*. New York: Oxford University Press, 2013.

Bessegato, Ludovico, and Ludovico Di Martino, dir. *SKAM Italia* (TV). TIMvision and Cross Productions, 2018–present.

cinemagay.it. '*I film più amati (dagli utenti)*.' Accessed 13 April 2023. www.cinemagay.it/film/ordinaper/i-piu-amati/desc/.

Cotroneo, Ivan, dir. *Un bacio* (*One Kiss*). Indigo Films, Titanus, Lucky Red, 2016.

De Sica, Andrea, Anna Negri and Letizia Lamartire, dir. *Baby* (TV). Fabula Pictures, 2018–2020.

Debruge, Peter. 'Film Review: *Call Me by Your Name*.' *Variety*, 23 January 2017. https://variety.com/2017/film/reviews/call-me-by-your-name-review-1201966646.

Driscoll, Catherine. *Teen Film: A Critical Introduction*. Oxford and New York: Berg, 2011.

Duncan, Derek. 'The Geopolitics of Spectatorship and Screen Identification: What's Queer About Italian Cinema?' *The Italianist* 33, no. 2 (2013): 256–61.

Duncan, Derek. 'The Queerness of Italian Cinema.' In *A Companion to Italian Cinema*, edited by Frank Burke, 467–83. Chichester and Malden: John Wiley & Sons, 2017.

Edelman, Lee. *No Future: Queer Theory and the Death Drive*. Durham: Duke University Press, 2004.

Elsaesser, Thomas. 'Tales of Sound and Fury: Observations on the Family Melodrama.' In *Imitations of Life: A Reader on Film & Television Melodrama*, edited by Marcia Landy, 68–91. Detroit: Wayne State University Press, 1991.

Ezra, Elizabeth, and Terry Rowden. 'General Introduction: What Is Transnational Cinema?' In *Transnational Cinema: The Film Reader*, edited by Elizabeth Ezra and Terry Rowden, 1–12. London and New York: Routledge, 2006.

Freeman, Elizabeth. *Time Binds: Queer Temporalities, Queer Histories*. Durham: Duke University Press, 2010.

Garrett, Stephen. 'Director Luca Guadagnino on *Why Call Me by Your Name* Is Making Everyone Cry.' *Observer*, 13 October 2017. https://observer.com/2017/10/interview-luca-guadagnino-on-why-call-me-by-your-name-makes-people-cry/.

Gray, Tim. '*Call Me by Your Name*: A Global Effort to Create a Simple, Well-Told Tale.' *Variety*, 8 November 2017. variety.com/2017/film/awards/call-me-by-your-name-global-effort-1202607919/.

Guadagnino, Luca, dir. *Call Me by Your Name*. Frenesy Film Company, La Cinefacture, RT Features, 2017.

Halberstam, Judith. *In a Queer Time and Place: Transgender Bodies, Subcultural Lives*. New York and London: New York University Press, 2005.

Haynes, Todd, dir. *Carol*. Film 4 Productions, Number 9 Films, Killer Films, 2015.

Higson, Andrew. 'The Limiting Imagination of National Cinema.' In *Transnational Cinema: The Film Reader*, edited by Elizabeth Ezra and Terry Rowden, 15–25. London and New York: Routledge, 2006.

Holdaway, Dom. 'The Queer Potential of Mainstream Film.' In *Queering Italian Media*, edited by Sole Anatrone and Julia Heim, 75–96. New York: Lexington Books, 2020.

Jenkins, Barry, dir. *Moonlight*. A24, PASTEL, Plan B Entertainment, 2016.

Kornhaber, Spencer. 'The Shadow Over *Call Me by Your Name*.' *Atlantic*, 3 January 2018. https://www.theatlantic.com/entertainment/archive/2018/01/the-shadow-over-call-me-by-your-name/549269/.

Lear, Andrew. 'Ancient Pederasty: An Introduction.' In *A Companion to Greek and Roman Sexualities*, edited by Thomas K. Hubbard, 106–30. Chichester: Blackwell Publishing Ltd, 2014.

Lee, Ang, dir. *Brokeback Mountain*. River Road Entertainment, Focus Features, 2005.

Lee, Ashley. 'Why Luca Guadagnino Didn't Include Gay Actors or Explicit Sex Scenes in *Call Me by Your Name* (Q&A).' *The Hollywood Reporter*, 8 February 2017. https://www.hollywoodreporter.com/news/general-news/call-me-by-your-name-why-luca-guadagnino-left-gay-actors-explicit-sex-scenes-q-a-973256/.

Miller, D. A. 'Elio's Education.' *Los Angeles Review of Books*, 19 February 2018. https://www.lareviewofbooks.org/article/elios-education/.

Miz Cracker. 'Why Do Gays Keep Falling for *Call Me by Your Name*?' *Slate*, 28 November 2017. https://slate.com/human-interest/2017/11/call-me-by-your-name-is-not-a-gay-movie.html.

Neale, Steve. 'Melodrama and Tears.' *Screen* 27, no. 6 (1986): 6–23.

Newman, Michael Z. '*Everyday Italian*: Cultivating Taste.' In *How to Watch Television*, edited by Ethan Thompson and Jason Mittell, 330–37. New York: New York University Press, 2013.

Özpetek, Ferzan, dir. *Saturno contro* (*Saturn in Opposition*). Medusa Emotion Pictures, R&C Produzioni, Faros Film, UGCYM, AFS Film – Istanbul, 2007.

Padva, Gilad. *Queer Nostalgia in Cinema and Pop Culture*. New York: Palgrave Macmillan, 2014.

Paul, Daniel. 'Marking Their Territory: Male Adolescence Abroad in Recent Italian Teen Film.' *California Italian Studies* 7, no. 1 (2017): 1–18.

Pickering, Michael, and Emily Keightley. 'The Modalities of Nostalgia.' *Current Sociology* 54, no. 6 (2006): 919–41.

Pivetti, Veronica, dir. *Né Giulietta né Romeo* (*A Little Lust*). Pigra s.r.l., 2015.

Placido, Michele, Andrea Molaioli, Giuseppe Capotondi, Piero Messina and Arnaldo Catinari, dir. *Suburra: Blood on Rome* (TV). Cattleya, Rai Fiction, Bartleby Film, 2017–2020.

Rawle, Steven. *Transnational Cinema: An Introduction*. London: Palgrave Macmillan, 2018.

Rigoletto, Sergio. 'Against the Teleological Presumption: Notes on Queer Visibility in Contemporary Italian Film.' *The Italianist* 37, no. 2 (2017): 212–27.

Sims, David. 'The Sumptuous Love Story of *Call Me by Your Name*.' *Atlantic*, 29 November 2017. https://www.theatlantic.com/entertainment/archive/2017/11/call-me-by-your-name-review/546872/.

Stambrini, Monica, dir. *Benzina* (*Gasoline*). Digital Film, Ministero per i Beni e le Attività Culturali, 2001.

Stevens, Sufjan. 'Visions of Gideon.' In Various, *Call Me by Your Name: Original Motion Picture Soundtrack*. Madison Gate Records/Masterworks/Sony Music Entertainment, 2017.

Wheeler, André-Naquian. 'The *Call Me by Your Name* Soundtrack Is Its Own Queer Love Story.' *i-D*, 18 December 2017, i-d.vice.com/en_au/article/9knwzv/the-call-me-by-your-name-soundtrack-is-its-own-queer-love-story.

8

Plato to Elio:
Ancient and Modern Sexualities
in *Call Me by Your Name*

Nikolai Endres

Like many gay texts of the past (*The Picture of Dorian Gray, Death in Venice, Maurice*, the novels of Mary Renault and Gore Vidal ...),[1] *Call Me by Your Name* evokes classical antiquity. The love story between 17-year-old Elio (Timothée Chalamet) and 24-year-old Oliver (Armie Hammer) seems to follow the pederastic paradigm, the Platonic relationship between *erastes* (lover) and *eromenos* (beloved). However, director Luca Guadagnino greatly complicates this matter. As a (graduate) *student*, Oliver reluctantly fits the *erastes*, and Elio, impossibly precocious, seems to need little instruction. Yet there is one aspect that Elio learns profoundly, *ta erotika*, the arts of love. *Call Me by Your Name* retells Plato's *Phaedrus* (rather than the *Symposium*, a dinner party at which the guests sing the praises of Eros, the God of Love), which engages with questions of love, sex, the good life, and erotic reciprocity – the prevalent romantic model for our time. Moreover, because of its setting in Italy, *Call Me by Your Name* also recalls Roman sexualities, extensions of Platonic love that hit much closer to present-day notions of queer identities. Studying ancient sexualities thus helps understand that the film should not be dismissed (as some critics have done) for its relationship between a teenager and an adult and for the issue of (consensual) sex. *Call Me by Your Name* asks a simple yet in cinematic history almost unprecedented question: how to negotiate a meaningful (albeit brief) erotic relationship between two men? Because the question is so momentous, the text cannot but turn to ancient models. By evoking Plato, Sappho, Heraclitus, the Star of David, ancient Rome ..., *Call Me by Your Name* offers an erotic palimpsest that merges ancient and modern sexualities into something exciting and relevant. What started in 1983, somewhere in northern Italy, takes us from Plato to Elio.

Paiderastia *and the peach*

On 10 September 2017, actor James Woods retweeted a post that read '24-year-old man. 17-year-old boy. Stop', adding the hashtag '#NAMBLA'.[2] The tweet thus paired *Call Me by Your Name*'s 17-year-old Elio and 24-year-old Oliver with the North American Man/Boy Love Association, which on its website lists the following mission: 'NAMBLA's goal is to end the extreme oppression of men and boys in mutually consensual relationships'. NAMBLA later explains man/boy love by quoting Oscar Wilde's famous speech in court:

> The 'Love that dare not speak its name' in this century is such a great affection of an elder for a younger man as there was between David and Jonathan, such as Plato made the very basis of his philosophy, and such as you find in the sonnets of Michelangelo and Shakespeare. It is that deep, spiritual affection that is as pure as it is perfect. It dictates and pervades great works of art like those of Shakespeare and Michelangelo.[3]

Wilde is alluding here to Greek *paiderastia* (which is best left untranslated, for 'pederasty' is such a loaded term),[4] the relationship between an older man, *erastes*, and a younger man, *eromenos*. (Just how young the *eromenos* was remains contested, but we know that Greek girls got married as early as age 14, when they were able to conceive; the most probable range for the *eromenos* is thus from 14 to 20 – the *terminus ante quem* being the growth of a beard – while the *erastes* normally was between 20 and 30 years old.) What brought them together? The *erastes* taught the *eromenos* about politics, civics, warfare, philosophy and much more. Just as Wilde evoked literary ancestors of *paiderastia* (Plato, Michelangelo, Shakespeare), so the *erastes* would have talked about Zeus and Ganymede, Achilles and Patroclus, Harmodius and Aristogeiton and other famous homoerotic pairs. In return, the *eromenos* would grant his teacher erotic favors, ranging from kisses to sexual passivity.[5]

What is the role of *paiderastia* in the movie? Elio and Oliver retain their age, but by casting 20-year-old Timothée Chalamet and 29-year-old Armie Hammer, Luca Guadagnino seems to offer a more 'acceptable' couple age-wise. However, the age gap is thus nine years rather than seven, and as was widely pointed out, Hammer seems miscast as a 24-year-old, looking much older, while Chalamet could pass for younger. Jeffrey Bloomer in *Slate* remarks: 'In the book, one has the sense that while Oliver carries a sort of broad-shouldered "American" manliness compared with Elio, the two are not in such wildly different ZIP codes physically. The film exaggerates that difference.'[6] In the movie, in an early scene, we see Elio shaving some almost non-existent stubble, while his chest remains smooth and armpits virtually hairless. (Oliver, of course, is more hirsute, which not only recalls the prevalence of beards in Greek society but also seems suitable for the '80s, when men had more hair.) Later, Elio's father (Michael Stuhlbarg) recalls a famous pederastic couple, Hadrian and Antinous (Antinous died young, drowning in the Nile), and Benjamin Eldon Stevens, in a pioneering blog, exhaustively studies all the other pederastic allusions in *Call Me by Your Name*.[7] However, I argue that *paiderastia* plays much less of a role. (It will be instructive to compare novel and film throughout.)

Elio, even at the tender age of 17 years, hardly fits the bill of *eromenos*. Just on the first pages of the book, he blows the reader away with Haydn, Carlo Levi, Liszt, Busoni, Bach, Heraclitus and *Tristan* (without Isolde). He speaks English, French, Hebrew, German, Ancient Greek, Italian (both the standard Florentine and the Roman and Neapolitan dialects) and probably other languages. What could Oliver possibly teach him? In the movie (which somewhat tempers Elio's precocity), after Elio enlightens Oliver about the Battle of Piave, an exasperated Oliver enquires: 'Is there anything you don't know?' The movie thus does well presenting Oliver as a graduate student, for in the novel, he seems impossibly accomplished: Harvard undergraduate, Columbia PhD, having already written a book, that is already being translated into Italian, that by Christmas has already been published in England, Germany and France – all that at age 24. Another problem is the story itself, narrated by Elio, for an *eromenos* rarely had a voice, was supposed to remain passively receptive to the *erastes*' instruction. Most crucially, according to ancient sexuality, the *eromenos* was not supposed to be attracted to his teacher, was expected to feel *philia*/friendship rather than *eros*/love (which was the *erastes*' prerogative).[8] Showing Elio masturbating or grabbing Oliver's member in a beautiful meadow, the movie powerfully undermines such ancient notions. In fact, may I proclaim a heresy here (with apologies to Chalamet)? Elio isn't particularly beautiful, or at least he has nothing in common with the Greek statues displayed early on: no definition, no muscles (he prefers to watch rather than practice sports, as we see in the volleyball game), no chiselled face; he simply does not meet the (idealized) expectations of beauty so valued in Greek *paiderastia*.[9]

However, there *is* something Oliver teaches Elio, *ta erotika*, the arts of love. In response to Oliver's question earlier about the Battle of Piave, Elio says: 'I know nothing, Oliver'. As any Socratic dialogue makes clear, an admission of ignorance is the prerequisite for knowledge. Whatever homoerotic feelings Elio may have had in the past, he has a homophobic streak, as he reveals with the gay couple Isaac and Mounir. Elio greets them by kissing Marzia (Esther Garrel), and her dishevelled hair and hastily put-on dress give Isaac and Mounir a good idea of post-orgasmic heterosexual bliss; having donned the flowery shirt they gave him as a gift, Elio puts on an uncharacteristic flamboyancy (one hopes he is not trying to 'act gay');

behind their back, he calls them 'Sonny and Cher'. His father duly chides him, 'You're too old not to accept people for who they are' (although Papa has his own homophobic hang-ups, admitting that they're 'ridiculous'). Elio needs to learn *ta erotika. Call Me by Your Name* therefore conjures up a celebrated text in the history of sexuality, Plato's *Phaedrus*.

The *Phaedrus* tells the story of a happy summer day. Sparkling (that is how the title translates) with erotic energy, its setting is unusual: outside the city in a *locus amoenus*, where amorous Pan has a sacred shrine, in the heat of the day. Accompanied by his young friend Phaedrus, Socrates is on vacation from philosophy because nature, unlike human beings, normally cannot teach him anything. They are barefoot, in touch with the soil on which they are treading (rather than Socrates' usual ethereal speculations that point heavenward). Phaedrus suggests that they lie down in the grass, and Socrates agrees:

> Feel the freshness of the air; how pretty and pleasant it is; how it echoes with the sweet song of the cicadas' chorus! The most exquisite thing of all, of course, is the grassy slope: it rises so gently that you can rest your head perfectly when you lie down on it. You've really been the most marvelous guide, my dear Phaedrus.[10]

Later, Socrates asks Phaedrus: 'Where, then, is the boy to whom I was speaking?' Phaedrus replies: 'He is here, always right by your side, whenever you want him'.[11] The iridescent sun, fragrant budding trees, chirping cicadas, bodies covered with sweat yet barely clothed, next to the moisture of a flowing stream – this is where Socrates teaches Phaedrus *ta erotika*.

And he teaches Phaedrus something quite unheard of. In his allegory of the charioteer, an account of the soul driven by a charioteer and two horses, Socrates describes the lover in the presence of his beloved:

> After the lover has spent some time doing this, staying near the boy [...], then the spring that feeds the stream Zeus named 'Desire' when he was in love with Ganymede begins to flow mightily in the lover and is partly absorbed by him, and when he is filled it overflows and runs away outside him. Think how a breeze or an echo bounces back from a smooth solid object to its source; that is how the stream of beauty goes back to the beautiful boy and sets him aflutter. It enters through his eyes, which are its natural route to the soul; there it waters the passages for the wings, starts the wings growing, and fills the soul of the loved one with love in return. Then the boy is in love, but has no idea what he loves. He does not understand, and cannot explain, what has happened to him. It is as if he had caught an eye disease from someone else, but could not identify the cause; he does not realize that he is seeing himself in the lover as in a mirror.[12]

The *eromenos* is in love, feels *eros*! The sexual flow between the two lovers echoes the transfer of knowledge from the *erastes* to the *eromenos*, but here the flow seems to be going astray, for the particles stream in both directions. According to the *Phaedrus* and unlike in *paiderastia*, love is now reciprocated as *anteros* or 'counter-love'. The beloved responds to his lover with a mirror-image, *eidolon*, of love (dare we say they call each other by their names?) When the charioteer sees his *eromenos*, he overflows with such joy that he seems to be ejaculating: 'the whole soul throbs and palpitates [...] it is moistened and warmed'.[13] Is this still Plato, who gives us the idea of 'Platonic'/asexual love (obviously quite a misnomer)? True, to give in to sexual desire is never ideal for Plato, but it need not be too bad:

> If [...] they live a life less noble and without philosophy, but yet ruled by the love of honour, probably, when they have been drinking, or in some other moment of carelessness, the two unruly horses, taking the souls off their guard, will bring them together and seize upon and accomplish that which is by the many accounted blissful.[14]

In a striking departure from his proverbial distrust of the body, Socrates contends that these lovers will attain blessedness as well, that sex can be a happy choice. According to Socrates, the couple in the *Phaedrus* is in love with each other and they (occasionally) 'accomplish that which is by the many accounted blissful'.[15]

It is this fundamental erotic reciprocity that critics of the relationship seem to have missed. Emily Rutherford, in 'Dare to Speak Its Name: Pederasty in the Classical Tropes of *Call Me by Your Name*', issues a caveat:

> James Ivory's and Luca Guadagnino's efforts to translate André Aciman's novel to the screen are steeped in a set of tropes about elite male homoeroticism whose entire point is the seduction of the adolescent *pais kalos* [beautiful boy]. So go to see the film, marvel at its luscious beauty, and maybe along the way ask yourself some questions about how it is that, in the course of our present public conversation about gender, sexuality, and the rich and famous, *this* film has been nominated for a Best Picture Oscar.[16]

I hope to address some of those questions below. Steven D. Greydanus, who as a Christian advocate is admittedly more hostile to a gay relationship, glosses over all the intricacies of Platonic *eros* that I just tried to point out:

> From a Catholic perspective – but also in the best philosophical and literary traditions of the classical world [sic] – human sexuality is ordered toward union with the other: sexual union with the sexually other. The goods of both friendship and eros present in same-sex relationships are stunted and distorted by sexual acts where no true union of two in one flesh is possible.[17]

Renee Sorrentino and Jack Turban, in '*Call Me by Your Name*: Not Pedophilia, Still Problematic', contend: 'The power disparity in the relationship is clear. Elio is fragile and sexually naive. Oliver is experienced and directive in the relationship.'[18] Yes, Oliver is attracted to Elio, and he makes a first move by massaging his shoulders, but when he senses that Elio is uncomfortable, he stops. They continue: 'One could argue that Oliver grooms Elio by moving into the household, spending time with him, endearing trust before advancing to a sexual relationship that is secretive. Elio's parents are portrayed as supportive of the relationship.'[19] How can the relationship be secretive if Elio's parents are aware of it (how else could they be 'supportive'?)? And just the idea that Oliver visited the Perlmans in order to 'groom' their son defies reason.

I need to mention that Aciman, unlike Guadagnino, acknowledges the issue of consent more directly, but he characteristically does so in the context of ancient rather than modern sexualities: Elio recalling the many rape stories in Ovid.[20] Discussing the peach scene in the movie, Rutherford opines: 'Oliver and Elio's affair exists in a world in which rape can be translated into something sexy, something pornographic'.[21] She continues: 'Elio's reaction to Oliver's attentions is mostly thrilled and anxious silence – he never verbally expresses consent'.[22] First of all, Rutherford makes an error here. Elio, responding to Oliver's request in the bedroom to kiss him, says 'Yes, please' – clearly consenting. Second, is it appropriate to apply a #MeToo lens to a text set in the '80s? (As has been rehashed ad absurdum, in Italy the age of consent was and is fourteen – and it is at precisely that age that Elio, in the novel, is sexually propositioned by a 'young man' in Rome, followed at age fifteen by Maynard, one of Oliver's predecessors.)[23] Is it not Victorian to expect something like 'Reader [or Viewer], I consented'? In fact, Ovid works on a different level as well. Considering the Narcissus/Echo myth, Zachary J. Gianelle notes that 'the anagrammatic relationship of the names "Elio" and "Oliver" (O-L-I-V-E-R) emphasizes the interchangeable roles of the two central characters'.[24] *Call Me by Your Name* thus turns one of the most famous myths of one-sided love into a consensual and meaningful relationship. True, Guadagnino never references Ovid explicitly, but he does feature a homoerotic couple from antiquity. Sufjan Stevens' soundtrack 'Mystery of Love' singles out Alexander and Hephaestion. Alexander and Hephaestion are famous for reciprocal rather than pederastic *eros*. Oliver Stone's heterosexualization/ bisexualization of the Macedonian warrior in his *Alexander* of 2004 notwithstanding, Mary Renault, in *Fire from Heaven*[25] and *The Persian Boy*, offers one of the queerest modern portraits; drawing on the historian Diodorus, when the captured Persian Queen Sisygambis made obeisance to Hephaestion, mistaking him for the king, Alexander famously replied: 'Never mind, mother, you weren't far out; he is Alexander too'.[26] Alexander and Hephaestion echo each other, so to speak.

According to Guadagnino, at the heart of the film is something very Platonic and ancient, the 'transmission of knowledge'. He elaborates: 'I like the idea that the other changes you – and that there is no boundary; the power and the beauty of change coming from meeting another'. This sounds very different from Sorrentino and Turban's problematic power dynamics, who fail to pick up even on the title *Call Me by Your Name*. Guadagnino finishes: 'In the movie, everything that you believe, you get the privilege to pass to the other'.[27] It shows. On their final night together in Bergamo, as Joanna Di Mattia perceptively observes,

> In a darkened corner of the city, [Elio and Oliver] share a passionate kiss and embrace. As he does when Elio and Oliver kiss prior to first sleeping together, Guadagnino momentarily pulls the shot out of focus, which has the extraordinary effect of blurring their bodies into one.[28]

This makes a lot more sense than this:

> Without Elio's express consent given through his own narration of the events, the film's final scene in Rome [*sic*] looks disturbingly like a man taking advantage of a drunk teenager in the streets late at night, as the youth's perceptions blur into a haze.[29]

A compromise is needed, and Jeffrey Bloomer puts it best:

> In my view, it's reasonable to be disturbed by the unconventional relationship in *Call Me by Your Name*, but it's not reasonable to say the movie endorses pedophilia, or really any kind of power-based abuse, just because it depicts that relationship. If we go down that censorious and unnuanced path with our art, very little will survive the trip.[30]

Alas, the summer of love ends soon enough, and Oliver gets the privilege to pass everything that he believes to someone else, his wife. Why does Oliver get married? He cryptically refers to his father carting him off 'to a correctional facility', alluding to the horrific practice of conversion therapy that is now widely discredited but was certainly practiced in the '80s and later (as recently depicted in Kerstin Karlhuber's *Fair Haven* of 2016 and Joel Edgerton's *Boy Erased* of 2018). However, he is a graduate student of classics, a field that has long acknowledged (though not always approved of) Greek and Roman same-sex desire, home in New York or New England, and middle-class (with money to spare for poker games). Unmarried, he could have lived discreetly in the ivory tower of academia (and as the *wunderkind* that he is, he might have been granted even more licence). It is therefore difficult to imagine a more sympathetic environment.[31] Now in terms of ancient sexualities, his choice makes perfect sense. Pederastic relationships were temporary, the *eromenos* becoming an *erastes* once he had mastered his instruction and eventually getting married. However, this continuum from *eromenos* to *erastes* to husband clearly fails to satisfy in the twenty-first century (plus there is no evidence of Oliver ever having been an *eromenos*) – and it even fails to satisfy the terms of the *Phaedrus*. Unlike the *Symposium*, which mostly affirms the pederastic paradigm, the *Phaedrus* gestures towards modern notions of love and sex.[32] Even if we assume Oliver is bisexual, his marriage remains an erotic riddle (to be solved in a sequel?).

As I hope to have shown, when we turn to ancient sexualities, *Call Me by Your Name* cannot be reduced to *paiderastia*. Arguably, it manifests itself at the end: Elio's 'talk' with his father. The *erastes* is often cast in the role of a father figure (and Socrates is the perfect example for a *paiderastia* that always includes instruction but need not involve sex). 'You two had a nice friendship. [...] He was good, and you were both lucky to have found each other, because you too are good.' Yet even among such beautiful discourse, Elio is ready to deny the beautiful friendship he had (with a lame 'yeah'). The father gently prods on, admitting that he himself had once been in love with another man but too afraid to act on his feelings. Instead, he now offers himself as the conveyor of *ta erotika* to his son: 'We may never speak about this again. But I hope you'll never hold it against me that we did. I will have been a terrible father if, one day, you'd want to speak to me and felt that the door was shut or not sufficiently open.' Despite the almost universal praise of this scene – 'It's a beautiful declaration and one that engenders deeply emotional reactions from the audience'[33] – with the father's admission that he is to some extent in the closet (and also seems to have a crush on Oliver, from the way he jumps up and down the bus when Oliver departs for Bergamo to the way he reacts to Oliver's wedding announcement, at first theatrical, then sad) and never told his wife, we now learn that the happiest relationship presented in *Call Me by Your Name* seems to have been a gay one all along: Isaac and Mounir. It is a shame that they have received little attention, for Guadagnino does a wonderful job of bringing out their loving complementarity through clothing, facial expressions, and gesture; what seems to have been noticed even less is that they are played by co-producer Peter Spears and André Aciman himself. Elio would have done well to get to know them better.

D. A. Miller, in a scathing review, after admitting that Elio's parents are sympathetic – 'most parents in their place would be too busy worrying about an older man "preying" on their son to recognize the fact that their Tadzio might be the one cruising him' (although the *Death in Venice* comparison is singularly misguided here, for Elio is three years older than his Polish counterpart and Oliver decades younger than Gustav von Aschenbach) – finds the speech 'repulsive':

[I]t seeks to drive away every possible understanding that might make the relation with Oliver a serious *sexual* experience for Elio – and thus also make it that significant *social* experience we call 'coming of age'. The father's knowingness (capped with this masterful finishing touch: 'Have I spoken out of turn?') leaves no breathing room for the son's self-knowledge.[34]

I agree that this scene is not unproblematic but read it very differently: the father is acknowledging his son's sexuality (whatever it is exactly, but that's the point) but also preparing Elio for various significant social experiences: the heartbreak of being gay in the '80s, notably the devastation of AIDS, Ronald Reagan, and what B. Ruby Rich has referred to in *New Queer Cinema* as 'a new conservative Christian version of the Republican Party devoid of compassion, moral compass, or love of New York, queers, or the arts';[35] the problematics of bisexuality (is Marzia really out of the picture?); Oliver's eventual marriage (it should be recalled that Oliver's primary purpose of the visit is to help Professor Perlman, so they would have spent a lot of time together, and Oliver may well have mentioned his girlfriend back in the States, although one wonders whether he would have admitted to cheating on her; moreover, when Oliver calls for Hanukkah with 'news', Elio already knows what it is about); and, foremost, the uniqueness of their love. As an example of pederastic instruction, this speech encompasses a moral universe that goes well beyond sex.

And that brings us to the peach, that hilarious emoji on Grindr and other gay dating sites for the behind. Plato, of course, would have never engaged in such juicy pleasures, but Aciman and Guadagnino are paying homage to that other queer icon from classical antiquity, Sappho, whose poetry is permeated by lushness. *Melon*, conventionally translated as 'apple', really connotes 'fleshy fruit – apricots, peaches, apples, citron, quinces, pomegranates'.[36] It would have been difficult for Elio to do what he did with an apple, but it is the fleshy fruit's sensitivity that matters. Elio is fantasizing about Oliver inside him by penetrating a substance that offers little resistance, that accommodates his desire wholly, that leaves him covered in sweet pulp – filmed in a scene drenched in sunlight. It is the apricock, a cock to be sure, but going along with playful etymology, it also involves the act of opening (Italian *aprire* or *aprirsi*) in all its meanings. Unlike the crudeness of carrots or cucumbers (or Grindr's eggplants), Sappho's peaches show the tender moments of ancient sexualities, where phallic hardness yields to something more feminine, more gentle, more queer. Guadagnino has mused that his film 'is about the mother within the father', which he defines as 'an element of femininity that is so fecund, so powerful and so full of the capacity of fertilisation that it is within each of us'.[37] Dare we call Oliver ingesting the peach with Elio's semen a transmission of knowledge (note the reversed flow, from younger to older), a moment of Platonic spiritual begetting, a fertilization of a relationship that in the '80s would have been widely viewed as 'sterile' (Figure 8.1)?

FIGURE 8.1: Oliver (Armie Hammer) contemplates Elio's (Timothée Chalamet) peach. Luca Guadagnino (dir.), *Call Me by Your Name*, 2017. Italy/France/USA/Brazil. © Frenesy, La Cinefacture.

From Athens to AIDS

The movie opens with a collection of postcards: ancient statuary, classical masks, drinking vessels and urns, reinforced by the later excavation of a severed arm and a torso with a head out of a lake, followed at midpoint by a slide show of 'sensual' statues sculpted under the influence of Praxiteles and of 'ageless ambiguity'. As Molly Haskell notes:

> The atmosphere is pagan, the time not just BCE but BCP – Before Cell Phones. Oliver appears rather like a deus ex machina (almost literally: climbing out of a car, blond head rising and rising some more), an Adonis who moves as if by divine right among the French-Italian admirers.[38]

Alas, as pagan literature makes clear, Adonis, beloved by Venus, dies young. Time is not on Elio and Oliver's side, and this is nowhere clearer than in the subject of Oliver's book: Heraclitus. This pre-Socratic philosopher survives in fragments and is remembered in the popular imagination for his dictum that one cannot step into the same river twice. From Socrates to Shakespeare, from John Donne to Dorian Gray, time's winged chariot inexorably bears down on the lovers. But why would a 17-year-old (or even a 24-year-old) worry about time? Why this nostalgia? As we saw, time is always an issue in *paiderastia*, for there comes a moment when the *eromenos* graduates to *erastes* and then to husband. In terms of ancient sexualities, the *Phaedrus* offers a solution to this issue, but in modern times, in the '80s, a new threat to time arose.

The movie starts in 1983, not as a flashback two decades later (as in the novel), and thus diminishes Elio's backward gaze (although I think the director is alluding to it in the painful and seemingly endless scene of Elio gazing into the fireplace at the end), but the greatest moment of nostalgia is probably something that is never mentioned, a summer of making love with impunity: AIDS. It cannot have been for lack of knowledge. On 3 July 1981, Oliver, presumably a reader of his current city's newspaper (since he purchases its international edition abroad, the *Herald Tribune*), would have come across the now famous headline in the *New York Times*: 'Rare Cancer Seen in 41 Homosexuals'.[39] Shortly afterwards, the Gay Men's Health Crisis was founded by Larry Kramer, Edmund White and others. In 1982, the Centers for Disease Control established the term AIDS, replacing the former 'gay-related immune deficiency' or GRID. On 14 March 1983, Kramer published '1,121 and Counting' in the *New York Native*, attacking the government and the pharmaceutical industry for ignoring the crisis affecting the gay community.[40] (In 1987, he would found ACT UP.) Oliver might have even heard of (or been to) the first major AIDS fundraiser on 30 April 1983, a benefit performance of the Ringling Bros. and Barnum & Bailey Circus. On 3 May, the Kaposi's Sarcoma Foundation held the first AIDS Candlelight Vigil in New York (and San Francisco), whose poignant images went around the world. On 25 May, the *New York Times* published its first front-page story on AIDS, 'Health Chief Calls AIDS Battle "No. 1 Priority"'.[41] By then, 1,450 cases of AIDS had been reported and 558 individuals had died.

A couple of weeks later, Oliver packed his bags and flew to Italy. (The exact date is unknown but probably late June to early August, from the general election of 23 June to the beginning of the premiership of Bettino Craxi on 4 August that Annella [Amira Casar] and her friends talk about.) It seems that not only does Elio not use condoms for sex with Oliver (even in the novel, the 'tactful health question' remains elusive),[42] but Guadagnino actually turns back time, the camera shifting from 1983 to a poster of the 24h car race in Le Mans in 1982 to a crude drawing with the year 1981 to the fade of the timelessness of an ancient tree, pre-AIDS. However, *Call Me by Your Name* is nostalgic, not escapist. The monument to the First World War, as Pamela Hutchinson points out, recalls the mass extermination of people of Elio and Oliver's age,[43] as do images of flies (short-lived creatures), blood, infection or Elio's Keith Haring-like T-shirts.[44] AIDS hangs in the air, but it doesn't quite intrude.

A Merchant Ivory movie?

I would like to elaborate a bit on nostalgia. *Call Me by Your Name* comes with a certain baggage. James Ivory, formerly the business and erotic partner of Ismail Merchant until Merchant's demise in 2005, wrote the script and co-produced the movie. Merchant Ivory movies have a reputation as period pieces – and therefore 'conservative', maybe even 'politically incorrect'. However, in *Heritage Film Audiences: Period Films and Contemporary Audiences in the UK*, Claire Monk clarifies this assumption. While Merchant Ivory films may emphasize tropes of a golden past and upper-class privilege, their viewers rarely share those traits:

> [T]he real audiences who enjoyed 'heritage films' and other 'quality' period films were more diverse – demographically, culturally, politically and in their broader film tastes – than the narrow, bourgeois, 'older' heritage audience projected in the founding critiques of heritage cinema and some sections of the media.[45]

How about *Call Me by Your Name* and its depiction of sexuality? (Claire Monk's chapter in this collection says more on Merchant Ivory in relation to *Call Me by Your Name*.)

When we look at audience reactions[46] to the two most contentious aspects of the movie, an equally complex picture emerges. On the one hand, there is Elio's age, but whatever one thinks of it, one cannot describe its depiction as conservative; if anything, for a film to show a relationship that to some borders on (statutory) rape is nothing but absolutely radical. On the other hand, for a movie to envision a relationship between a teenager and an adult that is erotically reciprocated is equally visionary. How about the sex? According to Armond White in the *National Review*, 'Ivory's own cache – an old-fashioned refinement of lust – disguises what is, essentially, Guadagnino's porno-chic',[47] while others have complained about the movie's supposed coyness: 'there is in *Call Me by Your Name* a neutering restraint when it comes to depicting man-to-man physical insatiability, a greater aversion of the camera from gay intimacy than even 2005's *Brokeback Mountain*, which included a memorable, and chafing, moment of spontaneous anal sex'.[48] This needs nuance. Unlike the stereotype of Merchant Ivory reticence toward sex, I suggest, Guadagnino refuses to overrate it: the pre-AIDS world of sex, drugs and rock 'n' roll, the proverbial Mediterranean laxness, the Bloomsbury atmosphere of the Perlman household (where a teenager, unprompted, tells his parents 'We almost had sex last night – Marzia and me') – the opportunities for a sexual feast would have been there, but Guadagnino did not walk into that trap.

What makes *Call Me by Your Name* different is that it encompasses a nostalgia for ancient sexualities without limiting itself to contemporary queerness. Several critics mention this (although often in passing). For Manohla Dargis, '*Call Me by Your Name* is less a coming-of-age story, a tale of innocence and loss, than one about coming into sensibility. In that way, it is about the creation of a new man who, the story suggests, is liberated by pleasure that doesn't necessarily establish sexual identity.'[49] Joanna Di Mattia says it slightly differently: 'Elio and Oliver express their desire for each other without labels; the words "gay", "bisexual" or "queer" are never used in the film'. (To be totally accurate, Elio's father does refer to Isaac and Mounir as 'gay'.)[50] Brett Easton Ellis goes even further: '*Call Me by Your Name* can easily be heralded as a post-gay movie because it's not about the closet or AIDS or bullying or politics or being a victim'.[51] Here is a movie, admired by many, criticized by some, that seems to strike a nerve, yet in its engagement with ancient sexualities, it goes beyond the very cornerstone of the modern gay rights movement – identity politics. How queer is that?

Like a prayer

The *Phaedrus* ends with a prayer by Socrates: 'O dear Pan and the other gods of this place, grant that I may be beautiful inside'.[52] So, in a way, does *Call Me by Your Name*, as in Sufjan Stevens' evocative soundtrack 'Visions of Gideon'. The judge Gideon (who gives his name to the Gideons, distributors of free bibles) received visions from Yahweh about freeing the chosen people from oppression. I mention this because *Call Me by Your Name* is also a deeply spiritual text, although little attention has been paid beyond the obvious. Frederick S. Roden's 'Queer Jewish Memory' is the exception: 'The narrative consistently blurs the Abrahamic generative/generational imperative with a Platonic love of beauty'.[53] Obviously, one reason gay people have turned to classical antiquity is its validation of same-sex desire, in stark contrast to biblical interdictions. So when we look at relevant ancient sexualities in *Call Me by Your Name*, we cannot ignore the Hebrew Bible, its obsessive procreative mandate and its most notorious injunction against same-sex acts: Sodom and Gomorrah.[54] Everyone knows the story, the sin of sodomy, and the Lord raining brimstone and fire upon the cities of the plain and condemning homosexuals to eternal hellfire. But how can we explain the improbability of a biblical city comprised of gay people – like a modern-day subculture of San Francisco's Castro or London's Soho or Paris's Marais – or of Lot offering his daughters to pacify aroused homosexuals? As a result, many biblical scholars[55] have concluded that at the core of the Sodomites' sin is the violation of guest-friendship or hospitality, not homosexuality (and in keeping with ancient norms, the punishment for not honouring such an obligation in a shame culture is gang rape). Guadagnino, I think, turns the story upside down: *Call Me by Your*

Name offers a narrative of impeccable hospitality. When Oliver arrives (in the possibly threatening guise of a 'usurper') and after the usual pleasantries have been dispensed with, Professor Perlman's words are 'Our home is your home', to which Elio adds 'My room is your room'. The Perlmans could have put Oliver in the guest room, but they go far beyond it: in almost biblical proportions, Elio offers his bedroom to a perfect stranger, just as Sam and Annella treat Oliver 'almost like a son-in-law'. *Nostos*, nostalgia, a desire for home, finally finds a home for Elio and Oliver's gay relationship (almost gay marriage, considering the 'almost like a son-in-law'). Moreover, not only are Oliver and Elio freed from the oppression of Sodom and Gomorrah, we actually find a story of positive same-sex love in the Hebrew Bible that *Call Me by Your Name* references.

There is the Star of David, Elio and Oliver's ineffable yet deeply intimate bond. David had a relationship with Jonathan (mentioned earlier by Wilde in his courtroom defence). After Jonathan's demise, David memorably lamented: 'I am distressed for thee, my brother Jonathan: very pleasant hast thou been unto me: thy love to me was wonderful, passing the love of women'.[56] Whatever union they had,[57] David and Jonathan were peers (future king and crown prince), not pederastic lovers. Socrates and Phaedrus, Alexander and Hephaestion, David and Jonathan – the ancient evidence evoked in *Call Me by Your Name* points toward erotic reciprocity.

From Rome with love

In the novel, Elio and Oliver end their summer of love in Rome, which is not in the movie, but since there is talk of a sequel and by way of a conclusion, let us take a look at its significance. (The movie has them hike the Bergamo Alps – a tribute to *Brokeback Mountain?*) For a romantic getaway, they could have done much better: Paris, Venice, even Naples, but not Rome. Why does Aciman send them there? While I pointed out earlier that ancient Greek sexualities differ considerably from modern queer identities (with the possible exception of the *Phaedrus*), when we turn to the Roman sources, the difference becomes less pronounced.[58] Rome continued the Greek tradition of *paiderastia*, but it never had the same social status. What we do find, instead, are relationships between peers (without a significant age difference), sometimes long-term (well beyond the growth of a beard, which Romans tended to shave anyway) and often reciprocated (rather than the elaborate *eros/philia* dichotomy). Classical scholar Amy Richlin has challenged Michel Foucault's idea of (homo)sexuality as a construct. She argues that what we call a 'homosexual' nowadays was in Rome a 'male penetrated by choice'[59] (the *cinaedus* or *mollis*), characterized by 'a social identity and a social burden',[60] and at home in a subculture surrounded by 'homophobia'.[61] How fitting then that the Basilica of San Clemente (subject of the third part of the novel, the San Clemente Syndrome), formerly on Via di San Giovanni in Laterano, is now on Gay Street – literally. This pedestrian stretch east of the Colosseum has long been the meeting place of Rome's LGBTQ population, so much so that on 2 March 2007 (the year of *Call Me by Your Name*'s publication), the first 300 meters of Via di San Giovanni were officially christened as 'Gay Street', housing favourites such as Coming Out Club, shops, bars and restaurants. Literally overshadowed by one of Rome's most ancient monuments, it is here that queer people meet strangers, pursue *philia* or *eros*, transmit knowledge or watch movies.

So to return to the texts I listed in the introduction – *The Picture of Dorian Gray*, *Death in Venice*, *Maurice*, the novels of Mary Renault and Gore Vidal – they all engage with ancient sexualities but ultimately dismiss them as non-viable for the present (with the possible exception of Renault's *The Charioteer*).[62] *Call Me by Your Name* is different. It weaves the *Phaedrus' anteros*, Sappho's peach, the Heraclitean concern with time, the story of Sodom, and David and Jonathan into a modern picture of a relationship between a teenager and an adult that is reciprocated/consensual in its love and sex (and, despite Oliver's marriage, may hold out the promise of longevity), of a harbinger of AIDS, and of gay hospitality. Plato to Elio.

NOTES

1. Oscar Wilde, *The Picture of Dorian Gray* (*Lippincott's Monthly Magazine*, 1890 [novella]; London: Ward, Lock and Company, 1891 [novel]); Thomas Mann, *Der Tod in Venedig* (*Death in Venice*, Berlin: S. Fischer Verlag, 1912); E. M. Forster, *Maurice* (London: Hodder Arnold, 1971).

2. See Amanda Keats, '*Call Me by Your Name* "Controversy" is Pure Nonsense: It's a Romantic Masterpiece, Plain and Simple', *Metro*, 13 October 2017, https://metro.co.uk/2017/10/13/call-me-by-your-name-controversy-is-pure-nonsense-its-a-romantic-masterpiece-plain-and-simple-6990122/.

3. Quoted in https://www.nambla.org/whatis.html. NAMBLA has become irrelevant in terms of membership: see https://en.wikipedia.org/wiki/North_American_Man/Boy_Love_Association.

4. A recent engagement with the problematics of modern pederasty is Kadji Amin, *Disturbing Attachments: Genet, Modern Pederasty, and Queer History* (Durham: Duke University Press, 2017).

5. On Greek homosexuality, see Kenneth J. Dover, *Greek Homosexuality* (Cambridge: Harvard University Press, [1978] 1989).

6. Jeffrey Bloomer, 'What Should We Make of *Call Me by Your Name*'s Age-Gap Relationship?', *Slate*, 8 November 2017, https://slate.com/human-interest/2017/11/the-ethics-of-call-me-by-your-names-age-gap-sexual-relationship-explored.html.

7. Benjamin Eldon Stevens, 'Classical Desires in *Call Me by Your Name* (dir. Luca Guadagnino 2017)', *Antiquipop: Antiquity, Pop Culture & Politics*, https://antiquipop.hypotheses.org/eng/3264eng.

8. See Dover, *Greek Homosexuality*, 91–99.

9. Elio does fit the profile of a twink, which is more in keeping with contemporary stereotypical gay pairings, but there is also the twunk (a hunky/muscular twink).

10. Plato, *Phaedrus*, trans. Alexander Nehamas and Paul Woodruff (Indianapolis: Hackett, [*c.*370 BCE] 1995), 230c.

11. Plato, *Phaedrus* 243e.

12. Plato, *Phaedrus* 255b–d.

13. Plato, *Phaedrus* 251c.

14. Plato, *Phaedrus* 256b–c.

15. Plato, *Phaedrus* 256c.

16. Emily Rutherford, 'Dare to Speak Its Name: Pederasty in the Classical Tropes of *Call Me by Your Name*', *Eidolon*, 12 February 2018, https://eidolon.pub/dare-to-speak-its-name-819a05b358f.

17. Steven D. Greydanus, 'Artful Veneer of *Call Me by Your Name* Masks Shallow, Distorted View of Sexuality', *Catholic World Report*, 13 February 2018, https://www.catholicworldreport.com/2018/02/13/artful-veneer-of-call-me-by-your-name-masks-shallow-distorted-view-of-sexuality/.

18. Renee Sorrentino and Jack Turban, '*Call Me by Your Name*: Not Pedophilia, Still Problematic', *Psychiatric Times* 35, no. 9 (September 2018): 16E.

19. Sorrentino and Turban, 16E-F.

20. See, for example, André Aciman, *Call Me by Your Name* (London: Atlantic Books, [2007] 2009), 147.

21. Rutherford, 'Dare to Speak'.

22. Rutherford.

23. See Aciman, *Call Me*, 176 and 221 respectively.

24. Zachary J. Gianelle, 'Sympotic Love?: Classical Reception in *Call Me by Your Name*', Master's thesis, University of Arizona, 2019, https://repository.arizona.edu/bitstream/handle/10150/633123/azu_etd_17218_sip1_m.pdf?sequence=1, 28.

25. Mary Renault, *Fire from Heaven* (New York: Pantheon Books, 1969).

26. Mary Renault, *The Persian Boy* (New York: Vintage, [1972] 1988), 35. There is actually a variation on this in Stone's film, but without the sexual implications.

27. Quoted in Pamela Hutchinson, 'My Summer of Love', *Sight and Sound* 27, no. 11 (November 2017): 35.

28. Joanna Di Mattia, 'Beating Hearts: Compassion and Self-Discovery in *Call Me by Your Name*', *Screen Education* 91 (2018): 10.

29. Gianelle, 'Sympotic Love?', 53.

30. Bloomer, 'What Should We Make'.

31. Thank you to Judy Hallett here, who provided valuable information on openly gay classics professors in the '80s.

32. On the role of the *Symposium* in the movie, see Gianelle, 'Sympotic Love?', 51–53.

33. Erick Neher, 'A Revolution in Progress', *Hudson Review* 71, no. 1 (Spring 2018): 102.

34. D. A. Miller, 'Elio's Education', *Los Angeles Review of Books*, 19 February 2018, https://www.lareviewofbooks.org/article/elios-education/.

35. B. Ruby Rich, *New Queer Cinema: The Director's Cut* (Durham: Duke University Press, 2013), xvi.

36. John J. Winkler, *The Constraints of Desire: The Anthropology of Sex and Gender in Ancient Greece* (New York: Routledge, 1990), 183.

37. Quoted in Hutchinson, 'My Summer', 34.

38. Molly Haskell, '*Call Me by Your Name*', *Film Comment* 53, no. 6 (November–December 2017): 68.

39. Anon., 'Rare Cancer Seen in 41 Homosexuals', *New York Times*, 3 July 1981, Section A, 20.

40. Larry Kramer, '1,121 and Counting', *New York Native* 59 (14–27 March 1983).

41. Robert Pear, 'Health Chief Calls AIDS Battle "No. 1 Priority"', *New York Times*, 25 May 1983, Section A, 1.

42. Aciman, *Call Me*, 133.

43. Hutchinson, 'My Summer', 35.

44. See Spencer Kornhaber, 'The Shadow Over *Call Me by Your Name*', *Atlantic*, 3 January 2018, https://www.theatlantic.com/entertainment/archive/2018/01/the-shadow-over-call-me-by-your-name/549269/.

45. Claire Monk, *Heritage Film Audiences: Period Films and Contemporary Audiences in the UK* (Edinburgh: Edinburgh University Press, 2011), 33.

46. On queer audiences specifically, see Tyler Quick, 'The Queer Public and Its Problem with Representation', *The Velvet Light Trap* 86 (Autumn 2020): 27–36; on fans, see Barb Mirell, ed., *Call Me by Your Name: How a Little Film Touched So Many Lives* (Philadelphia: Liberty Bell Publishers, 2018).

47. Armond White, '*Call Me by Your Name*: Idealized Sex between an Adult Man and a Nubile Teen', *National Review*, 1 December 2017, https://www.nationalreview.com/2017/12/call-me-your-name-hollywood-hypocrisy-teen-sex/.

48. Billy Gray, '*Call Me by Your Name, Moonlight*, and the Cost of Critical Success for Queer Films', *Slate*, 21 November 2017, https://slate.com/human-interest/2017/11/call-me-by-your-names-lack-of-explicit-sex-may-explain-its-critical-success.html.

49. Manohla Dargis, 'Review: A Boy's Own Desire in *Call Me by Your Name*', *New York Times*, 22 November 2017, https://www.nytimes.com/2017/11/22/movies/call-me-by-your-namereview-armie-hammer.html?referrer=google_kp.

50. Di Mattia, 'Beating Hearts', 10.

51. Brett Easton Ellis, 'Movie of the Year: Bret Easton Ellis on the Many Pleasures of *Call Me by Your Name*', *Out*, 18 December 2017, https://www.out.com/out-exclusives/2017/12/18/movie-year-bret-easton-ellis-many-pleasures-call-me-your-name.

52. Plato, *Phaedrus* 279b.

53. Frederick S. Roden, 'Queer Jewish Memory: André Aciman's *Call Me by Your Name*', *Journal of Modern Jewish Studies* 18, no. 2 (May 2019): 200.

54. Genesis 19:1–29.

55. See, for example, Martti Nissinen, *Homoeroticism in the Biblical World: A Historical Perspective*, trans. Kirsi Stjerna (Minneapolis: Fortress Press, 1998), 45–49.

56. 2 Samuel 1:26 (KJV).

57. For a queer reading, see David M. Halperin, *One Hundred Years of Homosexuality and Other Essays on Greek Love* (Abingdon and New York: Routledge, 1990), 75–87.

58. On Roman homosexuality, see Craig A. Williams, *Roman Homosexuality*, second edition (New York: Oxford University Press, [1999] 2010).

59. Amy Richlin, 'Not Before Homosexuality: The Materiality of the *Cinaedus* and the Roman Law against Love between Men', *Journal of the History of Sexuality* 3 (1993), 526.

60. Richlin, 530.

61. Richlin, 530.

62. See Nikolai Endres, 'Horses and Heroes: Plato's *Phaedrus* and Mary Renault's *The Charioteer*', *International Journal of the Classical Tradition* 19, no. 3 (2012): 152–64.

REFERENCES

Aciman, André. *Call Me by Your Name*. London: Atlantic Books, [2007] 2009.

Amin, Kadji. *Disturbing Attachments: Genet, Modern Pederasty, and Queer History*. Durham: Duke University Press, 2017.

Anon. 'Rare Cancer Seen in 41 Homosexuals.' *New York Times*, 3 July 1981, Section A, 20.

Bloomer, Jeffrey. 'What Should We Make of *Call Me by Your Name*'s Age-Gap Relationship?' *Slate*, 8 November 2017. https://slate.com/human-interest/2017/11/the-ethics-of-call-me-by-your-names-age-gap-sexual-relationship-explored.html.

Dargis, Manohla. 'Review: A Boy's Own Desire in *Call Me by Your Name*.' *New York Times*, 22 November 2017. https://www.nytimes.com/2017/11/22/movies/call-me-by-your-name-review-armie-hammer.html?referrer=google_kp.

Di Mattia, Joanna. 'Beating Hearts: Compassion and Self-Discovery in *Call Me by Your Name*.' *Screen Education* 91 (October 2018): 8–15.

Dover, Kenneth J. *Greek Homosexuality*. Cambridge: Harvard University Press, [1978] 1989.

Edgerton, Joel, dir. *Boy Erased*. Focus Features, Perfect World Pictures, Blue Tongue Films, Anonymous Content, 2018.

Ellis, Brett Easton. 'Movie of the Year: Bret Easton Ellis on the Many Pleasures of *Call Me by Your Name.*' *Out*, 18 December 2017. https://www.out.com/out-exclusives/2017/12/18/movie-year-bret-easton-ellis-many-pleasures-call-me-your-name.

Endres, Nikolai. 'Horses and Heroes: Plato's *Phaedrus* and Mary Renault's *The Charioteer.*' *International Journal of the Classical Tradition* 19, no. 3 (2012): 152–64.

Forster, E. M. *Maurice*. London: Hodder Arnold, 1971.

Gianelle, Zachary J. 'Sympotic Love?: Classical Reception in *Call Me by Your Name.*' Master's thesis, University of Arizona, 2019. https://repository.arizona.edu/bitstream/handle/10150/633123/azu_etd_17218_sip1_m.pdf?sequence=1.

Gray, Billy. '*Call Me by Your Name, Moonlight,* and the Cost of Critical Success for Queer Films.' *Slate*, 21 November 2017. https://slate.com/human-interest/2017/11/call-me-by-your-names-lack-of-explicit-sex-may-explain-its-critical-success.html.

Greydanus, Steven D. 'Artful Veneer of *Call Me by Your Name* Masks Shallow, Distorted View of Sexuality.' *Catholic World Report*, 13 February 2018. https://www.catholicworldreport.com/2018/02/13/artful-veneer-of-call-me-by-your-name-masks-shallow-distorted-view-of-sexuality/.

Guadagnino, Luca, dir. *Call Me by Your Name*. Frenesy Film Company, La Cinefacture, RT Features, 2017.

Halperin, David M. *One Hundred Years of Homosexuality and Other Essays on Greek Love*. Abingdon and New York: Routledge, 1990.

Haskell, Molly. '*Call Me by Your Name.*' *Film Comment* 53, no. 6 (November-December 2017): 67–69.

Hutchinson, Pamela. 'My Summer of Love.' *Sight and Sound* 27, no. 11 (November 2017): 32–35.

Karlhuber, Kerstin, dir. *Fair Haven*. Trick Candle Productions, Silent Giant Productions, 2016.

Keats, Amanda. '*Call Me by Your Name* "Controversy" is Pure Nonsense: It's a Romantic Masterpiece, Plain and Simple.' *Metro*, 13 October 2017. https://metro.co.uk/2017/10/13/call-me-by-your-name-controversy-is-pure-nonsense-its-a-romantic-masterpiece-plain-and-simple-6990122/.

Kornhaber, Spencer. 'The Shadow Over *Call Me by Your Name.*' *Atlantic*, 3 January 2018. https://www.theatlantic.com/entertainment/archive/2018/01/the-shadow-over-call-me-by-your-name/549269/.

Kramer, Larry. '1,121 and Counting.' *New York Native* 59 (14–27 March 1983).

Lee, Ang, dir. *Brokeback Mountain*. River Road Entertainment, Focus Features, 2005.

Mann, Thomas. *Der Tod in Venedig (Death in Venice)*. Berlin: S. Fischer Verlag, 1912.

Miller, D. A. 'Elio's Education.' *Los Angeles Review of Books*, 19 February 2018. https://www.lareviewofbooks.org/article/elios-education/.

Mirell, Barb, ed. *Call Me by Your Name: How a Little Film Touched So Many Lives*. Philadelphia: Liberty Bell Publishers, 2018.

Monk, Claire. *Heritage Film Audiences: Period Films and Contemporary Audiences in the UK*. Edinburgh: Edinburgh University Press, 2011.

Neher, Erick. 'A Revolution in Progress.' *Hudson Review* 71, no. 1 (Spring 2018): 96–102.

Nissinen, Martti. *Homoeroticism in the Biblical World: A Historical Perspective*. Translated by Kirsi Stjerna. Minneapolis: Fortress Press, 1998.

Pear, Robert. 'Health Chief Calls AIDS Battle "No. 1 Priority".' *New York Times*, 25 May 1983, Section A, 1.

Plato. *Phaedrus*. Translated by Alexander Nehamas and Paul Woodruff. Indianapolis: Hackett, [c.370 BCE] 1995.

Quick, Tyler. 'The Queer Public and Its Problem with Representation.' *The Velvet Light Trap* 86 (Autumn 2020): 27–36.

Renault, Mary. *Fire from Heaven*. New York: Pantheon Books, 1969.

Renault, Mary. *The Persian Boy*. New York: Vintage, [1972] 1988.

Rich, B. Ruby. *New Queer Cinema: The Director's Cut*. Durham: Duke University Press, 2013.

Richlin, Amy. 'Not Before Homosexuality: The Materiality of the *Cinaedus* and the Roman Law against Love between Men.' *Journal of the History of Sexuality* 3 (1993): 523–73.

Roden, Frederick S. 'Queer Jewish Memory: André Aciman's *Call Me by Your Name*.' *Journal of Modern Jewish Studies* 18, no. 2 (May 2019): 194–211.

Rutherford, Emily. 'Dare to Speak Its Name: Pederasty in the Classical Tropes of *Call Me by Your Name*.' *Eidolon* 2018. https://eidolon.pub/dare-to-speak-its-name-819a05b358f.

Sorrentino, Renee, and Jack Turban. '*Call Me by Your Name*: Not Pedophilia, Still Problematic.' *Psychiatric Times* 35, no. 9 (September 2018): 16A–16F.

Stevens, Benjamin Eldon. 'Classical Desires in *Call Me by Your Name* (dir. Luca Guadagnino 2017).' *Antiquipop: Antiquity, Pop Culture & Politics*. https://antiquipop.hypotheses.org/eng/3264eng.

Stone, Oliver, dir. *Alexander*. Warner Bros., Intermedia Films, Pacifica Film, 2004.

White, Armond. '*Call Me by Your Name*: Idealized Sex between an Adult Man and a Nubile Teen.' *National Review*, 1 December 2017. https://www.nationalreview.com/2017/12/call-me-your-name-hollywood-hypocrisy-teen-sex/.

Wikipedia. https://en.wikipedia.org/wiki/North_American_Man/Boy_Love_Association.

Wilde, Oscar. *The Picture of Dorian Gray*. *Lippincott's Monthly Magazine*, 1890 (novella). London: Ward, Lock and Company, 1891 (novel).

Williams, Craig A. *Roman Homosexuality*. Second Edition. Oxford: Oxford University Press, [1999] 2010.

Winkler, John J. *The Constraints of Desire: The Anthropology of Sex and Gender in Ancient Greece*. New York: Routledge, 1990.

9

'Daring You to Desire Them': Digital Classicism, Star Bodies and *Call Me by Your Name*

Michael Williams

This chapter explores how *Call Me by Your Name* (Luca Guadagnino, 2017) locates the characters of Elio (Timothée Chalamet) and Oliver (Armie Hammer) within a long history of queer classical reception, and in particular the way the film, and its active fanbase, brings ancient sculptural imagery and classical myth into dialogue with the digital present.

I begin by highlighting the way the film's opening titles work to frame the film within a queer history of classical receptions and, through the imagery presented, act as a guide to viewing the film that follows. I then explore sculptural references, implicit and explicit, that shape the bodies of Elio and Oliver on screen and place them within the film's languid topography of bathing pools, ancient ruins and artefacts, and intertextual cinematic heritage. The corollary of this, I argue, and a key reason for the astonishing international success of the film, lies not only in its use of the past but in how the film resonated with – and indeed actively solicited in its archaeological regime of on-screen sculptural comparisons and teasing postural allusions – an audience securely located in the digital present and versed in the evolving aesthetics of social media forms such as the YouTube 'coming-out' video. The film's appropriation of classical imagery and the audience's enthusiastic response to it are two sides of the same coin. In the latter sections of this chapter, I therefore turn to the fascinating ways in which the romance of Elio and Oliver was received by critics and then reworked by fans online, who have often brought ancient and modern juxtapositions to the fore with imagination and insight, aiding the film's word-of-mouth success in the process.

Queer classicism

A classical *objet d'art* on a film set or in the background of a publicity still can say a lot about a character or star, carefully encoding aspects of their identity for those with the inclination, or knowledge, to see it. There's nothing masked about the homoerotic impulses in *Call Me by Your Name*, but much of the film's imagery evokes how gay identity has historically often found an articulate but 'tasteful' voice when enunciated through a classical mask of one form or another. Richard Dyer has discussed how classical imagery was deployed in queer photography and early gay rights publications to communicate ideas about identity, eroticism and legitimation. This was, as he put it, 'a way of representing desire, both in the sense of imaging it to themselves and in the sense of arguing for it to the world'.[1] Art, identity and eroticism were thus intertwined in the reception of the classical nude in a queer lineage apparent in western visual culture particularly since the Enlightenment. As Robert Aldrich argues, this 'provided the archetype for male beauty and homosexual aesthetics' with authors and artists constructing the Mediterranean itself as a space of homoerotic possibility and 'conflating ancient and modern images'.[2] It is exactly this blending of the classical with the contemporary that intrigues. Whitney Davis has explored this palimpsestic historical process in his study of queer beauty, indicating how the canonical norm of classical beauty we receive, through thousands of prior readings that will include queer ones, is itself likely to have some element of the homoerotic 'dynamically integrated' into it.[3] Thus:

> Many testimonies suggest that queer beauty enabled homoerotically inclined viewers in the past two hundred years to reconstruct themselves [...]: in engaging the images projected in certain works of art, these beholders could retrace the teleology of queer beauty, presented officially or canonically as an aesthetic and social norm, back to its echo and origins or its content and conditions in homosexual judgments of taste. Indeed, they could (re)discover their *participation* in the dynamic constitution of ideals of beauty in their culture.[4]

The classical queer canon, as I will examine in a moment, is foregrounded in Guadagnino's film, setting up echoes that very much instil a participatory resonation in the film's online reception, which I examine in the second part of this chapter.

What we might now term 'celebrity' culture developed on a parallel trajectory to the timeline proposed by Aldrich. Those with the means to do so might be painted amid the ruined grandeur of the ancient past while on a Grand Tour in southern Europe or might pose next to props evoking ancient Greece and Rome in an artist's studio – all carrying a history of associations that were visually pleasing, culturally refining and deeply layered. As I've explored elsewhere, cinema stepped into this classical aesthetic tradition as the industry positioned itself as an art and entertainment industry in the early twentieth century, shaping tropes for star publicity and fan-magazine discourse that are still with us.[5] These tropes are versatile and ambiguous, whether foregrounding the allure and auratic stature of Gloria Swanson in a 1922 portrait standing next to a statuette of the *Venus de Milo*, whose pose she gently emulates,[6] or hinting to gay fans through oblique queer historical references to Antinous (the lover of Roman Emperor Hadrian), Alexander the Great or the pose of the Apollo Belvedere that stars such as MGM's Ramón Novarro might be 'one of us' (as indeed he was).[7]

Call Me by Your Name establishes its classical framework from the outset. The opening title credits designed by Chen Li are a series of still, self-consciously framed shots of photographs of classical sculptures scattered over a desk, presumably that of Elio's archaeologist father, Mr Perlman (Michael Stuhlbarg). The first shot (see Figure 9.1), captioned 'Starring Armie Hammer' in a font emulating hand-scrawled yellow chalk, presents fragmented images of the head of a heavily patinated bronze sculpture of a youth known as *The Athlete of Ephesos*, viewed in profile. The sculpture's gaze is downward and reflective in the main left-centre photograph, while the images to the right see it first angled to suggest his head is lifted before bending down in the close-up image on the right, focusing on his cheek and ear. The implied sense of movement and scrutiny of the athlete's body already suggest haptic sensuality and an ancient homoeroticism being brought 'to life' in Pygmalionesque fashion. The way the star's name is juxtaposed with his ancient counterpart establishes a process of association between ancient and modern bodies that continues through the titles and across the ensuing narrative. The next shot finds the same ancient youth facing the camera in the main photograph – his eyes blankly staring through Chalamet's name – resting upon three close-up images of the athlete's eye, lips and hair, as if an animated series portraying him having turned towards the viewer and what we might see if we kissed and embraced him (also Figure 9.1).

The *Athlete* is the most frequently occurring figure in the ensuing titles, which consist of fragmented views of predominantly nude male sculptures and some female ones. The striking bronze was discovered in Turkey in 1896 and identified as a Roman copy of a Greek original, and a rare survival that forms the centrepiece of Vienna's Ephesos Museum.[8] Another, almost intact, copy of the statue was discovered 100 years later off the Croatian coast and is the sole occupant of The Museum of Apoxyomenos at Lošinj, Croatia.[9] The auratic symbolism of this ancient youth could hardly be stronger. The miraculous survival of the Ephesos statue and rebirth as prized museum exhibit was arguably intensified by its having

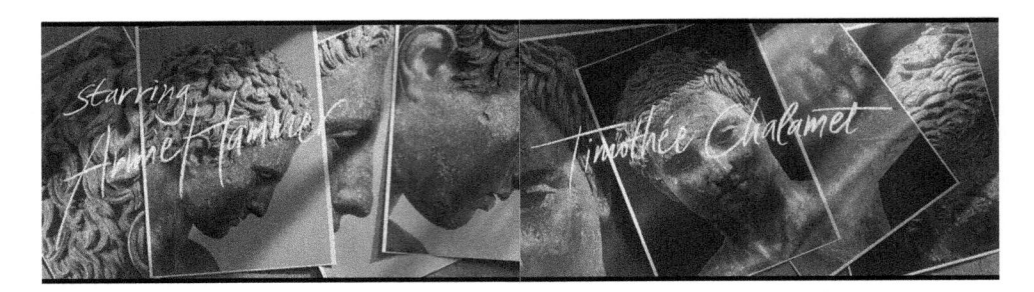

FIGURE 9.1: The bronze *Athlete* frames the introduction of Armie Hammer and Timothée Chalamet in the opening titles. Luca Guadagnino (dir.), *Call Me by Your Name*, 2017. Italy/France/USA/Brazil. © Frenesy, La Cinefacture.

been reconstructed from 234 fragments – like the still-broken sculptures we also see in the title sequence – across millennia and then reformed,[10] its patina and visible joins testifying to the rough passage of time, and thus to its authenticity. This reflects David Lowenthal's observation of the historical turn in perceptions of the past that began to see that

> [f]ragmented works seemed more intensely alive than intact antiquities. 'It is not that we prefer time-worn bas-reliefs, or rusted statuettes as such', said André Malraux, 'but the sense of life they impart, from the evidence of their struggle with Time'.[11]

The *Athlete* testifies to the beguiling power of fragments as well as the ancient predilection for making copies of sculptural types.

It is fitting that the *Athlete* connects the men just as the sculptural artefact removed from Lake Garda will do later, and visually links both their names in the manner of the film's title. This doubling resonates with the Platonic idea of the 'other half' that a lover needs to find to become whole once more, here felicitously rendered in archaeological form. The 'twin' athletes were actually brought together in 2015 for an exhibition, 'Power and Pathos: Bronze Sculpture of the Hellenistic World', that toured Italy and the USA, perhaps giving them a timely prominence in the consciousness of the filmmakers ahead of the film's production.[12] That the sculpture is also used for the next cast member, Michael Stuhlbarg, is perhaps also appropriate for the way in which it will be Mr Perlman who will use slideshow images of classical sculpture to refer obliquely to the men's queer relationship.

Reviewing the screening of the film at the Berlinale, *Mic*'s online review claimed:

> The film's title sequence features full-color slide images of classical Greek statuary, busts and chests and bodies of idealized young men, an inscrutable smile on

every face, hair carved into artful tousles; any one of them could have been carved after Elio.[13]

Not quite every statue, perhaps, but one gets the point. And the *Athlete*'s expression of wistful reverie is a good match for Elio's introspection and longing gazes at Oliver, although the sculpture's full body is of a muscular scale that better matches Oliver. Benjamin Eldon Stevens links these images to the long take of Elio's saddened face at the film's end, with its 'close association between gazing at ancient statues and desiring people in the present'.[14] However, if the bronze *Athlete* combines Oliver's muscular physique with Elio's melancholy, a better match for the latter in the title sequence is found in the *Spinario* – the much-copied Roman bronze of a boy pulling a thorn from his foot, housed in Rome's Palazzo dei Conservatori – which is included in six shots in the titles and is perhaps its most widely recognizable artwork.[15] I shall return to this reference later. Interestingly, one of the other most striking sculptures seen in the titles is a Greek bronze known as *The Charioteer of Delphi* or *Heniokhos*, which depicts a youthful chariot racer whose appearance also inspired the costume design and marketing imagery of the 1925 epic *Ben-Hur: A Tale of the Christ* (dir. Fred Niblo), starring the aforementioned queer icon Ramón Novarro in the title role. Most of the classical bodies are photographed to display full-frontal nudity; indeed, the titles present a cornucopia of ancient penises. There is a sense of the viewer being offered an inhibited gaze at these homoeroticized bodies which stand vicariously for the bodies of Oliver and Elio themselves, and form part of their erotic courtship.

As the titles progress, the domestic clutter of period objects – a cassette tape as Sufjan Stevens' name appears, a roll of 35 mm film, a tax disc for 1983, two Stars of David, etc. – strays further into the frame orientating the viewer towards a more recent past. As with any historical film, *Call Me by Your Name*'s opening titles have gently established its setting and atmosphere and a particular discourse of authenticity. We have been offered fragmented, analogue views of ancient sculptural bodies with an implied connection to the present, but first and foremost we have seen *images* of the past, brought into juxtaposition and play which, I would argue, provided templates for the digital fan art that proliferated as the film found its audience. The classical frame the film's titles place around the characters positions Elio and Oliver within a version of perceived Greek ideals of male–male love and sex, where the desired body of the youthful *erastes* is an object for the older *eromenos*.[16] André Aciman's novel is arguably unusual, as Stevens notes,[17] in adopting the perspective of the younger *erastes*, Elio, and his intense longing and lust for Oliver. (See Nikolai Endres's chapter in this collection for discussion that problematises these terms.) The film, though from the very first shot panning from a bed to the shirtless Elio, presents the youth, too, as the object of desire for the audience, ceaselessly repurposed in the film's reception. The titles thus provide a cinematic, and sculptural, guide for viewing within the parenthesis of queer classicism: a palimpsestic coupling of desiring bodies, past and present.

Palimpsestic coupling

The companion scene for the title sequence arrives when Elio's father projects a slide show of ancient sculptures for Oliver, which communicates in a code that is oblique but hardly subtle that the classical bodies might be read as stand-ins for Oliver and Elio, and vice versa. Indeed, the light shining towards the camera suggests a proxy cinema with Mr Perlman and Oliver alternating with us as audience. 'They're all so incredibly sensual', Oliver exclaims, curling his left arm behind his head in a curiously deliberate gesture that frames his head for the gaze, and mirroring the pose of the first statue slide seen, with its right arm raised. Mr Perlman's eulogizing of Praxiteles ('the greatest sculptor in antiquity') is intercut with Elio's discovery of Oliver's note upstairs, inviting him to meet at midnight, Elio's profile also inserted into the context of sculptural images. As the camera holds on a view of Elio's body, now reclined on his bed, we hear, somewhat incongruously, his father's description of the sculpture: 'Muscles are firm. Look at his stomach, for example. Not a straight body …' We then cut back to the slides 'in these statues, they're all curved. Sometimes impossibly curved. And so … nonchalant, hence their ageless ambiguity. As if they're daring you to desire them.' Mr Perlman turns to Oliver at this moment, and Oliver looks up, eyebrows raised as he picks up the subtext. The association had been foregrounded in the film's trailer where Mr Perlman's words are heard over images of the Lake Garda sequence with 'so … nonchalant' then juxtaposed with a shirtless Oliver, establishing the link between bodies of marble and flesh even before audiences had seen the film.

There's a play on 'straight' in the dialogue, of course, but the curve of the ancient Hellenistic bodies draws different lines to Oliver and Elio. In his Blu-ray commentary, Chalamet, channelling the perspective of his character, suggests that Mr Perlman's reference to 'ageless bodies' 'could be a description of Oliver'.[18] As Malparte argues in an online essay, the first two images in the slide sequence correspond to Oliver's '*eroico*' (heroic) body, rather than Elio's, who corresponds more to the ephebe type characteristic of the opening sequence. After we have cut away to Elio's profile and discovery of Oliver's note inviting him to meet him later, we see a slide of *The Dancing Satyr*, a light and ephebic body recalling Elio and which Malparte argues suggests that Oliver is projecting the object of his desire, having been stirred by Mr Perlman's words.[19]

Elio does not possess the upright, *contrapposto*, pose seen in the slides and which seems closer to the more 'statuesque' frame of Hammer's Oliver, who appears outsized, of heroic proportion. 'Oh my goodness, you're bigger than your picture', exclaims Mr Perlman upon the American's arrival. Elio reaches towards him for the handshake, which emphasizes their contrast in build, and age. Later, Mafalda (Vanda Capriolo), the housekeeper, exclaims to Mrs Perlman (Amira Casar), 'What a movie star!' in the garden, a Romanesque statue punctuating their view of Oliver playing tennis in the background. The physical and iconographic contrast is apparent in the scene in which a shirtless Elio charms Oliver with his virtuosity at the piano, copying classical musical styles as their bodies emulate sculptural ones. Oliver listens in the doorway in the background, standing *contrapposto* with hand on hip and weight on one leg, turning his head in a manner that closely resembles the *Farnese Hermes*.[20] Elio's slender body is in the foreground, his back curved, leaning over the piano as he plays; if he raised a foot onto his knee, he would be the picture of the *Spinario* (the way he had been playing the guitar amid the trees immediately beforehand, sat on a stone seat, adding an Arcadian air suiting this association). By the end of the scene, Oliver is drawn towards the younger man, slumping onto a chair below Elio in the frame, losing his statuesque height and posture as Elio's precocious teasing vexes, but utterly charms him (Figure 9.2). There, after a moment when his turned head strikes a resemblance to a seated sculpture such as *The Ludovisi Ares*, displayed in Rome's Palazzo Altemps, Oliver becomes less the image of the imposing athlete and instead emulates Elio's posture, albeit somewhat broken, the two sculptural forms in dialogue, tuning in to one another.

Following his passion for playing variations, there are other moments in the film when Elio sits with one leg raised, or with crossed legs, or presents the serpentine

FIGURE 9.2: The '*Farnese* Oliver' and '*Spinario* Elio': Oliver (Armie Hammer) stands *contrapposto* in the doorway as Elio (Timothée Chalamet) plays the piano; at the end of the scene Oliver is mirroring Elio's pose. Luca Guadagnino (dir.), *Call Me by Your Name*, 2017. Italy/France/USA/Brazil. © Frenesy, La Cinefacture.

curve of his back in a way that evokes the *Spinario* – for example when he plays the piano for his family or writes outside or at his desk, watches TV or sits, cross-legged, on his bed. This sculpture has a long history of display and celebration, recorded for nearly 900 years. The bronze of a youth, sat upon a tree stump, pulling a thorn from his foot was one of the first ancient statues to be copied in the Renaissance, with reproductions appearing in great houses across Europe.[21] The subject of the sculpture has been the subject of much speculation, from Absolom, 'the best-known male beauty of the Old Testament', to a Greek athlete or a Roman shepherd boy called Martinus,[22] and it has even been read as a metaphor for 'the crippling power of Eros',[23] presumably due to the injured foot and hunched posture of the youth. Whatever the origins, the young man connotes beauty, muted heroism and a naïve pastoral charm.

That moment when Elio reclines on the bed during the slideshow sequence also resonates with representations in art of Endymion, the youth (another shepherd figure) who captivated the Greek moon goddess Selene, and who was sent into eternal sleep so that she could gaze endlessly upon him. Anne-Louis Girodet de Roussy-Trioson's painting *The Sleep of Endymion* (1791) and Canova's sculpture *The Sleeping Endymion* (1819–22) are among the best-known examples, both portraying the youth reclining with one arm raised behind his turned head to display his torso to the goddess above. Elio obliquely emulates the pose several times in the film, often when lying in dappled sunshine or moonlight on his bed, as when he reaches down his shorts to masturbate before Oliver interrupts him. Elio is always the languid youth, the ephebe.

When Oliver gives the reclining Elio a foot massage, troubled by a nosebleed rather than a thorn, it seems the culmination of this imagery and – recalling that link through the *Spinario* to the burden of Eros – consolidates a sensual bonding between the men that acknowledges that this is a bittersweet summer romance. The statue-light shining into the lens during the slideshow connects to several Baroque photographic flourishes in the film, namely the play of moonlight transformed into lens flare as Elio awaits Oliver, leaning back and looking up, the flickering slow motion as the statue emerges from the lake, and Oliver's nostalgic flashbacks later in the film as he stands on the balcony in silhouette. That moment, like the earlier silhouetted image of Elio before the balcony at home noted by Stevens,[24] is strikingly statuesque. Like the pivotal, titular scene of queer discovery in Barry Jenkins' 2016 *Moonlight*, these moments take us to liminal, ageless spaces, and of course to that much-discussed camera pan towards the beckoning moonlight as Elio and Oliver finally sleep together; Endymion is awake and is no longer the passive object offered up to the gaze of Selene, or the camera.

The day after they sleep together the men visit the town, and here we find a visual connection being made to more contemporary icons and a discourse of celebrity that I will return to later. Oliver is framed in another doorway surrounded by magazines, the nearest displaying a shirtless and muscle-flexing John Travolta on the cover of *Rolling Stone* magazine. 'Sex and the Single Star', its headline reads. Here Oliver is associated with contemporary Hollywood idols in addition to ancient ones, and perhaps it is the Americanness of the character, as well as Hammer, that contrasts with Chalamet. As Francesca Sobande has noted, Chalamet's Hollywood image 'cuts a familiar and normative shape in Hollywood, as a young, white, cisgender American man, while also being regarded as embodying a Frenchness and European sartorial flare that fixates the transnational media and fandom that follows him'.[25] Through the palimpsestic coupling of Elio and Oliver, therefore, the viewer is presented with an intriguingly ambiguous icon-play of classical sculpture and modern Hollywood, whether juxtaposed within the *mise en scène* or editing, or embodied within the stars' performances themselves.

Sculptural touch

The most overt of these sculptural mediations occurs when Elio and Oliver accompany Mr Perlman to Sirmione to oversee the recovery of a statue from the lake. This scene is not part of Aciman's source novel but was, Chalamet relates, the first scene planned by Ivory and Guadagnino before production began,[26] and is thus the film's foundational ur-scene. The sequence follows some prickly conversation between the men that morning following Elio's jealousy at watching Oliver dance with Chiara (Victoire du Bois) the previous evening – *The Dancing Satyr*, perhaps, or even better, *The Dancing Faun* from Pompeii, with its raised arms strongly reminiscent of Oliver's dance moves – with Elio recounting how he nearly had sex with Marzia (Esther Garrel) if only he had found 'the courage to reach out and touch'. But on the shore of Lake Garda the men are reconciled through another moment of sculptural performance as Elio offers a 'truce' via a prosthetic of ancient bronze, as Oliver holds up the arm of the ancient sculpture and they shake hands, echoing their first meeting. The image – a literal rendering of gay identity mediated through the classical past – became central to the film's marketing and reception. Laura Marcus reads the sequence in the context of the Platonic search for the 'lost half' referenced in Aciman's writing, including the source novel where Elio asks himself 'When had they separated us, you and me, Oliver?'[27] In the film, Marcus argues, the 'reparative conjoining' performed by Elio and Oliver through their handshake with the detached arm 'becomes a reminder of the "amputated limb" which for Aciman represents the ways in which "we are torn in two"'.[28]

The handshake precipitates more of the past to surface. On the boat above the dive site Mr Perlman relates the history of the sculpture, which belongs to one of four known sets based on the Praxiteles originals, with previous owners including the Roman Emperor Hadrian, famous to queer history for his relationship with the young and handsome Antinous. As the statue breaks the surface, a slow-motion effect creates a dream-like moment that, combined with its beautifully patinated surface, emphasizes the miraculous nature of its return. We hear that Hadrian's pair had been melted down by one of the Farnese Popes to form 'a particularly voluptuous Venus', making the statue's recovery an act that resists the historical erasure of queer desire. As Galt and Schoonover note, the 'rhyming of these bodies across millennia' is not only about queer desire but about 'raising the specter of a violently heteronormalized history in the intervening centuries'.[29] Mr Perlman later refers to the statue as 'our boxer', but it most closely resembles *Victorious Youth*,[30] a 300–100 BCE Greek bronze now in the Getty Villa, Malibu.[31]

The find in the lake takes place before the ruins of the Grotto of Catullus, a picturesquely located Roman villa, situating this exchange within a history of Grand Tours and their posturing amid the past. Elio and Oliver are connected by the hand of this ancient bronze youth; the lively piano on the soundtrack – which Kingsley Marshall notes in this collection is associated with 'discovery' in the film – here echoes the music from the opening titles. Chalamet spent a week with James Ivory prior to production and watched the 1987 Merchant-Ivory production, *Maurice*, with him.[32] That is another film which uses the ancient past as a reference point, with Hugh Grant's Clive figuring out his feelings about Maurice (James Wilby) while wandering in Greek ruins. Chalamet has described the scene of Elio and Oliver in a field as being 'almost a direct homage' to *Maurice*,[33] which had its thirtieth anniversary re-release four months after *Call Me by Your Name*'s Sundance premiere. At the end of the lake scene the three men go bathing in the lake, whooping as they splash in the water, perhaps a knowing reference to the famous full-frontal nudity of the 'Sacred Lake' scene from *A Room with a View* (James Ivory, 1985), an idyllic space conceived by closeted gay author E. M. Forster to escape the confines of Edwardian society. In that film, the lake had been constructed specifically for the production,[34] as was the small pool at Elio's house where the men idly develop their relationship,[35] Oliver rolling, stiff-limbed and statue-like, into the water at one point, foreshadowing the lake scene where his sculptural avatar rises back to the surface.

At the lake, having bonded in the arm(s) of the Greek youth, Oliver and Elio begin to stroke its recovered body as it lays, still bound in ropes, on the shore. Elio probes the glistening moisture on its torso in fascination, as if the ancient youth were coming to life through this Pygmalionesque ritual; the imagery anticipates the peach juices, sweat and semen upon his and Oliver's bodies in later scenes. Oliver's tactile gestures, in turn, are mirrored in the scene in the field where the couple lay in the sun after a bike ride. As Elio lies with his arms resting behind his head once

FIGURE 9.3: Reaching out and touching: interchangeable views of the statue/Elio (Timothée Chalamet). Luca Guadagnino (dir.), *Call Me by Your Name*, 2017. Italy/France/USA/Brazil. © Frenesy, La Cinefacture.

more, Oliver touches Elio's mouth in almost the same way he earlier caressed the statue at the lake, as if the points of view, and Elio/statue, were interchangeable or that he, indeed, is its missing sculptural twin (Figure 9.3). In *Call Me by Your Name*, the statues may bring abundant male nudity that is beautiful but somehow mundane; it is Oliver and Elio who connect the longing they evoke to human desire and intimacy. This trope of wistful longing and the mythical contemplation of the human body that would prove core to the film's social media fandom, as I will explore next, is perhaps nowhere more fully realized than in the film's final images.

Reaching/coming out

As Claire Monk's work on *Maurice* and 'Heritage 2.0' has indicated, the twenty-first-century digital environment provides a fertile space for fans to respond to films through writing and art: the 1987 film's original trailer promised 'an eternal pairing' which, combined with the openness of the film's ending and mythical approach, stimulated the imagination of a highly active online community.[36] *Call Me by Your Name* is perhaps even more conducive to fan appropriation, with its 'ageless ambiguity' and feeling for the 'iconic' in its imagery of the past, catalysed by its photogenic leads and the sheer proportion of screen time devoted to rising star Chalamet's face and body. This is nowhere more to the fore than in the film's much-discussed final shot in which Elio, having just spoken to Oliver on the telephone and learnt of his forthcoming marriage, stares tearfully into the glowing flames of the marble fireplace – the residual warmth of a long-gone summer, snow now falling outside. More than a simple continuation of the film's homoerotic framing of ancient and modern bodies, the 3.5-minute final shot advances the film into close alignment with contemporary digital aesthetics. In the reception of

Call Me by Your Name, Timothée Chalamet became a Greek god for the YouTube generation.

On the one hand, Elio is here once more the animated statue, adopting his familiar hunched-over, *Spinario*-esque, pose, lost in melancholy. On the other hand, he has never looked more *contemporary* in the context of the film's 1980s setting: new haircut, clothes, Walkman and all. Rather than the slow motion of the statue rising from Lake Garda, we have the stillness of a static shot fixed on a human face, tears wetting his face like those droplets of water carefully contrived to run down the features of the athlete from the water. This time, however, the face does not receive the lover's touch. Sufjan Stevens' song 'Visions of Gideon' plays over the sequence, its lyrics speaking of having touched someone for the final time and questioning whether these visions are memories or, significantly, a video. Echoing the 'visions' of the earlier slideshow, this time firelight plays over Elio's face as if he were the projected image, or if illuminated in the manner of a glowing screen today. Elio momentarily looks up at the camera before the screen fades to black, reflexively acknowledging both camera and audience. It is here that the film's iconography of lingering shots on Elio's face – perhaps the emotion of his longing gaze at the dancing Oliver its nearest counterpart – recalls the aesthetics of innumerable other LGBTQ+ people in the prolific YouTube genre of the 'coming-out video'. As a young fan coming to terms with his sexuality posted in reply to one of Chalamet's Instagram posts: 'In the final scene, when you broke the fourth wall and looked right at me, for the first time I felt seen'.[37] In coming-out videos YouTubers, often with an established relationship with their subscribers, reveal their sexuality to the camera, or come out to others while filming themselves. As John Wei has discussed, the genre had been growing though the 2010s,[38] and August 2017,[39] as *Call Me by Your Name* was between festival screenings and general release, saw the highest number of coming-out content in the platform's history. 'YouTube celebrity has thus become a central space not only for the representation of gay identities', Michael Lovelock asserts, 'but for the circulation of particular scripts of coming out'.[40]

One of the most prominent coming-out videos on YouTube is that of musician and actor Troye Sivan, whose original 8-minute 2013 video has received over 8.8 million views at the time of writing with a follow-up in 2015.[41] In the video, Sivan relates his experience of coming out as gay three years earlier at the age of 15, and particularly the (positive) occasion when, after a few moments when he couldn't speak, he had tearfully told his father about his sexuality. Sivan explains that 'I share every aspect of my life with the internet' and offers reassurance as well as a promise of support for his viewers. The image of Sivan on the screen is strikingly like that of Elio: the faces of two young LGBTQ+ men framed on a screen reflecting on their sexuality, the past and the future, and both look at the camera. Instead of the background of a dining table in the Perlmans' villa there is what looks like Sivan's modern bedroom, warm light shining on a TV screen in the background (Figure 9.4). As Losh and Alexander note of the coming-out genre, these videos as characterized by a 'temporary mastery of domestic space and control of the gaze of the viewing public looking in'.[42] Elio is practically sitting *in* the hearth at the end of the film when he makes this connection with the camera. There is also the odd similarity between the looks of the men, something that Sivan discussed in a 2018 interview (much quoted in the gay press) with digital entertainment website *PopCrush*, writing himself into the film's reception.[43] Sivan relates that he wished that he had auditioned for *Call Me by Your Name*, stating that Elio is the only character of which he could say that he could

> 100 percent relate to that person. Like every single thing, even down to his body type and the way that he looks. It's so strange. I look at his body and I'm like, 'That's my body.' Like skinny, small little nipples, pale. Like everything down to the nipples, it's me.[44]

In a *Time* magazine article later that year Sivan was described as 'queer, sensitive, thoughtful' and 'a true digital native' in his connection with the camera.[45] Again, his slight build is evoked as part of his popularity in seeking to create a space for 'people who look and act like him' rather than what Sivan terms all the 'hunky straight white male pop stars'.[46]

Likewise, Chalamet's slender body, which draws the camera in the film's first shot after the credits, marks difference not only from the body of Oliver but from the gym-built bodies that predominate among his male contemporaries on various forms of screen media. Sivan relates to *PopCrush* that he doesn't know 'if the world needs another sad gay album' and hoped that his forthcoming release

FIGURE 9.4: Elio (Timothée Chalamet) in the final shot of *Call Me by Your Name*. Luca Guadagnino (dir.), *Call Me by Your Name*, 2017. Italy/France/USA/Brazil. © Frenesy, La Cinefacture; Troye Sivan in his 2013 YouTube video, 'Coming Out'.

would offer some 'sonic relief'. His explanation that 'we've been through shit in the past and we're going to continue to go through shit, but we're always going to be okay' is clearly a reference to homophobia and perhaps more specifically that surrounding the HIV/AIDS pandemic, a crisis that arguably forms a structuring absence in *Call Me by Your Name*, and one that is yet to touch the life of Elio as he looks us in the eye at the end of the film. This is the 'projective temporality' of Oliver's parting mantra, 'Later', discussed by Galt and Schoonover, setting up a recursive connection with enfolding queer history.[47] Elio's haunted beauty presents the 'sad young man' queer archetype discussed by Richard Dyer in a way that he doesn't quite fit for the rest of the film.[48] Or rather, he is the sad ephebe, beautiful and yearning, and with a touch of a smile towards the end of the shot, because he *has* loved and lost, and will presumably love again. It is not because he was being marginalized by society and has been denied that love or, for that matter, its positive representation on screen.

Sivan's fans were swift to spot a resonance between his music and image and *Call Me by Your Name*. On YouTube there were fanvids (fan-made videos) posted from at least early December 2017, combining clips from the film edited to Sivan's songs, seamlessly blended with footage from his videos. Hundreds more would follow. The YouTube channel of style magazine *Dazed* even posted a video of Sivan reciting the lyrics of Stevens' 'Mystery of Love' in March 2018.[49] However, while the entwining of Sivan in the reception of *Call Me by Your Name* is fascinating as a marker of queer cultural production in the late 2010s, I would argue that the greater significance lies in the way that such implicit contemporary resonances with youth and queer-focused digital culture were carefully aligned to help the film reach and gain word-of-mouth success with young adult audiences. While Elio is resolutely in the analogue world, he casts an eye on the contemporary audience looking back from the digital world. Indeed, more than just being conducive to such appropriations it is likely that they were an active part of the film's marketing strategy.

Digital classicism

The film's critical and fan receptions were clearly drawn to its imagery and historical framings, particularly relating to Hammer and Chalamet, and each actor transitioned a higher magnitude of celebrity by association, one secured by an aura of arthouse prestige. For example, *British GQ Style* gave readers a choice of two covers of the *Call Me by Your Name* leads in late 2017, with Chalamet's headlined 'A Star Is Born', while Hammer became 'A Man of Power'. Hammer's cover for *The Hollywood Reporter*, meanwhile, read 'A Star Becomes an Actor'.[50]

The Economist's Toronto International Film Festival review amalgamated classical deities with superheroes in praise of Hammer's attributes: 'Confident and immovable, Oliver resembles a Greek god in human form, or perhaps Superman (Mr Hammer was once in consideration to play the Man of Steel)'.[51] Molly Haskell's *Film Comment* review, meanwhile, presented Oliver as 'an Adonis who moves as if by divine right among the French-Italian admirers'.[52] References to Greek gods would become ubiquitous in fan receptions, which seized the opportunities offered by digital media to deploy images and prose for effect, an approach anticipated in an evocative review in youth-focused digital publication *Mic*, reporting from the Berlinale film festival: 'Elio [...] looks like a Greek bronze statue come to life [...]. Several times in the film we see him draped across a sofa, the *Barberini Faun* in a Talking Heads T-shirt, Elio as a gay Pygmalion in reverse.'[53] Although recalling the Endymion type, *the Barberini Faun* – with what might be termed today 'manspreading' legs drawing the gaze to its genitals – is perhaps a touch too provocative an image for Elio, but the pop-culture costume reference is apt. This also aligns the film's aesthetic with the work of contemporary artists such as Leo Caillard, whose dressed statues from his 'Hipsters in Stone' photographic series (2012–16)[54] is part of a playful artistic trope that uses the absurd to mock prudishness about nude sculpture. *Mic*'s description of 'A gay Pygmalion in reverse' is fascinating, if a little confusing. The point is that we have a gay, rather than straight, version of the Pygmalion myth, with Chalamet the statue brought to life.

The film's best-known fan art comes from the 'Call Me by Monet' and 'chalametinart' Instagram accounts, which Joey Fathom argues has turned Chalamet into 'a sort of classical figure' online.[55] These images teleport Chalamet into various art history locales and are an excellent example of Henry Jenkins' notion of 'media convergence' and the porous borders between different media.[56] The star was filmed reacting to images from the latter account when he appeared on *The Tonight Show Starring Jimmy Fallon* to discuss his experience at the Academy Awards as a nominee for *Call Me by Your Name* as well as promoting his new film, *Beautiful Boy* (Felix Van Groeningen, 2018). In a clip that posted on the show's official YouTube channel (Figure 9.5), which has been viewed over 4 million times,[57] Chalamet indicates his familiarity with the images, and while he appears embarrassed and exclaims 'That is so weird' as the audience is presented with a close-up of an image skilfully blending his features into the statue of Michelangelo's *David* that had been posted earlier that year,[58] he also indicates appreciation to the anonymous fan for their creativity in producing it. The image in question had been posted on 9 July 2018 with the official account of Chalamet tagged on the face of what we might call 'Chalamet–*David*', and the film tagged on his torso. Fallon's show was the top late-night US show in the key ad-sales demographic of 18- to 49-year-olds in 2018, notably, *The Hollywood Reporter* claims, holding 'an edge

FIGURE 9.5: Timothée Chalamet encounters his 'chalametinart' Instagram composite on *The Tonight Show Starring Jimmy Fallon* (NBC), 10 October 2018.

in the digital afterlife' through its leading number of views for its YouTube clips.[59] The show was clearly exactly the right space for Chalamet not only to promote his career and Guadagnino's film but to further connect with the wider digital audience who are already engaging with images such as the 'Chalamet–*David*'.

Michelangelo's *David*, one of the world's most recognizable artworks, copied across innumerable postcards and souvenirs since the Grand Tour era, is in many ways an apt icon to be worked into Chalamet's image. The original placing of *David* outside the site of civic power that is now Florence's Palazzo Vecchio framed the statue within 'the widest range of interpretative messages', John T. Paoletti has argued, alluding to the city's foundational myths and recent history while drawing from 'Biblical history and classical mythology' with its 'ironic depiction of the weak adolescent of the biblical narrative as a heroic marble giant'.[60] The Biblical David, the youth famed for slaying Goliath and becoming the King of Israel, is another shepherd figure, and with a gift for soothing harp-playing in the way that Elio beguiles the more Herculean Oliver with the guitar or piano. Physically, however, while Chalamet shares the tousled hair and large eyes of the statue, their body types are markedly different; *David* is the opposite of Sivan's pithy description of a body that is 'skinny, small little nipples, pale'. The statue is certainly pale, constructing a marble Chalamet attuned to a bias towards whiteness in the reception of western art, but the differences miss the point. The low-angled photograph of *David*, taken from the perspective of a visitor beneath his pedestal, emphasizes the imposing 5.17-metre form and defiant expression of the sculpture, a hero 'capable of overcoming all adversity', as Paoletti observes of the Michelangelo original.[61] Mapped onto Chalamet, and in the context of *Call Me by Your Name*'s reception, Elio becomes an auratic art object even beyond the kind of associations we have seen in the film itself. Armed with a slingshot and newly muscled in an alternative, absurdly fetishized, version of his body, the Chalamet–*David* seems ready to face whatever the future throws at it. Still, the image is 'weird', as Chalamet says, and uncanny; it is clearly the avatar of both *David* and Chalamet – the heroically scaled union of both – and yet neither of them, and is photographically lifelike and yet also deathlike in cold stone with glazed-over eyes.

The Instagram image is exemplary of a trope that embraces statue-play in the reception of Chalamet, particularly as Elio. The Chalamet–*David* is deftly Photoshopped, but often the images produced by fans and circulated on platforms such as Instagram, Twitter (now X) and Pinterest are fragmentary collages of two or more images, often with a photograph of Chalamet from the film cropped diagonally to reveal a perfectly aligned sculpture of an ancient youth beneath, as if archaeologically excavated. These images belong to a long history of icon-play, including that of the aforementioned Gloria Swanson embodying Venus in the 1920s or, more closely, Clarence Sinclair Bull's 1931 'The Swedish Sphinx' photomontage that transposed Greta Garbo's face onto the body of the *Great Sphinx of Gisa*.[62] Nonetheless, there is perhaps something in the delicate structure of Chalamet's features, that youthful blend of masculine and feminine with that 'ageless ambiguity' constructed in the film, that makes the star so conducive to these images. There is now a virtual museum's worth of fan-curated sculptural Chalamets dispersed online, an example of the 'insistent reiteration' of online cultural production described by Carol Vernallis.[63] As well as precedents set by the film and other fans, these images were perhaps also inspired beyond the film by advertising using classical sculpture, such as in Paco Rabanne's 2018 'Olympéa' campaign; fragrance advertising having frequent recourse to classical sculpture to exploit the lucrative halo from centuries of reception as icons of beauty.[64] A fascinating match for the trope in which Chalamet's face is bisected by that of a sculpture can be found in Swatch's spring 2018 campaign for its 'Skin Irony' collection of watches, featuring the hashtag #FutureClassic. The main imagery consisted of the faces of three young men and one woman cut diagonally by the image of a silvered classical statue. Rome's historic centre was graced by at least two billboards from this campaign, one above the Fontana del Moro in Piazza Navona. At its launch reception in Antwerp in May 2018, the watches were displayed on marble pedestals overlooked by what looks like a full-sized Greek statue; on its wrist was one of the watches, of course.[65] It resembles one of the twin *Riace Warriors* that were discovered in the sea in southern Italy in 1972 and is likely one of the inspirations for the sculpture raised from the waters in *Call Me by Your Name*. Whether the advertising inspired the fan images or vice-versa is unknown, but again this evidences the way that the seemingly 'old-fashioned' classical iconography in *Call Me by Your Name* and its reception were closely aligned to contemporary uses of ancient heritage targeted at young audiences and consumers to effectively create a 'digital word-of-mouth' effect.

Although there is slash fiction online where fans extend the erotic experience of the characters – the hosting site Archive of Our Own currently lists 4,511 stories associated with the film's title[66] – and fan art can be explicit, for the most part the attraction of *Call Me by Your Name* is more sensual than sexual. Among fan images we find clever reworkings of the film poster transformed by Bernini's sculpture *David*, with Elio and Oliver each as *David* from a different angle. We also see Twitter being used in a way akin to a scholarly video essay, as in a tweet by critic Rhett Butler. The tweet juxtaposed an image of the tearful Elio in the car after leaving Oliver at the train station, his left hand held up to his right temple, next to its near exact double in the pose of the statue from the lake. 'That incredible subtle moment when @RealChalamet's pose mirrors that of the statue', read the caption.[67] Shared receptions such as this invite others to view the film in a similar fashion.[68] The film's official social media campaign can be seen to tacitly encourage, and recirculate, this meme-ing of characters, art objects and fetishizing of statues. In its 2018 Valentine's Day message a gif of the statue rising to the surface was given the caption 'I love you like Mr. Perlman loves statues'.[69] The much-pictured shirt James Ivory wore to the Academy Awards in March 2018, emblazoned with a sketch of Chalamet, is another form of this icon-play.[70] Sony Pictures' Facebook page for the film was initiated in August 2017 as it made the famous image of the meeting of ancient and modern hands its profile picture,[71] and its posting of a *Little White Lies* magazine cover featuring a painterly Chalamet later that month hinted at the way the imagery would be restyled in different artistic fashions in the coming months.[72]

The strongest influence on fan art was perhaps the music video for Sufjan Stevens' 'Mystery of Love', which was launched in early January 2018.[73] The visuals are loosely associative and are redolent of the place of the classical *objet d'art* within queer culture. Stills from the music video were often the source, and inspiration, for artist and fan-made juxtapositions, including one playful Pinterest image juxtaposing a profile portrait of Chalamet with a marble statue as proof that the star is, as the capitalized caption puts it, an 'ACTUAL GREEK GOD'. Like the fan work discussed by Monk with respect to *Maurice*, there is a strong use of 'digital "manips" (manipulations) of existing still images or screencaps' as well as a foregrounding of '"iconic" images' in the reception of *Call Me by Your Name*.[74] However, given the palimpsestic historical imagery of the film and a star in Chalamet who engenders particularly intense responses and identification, the generative impulse it seems to foster for fans to actively perform a kind of digital archaeology themselves in response is remarkable.

Conclusion

This chapter has argued that the cultural familiarity of classical sculpture in western culture enabled audiences to appreciate the intricate symbolism of *Call Me by Your Name* and to become participants in this ongoing mediation. Just as in classicism where, as Beard and Henderson put it, 'to copy an original is to *re*-create the original; but it is also to *create* an original',[75] the creative work performed by fans in creating fanart or fanvids (vidding) finds audiences digging deeper into the film's world while at the same time adding filigree layers of patina to create something that is ostensibly new in form but authentically old in tradition. As Tisha Turk observes, vidding, and I would argue the other forms discussed above, 'involves *both* interpreting commercial texts *and* producing new texts for an audience of fellow fans'.[76] Texts such as the Chalamet–*David*, like the photomontages of classic Hollywood, can at once be superficial in their entertaining play with the image *and* speak profoundly as the latest iterations of a palimpsestic, and at least partly queer-authored, history of reception.

Call Me by Your Name is not unique in having a strong and imaginative online following. However, the combination of its romantic Italian summer location and period setting, its young stars – Chalamet in particular – its poignant sense of longing and loss, and visuals rich in cultural patination, provide and arguably encourage abundant opportunities for audience engagement. Its release came at a moment – aided by other cross-over gay releases such as *God's Own Country* (Francis Lee) and *Moonlight* (Barry Jenkins) in 2017 – when the spotlight had been cast more directly onto the experience of young LGBTQ+ individuals, and the film has clearly helped many to articulate this experience and 'dare to desire', in inspiring them to embrace and rework its iconography.

NOTES

1. Richard Dyer, *The Matter of Images: Essays on Representations* (London: Routledge, 1993), 25.
2. Robert Aldrich, *The Seduction of the Mediterranean: Writing, Art and Homosexual Fantasy* (London: Routledge, 1993), x.
3. Whitney Davis, *Queer Beauty: Sexuality and Aesthetics from Winckelmann to Freud and Beyond* (New York: Columbia University Press, 2010), 44.
4. Davis, 50.

5. Michael Williams, *Film Stardom, Myth and Classicism: The Rise of Hollywood's Gods* (Basingstoke: Palgrave Macmillan, 2013).

6. Michael Williams, 'Gloria Swanson as Venus: Silent Stardom, Antiquity and the Classical Vernacular', in *The Ancient World in Silent Cinema*, ed. Pantelis Michelakis and Maria Wyke (Cambridge: University of Cambridge Press, 2013), 125–44.

7. Williams, *Myth and Classicism*, 76–81.

8. 'Athlet', Kunsthistorisches Museum, Vienna, accessed 13 April 2023, https://www.khm.at/en/objectdb/detail/67188/?offset=2&lv=list.

9. The Museum of Apoxyomenos, Lošinj, Croatia, accessed 13 April 2023, https://www.muzejapoksiomena.hr/en/.

10. Georg A. Plattner, Kurt Gschwantler and Bettina Vak, 'The Bronze *Athlete* from Ipanema', in *Artistry in Bronze: The Greeks and Their Legacy (XIXth International Congress on Ancient Bronzes)*, ed. Jens M. Daehner, Kenneth Lapatin and Ambra Spinelli, J. Paul Getty Museum, Getty Conservation Institute, 2017, https://www.getty.edu/publications/artistryinbronze/large-scale-bronzes/1-plattner-gschwantler-vak/.

11. David Lowenthal, *The Past Is a Foreign Country: Revisited* (Cambridge: Cambridge University Press, 2015), 244.

12. J. Paul Getty Museum, 'Power and Pathos: Bronze Sculpture of the Hellenistic World', accessed 13 April 2023, https://www.getty.edu/art/exhibitions/power_pathos/BRONZES_EXHIBITION_CHECKLIST.pdf.

13. John Sherman, 'Berlinale Review: *Call Me by Your Name* Is a Portrait of Homosexual Intimacy that Honors the Book', *Mic*, 14 February 2017, https://mic.com/articles/168595/berlinale-review-call-me-by-your-name-is-a-portrait-of-homosexual-intimacy-that-honors-the-book#.YjAYJmdmp.

14. Benjamin Eldon Stevens, 'Classical Desires in *Call Me by Your Name* (dir. Luca Guadagnino 2017)', *Antiquipop: Antiquity, Pop Culture & Politics*, https://antiquipop.hypotheses.org/eng/3264eng.

15. '*Spinario*', Musei Capitolini, accessed 13 April 2023, http://www.museicapitolini.org/it/percorsi/percorsi_per_sale/appartamento_dei_conservatori/sala_dei_trionfi/spinario.

16. Kenneth J. Dover, *Greek Homosexuality* (Cambridge: Harvard University Press, [1978] 1989), 16.

17. André Aciman, *Call Me by Your Name* (London: Atlantic Books, [2007] 2009); Stevens, 'Classical Desires'.

18. Timothée Chalamet and Michael Stuhlbarg, 'Commentary with Timothée Chalamet and Michael Stuhlbarg', *Call Me by Your Name* (London: Sony Pictures, 2018), Blu-ray Disc, SBR J0189UV.

19. Malparte, '*Les statues aiment aussi …*', *Overreading*, 5 May 2020, https://overreading.com/les-statues-aiment-aussi/.

20. See 'Object: *The Farnese Hermes*', British Museum, accessed 13 April 2023, https://www.britishmuseum.org/collection/object/G_1864-1021-1.

21. Francis Haskell and Nicholas Penny, *Taste and the Antique: The Lure of Classical Sculpture 1500–1900* (New Haven and London: Yale University Press, 2006), 308.

22. Haskell and Penny, 308.

23. Nigel Spivey, *Greek Sculpture* (Cambridge: Cambridge University Press, 2013), 308.

24. Stevens, 'Classical Desires'.

25. Francesca Sobande, 'The Internet's "Transnational" Boyfriend: Digital (Re)Presentations of Celebrity Men', *Feminist Media Studies* 21, no. 4 (2021): 8, https://doi.org/10.1080/14680777.2021.1900312.

26. Chalamet and Stuhlbarg, 'Commentary'.

27. Laura Marcus, '"In the Key of Loss": Aciman, Guadagnino, and *Call Me by Your Name*', *Journal of World Literature* 6, no. 3 (2021): 374, citing André Aciman, *Call Me by Your Name* (New York: Farrar, Straus and Giroux, 2007), 68.

28. Marcus, '"In the Key"', 377, citing André Aciman, *Alibis: Essays on Elsewhere* (New York: Farrar, Straus and Giroux, 2011), 191.

29. Rosalind Galt and Karl Schoonover, 'Untimely Desires, Historical Efflorescence, and Italy in *Call Me by Your Name*', *Italian Culture* 37, no. 1 (March 2019), https://doi.org/10.1080/01614622.2019.1609220, 10.

30. Malparte, '*Les statues*'.

31. 'Statue of a Victorious Youth', The J. Paul Getty Museum, accessed 13 April 2023, https://www.getty.edu/art/collection/objects/7792/unknown-maker-statue-of-a-victorious-youth-greek-300-100-bc/?dz=#68788f24efae95841e79b70adf1a8cc848572090.

32. Chalamet and Stuhlbarg, 'Commentary'.

33. Chalamet and Stuhlbarg, 'Commentary'.

34. See Michael Williams, 'Room with a Gay View?: Sexuality, Spectatorship and *A Room With a View*', in *Screen Methods: Comparative Readings in Screen Studies* (London: Wallflower Press, 2006), ed. Jacqueline Furby and Karen Randell, 91–101.

35. Chalamet and Stuhlbarg, 'Commentary'.

36. Claire Monk, 'Heritage Film Audiences 2.0: Period Film Audiences and Online Fan Cultures', *Participations: Journal of Audience & Reception Studies* 8, no. 2 (2011), http://www.participations.org/Volume%208/Issue%202/3h%20Monk.pdf.

37. Quoted in Tyler Quick, 'The Queer Public and Its Problem with Representation', *The Velvet Light Trap* 86 (Autumn 2020), 33.

38. John Wei, 'Out on YouTube: Queer Youths and Coming Out Videos in Asia and America', *Feminist Media Studies* (2021): 2.

39. Curtis M. Wong, 'Here's a Brief History of the YouTube Coming Out Video', *Huffington Post*, 12 October 2017, https://www.huffingtonpost.co.uk/entry/10-youtube-coming-out-videos_n_59dd1c60e4b04fc4e1e94082.

40. Michael Lovelock, '"Is Every YouTuber Going to Make a Coming Out Video Eventually?": YouTube Celebrity Video Bloggers and Lesbian and Gay Identity', *Celebrity Studies* 8, no. 1 (2017): 88.

41. Troye Sivan, 'Coming Out', YouTube, 7 August 2013, https://youtu.be/JoL-MnXvK80; Troye Sivan, 'Coming Out (Part 2)', YouTube, 17 May 2015, https://youtu.be/UfXEcpGCxiw.

42. Jonathan Alexander and Elizabeth Losh, '"A YouTube of One's Own?": "Coming Out" Videos as Rhetorical Action', in *LGBT Identity and Online New Media*, ed. Christopher Pullen and Margaret Cooper (New York: Routledge, 2010), 38.

43. Dana Getz, 'Troye Sivan: The World Doesn't Need a Sad Gay Album', 22 February 2018, *PopCrush*, https://popcrush.com/troye-sivan-interview-sophomore-album-the-new-a-list/.

44. Getz, 'Troye Sivan'.

45. Raisa Bruner, 'Troye Sivan Is a New Kind of Pop Icon', *Time*, 3–10 September 2018: 100.

46. Bruner, 101.

47. Galt and Schoonover, 'Untimely Desires', 14.

48. See Richard Dyer, 'Coming Out as Going In: The Image of the Homosexual as a Sad Young Man', in *The Culture of Queers*, by Richard Dyer (London: Routledge, 2002), 116–36.

49. Dazed, 'Troye Sivan Recites "Mystery of Love"', YouTube, 14 March 2018, https://youtu.be/dUBou48RL58.

50. *British CQ Style* 25 (launched October 2017), cover; *The Hollywood Reporter*, 20 November 2017, cover.

51. N.E.G., '*Call Me by Your Name* Is a Work of Beauty', *The Economist*, 8 September 2017, https://www.economist.com/prospero/2017/09/08/call-me-by-your-name-is-a-work-of-beauty.

52. Molly Haskell, '*Call Me by Your Name*', *Film Comment* 53, no.6 (November–December, 2017): 68.

53. Sherman, 'Berlinale Review'.

54. See Anne-Lise Desmas, 'Edme Bouchardon's *Sleeping Faun* Takes Up Residence in the Getty's Entrance Hall', *Getty Iris*, 14 December 2016, https://blogs.getty.edu/iris/edme-bouchardons-sleeping-faun-takes-up-residence-in-the-gettys-entrance-hall/.

55. Joey Fathom, '*Call Me by Your Name*: From Guadagnino's Film to the "Call Me by Monet" Instagram Account', *Film Matters* 11, no. 1 (1 March 2020), 169.

56. For discussion and examples of these Instagram accounts as well as on media convergence, see Fathom, '*Call Me*'; Fathom cites Henry Jenkins, 'Introduction: "Worship at the Altar of Convergence": A New Paradigm for Understanding Media Change', in *Convergence Culture: Where Old and New Media Collide*, ed. Henry Jenkins (New York and London: NYU Press, 2006), 1–24.

57. *The Tonight Show Starring Jimmy Fallon*, 'Timothée Chalamet Reacts to Being Photoshopped into Artwork Memes', YouTube, 10 October 2018, https://youtu.be/MrPuw_F-dXA.

58. Chalametinart, '*David*, 1501–1504 by Michelangelo', Instagram, 9 July 2018.

59. Rick Porter, 'Colbert Increases Late-Night Viewer Lead in 2018, Fallon Still Tops Demos', *The Hollywood Reporter*, 18 December 2018, https://www.hollywoodreporter.com/tv/tv-news/tonight-show-late-show-ratings-fall-2018-1170567/.

60. John T. Paoletti, *Michelangelo's* David: *Florentine History and Civic Identity* (Cambridge: Cambridge University Press, 2015), 174.

61. Paoletti, 174.

62. See Michael Williams, *Film Stardom and the Ancient Past: Idols, Artefacts and Epics* (London: Palgrave Macmillan, 2017), 26–31.

63. David McGowan, 'Nicolas Cage – Good or Bad? Stardom, Performance, and Memes in the Age of the Internet', *Celebrity Studies* 8, no. 2 (2017): 215, citing Carol Vernallis, *Unruly Media: YouTube, Music Video, and the New Digital Cinema* (New York: Oxford University Press, 2013), 131.

64. See 'Olympéa | PACO RABANNE', Official YouTube channel, 16 January 2018, https://youtu.be/oH7axwK5YTY.

65. Bert Buijsrogge, 'Swatch Skin Irony Launch Party (In Antwerp) Report', *Watch-Insider*, 28 May 2018, https://watch-insider.com/swatch/launch-of-swatch-skin-irony-collection/.

66. See Archive of Our Own, accessed 18 December 2023, https://archiveofourown.org.

67. Rhett Bartlett (@dialmformovies), Twitter, 26 January 2018.

68. A book of Facebook fan posts was published in 2018: Barb Mirell, ed., *Call Me by Your Name: How a Little Film Touched So Many Lives* (Philadelphia: Liberty Bell Publishers, 2018).

69. @CMBYNFilm, Twitter, 14 February 2018.

70. See Hilary Weaver, 'The Story Behind James Ivory's Timothée Chalamet Shirt', *Vanity Fair*, 4 March 2018, https://www.vanityfair.com/style/2018/03/james-ivory-is-wearing-timothee-chalamet-face.

71. @CallMeByYourNameMovie, Facebook, 4 August 2017.

72. See Facebook posting on 31 August 2017 of the September–October issue of *Little White Lies*; see also '*Call Me by Your Name*', *Little White Lies*, October 2017, https://lwlies.com/back-issues/call-me-by-your-name/.

73. See 'Sufjan Stevens – "Mystery of Love" (from *Call Me by Your Name* Soundtrack)', SonySoundtracksVEVO channel, YouTube, 12 January 2018, https://youtu.be/gVVhHjyC04k.

74. Monk, 'Audiences 2.0', 453.

75. Mary Beard and John Henderson, *Classical Art: From Greece to Rome* (Oxford: Oxford University Press, 2001), 6.

76. Tisha Turk, 'Transformation in a New Key: Music in Vids and Vidding', *Music, Sound, and the Moving Image 9*, no. 2 (2015): 164, cited in E. Charlotte Stevens, *Fanvids: Television, Women, and Home Media Re-Use* (Amsterdam: Amsterdam University Press, 2020), 9, original emphasis.

University of Southampton ERGO Submission ID: 62556

REFERENCES

Aciman, André. *Call Me by Your Name*. New York: Farrar, Straus and Giroux, 2007.

Aciman, André. *Call Me by Your Name*. London: Atlantic Books, [2007] 2009.

Aciman, André. *Alibis: Essays on Elsewhere*. New York: Farrar, Straus and Giroux, 2011.

Aldrich, Robert. *The Seduction of the Mediterranean: Writing, Art and Homosexual Fantasy*. London: Routledge, 1993.

Alexander, Jonathan, and Elizabeth Losh. '"A YouTube of One's Own?": "Coming Out" Videos as Rhetorical Action.' In *LGBT Identity and Online New Media*, edited by Christopher Pullen and Margaret Cooper, 37–50. New York: Routledge, 2010.

Beard, Mary, and John Henderson. *Classical Art: From Greece to Rome*. Oxford: Oxford University Press, 2001.

Bruner, Raisa. 'Troye Sivan Is a New Kind of Pop Icon.' *Time*, 3–10 September 2018: 99–101.

Buijsrogge, Bert. 'Swatch Skin Irony Launch Party (In Antwerp) Report.' *Watch-Insider*, 28 May 2018. https://watch-insider.com/swatch/launch-of-swatch-skin-irony-collection/.

Chalamet, Timothée, and Michael Stuhlbarg. 'Commentary with Timothée Chalamet and Michael Stuhlbarg.' In *Call Me by Your Name*. London: Sony Pictures, 2018. Blu-ray Disc. SBR J0189UV.

Davis, Whitney. *Queer Beauty: Sexuality and Aesthetics from Winckelmann to Freud and Beyond*. New York: Columbia University Press, 2010.

Desmas, Anne-Lise. 'Edme Bouchardon's *Sleeping Faun* Takes Up Residence in the Getty's Entrance Hall.' *Getty Iris*, 14 December 2016. https://blogs.getty.edu/iris/edme-bouchardons-sleeping-faun-takes-up-residence-in-the-gettys-entrance-hall/.

Dover, Kenneth J. *Greek Homosexuality*. Cambridge: Harvard University Press, [1978] 1989.

Dyer, Richard. *The Matter of Images: Essays on Representations*. London: Routledge, 1993.

Dyer, Richard. *The Culture of Queers*. London: Routledge, 2002.

Fathom, Joey. '*Call Me by Your Name*: From Guadagnino's Film to the "Call Me by Monet" Instagram Account.' *Film Matters* 11, no. 1 (1 March 2020): 165–71.

Galt, Rosalind, and Karl Schoonover. 'Untimely Desires, Historical Efflorescence, and Italy in *Call Me by Your Name*.' *Italian Culture* 37, no. 1 (March 2019): 64–81. https://doi.org/10.1080/01614622.2019.1609220.

Getz, Dana. 'Troye Sivan: The World Doesn't Need a Sad Gay Album.' *PopCrush*, 22 February 2018. https://popcrush.com/troye-sivan-interview-sophomore-album-the-new-a-list/.

Guadagnino, Luca, dir. *Call Me by Your Name*. Frenesy Film Company, La Cinefacture, RT Features, 2017.

Haskell, Francis, and Nicholas Penny. *Taste and the Antique: The Lure of Classical Sculpture 1500–1900*. New Haven and London: Yale University Press, 2006.

Haskell, Molly. 'Call Me by Your Name.' Film Comment 53, no. 6 (November-December 2017): 67–69.

Ivory, James, dir. A Room with a View. Goldcrest Films International, Merchant Ivory Productions, 1985.

Ivory, James, dir. Maurice. Merchant Ivory Productions, Cinecom Pictures, Channel 4, 1987.

Jenkins, Barry, dir. Moonlight. A24, PASTEL, Plan B Entertainment, 2016.

Jenkins, Henry. 'Introduction: "Worship at the Altar of Convergence": A New Paradigm for Understanding Media Change.' In Convergence Culture: Where Old and New Media Collide, edited by Henry Jenkins, 1–24. New York and London: New York University Press, 2006.

Lee, Francis, dir. God's Own Country. BFI, Creative England, Shudder Films, Inflammable Films, 2017.

Lovelock, Michael. '"Is Every YouTuber Going to Make a Coming Out Video Eventually?": YouTube Celebrity Video Bloggers and Lesbian and Gay Identity.' Celebrity Studies 8, no.1 (2017): 87–103.

Lowenthal, David. The Past Is a Foreign Country: Revisited. Cambridge: Cambridge University Press, 2015.

Malparte. 'Les statues aiment aussi …' Overreading, 5 May 2020. https://overreading.com/les-statues-aiment-aussi/.

Marcus, Laura. '"In the Key of Loss": Aciman, Guadagnino, and Call Me by Your Name.' Journal of World Literature 6, no. 3 (2021): 365–80.

McGowan, David. 'Nicolas Cage – Good or Bad? Stardom, Performance, and Memes in the Age of the Internet.' Celebrity Studies 8, no. 2 (2017): 209–27.

Mirell, Barb, ed. Call Me by Your Name: How a Little Film Touched So Many Lives. Philadelphia: Liberty Bell Publishers, 2018.

Monk, Claire. 'Heritage Film Audiences 2.0: Period Film Audiences and Online Fan Cultures.' Participations: Journal of Audience & Reception Studies 8, no. 2 (2011): 431–77. http://www.participations.org/Volume%208/Issue%202/3h%20Monk.pdf.

N.E.G. 'Call Me by Your Name Is a Work of Beauty.' The Economist, 8 September 2017. https://www.economist.com/prospero/2017/09/08/call-me-by-your-name-is-a-work-of-beauty.

Niblo, Fred, dir. Ben-Hur: A Tale of the Christ. M-G-M, 1925.

Paoletti, John T. Michelangelo's David: Florentine History and Civic Identity. Cambridge: Cambridge University Press, 2015.

Plattner, Georg A., Kurt Gschwantler and Bettina Vak. 'The Bronze Athlete from Ipanema.' In Artistry in Bronze: The Greeks and Their Legacy (XIXth International Congress on Ancient Bronzes), edited by Jens M. Daehner, Kenneth Lapatin and Ambra Spinelli. J. Paul Getty Museum, Getty Conservation Institute, 2017. www.getty.edu/publications/artistryinbronze/large-scale-bronzes/1-plattner-gschwantler-vak/.

Porter, Rick. 'Colbert Increases Late-Night Viewer Lead in 2018, Fallon Still Tops Demos.' *The Hollywood Reporter*, 18 December 2018. https://www.hollywoodreporter.com/tv/tv-news/tonight-show-late-show-ratings-fall-2018-1170567/.

Quick, Tyler. 'The Queer Public and Its Problem with Representation.' *The Velvet Light Trap* 86 (Autumn 2020): 27–36.

Sherman, John. 'Berlinale Review: *Call Me by Your Name* Is a Portrait of Homosexual Intimacy that Honors the Book.' *Mic*, 14 February 2017. https://mic.com/articles/168595/berlinale-review-call-me-by-your-name-is-a-portrait-of-homosexual-intimacy-that-honors-the-book#.YjAYJmdmp.

Sivan, Troye. 'Coming Out.' YouTube, 7 August 2013. https://youtu.be/JoL-MnXvK80.

Sivan, Troye. 'Coming Out (Part 2).' YouTube, 17 May 2015. https://youtu.be/UfXEcpGCxiw.

Sobande, Francesca. 'The Internet's "Transnational" Boyfriend: Digital (Re)Presentations of Celebrity Men.' *Feminist Media Studies* 21, no. 4 (2021): 539–55. https://doi.org/10.1080/14680777.2021.1900312.

Spivey, Nigel. *Greek Sculpture*. Cambridge: Cambridge University Press, 2013.

Stevens, Benjamin Eldon. 'Classical Desires in *Call Me by Your Name* (dir. Luca Guadagnino 2017).' *Antiquipop: Antiquity, Pop Culture & Politics*. https://antiquipop.hypotheses.org/eng/3264eng.

Stevens, E. Charlotte. *Fanvids: Television, Women, and Home Media Re-Use*. Amsterdam: Amsterdam University Press, 2020.

Tonight Show Starring Jimmy Fallon, The. 'Timothée Chalamet Reacts to Being Photoshopped into Artwork Memes.' YouTube, 10 October 2018. https://youtu.be/MrPuw_F-dXA.

Turk, Tisha. 'Transformation in a New Key: Music in Vids and Vidding.' *Music, Sound, and the Moving Image* 9, no. 2 (2015): 163–76.

Van Groeningen, Felix, dir. *Beautiful Boy*. Amazon Studios, Big Indie Pictures, Plan B Entertainment, 2018.

Vernallis, Carol. *Unruly Media: YouTube, Music Video, and the New Digital Cinema*. New York: Oxford University Press, 2013.

Weaver, Hilary. 'The Story Behind James Ivory's Timothée Chalamet Shirt.' *Vanity Fair*, 4 March 2018. https://www.vanityfair.com/style/2018/03/james-ivory-is-wearing-timothee-chalamet-face.

Wei, John. 'Out on YouTube: Queer Youths and Coming Out Videos in Asia and America.' *Feminist Media Studies* (2021): 1–16.

Williams, Michael. 'Room with a Gay View?: Sexuality, Spectatorship and *A Room with a View*.' In *Screen Methods: Comparative Readings in Screen Studies*, edited by Jacqueline Furby and Karen Randell, 91–101. London: Wallflower Press, 2006.

Williams, Michael. *Film Stardom, Myth and Classicism: The Rise of Hollywood's Gods*. Basingstoke: Palgrave Macmillan, 2013.

Williams, Michael. 'Gloria Swanson as Venus: Silent Stardom, Antiquity and the Classical Vernacular.' In *The Ancient World in Silent Cinema*, edited by Pantelis Michelakis and Maria Wyke, 125–44. Cambridge: University of Cambridge Press, 2013.

Williams, Michael. *Film Stardom and the Ancient Past: Idols, Artefacts and Epics*. London: Palgrave Macmillan, 2017.

Wong, Curtis M. 'Here's a Brief History of the YouTube Coming Out Video.' *Huffington Post*, 12 October 2017. https://www.huffingtonpost.co.uk/entry/10-youtube-coming-out-videos_n_59dd1c60e4b04fc4e1e94082.

10

Call Me Bi Any Other Name: Anal Monstration, Formal Bisexualization, Gay Indigestion

Jacob Engelberg

For some viewers, *Call Me by Your Name* (Luca Guadagnino, 2017) just wasn't gay enough. Though the film centres on the desire and love between two men, its gay or queer credentials were called into question by a variety of critics, journalistic and scholarly alike. For *The Advocate*'s Ben Ratskoff, the film 'depicts an enchanted utopia where the social realities of gayness cannot intrude'; for the *Washington Post*'s Garrett Schlichte, *Call Me by Your Name* is 'indicative of how media ensconces queer life and is inherently shaming of gay sex'; in a guest article for *Slate* magazine, drag performer Miz Cracker pronounces that gay men have 'fallen for this ungay romance because it's so straight – and if we gays love anything, it's chasing after straight guys'.[1] Sentiments around these purported deficiencies were echoed by veteran scholar D. A. Miller, who declared the film typical of the 'mainstream gay-themed movie' in its supposed elision of images of sex between men: '[T]he beautification campaign in and around *Call Me by Your Name* runs gay sex through such grandiose sentimental misrecognitions that we would no longer know it even if we did see it'.[2] The troubling unrecognizability of gayness in the film is compounded, for Miller, by the visibility of what he calls its 'hetero-consummations', sex between men and women.[3] Here we get a clue as to what undergirds these critics' misgivings around the film's nongayness: a fundamental anxiety around bisexuality.

By bisexuality, I am not referring to one certain identity formation or sexuality label. Rather, I use this term in a capacious sense – similarly to its use by scholars of bisexual theory and many bisexual activists – to describe desire towards people of more than one gender.[4] Though I wish to articulate these kinds of desires with specificity, those bisexual potentialities between and beyond the gay–straight binary are expansive, resisting the presumed univocality of dominant categories of sexual orientation. The discomfort articulated by those decrying *Call Me by Your Name*'s lack of gayness is characterized, I contend, by three phenomena: an investment in the visualization of queer sexuality through the cinematic monstration of certain sex acts, which are treated as representational paradigms par excellence; the transgressions of formal bisexualization, wherein a film departs from established codes of sexual signification that work to reify gay and straight sexualities (monosexuality); and the troubling presence of nongay queers in queer space, which is, in turn, conceptualized as *putatively* gay.[5] Analysis of the roots of this discomfort not only reveals the ideological, identarian and intellectual limitations of certain queer methodologies but also uncovers the centrality of bisexuality to *Call Me by Your Name*'s cinematic project.

While one should be wary of overstating declarations of authorial intention, it is remarkable that two of *Call Me by Your Name*'s 'authors' have suggested bisexuality as a term through which to understand the text. In an interview with *Playboy*, André Aciman reflects, 'People don't talk about [*Call Me by Your Name*] as *bisexual*, do they? […] They want to see it as […] a gay story.'[6] At the Toronto International Film Festival, Luca Guadagnino proffered a similar interpretive framework: 'Maybe we are making the first bisexual movie'.[7] Though Guadagnino's claim to pioneership is obviously contestable, both his and Aciman's suggestion of bisexuality as a possible frame of interpretation is worth taking up. Similarly, Aciman's identification of certain viewers' *volition* to find in this story a knowable form of gayness is instructive. What might a queer text look like were it to exceed knowable forms of gayness? Bisexuality, I suggest, is at once an expansive and particularizing lens through which to approach *Call Me by Your Name*'s status as a nongay yet queer film. As an analytic approach, bisexuality lays bare the strictures of gay hermeneutics and monosexist representational paradigms that have stymied discussions of *Call Me by Your Name*.[8] A bisexual sensibility allows us to comprehend the film's queerness not as a truncated or inadequate form of gayness but as a portrait of sexuality's mutability.

Anal monstration

The most troubling moment for many of the film's gay critics occurs when Elio (Timothée Chalamet) and Oliver (Armie Hammer) caress one another in Elio's bedroom and undress. From the bed where the two of them embrace, the camera pans – past Eduardo Arroyo's poster for the 1981 Roland Garros tennis championship, pasted to the wall – towards an open window. The camera rests gazing out the window at a moonlit tree, Elio and Oliver's soft moans blending with the sounds of nature's Orthoptera. The turning away of the film from this carnal moment spells a problem for these critics. For Ratskoff, the film refuses 'the salacious filth and sexualized male flesh that give gay culture its radical power. [...] The post-gay world is too civilized for naughty gay boys and certainly cannot be bothered by the unfortunate deviancy of gay culture.'[9] Here, Ratskoff locates in the *visualization* of sex between men a deviant, radical power whose elision can only be assimilatory. In a similar vein, this moment reminds *Guardian* reviewer Guy Lodge of 'the kind of tasteful dodge that practically nods to Code-era Hollywood', by which he means the Production Code – effectively enforced to varying degrees between 1934 and 1968 – which prohibited the inference of 'sex perversion'.[10] Miller characterizes the camera's movement here as a 'demure retreat from the sex act', which shields a spectator from 'the unlovely spectacle of blood, shit, and pain' that he surmises to be taking place off screen.[11] For Ratskoff, Lodge and Miller alike, this pan can only be understood as a conservative and regressive gesture; not to depict what they assume to be anal penetrative sex between men is deemed classically homophobic.

These readings have, however, met contestation. David Greven, in his response to Miller's article, asserts that

> [i]t's impossible for Miller to imagine that, perhaps, the film is employing a certain level of decorum here to frustrate our appetites for full-on consummation in a manner that is commensurate with its larger, painstakingly maintained themes and aesthetics of longing to the point of deprivation.[12]

In Greven's reading, the film transposes the aches of its protagonists onto the spectator, whose potential longing to see 'full-on consummation' – to potentially look upon these actors' naked bodies and *see* them engaged in anal sex – is frustrated, leaving us with a bathos akin to that of our characters.[13] The lack of consideration given to the affective functions this scene performs is reflected in Greven's broader critique of Miller's essay, which he sees as typifying a tendency among certain gay male queer theorists: 'that anything that smacks of personal investment – emotional ties, personal and mutual – must be evacuated from any depiction of sex and sexuality'.[14] Through Greven's critique, we can thus understand the reverence of the sex act as superlative queer cinematic representation as the natural conclusion of an approach which denies the representational meaningfulness of emotionality. Within this interpretive framework, longing, pleasure, joy and melancholy are small fry when compared to the *image* of messy, abject, visceral homosex.

The privileging of the sex act among *Call Me by Your Name*'s critics is also interrogated by Rosalind Galt and Karl Schoonover in their observation that '[d]ebates around leaving the central sex scene off screen reveal a persistent anxiousness about the monstration of gay sex, a demand and sometimes a pressure for queer films to show sex acts in a declarative fashion'.[15] This investment in declarative sex acts, which they term 'queer monstration', presents itself as an imperative for queerness to be made visible. Monstration was first conceptualized in film studies by André Gaudreault, who uses the term to describe an early mode of narrative communication 'which consists of *showing* characters [...] who *act out* rather than *tell* the vicissitudes to which they are subjected'.[16] This showing rather than telling is a specifically *visual* mode of representation, the 'Here it is! Look at it' that characterized early cinema's display of attractions.[17] To be invested in a cinema of queer monstration is to forge a yardstick of queer representation with reference to a visual economy. In this economy, queer value is found in those images most identifiably *gay*.

But what 'counts' for these critics as an identifiably gay image? It is wrong to suggest that *Call Me by Your Name* never deploys a monstrative narrative mode in relation to sex – it is deployed in some instances and not in others. The film's refusal of monstration in *this moment* is a refusal of the scene of potential penetrative anal sex, that, with respect to the film *in toto*, cannot be read as a closeting of *any sex* between men. Accusations of *Call Me by Your Name*'s assimilationism, self-censorship or regressiveness are complicated by the visualization of carnal desire between Elio and Oliver at other moments in the film: from massaging to kissing to groping to cock-sucking to cum-licking. These moments *are* salacious and sexual, and, no, they would not meet the strictures of Hollywood's Production Code. There is nothing that would suggest to me that the image of a man licking a mingling of peach juice and cum off his finger is any more deferential to the sensibilities of a heterosexual or homophobic audience than the scenes of penetrative anal sex between men that can be found in successful 'gay' films like *Weekend* (Andrew Haigh, 2011) or *Kill Your Darlings* (John Krokidas, 2013). It would seem, therefore, that the complaint is not that the film elides the portrayal of sex between men but that it does not show us the scene of what many assume to be penetrative anal sex. The gay representational paradigm yearned for and politicized by these critics is not simply queer monstration, but *anal* monstration.

The image that Miller purports to have been denied – that of bloody, shitty penetrative anal sex and 'Elio's desiring asshole' – is, tellingly, one he *imagines* having taken place.[18] Nowhere does the film evidence precisely what kind of sex Elio and Oliver partook in that night.[19] Miller's secondary assumption – that Elio bottomed and Oliver topped – betrays further the limitations of his interpretive approach: the skinny, shorter ephebe must be the bottom, the muscular, taller 20-something must be the top. These imagined details are symptomatic of a normalizing undercurrent in Miller's essay, which surmises both the kind of sex that took place and the roles taken therein with reference to normative notions of what 'gay sex' *is* and which 'type' of men *do what*. We can thus come to understand Miller and other critics' identification of homophobia in the unseen (and fundamentally imagined) image of anal penetrative sex as an ideologically inflected hermeneutic bound by its own normalizing prejudices.

This hermeneutic reveals itself to be undergirded by the normative and fundamentally anti-queer assumption that anal penetrative sex is *the* gay sex act par excellence. In Miller's undeniably most well-known article, 'Anal Rope', he describes the anus as

> the popularly privileged site of gay male sex, the orifice whose sexual use general opinion considers (whatever happens to be the state of sexual practices among gay men and however it may vary according to time and place) the least dispensable element in defining the true homosexual.[20]

It would seem that, with time, Miller's sense of what 'gay male sex' is has shifted away from the variety and proteanism of sexual practices among gay men, instead seeking, in queer film representation, that which is 'popularly privileged' by 'general opinion' as meaning 'gay male sex'. It is through this allegiance to dominant sexual epistemology that Miller is now content to conflate anal penetrative sex with gayness as a whole (pun perhaps intended). Miller's surmising of a bottom and a top through qualities of these characters that one can only guess – perhaps physicality, age, demeanour – is not incidental: it is part and parcel of an epistemology of sexuality that remains tied to normative categories. To take up this epistemology of sexuality is to be limited by a rigid, overdetermined taxonomy through which sexuality is necessarily organizable into binaries of male/female, masculine/feminine, gay/straight, active/passive. These are the very structures queer enquiry has sought to unsettle.

The film, however, provides us with something more expansive than this taxonomical approach permits. *Call Me by Your Name*'s turning away from a *potential* site of anal penetrative sex occurs alongside the explicit visualization of other kinds of queer carnal relation. Consider the moment which is, for Greven, 'the film's most achingly, overpoweringly sexual scene':

> Oliver systematically cracks each of Elio's toes in order – so the older man says – to soothe his pain over a nosebleed. Elio's breath hisses out with each crack, but he submits; it's sweetly sadomasochistic. There are many ways of depicting the erotic onscreen; doesn't this one deserve recognition?[21]

Far from assimilatory, the film's depiction of moments like these, and its avoidance of that which comes to mind first when many think 'gay sex', in fact broadens the scope of queer cinematic erotics. For Greven, there is an overwhelming erotic power in this scene of toe-cracking. For me, it's Elio's perverse encounter with Oliver's swimming trunks. His face shrouded in them, he inhales the fabric that has touched the genitals he desires; as he worships this fetish object – stretched out on all-fours, yogi-like – his concupiscence is briefly assuaged in a moment of sensory abandon. My stressing of the queer import of this moment of protracted, fetishistic sexuality is grounded in my agreement with Lisa Downing 'that a queer theory that does not embrace the energies of the "perverse" is missing a trick in failing to celebrate the "twistedness," the "athwart-ness," of which perverts have long been accused'.[22] In this sense, the film's expansion of carnality *beyond* sites of penetrative sex should be understood as quintessentially perverse in its fetishistic turning towards a nonnormative object. It's moments like these, which fleetingly orient us around a heady fetish object, that offer a queer expansion of erotics. As Oliver remarks upon noticing Elio has masturbated using a peach, 'You've moved onto the plant kingdom already. What's next? Minerals?' Perhaps.

The misgivings of the critics who bemoan *Call Me by Your Name*'s lack of 'gay sex' – emblematized, for them, in the camera's turning away from a site of potential anal penetrative sex – are, in fact, parochialism. Their approach reveals what might be termed an axiology of representation, which privileges sex involving penile penetration and devalues the sexuality and eroticism of other perverse, inventive, queer kinds of carnal relation. The film itself, however, makes space for what Galt and Schoonover call 'the heterotopic and anti-reifying forces of queer desire, where queerness resists any stable mapping of bodies to identities'.[23] This queer instability is unrecognizable to some as gayness, but perhaps it is not gayness at all.

Formal bisexualization

Michael du Plessis, in his survey of discourses around bisexuality, observes that 'bisexuality seems to lend itself to exaggeration – all or nothing; everyone is bisexual or no one is'.[24] These biphobic adages have been articulated in starkly gendered ways when positioned against women and men respectively. Vis-à-vis women, the assumption is that *all* have bisexual capacity, rendering female bisexual specificity meaningless. It is from this position that female bisexuality is, in the words of Shiri Eisner, 'converted and rewritten into [...] something that's both palatable and convenient to patriarchy'.[25] Often, this conceptualization of female bisexuality treats it simply as a component or an extension of female heterosexuality: an unserious phase or an erotic spectacle for heterosexual men. When turning to critical engagements with film, we can observe this tendency in the reluctance to think cinematic representations of female bisexuality through the lens of queerness, a tendency which Maria San Filippo subverts in her reparative bisexual readings of *Persona* (Ingmar Bergman, 1966) and *Mulholland Drive* (David Lynch, 2001).[26] The nonexistence of male bisexuality, however, is conceptualized differently. As bisexual scholars and activists alike have observed, whereas women's desire towards other women is neutralized (often through hypersexualization) into 'heterosexuality', bisexual men's desire towards other men is treated as a *disqualification* of attraction towards women, yoking such desires to gayness indelibly.[27]

A symptom of this tendency can, similarly, be found in both critical and vernacular discussions around *Brokeback Mountain* (Ang Lee, 2005), the majority of which diminish the film's representations of its main characters' desires towards their wives in a strategic effort to read them as gay. These kinds of presumptions should be understood as rooted in dominant ideology's epistemological frameworks: patriarchal in their androcentrism, cissexist in their gender binarism and monosexist in their insistence on a gay-straight binary. We can understand these frameworks, in Louis Althusser's terms, as part of an ideology that *hails* sexual subjects into intelligibility, a process he calls interpellation.[28] To recognize monosexism as a constituent part of dominant sexual ideology is to better understand how bisexuality has been conceptualized as nonexistent. In other words, it is not bisexuality that is impossible, but bisexual *interpellation* within an ideology of sexuality defined by monosexism.[29]

It is evident that the dominant monosexualities are often naturalized on film, but this phenomenon is not simply a symptom of spectators' own ideological presumptions. Cinema has also worked on the level of *form* to naturalize monosexual signification. Most are familiar with the classical narrative structure deployed by many Hollywood films, in which heterosexual marriage is established as a telos reifying heteromonogamous norms.[30] Yet, comparatively, certain 'gay' narratives adhere to structures that establish a coming out temporality journeying from inauthentic closetedness to authentic outness. These kinds of 'sexual journeys' can be seen, for example, in Evie (Nicole Ari Parker) from *The Incredibly True Adventure of Two Girls in Love* (Maria Maggenti, 1995) or in Howard (Kevin Kline) from *In & Out* (Frank Oz, 1997); a character's past extragender relationship is repudiated in order to effect the coming out narrative's telos: the acceptance of the true gay self. In these narratives, as Esther Saxey argues in relation to literature, 'the archetypal story uses the exclusion of any bisexual potential as one of its key dramatic and moral incidents', in order to buttress 'an ethical battle between enforced, inauthentic heterosexuality and redemptive gay honesty'.[31] It is through the deployment of certain narrative structures that film can exclude and subsume its characters' bisexual behaviour into narrative structures that reify notions of monosexual authenticity.

It is in such narratives that a (usually female) character's intragender desires are treated as experimental phases on the way to heterosexuality, or a character's extragender desires are treated as confused or inauthentic periods on the way to homosexuality.[32] As Beth Carol Roberts discerns,

> [i]n films where the protagonist has a relationship with someone of one sex and then one with someone of the other sex, movie critics tend to read her sexual journey as one of conflict and resolution, often utilizing tropes associated with the narratives of Coming Out or Going Straight, depending on the ordering of her partners.[33]

Roberts understands these readings as a means through which critics 'sort out (quite literally) the unruly sexual histories these films depicted'.[34] Although Roberts is describing spectatorial interpretations, it is, crucially, through a film's formal qualities – here, narrative temporality – that such interpretations become either amenable to or troubling for monosexual interpretation. I contend that part of what has rendered *Call Me by Your Name* irksome for critics looking to ascribe gayness to the film is its *textual treatment* of Elio and Oliver's desire towards women. The structuring of these characters' desires resists the models of 'Coming Out' and 'Going Straight' that Roberts identifies, instead deploying a transgressive mode of textuality which confounds expectations regarding narrative and *mise en scène*. Where such cinematic systems have been used, conventionally, to signify stable monosexual subjects, their inventive and subversive deployment *against* such a signification effects what might be termed formal bisexualization.

Monosexual signification on film is conventionally achieved through reference to the dominant epistemology of sexuality which reifies the gay-straight binary. Within this epistemology, aspersions are cast on the veracity of desire towards women when expressed by a man who also desires men. For a man, Michael Amherst writes, 'a single kiss with a man can be taken as symptomatic of closeted homosexuality'.[35] That a man who has once expressed desire towards men might *retain* his desire towards women – or experience desire towards women *later* – is rendered both conceptually and epistemologically unthinkable. It is within this monosexist ideology of sexuality that *Call Me by Your Name*'s visualization of sex acts between Elio and Marzia (Esther Garrel) takes on a specific significance. Rather than be understood simply as a symptom of the 'acceptability' of images of sex between men and women in cinema, these scenes must be understood in two contexts: first, the ideological context, where it dashes presumptions around queer men's potential to desire women and, second, the textual context, wherein the film presents these scenes in concert with its narrativizing of the burgeoning love between Elio and Oliver. *Call Me by Your Name*'s visualization of sex between

Elio and Marzia thus provides an affirmative visualization of male bisexual possibility against the doctrine of monosexist ideology and the conventions of narratives of sexual becoming.

The sex scenes between Elio and Marzia are tender in their unpretentiousness. The first time they have sex is outside at night. Their figures occupy a corner of the frame against a backdrop of dimly moonlit grass. It's Elio's first time doing this, and he ejaculates prematurely. Elio is mortified but Marzia is playful and nonplussed; she laughs and reassures him that this is fine. The second time they have sex is in a stony garret atop the Perlmans' villa. Elio throws a dusty mattress to the floor and turns on the radio; F. R. David's Europop classic 'Words' plays out, Marzia removes her bikini top and Elio kisses her abdomen. The two stumble onto the dirty mattress and Elio folds down Marzia's bikini bottoms; intermittently, he kisses her mons pubis and looks directly up at her. We cut to the radio, which tinnily hisses the cheesy tune.

Watching these scenes carefully, it becomes apparent that certain critics' assertions of their graphicness – what Miller calls 'the explicitness reserved for hetero-consummations' in the film – are hyperbole.[36] The outdoor sex between Elio and Marzia is barely perceptible; their bodies flank the frame as we witness a moment not of idealized sexual union but of sweet sexual clumsiness (Figure 10.1). Although the second sex scene between the two depicts them in a less concealed manner, it cuts away to a radio just as the sex between them is beginning. When Miller writes that '[t]o gaze on love-making had been perfectly acceptable when Elio lost his (heterosexual) virginity with Marzia', and that the film treats sex between Elio and Oliver as 'the wrong kind of fuck', he cynically exaggerates the former scene's explicitness in the service of a reading unsupported by the film itself.[37] What Greven calls the 'decorum' exercized in the sex scene between Elio and Oliver is just as discernible in the scenes between Elio and Marzia: in the hiddenness of their decentred bodies in the grass and in the cutaway to the radio in the midst of their passion. Therefore Miller is, again, treating the visualization – even the nonexplicit, barely perceptible visualization – of *penetrative* sex *as* sex, as the prized form of fucking.

The placement of these scenes within the film's narrative structure poses further challenges to Miller and other critics' readings of the film's 'straightness'. Consider that the outdoor sex scene cuts to Elio hunched over at a desk, scribbling messages to Oliver declaring his desire for him; Elio and Marzia's second tryst occurs on the same day as his first with Oliver. In her consideration of different narrative temporalities and their relation to bisexual intelligibility on film, Roberts proposes that

[t]ypically we are shown (bi) characters oscillating between, or partaking in, same- and other-sex attractions, particularly in narratives where plot and/or story unfold

FIGURE 10.1: Elio (Timothée Chalamet) and Marzia (Esther Garrel): a (barely perceptible) moment not of idealized sexual union but of sweet sexual clumsiness. Luca Guadagnino (dir.), *Call Me by Your Name*, 2017. Italy/France/USA/Brazil. © Frenesy, La Cinefacture.

> in chronological order and/or within a homogenous setting. [This] strategy ensures that one sexual event is not perceived as more authentic or less definitive than the other [...]. [T]he (sexual and) narrative conditions anticipate those of the cinema, a medium in which the importance of same- and other-sex activities is weighted through temporal and spatial relations.[38]

This oscillatory approach to depicting sexual desire wherein intra- and extragender attractions occur in succession spells a bisexualization of narrative temporality; these moments' spatial contingency works to support their contextual equability. In this sense, *Call Me by Your Name* can be understood as anticipating the tendency of a monosexual spectatorial hermeneutic to disqualify certain representations of desire with the support of narrative justification, and to deny it this justification.

The temporal presentation of these desires in an oscillatory fashion, twinned with their taking place within the same milieu, frustrates attempts to read them monosexually. It is this cinematic quality that inspires critic Anthony Lane to remark,

> you don't think, Oh, Elio's having straight sex, followed by gay sex, and therefore we must rank him as bi-curious. [...] Desire is passed around the movie like a dish, and the characters are invited to help themselves, each to his or her own taste.[39]

Lane's observation that the film's portrayal of Elio's desirous excesses resists ranking this character's sexuality is accurate. However, we should not consider bisexuality (or even 'bi-curiousness') as a ranking akin to the dominant monosexualities. Bisexuality, instead, signals possibility beyond a hegemonic binary of sexuality, not an alternate model of sexual subjectivity that can be just as easily signified on film as heterosexuality and homosexuality. *Call Me by Your Name*'s formal presentation of its characters' desires frustrates monosexual taxonomy as it ushers in bisexual potentiality.

Yet it is not simply through sex scenes that *Call Me by Your Name* conveys this potentiality but also in some notable shots where the film visualizes these extensive desires through the positioning of actors' bodies as constituent parts of the *mise en scène*. We can sense this bisexual potentiality when Elio watches Oliver and Chiara (Victoire du Bois) dancing and kissing, later gazing upon their embrace the morning after the party (Figure 10.2). Yes, there is sexual jealousy here, but this is not simply the Girardian heterosexual erotic rivalry.[40] As Elio's later comments about Chiara reveal, his are sexual jealous*ies* directed towards both Chiara and Oliver, a simultaneous desire to be the one kissing *either* of them.

Or perhaps we can discern a similar organization of bodies in the *mise en scène* when Oliver beckons Marzia to feel a knot in Elio's back; the three of

FIGURE 10.2: Elio (Timothée Chalamet) gazing upon the embrace of Chiara (Victoire du Bois) and Oliver (Armie Hammer) the morning after the party. Luca Guadagnino (dir.), *Call Me by Your Name*, 2017. Italy/France/USA/Brazil. © Frenesy, La Cinefacture.

FIGURE 10.3: Marzia (Esther Garrel), Oliver (Armie Hammer) and Elio (Timothée Chalamet) touch in a moment equally caring and erotic. Luca Guadagnino (dir.), *Call Me by Your Name*, 2017. Italy/France/USA/Brazil. © Frenesy, La Cinefacture.

them touch – briefly – in a moment equally caring and erotic (Figure 10.3). These tableaux speak to the unique bisexual legibility of the triangle. A recurrent observation of bisexual theorists, including Catherine Deschamps, Marjorie Garber, Clare Hemmings, Maria Pramaggiore and Maria San Filippo, the triangular image carries the potential to convey bisexual desirous simultaneity.[41] Yes, this image is structured according to a cisnormative gender binary – its display of desire towards a man and a woman *simultaneously* – but its subversiveness lies in its *structural rejection* of compulsory monosexuality. Images of triangles featuring two men and one woman carry two subversive potentials: first, they work against the ideological denial of male bisexuality's possibility, and second, they depict a *multiplicity* of desire in a male subject, thus defying the masculinist notion of male oneness, famously theorized by Luce Irigaray.[42] We can find these subversive triangular images of male bisexuality in film examples ranging from Coline Serreau's *Pourquoi pas!* (*Why Not!*, 1977) and Eloy de la Iglesia's *El Diputado* (*Confessions of a Congressman*, 1978) to John Akomfrah's *Speak Like a Child* (1998) and Alfonso Cuarón's *Y tu mamá también* (*And Your Mother Too*, 2001). In the context of a monosexist epistemology of sexuality that denies male bisexuality's possibility and asserts the oneness of masculinity, these cinematic images are disruptive. By making this observation, I do not mean to say the image of the bisexual triangle is the ideal bisexual image. (In fact, it indicates the stringent limitations of bisexual legibility on screen.) The image of the bisexual triangle image might be understood, instead, as a means through which film has made bisexuality knowable. In a visual economy in which sexuality must be seen to be believed, the bisexual triangle image beats a monosexist visual logic at its own game.

Call Me by Your Name's handling of desire through systems of narrative temporality and *mise en scène* indicates a kind of formal bisexualization at play. Through these unconventional deployments of form, the film takes the systems of sexuality's signification on screen and perverts them to such an extent that the semiotic clues through which sexuality is usually read on screen become unreliable in their multivocality. A similar kind of sexual-semiotic polyvalence also animates Guadagnino's limited series *We Are Who We Are* (2020). Here, the sexualities of the characters Fraser and Caitlin/Harper (both of whom are played by bisexual-identified actors: Jack Dylan Grazer and Jordan Kristine Seamón, respectively) are rendered expansive through a proliferation of differently gendered desirous encounters and, with Caitlin/Harper, the unintelligibility of the character's gender.[43] Semiotic instability is a theme that *Call Me by Your Name* also touches upon in dialogue. In her compelling reading of Oliver and Samuel's (Michael Stuhlbarg) discussion of the word apricot's etymological roots, Jaishikha Nautiyal finds parallels with the film's treatment of sexuality:

> The incongruities, the repetitions, and the arbitrariness of the word apricot's signification across the seven seas catalyze the preripened, tart juiciness of desire that ironically blooms prior to and alongside the identity-fixing confines of its transnational markers [...]. Among several other moments in the film, this moment of intrigue rearranges and mobilizes what might otherwise be limited as heterosexed sensory objects of desire – opening into feeling before calling and naming the inexplicable, desire-bending-love-breaking-heart-barking-love.[44]

This desirous unnameability – metaphorized through 'apricot' as a Saussurian arbitrary sign – speaks to sexuality's potential for extensibility.[45] When queerness is articulated as being one certain thing – a *gay* thing, with a concomitant language and symbolic economy that secure its knowability – desire's extensibility becomes something to be purged. And, like the overzealous eater who has gorged themselves on apricots, peaches and eggs, these erotic excesses leave some dyspeptic.

Gay indigestion

During Oliver's first breakfast with the Perlmans, Annella (Amira Casar) offers him a second egg in a gesture of hospitality. Oliver refuses the offer, however, cautioning, 'I know myself too well. If I have a second, I'm just gonna have a third, and then a fourth, and then you're just gonna have to roll me out of here'. Oliver's awareness of his own propensity towards overindulgence serves as a rich metaphor for the bisexual desirous excesses that will come to be revealed; this is a metaphor that bisexual theorist Jo Eadie sees played out in other cinematic contexts wherein bisexual figures on film are made meaningful through their signifying 'the threats of unchecked appetite'.[46] For Eadie, filmic representations of bisexual gluttony emanate 'not out of a general emotion of "biphobia" but through [bisexuality's] implication in very particular discourses of anxiety'.[47]

One anxious discursive drama in which the bisexual figure can be found is what Eadie calls '[t]he pull between uncontainable appetite and dour asceticism'.[48] It is within this conflict between temperance and voracity that bisexuality is rendered knowable, the feared excesses of bisexual desire metaphorized in the excesses of ingurgitation. Yet further, *Call Me by Your Name*'s use of eggs as the objects through which this conflict is analogized recalls the most renowned eggs of classical literature: those served at Trimalchio's feast in Petronius's *Satyricon*. In this memorable episode, the grotesque half-hatched viscera beneath the eggs' shells signify the orgiastic excesses – both sexual and gastronomical – of Trimalchio and his guests' celebrations.[49] That the ovular excesses to which Oliver alludes might evoke this scene of antiquitarian excess speaks to the rich layers of metaphor within the film. It is, therefore, apposite that within *Call Me by Your Name*'s milieu – idyllic, leisurely, replete with knowledge of classical literature and abundant with eggs aplenty – bisexuality's own excesses come into view. With his comments, Oliver announces a propensity for desirous excess while imposing temperate limitations herein. Beneath their joviality, Oliver's words evoke the struggle between appetite and asceticism, which Eadie finds so typical of cinematic bisexualities, and an awareness of the laws of decorum governing his present surroundings. The abject image of being 'rolled out' following overconsumption is not becoming of breakfast on the veranda; Oliver saves his overindulgences to be shared privately with his allies in excess.

A focus on *Call Me by Your Name*'s metaphorization of bisexuality through excess gives us a clue as to an additional aspect of certain critics' discomfort with the film, what, I contend, is a gay discomfort with bisexuality more broadly. In his polemical and astute consideration of anti-bisexual sentiment within gay discourses, Jo Eadie proclaims:

Indigestion is at the core of the gay body politic. Its constant invitation to queers to come and join the party (in either sense of the word) results in a discomforting mass of foreign bodies lodged inside, stuck in its throat, or undigested in its stomach. The cure would be to recognize that the signs which have been collected around the figure of the homosexual [...] in fact secure nothing [...]. They do not – and this is crucial because it is the very opposite of how those signs are usually read – *tell us anything*.[50]

Here, Eadie parses precisely the threat that bisexuality poses a certain form of gay politics, that which San Filippo terms 'bisexuality's ontological, epistemological and representational polysemy that generates its subversive potential to lay bare the mutability, contingency and inherent transgressiveness of desire'.[51] *Polysemous excess is the enemy of a gay representational politics predicated on knowable signs.* To view Elio's face – in one instant enshrouded in Oliver's swimming trunks, inhaling a trace of the cock and balls he desires, and, in another, hovering above Marzia's vulva, transfixed in anticipation of the pleasures that await him – is to view a figure desirously polymorphous and semiotically polysemous.

The threat of bisexuality to a certain kind of gay politics has been theorized by Kenji Yoshino in his hypothesis that straight and gay people 'have mutual investments in the erasure of bisexuals'.[52] The causes of these investments are outlined by Yoshino as, first, an unwillingness or an inability to understand phenomena beyond binaries (both philosophically and cognitively), and, second, a political investment in stabilizing categories of sexual orientation, maintaining the alleged 'primacy' of sex binarism, and preserving the norm of monogamy.[53] The specifically gay investment in bisexual erasure is also characterized, according to Yoshino, by an 'interest in guarding the stability of homosexuality, insofar as [gay people] view that stability as the predicate for the "immutability defense" or for effective political mobilization'.[54] Bisexual erasure can thus be understood as an epistemic tool through which homosexuality can shore up its pretence of immutability and position its politics with reference to a stable contingent.

Eve Kosofsky Sedgwick argues, in one of queer theory's foundational texts, that heterosexuality's meaning is dependent on the 'simultaneous subsumption and exclusion' of homosexuality.[55] While this observation is, as Sedgwick would say, axiomatic, we must also account for a homologous process to that which she describes. In this process, homosexuality is made meaningful through the subsumption and exclusion of heterosexuality. These contrapuntal straight and gay processes are contingent upon what Clare Hemmings calls the 'due process of repudiation in the formation of a gendered and sexual self'.[56] The repudiation of one or other gender thus works to establish monosexual subjectivity as immutable: innate, natural, unchanging. For a gay politics or theory to acknowledge bisexual possibility is to lose grip of certain binary structures of which it has made strategic use in asserting its immutability: straight/gay, male/female, monogamous/nonmonogamous. It is through these binaries that mainstream gay politics has made some of its legislative gains, from same-sex marriage to asylum-seeking on the basis of sexual orientation.[57] Yet texts hold the potential to remind us of the excesses of desire disavowed by this kind of gay politics, and to render discernible those it excludes. In these troubling bisexual images, desire's mutability manifests itself in ways that undermine a sexual politics of immutability.

However, these strategies are not limited to a mainstream gay politics but can also be found in certain strands of queer theory where, ironically, the former is often critiqued. David Halperin's cutting assertion in 2009 that *'queer* has lost its sense of unassimilable and irredeemable sexual deviance, and subsided into a mere synonym of gay' can help us to identify certain monosexist trends in queer theory.[58] I'm talking about those works of queer scholarship predicated on a critical and theoretical oppositionality to heterosexuality, a reclamation of medico-juridical models of 'the sodomite' or 'the homosexual' and the centring of those intragender sex acts allegedly most discomforting for straight sensibilities. The predominance of these gay critical foci constrains queer studies' potential to find meaningful those expressions of sexuality that fall outside dominant models of sexual epistemology.

With consideration of this dominant formulation of gay politics and the assumption of a gay position in queer studies, we can better understand the eschewal of bisexuality in critical responses to texts like *Call Me by Your Name*, which fail to signify gayness in a univocal manner. A useful parallel can be drawn here through Joseph Ronan's critical analysis of the reception of Alan Hollinghurst's novel *The Stranger's Child* (2011). Ronan posits that '[t]he novel's bisexualities stage a critique of their inevitable interpretation within the terms of the Gay Novel'.[59] Ronan expands that these terms are defined by an overdetermined reading position that seeks the depiction of explicit sex between men, and a notion of 'Gay Truth'.[60] Importantly, the encounter between what Ronan calls the 'Gay Reader' and the bisexual text 'is frustrating [...]. It refuses to provide what it sets the Gay Reader up to want – particularly in the way sex is presented.'[61] The similarities between this text's reception and that of *Call Me by Your Name* are stark; accordingly, we might say that the 'Gay Spectator' seeks 'Gay Truth' in the 'Gay Film'. Neither Ronan nor I are positing these terms as essentialized categories of subjectivity or ontology; rather, these are hermeneutic and epistemological positions rooted in a monosexist understanding of sexuality. It is within this epistemology that bisexuality must be cast aside, lest it threaten a monosexual reading tradition.

This critical move is nowhere more observable than in Miller's article's only mention of bisexuality, which is literally parenthetical. In these parentheses, he writes that, in the 'mainstream gay movie', 'gay protagonists regularly pass through the bisexual antechamber'.[62] In order to be accounted for, bisexuality must be figuratively *siloed*. It must be banished to a conceptual antechamber – a place of transition, smallness, indeterminacy. Steven Angelides writes, in his historiographic consideration of bisexuality, 'Bisexuality has functioned as the structural Other to figurations of sexual identity and has represented the very uncertainty of the hetero/homosexual division'.[63] If Miller were to grant bisexuality the status of a *room*, this would be to *render uncertain* that upon which his critique is predicated: the conceptualization of sexual identity through the heterosexual/homosexual binary.

The space *Call Me by Your Name* affords these excesses, however, is roomy. Alcohol is drunk to excess, fruit is put to use in excess of its dietary function, desire exceeds monosexual frameworks. The film evokes the abandon of excess, while simultaneously figuring its aching unreachability. Joyous inebriation becomes vomiting, the peach once so appealing becomes the object of sexual shame, the person one desires must leave. Where the film choreographs various dances between excessive abandon and sobering bathos, we can perhaps find a dynamic akin to that between bisexual desire and the epistemological frameworks that structure its experience. To know a desire towards Elio, Oliver, Marzia and Chiara is to know the difficulty of these desires being expressed or signified, read or known. Perhaps one of the most meaningful ways *Call Me by Your Name* enjoins bisexual specificity is through the starkness with which it conveys yearning. To desire bisexually in a world structured by monosexual epistemology is to yearn for a world anew.

Elio, Oliver and Mario

If Elio and Oliver were to take a trip from the Perlmans' villa, around an hour's drive northwest, they would find the city of Milan. There, in the summer of 1983, they might have encountered the group of volunteers who were in the process of creating the *Circolo di cultura omosessuale Mario Mieli* [Circle of Homosexual Culture Mario Mieli]. This group, which remains in existence to this day, was founded shortly after the suicide of their namesake, Mario Mieli, an Italian theorist, performer and activist. Were Elio and Oliver to speak with these volunteers, they perhaps would have told the two lovers about the ideas of their friend Mario. Perhaps they would have shared with them an Italian copy of his groundbreaking 1977 monograph *Elements of Homosexual Critique*. Delving into this explosive book, Elio and Oliver might have discerned something they recognized in themselves.

Mieli was a radical, communist utopian whose work pulses to this day with a longing to see the world otherwise. Mieli's invective railed against the state, the heteronormative family and the rigidity of gender norms. In theoretical manoeuvres that made use of Sigmund Freud's conception of polymorphous perversity, he sketched the contours of a better future.[64] In *Elements*, Mieli contends that 'everyone is born endowed with a complete range of erotic capability [...]. They become either heterosexual or homosexual only as a result of educastration (repressing their homoerotic impulses in the first case, and their heterosexual ones in the second).'[65] We can understand Mieli's neologism, educastration, as akin to what I have described as a monosexist epistemology of sexuality, a system of knowledge that renders homo- and heterosexuality meaningful and renders bisexual potentialities unthinkable. Mieli's book ends with a rallying call to embrace that which educastration has denied us in favour of a kind of gay sexuality that does not disavow extragender desire. Mieli polemicizes:

> The liberation of sexuality [...] includes the complete recognition and the concrete manifestation of erotic desire for persons of the other sex on the part of homosexual men and women, and the realisation of a new gay way of loving between women and men.[66]

Mieli's vision of a sexual utopia can and should be recognized today as one with pertinence vis-à-vis bisexuality. Reading Mieli's text, Elio and Oliver would likely recognize a capacity they know in themselves, and perhaps – were they to part ways with some bourgeois tendencies – they might even be convinced of its political power. The recognition and manifestation of desires towards people of different genders is, indeed, something both know intimately.

I conclude with Mieli's ideas not simply for the diversion of imagining Elio and Oliver's encountering them (pleasurable as it may be) but as a reminder that models of queerness undergirded by monosexual assumptions have not always been prioritized by those seeking to comprehend and change the world queerly. Instead, there is a rich tradition – within bisexual politics, queer politics and even gay politics – in thinking queerly about the plasticity and mutability of desire. The responses to *Call Me by Your Name* that I have critiqued in this chapter betray a commitment to monosexual models of sexual epistemology and a failure to imagine queer desire in more expansive terms. The symptoms of this failure can be found in the commitment to penetrative anal sex between men as the preeminent form of queer cinematic monstration, the disdain with which bisexualized forms of narrative and *mise en scène* are dismissed as only ever the product of heterosexuality, and the vociferous discomfort of the gay critic irritated by the nongay queers, who are first hungered for, then become lodged in his gullet.[67] In the critical reception of *Call Me by Your Name* we can find, 40 years after Mieli's theorization, a reification of queerness as what he calls a 'homosexuality [...] in large part subject to the dictatorship of [a heterosexual] Norm'.[68] *Call Me by Your Name* – a film exuding a polymorphous perversity that exceeds singular forms of gayness – warrants a different critical approach to that taken up by these detractors, one through which extensive bisexual possibilities might be discerned, and educastration unlearned.

NOTES

1. Ben Ratskoff, '*Call Me by Your Name*: Gorgeous, But Is It Gay?' *Advocate*, 5 January 2018, https://www.advocate.com/commentary/2018/1/05/call-me-your-name-gorgeous-it-gay; Garrett Schlichte, '*Call Me by Your Name* Is a Gay Love Story. The Film Should Have Included Gay Sex', *Washington Post*, 18 December 2017, https://www.washington-post.com/news/soloish/wp/2017/12/18/why-call-me-by-your-name-should-have-included-gay-sex/; Miz Cracker, 'Why Do Gays Keep Falling for *Call Me by Your Name*?', *Slate*, 28 November 2017, https://slate.com/human-interest/2017/11/call-me-by-your-name-is-not-a-gay-movie.html.

2. D. A. Miller, 'Elio's Education', *Los Angeles Review of Books*, 19 February 2018, https://www.lareviewofbooks.org/article/elios-education/.

3. Miller, 'Elio's Education'.

4. Bisexual activists have used a variety of terms to indicate this broad usage, including bi+, bisexual*, the bisexual umbrella, nonmonosexuality and the multi-attraction spectrum. Although this word contains a bi- prefix, bisexual activists, since the 1970s, and theorists, since the 1990s, have put forward nonbinaristic definitions of bisexuality.

5. This chapter uses 'queer' to describe any forms of sexuality and gender beyond heterosexuality and/or cisness. My use of it is slightly different when I discuss queer theory, referring to that specific theoretical tradition which, at times, has embraced the multivalent potentials of 'queer' and, at others, has subsumed these under an assumptive cisgender gayness.

6. Quoted in Mary Katharine Tramontana, 'André Aciman Wants "Total Fluidity"', *Playboy*, 29 October 2019, https://www.playboy.com/read/andre-aciman-total-fluidity.

7. Quoted in TIFF Originals, 'CALL ME BY YOUR NAME Press Conference | Festival 2017', YouTube, 8 September 2017, https://www.youtube.com/watch?v=mDvj0XnYcFs.

8. Monosexism is defined by Shiri Eisner as 'a social structure operating through a presumption that everyone is, or should be, monosexual'. Shiri Eisner s.v., 'Monosexism', in *The SAGE Encyclopedia of LGBTQ Studies*, ed. Abbie E. Goldberg (London: SAGE Publications, 2016), 792.

9. Ratskoff, 'Gorgeous'.

10. Guy Lodge, 'Why Is *Call Me by Your Name* So Coy About Gay Sex?', *The Guardian*, 23 November 2017, https://www.theguardian.com/film/2017/nov/23/call-me-by-your-name-gay-sex-oscars. The Production Code articulated this rule in different ways across its history. In 1927, it prohibited 'Any inference of sex perversion', and in 1930, it forbade 'Sex perversion or any inference to it'. Reproduced in Jon Lewis, *Hollywood v. Hard Core: How the Struggle over Censorship Saved the Modern Film Industry* (New York and London: New York University Press, [2000] 2002), 301, 304.

11. Miller, 'Elio's Education'.

12. David Greven, 'Unlovely Spectacle: D. A. Miller on *Call Me by Your Name*', *Film International*, 13 March 2018, http://filmint.nu/unlovely-spectacle-miller/.

13. Rosalind Galt and Karl Schoonover read this moment in relation to the burgeoning HIV/AIDS pandemic, a reading supported, I contend, by the large 1981 on Elio's poster, this being the year that the first recorded AIDS deaths took place. They find in the pan

> a deferral that reflects the larger stakes of historical representation and the film's ability to speak of a moment ripe with potentialities that would be so soon foreclosed [...]. It asks whether the experience of pre-AIDS sex can be visible to us at all.

'Untimely Desires, Historical Efflorescence, and Italy in *Call Me by Your Name*', *Italian Culture* 37, no. 1 (March 2019), https://doi.org/10.1080/01614622.2019.1609220, 72–73.

14. Greven, 'Unlovely Spectacle'.

15. Galt and Schoonover, 'Untimely Desires', 70.

16. André Gaudreault, *From Plato to Lumière: Narration and Monstration in Literature and Cinema*, trans. Timothy Barnard (London: University of Toronto Press, [1988] 2009), 7, 69. Gaudreault is drawing upon similar uses of this term in linguistics, namely Catherine Kerbrat-Orecchioni, *L'Énonciation: De la Subjectivité dans le langage* (Paris: Armand Colin, 1980).

17. Tom Gunning, '"Now You See It, Now You Don't": The Temporality of the Cinema of Attractions', *The Velvet Light Trap* 32 (1993), 6.

18. Miller, 'Elio's Education'.

19. The sex between Elio and Oliver is described, in detail, in Aciman's novel, in which both characters top and bottom. However, it is important not to conflate the novel with the film.

20. D. A. Miller, 'Anal Rope', *Representations* 32 (1990): 127.

21. Greven, 'Unlovely Spectacle'.

22. Lisa Downing, 'Perversion and the Problem of Fluidity and Fixity', in *Clinical Encounters in Sexuality: Psychoanalytic Practice & Queer Theory*, ed. Noreen Giffney and Eve Watson (Earth: punctum books, 2017), 140.

23. Galt and Schoonover, 'Untimely Desires', 71.

24. Michael du Plessis, 'Blatantly Bisexual; Or, Unthinking Queer Theory', in *RePresenting Bisexualities: Subjects and Cultures of Fluid Desire*, ed. Donald E. Hall and Maria Pramaggiore (London: New York University Press, 1996), 19.

25. Shiri Eisner, *Bi: Notes for a Bisexual Revolution* (Berkeley: Seal Press, 2013), 143.

26. Maria San Filippo, *The B Word: Bisexuality in Contemporary Film and Television* (Bloomington and Indianapolis: Indiana University Press, 2013), 66–91.

27. For extensive consideration of the gendered dynamics of bisexuality and biphobia, see Eisner, *Bi*, 136–259.

28. Louis Althusser, *Lenin and Philosophy and Other Essays*, trans. Ben Brewster (New York, NY: Monthly Review Press, [1971] 2001). In making this theoretical move, I am, of course,

indebted to Judith Butler, whose use of Althusserian interpellation to theorize processes of sexual intelligibility instructs me: *Gender Trouble: Feminism and the Subversion of Identity* (London: Routledge, [1990] 2007).

29. Clare Hemmings suggests a similar theoretical framework to mine when she suggests that 'The "I" in "I am bisexual" is not simply an insubstantial assumption of fixed identity, as in "I am lesbian" – rather, it signifies transition and movement in itself. To say "I am bisexual" is to say "I am not 'I'".' 'Resituating the Bisexual Body: From Identity to Difference', in *Activating Theory: Lesbian, Gay, Bisexual Politics*, ed. Joseph Bristow and Angelia R. Wilson (London: Lawrence & Wishart, 1993), 129.

30. This phenomenon has been most famously theorized by Rick Altman and Virginia Wright Wexman. See Altman, *The American Film Musical* (Bloomington and Indianapolis: Indiana University Press, 1987); Wright Wexman, *Creating the Couple: Love, Marriage, and Hollywood Performance* (Chichester: Princeton University Press, 1993).

31. Esther Saxey, *Homoplot: The Coming-Out Story and Gay, Lesbian and Bisexual Identity* (Oxford: Peter Lang, 2008), 10, 130. I am grateful to Joseph Ronan for alerting me to Saxey's argument here.

32. I am using the terms intragender and extragender as a means of accounting for same/similar-gender desire and different-gender desire beyond the constraints of the gender and the sexuality binaries. Admittedly, intragender/extragender is itself another binary; however, it avoids reifying the gender/sexuality binaries I am critiquing while attending to the social separation of different kinds of gendered desiring.

33. Beth Carol Roberts, 'Neither Fish Nor Fowl: Imagining Bisexuality in the Cinema', PhD thesis, New York University, 2013, viii.

34. Roberts, 169.

35. Michael Amherst, *Go the Way Your Blood Beats: On Truth, Bisexuality and Desire* (London: Repeater Books, 2018), 46.

36. Miller, 'Elio's Education'.

37. Miller, 'Elio's Education'.

38. Roberts, 'Neither Fish Nor Fowl', 152.

39. Anthony Lane, '*Call Me by Your Name*: An Erotic Triumph', *New Yorker*, 4 December 2017, https://www.newyorker.com/magazine/2017/12/04/call-me-by-your-name-an-erotic-triumph.

40. René Girard theorizes literary romantic triangles as dramatizing a male character's expression of his desire to be like another man through a rivalry over a female object. *Deceit, Desire & the Novel: Self and Other in Literary Structure*, trans. Yvonne Freccero (London: Johns Hopkins University Press, [1961] 1976).

41. Catherine Deschamps, *Le Miroir bisexuel: Une Socio-anthropologie de l'invisible* (Paris: Balland, 2002); Marjorie Garber, *Vice Versa: Bisexuality and the Eroticism of Everyday Life* (London: Penguin, 1995/1997); Clare Hemmings, *Bisexual Spaces: A Geography of Sexuality and Gender* (London: Routledge, 2002); Maria Pramaggiore, 'Straddling the Screen: Bisexual Spectatorship and Contemporary Narrative Film', in *RePresenting Bisexualities:*

Subjects and Cultures of Fluid Desire, ed. Donald E. Hall, and Maria Pramaggiore, 272–300 (London: New York University Press, 1996); and San Filippo, *The B Word*.

42. Luce Irigaray, *This Sex Which Is Not One*, trans. Gillian C. Gill (New York, NY: Cornell University Press, [1974] 1985).

43. Jamie Tabberer, '*Luca* Star Jack Dylan Grazer Comes Out as Bisexual, Shares Pronouns', *Attitude*, 5 July 2021, https://www.attitude.co.uk/culture/film-tv/luca-star-jack-dylan-grazer-comes-out-as-bisexual-shares-pronouns-303213/; Nikki Onafuye, 'Start Paying Attention to *We Are Who We Are*'s Breakout Star Jordan Kristine Seamón', *gal-dem*, 22 November 2020, https://gal-dem.com/we-are-who-we-ares-jordan-kristine-seamon-is-stepping-into-her-power/.

44. Jaishikha Nautiyal, 'Queer Aesthetics, Playful Politics, and Ethical Masculinities in Luca Guadagnino's Filmic Adaptation of André Aciman's *Call Me by Your Name*', in *The Routledge Handbook of Gender and Communication*, ed. Marnel Niles Goins, Joan Faber McAlister and Bryant Keith Alexander (Abingdon and New York: Routledge, 2021), 216.

45. Ferdinand de Saussure, *Course in General Linguistics*, trans. Wade Baskin, ed. Perry Meisel and Haun Saussy (New York: Columbia University Press, [1916] 2011). In my articulation of sexuality's potential for extensibility, I am thinking of the extensibility of the self in the desired other as theorized by Leo Bersani in 'Sociality and Sexuality', *Critical Inquiry*, 26, no. 4 (2000): 641–56.

46. Jo Eadie, '"That's Why She Is Bisexual": Contexts for Bisexual Visibility', in *The Bisexual Imaginary: Representation, Identity and Desire*, ed. Bi Academic Intervention (London: Cassel, 1997), 156.

47. Eadie, '"That's Why"', 155.

48. Eadie, '"That's Why"', 157.

49. Gaius Petronius Arbiter, *The Satyricon*, trans. J. P. Sullivan (London: Penguin, [*c*.64 BCE] 2011), 21–66. If Trimalchio's feast proposes anything, it is that objects may not be as they seem; foods that appear to be one thing are revealed to be something else. This axiom chimes with one proposed across bisexual politics and theory: that sexuality cannot be read solely through the visible, that the potential for bisexual desire can lurk beneath subjects conventionally read as monosexual.

50. Jo Eadie, 'Indigestion: Diagnosing the Gay Malady', in *Anti-Gay*, ed. Mark Simpson (London: Cassel, 1996), 83, original emphasis.

51. Maria San Filippo, 'The Politics of Fluidity: Representing Bisexualities in Twenty-First-Century Screen Media', in *The Routledge Companion to Media, Sex and Sexuality*, ed. Clarissa Smith, Feona Attwood, and Brian McNair (Oxon: Routledge, 2018), 78.

52. Kenji Yoshino, 'The Epistemic Contract of Bisexual Erasure', *Stanford Law Review*', 52 (2000): 388.

53. Yoshino, 399.

54. Yoshino, 362.

55. Eve Kosofsky Sedgwick, *Epistemology of the Closet* (London: University of California Press, [1990] 2008), 9–10.

56. Hemmings, *Bisexual Spaces*, 25.

57. See Clifford J. Rosky and Lisa M. Diamond, 'Scrutinizing Immutability: Research on Sexual Orientation and U.S. Legal Advocacy for Sexual Minorities', *The Journal of Sex Research*, 53, nos. 4–5 (2016): 363–91; Jessica A. Clarke, 'Against Immutability', *The Yale Law Journal*, 125, no. 2 (2015): 1–325.

58. David M. Halperin, 'Thirteen Ways of Looking at a Bisexual', *Journal of Bisexuality* 9, nos. 3–4 (2009): 454. Halperin advocates for the critical functions of both queer and bisexual theory in resisting this tendency, but he does not comment directly on the susceptibility of queer theory to reproducing critical positions synonymous with gayness.

59. Joseph Ronan, '"Sometimes I Fear That the Whole World is Queer": What Bisexual Theories, Identities and Representations Can Still Offer Queer Studies', PhD thesis, University of Sussex, 2014, 165.

60. Ronan, 165–66.

61. Ronan, 166.

62. Miller, 'Elio's Education'.

63. Steven Angelides, *A History of Bisexuality* (Chicago and London: The University of Chicago Press, 2001), 16.

64. Mieli primarily draws upon Freud's ideas from 'Three Essays on the Theory of Sexuality', in *The Standard Edition of the Complete Psychological Works of Sigmund Freud, Volume VII*, by Sigmund Freud, trans. James Strachey (London: The Hogarth Press and the Institute of Psycho-Analysis, [1905] 1981), 125–248.

65. Mario Mieli, *Towards a Gay Communism*, trans. David Fernbach and Evan Calder Williams (London: Pluto Press, [1977] 2018), 5.

66. Mieli, 254.

67. Here, I am drawing upon Eadie's assertion that what leads to 'gay indigestion' is

> their craving for us [bisexuals] [...] the indigestible morsel that sticks in the throat [...] as with all indigestible food, the blame falls on us: on the way we taste, on the way we make ourselves unpalatable. The problem lies not with the food, but with the appetite: with a body which cannot digest us, but which wants to devour us.

Eadie, 'Indigestion', 72.

68. Mieli, *Towards*, 254.

REFERENCES

Akomfrah, John, dir. *Speak Like a Child*. BFI, Leda Serene Films, 1998.

Althusser, Louis. *Lenin and Philosophy and Other Essays*. Translated by Ben Brewster. New York: Monthly Review Press, [1971] 2001.

Altman, Rick. *The American Film Musical*. Bloomington and Indianapolis: Indiana University Press, 1987.

Amherst, Michael. *Go the Way Your Blood Beats: On Truth, Bisexuality and Desire*. London: Repeater Books, 2018.

Angelides, Steven. *A History of Bisexuality*. Chicago and London: The University of Chicago Press, 2001.

Bergman, Ingmar, dir. *Persona*. AB Svensk Filmindustri, 1966.

Bersani, Leo. 'Sociality and Sexuality.' *Critical Inquiry* 26, no. 4 (2000): 641–56. https://doi.org/10.1086/448986.

Butler, Judith. *Gender Trouble: Feminism and the Subversion of Identity*. London: Routledge, [1990] 2007.

Clarke, Jessica A. 'Against Immutability.' *The Yale Law Journal* 125, no. 2 (2015): 1–325.

Cuarón, Alfonso, dir. *Y tu mamá también* (*And Your Mother Too*). Anhelo Producciones, Besame Mucho Pictures, Producciones Anhelo, 2001.

de la Iglesia, Eloy, dir. *El Diputado* (*Confessions of a Congressman*). Figaró Films, Ufesa, Prozesa, 1978.

Deschamps, Catherine. *Le Miroir bisexuel: Une Socio-anthropologie de l'invisible*. Paris: Balland, 2002.

Downing, Lisa. 'Perversion and the Problem of Fluidity and Fixity.' In *Clinical Encounters in Sexuality: Psychoanalytic Practice & Queer Theory*, edited by Noreen Giffney and Eve Watson, 123–44. Earth: Punctum Books, 2017.

du Plessis, Michael. 'Blatantly Bisexual; Or, Unthinking Queer Theory.' In *RePresenting Bisexualities: Subjects and Cultures of Fluid Desire*, edited by Donald E. Hall and Maria Pramaggiore, 19–54. London: New York University Press, 1996.

Eadie, Jo. 'Indigestion: Diagnosing the Gay Malady.' In *Anti-Gay*, edited by Mark Simpson, 66–83. London: Cassel, 1996.

Eadie, Jo. '"That's Why She Is Bisexual": Contexts for Bisexual Visibility.' In *The Bisexual Imaginary: Representation, Identity and Desire*, edited by Bi Academic Intervention, 142–60. London: Cassel, 1997.

Eisner, Shiri. *Bi: Notes for a Bisexual Revolution*. Berkeley: Seal Press, 2013.

Eisner, Shiri. s.v. 'Monosexism.' In *The SAGE Encyclopedia of LGBTQ Studies*, edited by Abbie E. Goldberg, 793–96. London: SAGE Publications, 2016.

Freud, Sigmund. 'Three Essays on the Theory of Sexuality.' In *The Standard Edition of the Complete Psychological Works of Sigmund Freud, Volume VII*. Translated by James Strachey and edited by Sigmund Freud, 125–248. London: The Hogarth Press and the Institute of Psycho-Analysis, [1905] 1981.

Galt, Rosalind, and Karl Schoonover. 'Untimely Desires, Historical Efflorescence, and Italy in *Call Me by Your Name*.' *Italian Culture* 37, no. 1 (March 2019): 64–81. https://doi.org/10.1080/01614622.2019.1609220.

Garber, Marjorie. *Vice Versa: Bisexuality and the Eroticism of Everyday Life*. London: Penguin Books, [1995] 1997.

Gaudreault, André. *From Plato to Lumière: Narration and Monstration in Literature and Cinema*. Translated by Timothy Barnard. London: University of Toronto Press, [1988] 2009.

Girard, René. *Deceit, Desire & the Novel: Self and Other in Literary Structure*. Translated by Yvonne Freccero. London: Johns Hopkins University Press, [1961] 1976.

Greven, David. 'Unlovely Spectacle: D. A. Miller on *Call Me by Your Name*.' *Film International*, 13 March 2018. http://filmint.nu/unlovely-spectacle-miller/.

Guadagnino, Luca, dir. *Call Me by Your Name*. Frenesy Film Company, La Cinefacture, RT Features, 2017.

Guadagnino, Luca, dir. *We Are Who We Are* (TV). HBO, Sky Italia, Wildside, The Apartment, 2020.

Gunning, Tom. '"Now You See It, Now You Don't": The Temporality of the Cinema of Attractions.' *The Velvet Light Trap* 32 (1993): 3–12.

Haigh, Andrew, dir. *Weekend*. Glendale Picture Company, The Bureau, 2011.

Halperin, David M. 'Thirteen Ways of Looking at a Bisexual.' *Journal of Bisexuality* 9, nos. 3–4 (2009): 451–55. https://doi.org/10.1080/15299710903316679.

Hemmings, Clare. 'Resituating the Bisexual Body: From Identity to Difference.' In *Activating Theory: Lesbian, Gay, Bisexual Politics*, edited by Joseph Bristow and Angelia R. Wilson, 118–38. London: Lawrence & Wishart, 1993.

Hemmings, Clare. *Bisexual Spaces: A Geography of Sexuality and Gender*. London: Routledge, 2002.

Hollinghurst, Alan. *The Stranger's Child*. London: Picador, 2011.

Irigaray, Luce. *This Sex Which Is Not One*. Translated by Gillian C. Gill. New York: Cornell University Press, [1974] 1985.

Kerbrat-Orecchioni, Catherine. *L'Énonciation: De la Subjectivité dans le langage*. Paris: Armand Colin, 1980.

Krokidas, John, dir. *Kill Your Darlings*. Killer Films, Rose Pictures, 2013.

Lane, Anthony. '*Call Me by Your Name*: An Erotic Triumph.' *New Yorker*, 4 December 2017. https://www.newyorker.com/magazine/2017/12/04/call-me-by-your-name-an-erotic-triumph.

Lee, Ang, dir. *Brokeback Mountain*. River Road Entertainment, Focus Features, 2005.

Lewis, Jon. *Hollywood v. Hard Core: How the Struggle over Censorship Saved the Modern Film Industry*. New York and London: New York University Press, [2000] 2002.

Lodge, Guy. 'Why Is *Call Me by Your Name* So Coy About Gay Sex?' *The Guardian*, 23 November 2017. https://www.theguardian.com/film/2017/nov/23/call-me-by-your-name-gay-sex-oscars.

Lynch, David. dir. *Mulholland Drive*. Les Films Alain Sarde, Asymmetrical Productions, Babbo Inc., 2001.

Maggenti, Maria, dir. *The Incredibly True Adventure of Two Girls in Love*. Fine Line Features, Smash Pictures, 1995.

Mieli, Mario. *Towards a Gay Communism*. Translated by David Fernbach and Evan Calder Williams. London: Pluto Press, [1977] 2018.

Miller, D. A. 'Anal Rope.' *Representations* 32 (1990): 114–33. https://doi.org/10.2307/2928797.

Miller, D. A. 'Elio's Education.' *Los Angeles Review of Books*, 19 February 2018. https://lareviewofbooks.org/article/elios-education/.

Miz Cracker. 'Why Do Gays Keep Falling for *Call Me by Your Name*?' *Slate*, 28 November 2017. https://slate.com/human-interest/2017/11/call-me-by-your-name-is-not-a-gay-movie.html.

Nautiyal, Jaishikha. 'Queer Aesthetics, Playful Politics, and Ethical Masculinities in Luca Guadagnino's Filmic Adaptation of André Aciman's *Call Me by Your Name*.' In *The Routledge Handbook of Gender and Communication*, edited by Marnel Niles Goins, Joan Faber McAlister, and Bryant Keith Alexander, 206–22. Abingdon and New York: Routledge, 2021.

Onafuye, Nikki. 'Start Paying Attention to *We Are Who We Are*'s Breakout Star Jordan Kristine Seamón.' *gal-dem*, 22 November 2020. https://gal-dem.com/we-are-who-we-ares-jordan-kristine-seamon-is-stepping-into-her-power/.

Oz, Frank, dir. *In & Out*. Paramount Pictures, Spelling Films, 1997.

Petronius Arbiter, Gaius. *The Satyricon*. Translated by J. P. Sullivan. London: Penguin, [*c*.64 BCE] 2011.

Pramaggiore, Maria. 'Straddling the Screen: Bisexual Spectatorship and Contemporary Narrative Film.' In *RePresenting Bisexualities: Subjects and Cultures of Fluid Desire*, edited by Donald E. Hall and Maria Pramaggiore, 272–300. London: New York University Press, 1996.

Ratskoff, Ben. '*Call Me by Your Name*: Gorgeous, But Is It Gay?' *Advocate*, 5 January 2018. https://www.advocate.com/commentary/2018/1/05/call-me-your-name-gorgeous-it-gay.

Roberts, Beth Carol. 'Neither Fish Nor Fowl: Imagining Bisexuality in the Cinema.' PhD thesis, New York University, 2013.

Ronan, Joseph. '"Sometimes I Fear That the Whole World Is Queer": What Bisexual Theories, Identities and Representations Can Still Offer Queer Studies.' PhD thesis, University of Sussex, 2014.

Rosky, Clifford J., and Lisa M. Diamond. 'Scrutinizing Immutability: Research on Sexual Orientation and U.S. Legal Advocacy for Sexual Minorities.' *The Journal of Sex Research*, 53, nos. 4–5 (2016): 363–91. https://doi.org/10.1080/00224499.2016.1139665.

San Filippo, Maria. *The B Word: Bisexuality in Contemporary Film and Television*. Bloomington and Indianapolis: Indiana University Press, 2013.

San Filippo, Maria. 'The Politics of Fluidity: Representing Bisexualities in Twenty-First-Century Screen Media.' In *The Routledge Companion to Media, Sex and Sexuality*, edited by Clarissa Smith, Feona Attwood and Brian McNair, 70–80. Oxon: Routledge, 2018.

Saussure, Ferdinand de. *Course in General Linguistics*. Translated by Wade Baskin and edited by Perry Meisel and Haun Saussy. New York: Columbia University Press, [1916] 2011.

Saxey, Esther. *Homoplot: The Coming-Out Story and Gay, Lesbian and Bisexual Identity*. Oxford: Peter Lang, 2008.

Schlichte, Garrett. '*Call Me by Your Name* Is a Gay Love Story. The Film Should Have Included Gay Sex.' *Washington Post*, 18 December 2017. https://www.washingtonpost.com/news/soloish/wp/2017/12/18/why-call-me-by-your-name-should-have-included-gay-sex/.

Sedgwick, Eve Kosofsky. *Epistemology of the Closet*. London: University of California Press, [1990] 2008.

Serreau, Coline, dir. *Pourquoi pas!* (*Why Not!*) Dimage, Société Nouvelle de Doublage, 1977.

Tabberer, Jamie. '*Luca* Star Jack Dylan Grazer Comes Out as Bisexual, Shares Pronouns.' *Attitude*, 5 July 2021. https://www.attitude.co.uk/culture/film-tv/luca-star-jack-dylan-grazer-comes-out-as-bisexual-shares-pronouns-303213/.

TIFF Originals. 'CALL ME BY YOUR NAME Press Conference | Festival 2017.' YouTube, 8 September 2017. https://www.youtube.com/watch?v=mDvj0XnYcFs.

Tramontana, Mary Katharine. 'André Aciman Wants "Total Fluidity".' *Playboy*, 29 October 2019. https://www.playboy.com/read/andre-aciman-total-fluidity.

Wright Wexman, Virginia. *Creating the Couple: Love, Marriage, and Hollywood Performance*. Princeton and Chichester: Princeton University Press, 1993.

Yoshino, Kenji. 'The Epistemic Contract of Bisexual Erasure.' *Stanford Law Review* 52 (2000): 353–461. https://doi.org/10.2307/1229482.

PART III

RECEPTION

11

Call Me by Your Name and Film Festivals

Ruby Cheung

Call Me by Your Name premiered at the Sundance Film Festival on 22 January 2017. The film's director Luca Guadagnino, an Italian filmmaker, had previously utilized film festivals to showcase *Io sono l'amore* (*I Am Love*, 2009) and *A Bigger Splash* (2015), the two other productions from his 'desire' trilogy. While the other two films had premiered at the Venice International Film Festival (IFF), Guadagnino chose Sundance as the launch pad for the third film of the trilogy. Established in 1932, the Venice IFF is the world's oldest international film festival and one of the 'A-list' competitive feature film festivals accredited by the International Federation of Film Producers Associations (FIAPF).[1] On the other hand, since its inaugural edition in 1978 in the previous incarnation as the US Film Festival,[2] the annual Sundance Film Festival (commenced under this name in 1985) has been providing a solid platform for independent filmmakers to promote their films.[3] Working on a small budget of only US$3.4 million (provided by financiers from Brazil, France, Italy and the USA),[4] Guadagnino arguably made a smart move in showcasing *Call Me by Your Name* at Sundance, where the film's independent spirit could be amplified.

The choice to premiere at a specialized film festival for independent films paid off. Regarded by the Sundance Institute, the host organization of Sundance, as an 'instant classic',[5] the beautifully shot film received rave reviews from major film trade publications, such as *Screen Daily*, *The Hollywood Reporter* and *Variety*, during the festival period of the 2017 Sundance. Most of the reviews focused on glorifying this coming-of-age, gay-related film that portrays the mesmerizing love between the two Jewish male protagonists, the 17-year-old Elio (Timothée Chalamet) and the 24-year-old Oliver (Armie Hammer), in the idyllic ambience of an unidentified countryside in northern Italy in the summer of 1983. Praise from film trade press for Guadagnino's achievement abounded: for instance, the director 'tantalises, seduces, teases with a sensuousness'[6] and offers 'unexpectedly deep wells of emotion and surges of insight into human nature and relationships',[7] to the effect of advancing 'the canon of gay cinema'.[8] From Sundance, *Call Me by Your Name* moved on to travel along the international film festival circuit. It was subsequently shown at more than 50 other film festivals in different countries.

Undoubtedly, through its participation in film festivals, *Call Me by Your Name* helped Guadagnino enhance further his global recognition. In addition, Guadagnino collaborated with the world's mainstream film distribution and exhibition system to achieve handsome box-office takings of US$43.1 million worldwide.[9] However, a closer scrutiny of the film festivals that chose to show this film tells a different story, suggesting the film's possible struggles amidst the harsh realities of global film industries. Drawing on ideas from film festival studies, this chapter provides a case study of *Call Me by Your Name* and its relationship with the international film festival circuit. In particular, I seek to answer two questions: (1) How did *Call Me by Your Name* make use of this circuit to achieve its success? (2) What would be the stumbling blocks for the film in this environment, and could they tell us more about the political-economic and sociocultural realities of this circuit? I argue that, while *Call Me by Your Name* has indeed benefitted from various distribution and exhibition channels to attract a large following across the world, it was its presence or absence at various international film festivals in non-Euro-American regions – for example, East Asia – that clearly visualized the layering of these dynamics. Such layering is still under-researched in the discipline of film festival studies.[10] The film thus offers a suitable case in point to spotlight possible hierarchies in this 'alternative' film distribution and exhibition system vis-à-vis Hollywood.

For the purpose of this chapter, I situate *Call Me by Your Name* amidst the international film festival circuit as a whole, instead of confining my discussion of the film to only identity-based, genre-based or regional sub-circuits/sub-segments of the main circuit (such as those including only LGBTQ+/queer film festivals or only European film festivals). This angle can give a holistic view of the interactions between this film and the circuit. This overview of what the whole circuit entails, and its functions and representations highlighted by film festival researchers over the past 30 years, aims to help readers appreciate the complexities that the circuit often presents to individual films. I follow this with a close investigation of the case of *Call Me by Your Name*.

The international film festival circuit and its alternativeness

Call Me by Your Name is one of those non-mainstream, independent films that successfully utilize the film festival network to reach a global audience. The term 'international film festival circuit' is now often used by film industry practitioners and film festival scholars to identify this network that consists of individual film festivals in different geographical regions and territories. These festivals do not only include those major international ones but also much smaller, themed and specialized film festivals. Arguably, this circuit being the main one could be subdivided into different segments and/or sub-circuits, based on specific criteria used by different researchers for such subdivision (see more below).[11]

Some essentials

The circuit now works as an indispensable element of global film industries, providing major platforms for filmmakers to obtain funding for their films, to promote them among potential film business partners and target audiences, and to exhibit their films to paying viewers at the festivals. The scheduling of this circuit is usually mentioned in terms of an annual calendar. Many festivals themselves serve as spectacles when showcasing various categories of films from around the world, often on a regular basis. They become 'nodes'[12] in a complex network of filmic events that, from a distance, looks like an exquisitely woven tapestry in which the recurring separate film festivals occupy stable, if not completely fixed, places in space and time. Regardless of their sizes, film festivals may have trouble sustaining themselves in an unchangeable format. For example, the Dubai IFF, inaugurated in 2004 to occupy a slot every December in the annual festival calendar, announced in 2018 that it was becoming a biennial event.[13]

Films that find it difficult to be marketed to a mass audience and circulated in mainstream cinema networks may find the international film festival circuit particularly useful with regard to gaining the public's awareness. Such difficulties may derive from their non-mainstream subject matter and genres, their little-known filmmakers and actors or, in some cases, a running time that does not fit normal cinema programming schedules. For example, with its nine hours of running time, the multi-award-winning *Shoah* (Claude Lanzmann, 1985), a Holocaust documentary that was shown at the international film festivals in Berlin and Venice among others, would have had difficulties finding mainstream commercial cinemas to screen it. At well-established film festivals, certain films are usually shown in clearly identified sections specially programmed to fulfil specific criteria and goals – be they political, economic, social, cultural and/or artistic. Film festivals also hold retrospectives to pay tribute to specific cinematic traditions, individual auteurs, actors or lesser-known film practitioners.

Along with exhibiting films to the paying public, some festivals focus on facilitating the global film business by running affiliated film markets and financing forums. In fact, many of the largest and most noticeable festivals along the circuit often have affiliated film markets running during the festival periods for members of global film industries exclusively. Attendees at these marketplaces include film business executives, financiers, distributors, sales agents, directors and so on. They come together at these film markets to negotiate deals, or simply to catch up with each other on the latest trends in global film industries and expand their professional networks.

More recently in this circuit, film festivals of different sizes and with diverse themes have both physical and online versions for the same edition, in order to ensure a broad range of festival experiences for a much wider spectrum of festivalgoers.[14] Some sections of these festivals are not confined to showing and showcasing films only. More and more festivals combine exhibiting films with showing other screen products, such as episodes of television series, video games and virtual reality experiences.[15] Film festivals along this circuit are in some cases part of a larger group of entertainment events presented by their host cities. For example, the Hong Kong IFF, which was established as a standalone event in 1977, became a founding member of the Entertainment Expo in Hong Kong in 2005.[16] The Venice IFF is one of the major artistic events organized by *La Biennale di Venezia* in Venice.[17]

In terms of the interrelationships between individual festivals in this circuit, larger festivals are usually run as standalone events. They provide spaces at specific times and places for attendees, including industry practitioners, journalists, government officials and audiences alike, to gather and engage with each other in all kinds of film-related activities. These festivals strive to establish and maintain themselves as distinct from other festivals. In normal times, film festivals of different scales may or may not work together.[18] They might not be in direct competition with each other either, as regards the films shown or the foot traffic they are proud to generate.

In addition to its contributions to global film industries, the circuit, with its network of 'nodes, flows and exchanges'[19] or 'nodal points',[20] confers political-economic importance to the festivals' host cities. In return, by acting as hosts to these festivals, cities with specific geopolitical and spatial settings or political-economic agendas enhance their reputation in a globalized economy.

All the elements highlighted above suggest that the international film festival circuit was a natural environment for the non-mainstream *Call Me by Your Name* to find its major target audiences easily. At the same time, these elements have drawn the attention of scholars who have studied different areas of this circuit closely and enlightened our understanding of the accompanying issues and phenomena. Although the world's oldest international film festival, the Venice IFF, was established in 1932, systematic scholarly studies of this circuit and individual film festivals did not start before the 1980s. Scholars and critics often emphasize this circuit's alternativeness, whether to the Hollywood distribution and exhibition network or to the ordinary viewing experience of audiences. However, many of these studies do not give nuances to this alternative quality and are hence an inadequate basis for discussing individual films, such as *Call Me by Your Name*, and their travels along the circuit (and/or its sub-circuits). The case of *Call Me by Your Name*'s circulation along this circuit thus gives us important evidence to challenge existing studies of this circuit and shed new light on related academic debates.

Scholarly opinions

To underscore how this study on *Call Me by Your Name*'s use of this circuit (and any of its related sub-circuits) could fill in the gaps among different existing film festival investigations, I present here some representative scholarly ideas over the years. Bill Nichols was among the first generation of academic researchers of film festivals. In an essay published in 1994, he highlights the interactions between films (such as Iranian New Wave) screened at important international film festivals (for instance, the Toronto IFF) and the film festivalgoers (the audience) who appreciate the films at these events.[21] Understandably, the aura of the major international film festivals adds value to what would otherwise be a normal viewing experience for the audience. Judging from a western viewpoint, Nichols writes, 'We learn about other portions of the world and acknowledge the ascendancy of new artists to international acclaim'.[22] Such a perspective would be considered problematic nowadays, considering that, over the last three decades, new film festivals have been established in countless cities across the globe. Film festivals are no longer just spectacles at which we discover unfamiliar, new national cinemas and witness their ascent to a global audience.

Nichols also remarks, 'We are invited to receive such films as evidence of artistic maturity [...] and of a distinctive national culture – work that remains *distinct from Hollywood-based norms* both in style and theme'.[23] This acknowledgement of the international film festival circuit's difference from the Hollywood distribution and exhibition system is echoed by other important scholars in this field. Thomas Elsaesser sees international film festivals, especially those in Europe, as a means for European films to transcend their national boundaries.[24] In Elsaesser's words,

> the festival circuit is [...] a crucial interface with Hollywood itself, because taken together, the festivals constitute (like Hollywood) a global platform, but one which (unlike Hollywood) is at one and the same time a 'marketplace' (though perhaps more like bazaar than a stock exchange), a cultural showcase (comparable to music or theatre festivals), a 'competitive venue' (like the Olympic Games), and a world body (an ad-hoc United Nations, a parliament of national cinemas, or cinematic NGO's, considering some of the various festivals' political agendas). [...] It explains

why this originally European phenomenon has globalized itself, and in the process has created not only a self-sustaining, highly self-referential world for the art cinema, the independent cinema and the documentary film, but a sort of 'alternative' to the Hollywood studio system in its post-Fordist phase.[25]

Elsaesser's proposition helps solidify the understanding of the 'alternativeness' of this circuit among other film festival scholars while stimulating discussions, such as those offered by Marijke de Valck and Dina Iordanova. De Valck acknowledges the European origins of the distinctness of this circuit from its main counterpart, the Hollywood distribution and exhibition system. However, instead of presenting the apparent difference between the two networks in terms of their functions in promoting film cultures and cinephilia, the global film business, the political agendas of governments, the celebrity system, etc., the author highlights the understudied working relations between Hollywood and individual film festivals, such as Cannes. To De Valck, the international film festival circuit is a 'successful' cinematic network, which 'operates both with and against the *hegemony of Hollywood* [...] it is, at the same time, vital to characterize the network as open to the *participation of Hollywood* and other entities'.[26] The ostensible contradiction here between 'hegemony' and 'participation' hints at a complex situation that the circuit creates vis-à-vis the global reach of the Hollywood film circulation system. Simultaneously, De Valck also challenges the absolute alternativeness of the film festival network. The glamour of film festivals and the festival exhibition of films are part and parcel of the commodity that film festivalgoers pay for and consume in the wider, global cultural economy.[27]

Further challenges to the supposed alternativeness of the circuit come from Iordanova. The author questions a number of elements in the postulation that this circuit is an alternative film distribution network. The 'economic viability'[28] of using this circuit for distributing films is one of the issues she brings up. She also problematizes the degree to which film festivals are networked.[29] The wishes of many filmmakers and film executives entering their films into festivals and getting distribution opportunities there might not come true, as many of these films are, in the film business terminology, 'festival films'. According to film critic Jonathan Rosenbaum, the term 'festival film' refers derogatively to a film 'destined to be seen by professionals, specialists, or cultists but not by the general public because some of these professionals decide it won't or can't be sufficiently profitable to warrant distribution'.[30] Regardless of their genres and contents, festival films would have a similar fate: instead of gaining alternative distribution opportunities along the international film festival circuit, these films shown at one festival would be introduced only to the organizers of other festivals who happen to be there. The films would then be chosen by these other festivals, getting stuck forever in the film festival environment, whose exhibition function might be sporadic rather than continuous. Festival films are therefore unlikely to become known to most members of the general public, who do not attend them. As Iordanova remarks, 'Screening the film at festivals is not a means of getting the film to real exhibition; it *is* the real exhibition'.[31] Although being circulated along the international film festival circuit initially like a festival film, *Call Me by Your Name* escaped the fate of getting stuck in this circuit forever when Hollywood's global distribution network was also mobilized to introduce the film to a mass audience at different places. I will return to this point in the next section on situating *Call Me by Your Name* to discuss the complications involved.

Initially arguing in 2009 that it was wrong to think of film festivals as a film distribution network,[32] Iordanova updates her opinion and sees film festivals as more than exhibition sites.[33] With film festivals getting involved in more and more film business activities, ranging from financing and talent development to production and distribution, film festivals, according to Iordanova, are 'cluster[s] of creativity and commerce' and 'node[s] in more general transnational infrastructures'[34] that emphasize cinema production and distribution.[35]

If we consider only those brightest nodal points of the circuit, such as the IFFs held annually in Venice, Cannes and Berlin, the implications of the alternative quality of this circuit could easily escape us. After all, these biggest film festivals offer annual exciting line-ups of many kinds of films that Hollywood's film circulation would fail to contain. But if we also consider the variations in scales of a wide array of nodal points within this circuit, their physical locations in relation to their host and neighbouring territories and countries, and their geopolitical situation in the past and now, investigations of the alternativeness of the circuit would need to go deeper. In her monograph on film festivals, Cindy Hing-Yuk Wong goes along a similar vein, discussing film festivals as alternative platforms for global independent films' production, distribution and exhibition.[36] She, however, also reminds us of the issues of Eurocentrism found in many existing studies of film festivals as components of a complex network of films, stakeholders, institutions, cultures and power at play.[37] Seeking to counteract Eurocentrism in these studies, Wong's lengthy case study of the Hong Kong IFF presents an extra dimension of this 'alternative' film network.[38] I argued elsewhere that the East Asian film markets attached to the IFFs in Busan (formerly Pusan), Hong Kong, Shanghai and Tokyo had formed a 'quasi-circuit'.[39] The specific regional circuit comprising only these East Asian film markets, the IFFs they are affiliated with, and their individual relationships with the major IFFs and affiliated film markets in the West (mainly Europe), tell blatantly of existing hierarchies along the international film festival circuit. This quasi-circuit of the East Asian film markets may not necessarily be an alternative to the main segments of the circuit. But in terms of its reputation in the global film business environment, it is obviously of secondary importance compared with the main segment of this circuit comprising the oldest international film festivals and their affiliated film markets in Europe.

The alternativeness that the international film festival circuit embraces in relation to the Hollywood film circulation system is therefore not smooth and flat but hierarchical. It is not seamlessly interconnected. Rather, it is characterized by disjointedness and disruptions in the form of multi-layers of quasi-circuits, secondary circuits and 'parallel circuits'[40] that loosely link similar (but smaller) film festivals together. Some theme-based film festivals are much less noticeable. They are known only to the immediate community residing in a remote local neighbourhood. Other film festivals operate as one-off events and then quickly sink into oblivion. They are so detached, independent and self-contained as to probably have no intention to be part of the perennial international circuit. How much alternativeness (or complicity) different segments of the circuit (and its related, sub-circuits) provide to counteract (or work with) the omnipresent Hollywood hegemony then depends very much on the geopolitical, economic, sociocultural, religious and technological specificities (or idiosyncrasies) that define these film festivals and the films they choose to screen and help circulate. *Call Me by Your Name* is one of the recent films that reveal the complexity of the alternativeness of the international film festival circuit.

Situating Call Me by Your Name *amidst hierarchies of alternativeness of the international film festival circuit*

Call Me by Your Name ticks all the boxes for what independent films represent and how they are broadly perceived.[41] It was made on a small budget and with no backing, during the production stage, from conglomerated major Hollywood film studios. It was made by a film director with personal and artistic vision, and starred a small cast that did not include expensive megastars; also, it featured a specialized subject matter. The film was adapted from a large part of André Aciman's much-admired 2007 novel of the same name, while leaving out the last portion of the original story where the two lovers, after parting in Rome, reunite several times.[42] *Call Me by Your Name* benefitted from James Ivory's Academy Award-winning adapted screenplay, on which Guadagnino and Walter Fasano collaborated at some point. Narrating mainly from the angle of Elio, the film highlights the emotional travels of the two main characters alongside universal themes, such as family, and 'the blossoming of love and desire'.[43] According to the director, 'It was important to me [Guadagnino] to create this powerful universality, because the whole idea of the movie is that the other person makes you beautiful – enlightens you, elevates you'.[44] The emotional impacts of several important episodes of their romantic relationship on the audience are thus amplified. The film closes with a long take of the close-up of Elio silently in tears by the fireplace in his parents' house after receiving the news of Oliver's wedding, a scene that creates a lingering impression of the poignancy of the teenager's doomed first love.[45]

All these important elements of the film culminated in a successful world premiere at the 2017 Sundance (19–29 January 2017), where the film received a long standing ovation after screening.[46] In addition, *Call Me by Your Name* was selected for the 'Panorama Main Program and Panorama Special' section of the 2017 Berlin IFF (9–19 February 2017).[47] Having a world or regional (continental) premiere at major film festivals often increases a film's opportunities to move into a promising exhibition cycle via mainstream theatrical and/or online releases. Official film festival recognitions will also allow a film with a limited budget to build its marketing activities targeted directly at end-users (film audiences). It is no wonder that in an interview with *The Hollywood Reporter* dated 8 February 2021, Guadagnino confidently remarks, 'We only submitted to Sundance and Berlin; I never thought of going beyond the winter festivals, and I'm glad they both picked the film'.[48] Beyond the initial plan of Guadagnino's team of showing the film at the 2017 Sundance and the Berlin IFF, more than 50 other film festivals were very interested in showing the film.[49] This resulted in *Call Me by Your Name*'s subsequent year-long circulation on the international film festival circuit. Most of these other festivals are not specialized in curating films with LGBTQ+ topics; in fact, they are IFFs that curate various types of films, including features, shorts, documentaries, etc., for audiences with a broad range of preferences.

Irrespective of its official theatrical releases in different places, a quick glance at *Call Me by Your Name*'s exhibition records on the international film festival circuit in 2017–18 shows that the film does seem like a typical 'festival film' initially getting stuck in a festival environment (see Table 11.1).

Regardless of *Call Me by Your Name*'s high profile, the festival journey of this seemingly festival film has unintentionally proffered a lead into my investigation of the hierarchies and peculiarities of the alternativeness of the international film festival circuit. At least two possible types of hierarchies of this alternativeness can be detected in Table 11.1. The hierarchies highlighted below are illustrative of my argument about the festival circuit's complexity. They are not meant to be exhaustive.

Hierarchy type 1: Film festivals' reputation

Among these more than 50 film festivals, only eight have obtained official accreditation from FIAPF. In the order of *Call Me by Your Name*'s screening schedules in 2017, these accredited festivals were those in Berlin (Germany), Sydney (Australia), Toronto (Canada), San Sebastián (Spain), Mumbai (India), Kyiv (Ukraine),

TABLE 11.1: *Call Me by Your Name* and its film festival screenings. The following list is for illustrative purposes only. The publicly available information is not enough to define the list as exhaustive.

Call Me by Your Name screening date	Film Festival (FF) or International Film Festival (IFF)	Main location(s)	FIAPF-accredited film festival (Y/N)	Competitive (C) / non-competitive (N) [*any specifics?*]
22 January 2017	Sundance FF	USA (Utah)	N	C + N [*for indies*]
13 February 2017	Berlin IFF	Germany (Berlin)	Y	C
15 June 2017	Sydney FF	Australia (Sydney)	Y	C
28 July 2017	New Zealand IFF	New Zealand (Auckland, Christchurch, Dunedin, Wellington and others)	N	*
4 August 2017	Melbourne IFF	Australia (Melbourne)	N	C
7 September 2017	Toronto IFF	Canada (Toronto)	Y	N
8 September 2017	Jameson CineFest – Miskolc IFF	Hungary (Miskolc)	N	C
14 September 2017	Helsinki IFF	Finland (Helsinki)	N	N
22 September 2017	San Sebastián IFF	Spain (San Sebastián)	Y	C
29 September 2017	Zurich FF	Switzerland (Zürich)	N	C
30 September 2017	Edmonton IFF	Canada (Edmonton)	N	N
October 2017	Festival du Nouveau Cinéma de Montréal	Canada (Montreal)	N	C [*for indies*]
October 2017	Vancouver IFF	Canada (Vancouver)	N	C
October 2017	Morelia IFF	Mexico (Morelia)	N	C

(Continued)

TABLE 11.1: *Call Me by Your Name* and its film festival screenings. The following list is for illustrative purposes only. The publicly available information is not enough to define the list as exhaustive. (Continued)

Call Me by Your Name screening date	Film Festival (FF) or International Film Festival (IFF)	Main location(s)	FIAPF-accredited film festival (Y/N)	Competitive (C) / non-competitive (N) [*any specifics?*]
1 October 2017	Athens International Film and Video Festival	Greece (Athens)	N	C
1 October 2017	Bergen IFF	Norway (Bergen)	N	C
3 October 2017	New York FF	USA (New York)	N	N
5 October 2017	FF Cologne	Germany (Cologne)	N	C
5 October 2017	Filmekimi	Turkey (Istanbul)	N	N
6 October 2017	Hamptons IFF	USA (New York)	N	C
6 October 2017	Rio de Janeiro IFF	Brazil (Rio de Janeiro)	N	C
7 October 2017	Adelaide FF	Australia (Adelaide)	N	C
7 October 2017	San Diego IFF	USA (California)	N	C
9 October 2017	BFI London FF	UK (London)	N	C
12 October 2017	Mill Valley FF	USA (California)	N	N
14 October 2017	Mumbai FF	India (Mumbai)	Y	C
16 October 2017	Film Fest Gent	Belgium (Ghent)	N	C
20 October 2017	American FF	Russia (Moscow)	N	N
20 October 2017	Middleburg FF	USA (Virginia)	N	N
20 October 2017	New Orleans FF	USA (Louisiana)	N	C
21 October 2017	La Roche-sur-Yon IFF	France (La Roche-sur-Yon)	N	C
22 October 2017	Kyiv IFF Molodist	Ukraine (Kyiv)	Y	C + N
25 October 2017	American FF	Poland (Wrocław)	N	N [*for American indies*]
25 October 2017	Chicago IFF	USA (Illinois)	N	C

(Continued)

TABLE 11.1: *Call Me by Your Name* and its film festival screenings. The following list is for illustrative purposes only. The publicly available information is not enough to define the list as exhaustive. (Continued)

Call Me by Your Name screening date	Film Festival (FF) or International Film Festival (IFF)	Main location(s)	FIAPF-accredited film festival (Y/N)	Competitive (C) / non-competitive (N) [*any specifics?*]
27 October 2017	SoIndependent FIlm Festival	USA**	N	–
28 October 2017	FilmColumbia Festival	USA (New York)	N	N
28 October 2017	MIX Copenhagen	Denmark (Copenhagen)	N	C [*LGBTQ+ film festival*]
29 October 2017	Festival de Cine de Montevideo	Uruguay (Montevideo)**	N	N
30 October 2017	Austin FF	USA (Texas)	N	C
2 November 2017	Hawai'i IFF	USA (Hawai'i)	N	C
5 November 2017	Taipei Golden Horse Film Festival (TGHFF)	Taiwan (Taipei)	N	N
6 November 2017	Denver FF	USA (Colorado)	N	N
8 November 2017	Ljubljana IFF	Slovenia (Ljubljana)	N	C
9 November 2017	Napa Valley FF	USA (California)	N	N
10 November 2017	AFI Fest	USA (California)	N	N [*competition for shorts only*]
10 November 2017	St. Louis IFF	USA (Missouri)	N	N
13 November 2017	Cinema One Originals Festival	The Philippines (Quezon City)	N	C
14 November 2017	Zagreb FF	Croatia (Zagreb)	N	C
16 November 2017	Stockholm IFF	Sweden (Stockholm)	Y	C
17 November 2017	Key West FF	USA (Florida)	N	C
26 November 2017	Singapore IFF	Singapore	N	C
8 December 2017	IFF & Awards Macao	China (Macao)	N	C

(Continued)

TABLE 11.1: *Call Me by Your Name* and its film festival screenings. The following list is for illustrative purposes only. The publicly available information is not enough to define the list as exhaustive. (Continued)

Call Me by Your Name screening date	Film Festival (FF) or International Film Festival (IFF)	Main location(s)	FIAPF-accredited film festival (Y/N)	Competitive (C) / non-competitive (N) [any specifics?]
10 December 2017	Tbilisi IFF	Georgia (Tbilisi)	N	C
14 December 2017	IFF of Kerala	India (Kerala)	Y	C
12 January 2018	Palm Springs IFF	USA (California)	N	C
14 February 2018	Festival Désir … Désirs	France (Tours)	N	N
25 February 2018	Belgrade IFF	Serbia (Belgrade)	N	C

Main sources:
- FIAPF 2018
- 'Accredited Festivals', FIAPF's official website, www.fiapf.org. Accessed 18 November 2023.
- Official websites of identified film festivals in this table (except SoIndependent FIlm Festival). Accessed 18 November 2023.
- 'Release Info' of *Call Me by Your Name*'s entry on IMDb.com. Accessed 18 November 2023.

Notes:
* Not enough info is available on the official website.
** No further info is available besides the info on IMDb.com.

Stockholm (Sweden) and Kerala (India). Of these, the one in Berlin is the most reputable from a global film business perspective, as it is one of the European festivals most-attended by global film industry practitioners, who are also likely to visit the festival's affiliated film market, the European Film Market (EFM). The EFM is one of the most important annual film markets for film business and related activities in the world.[50] As for the other seven FIAPF-accredited film festivals that screened *Call Me by Your Name* in 2017, even though they may have film industry-facing units, such as co-production forums, they are unlikely to generate as much foot traffic as the Berlin IFF and the EFM would normally have. In 2017, the Berlin IFF presented 356 films with 198 world premieres.[51] It recorded 1,721 sales companies and buyers. There were 9,539 participants at the EFM. For comparison, Table 11.2 presents the corresponding numbers of the other seven FIAPF-accredited film festivals where *Call Me by Your Name* was screened.

TABLE 11.2: FIAPF-accredited film festivals (2017 Edition) that screened *Call Me by Your Name*. For easy reference, the largest number in each column is in bold.

Film Festival (FF) or International Film Festival (IFF)	No. of films presented	No. of world premieres	No. of sales companies and buyers	No. of participants attending the festival's film market
Berlin IFF	356	198	1,721	**9,539**
Sydney FF	283	37	1,500	*
Toronto IFF	356	192	**5,675**	*
San Sebastián IFF	213	39	406	*
Mumbai FF	227	47	no info	*
Kyiv IFF Molodist	no info	no info	no info	*
Stockholm IFF	150	1	62	*
IFF of Kerala	190	7	35	*

Source: FIAPF 2018: 15, 30, 37, 41, 47, 48, 53, 54.

Note: *The film festival does not have any affiliated film market.

The numbers here are revealing. The Berlin IFF overshadowed the other seven by the sheer quantity of films and world premieres shown, as well as by the foot traffic of film industry practitioners it generated. Its closest counterpart was the one in Toronto, which is a non-competitive festival. The Toronto IFF presented the same total number of films as the Berlin IFF that year, but was attended by a much larger number of sales companies and buyers. Although regarded as the 'most important North American world cinema market',[52] the Toronto IFF does not have an officially attached film marketplace, such as the EFM at Berlin. However, the total number of participants (9,539) at the EFM and the number of sales companies and buyers (5,675) at the Toronto IFF are arguably comparable. In terms of the attendance of global film business practitioners at these two events, Berlin was in the lead.

The rest of the list in Table 11.1 are not FIAPF-accredited 'A-list' film festivals, although some are extremely reputable in their own categories, like Sundance being a must-enter film festival for independent films. Some of the film festivals are famous locally or regionally, and are audience-oriented, such as the New York Film Festival.[53] Film business executives would not consider audience-oriented film festivals very important platforms for film distribution and related business activities. Many other festivals in Table 11.1 are of much less importance to the global film trade when they have sections that facilitate film industry activities.

In addition, well-established film festivals and the films presented there enjoy international media coverage. *Call Me by Your Name*'s screening at eight FIAPF-accredited film festivals ensured the film's abundant public visibility via festival news coverage. Such amount of publicity in turn facilitated the film's distribution for local releases around the world. Particularly, Sony Pictures Classics is known to have acquired the rights for distributing *Call Me by Your Name* before the film's Sundance premiere.[54] The involvement of a Hollywood film distributor in *Call Me by Your Name*'s worldwide distribution complicates the analysis of the film's distribution via the international film festival circuit. I should also note that *Call Me by Your Name* was distributed throughout the world not only by Sony Pictures Classics: smaller, local distributors from various places, which may or may not have had any direct working relationship with Sony Pictures Classics, eventually also participated in *Call Me by Your Name*'s worldwide distribution. They included, for instance, ACME Film (operating in the Baltic states and partnering with big Hollywood studios like Sony Pictures), Bir Film (operating in Turkey) and Edko Films (Hong Kong-based and distributing films in Hong Kong and mainland China).[55]

Still looking at Table 11.1, many questions arise when we consider the importance and, indeed, the usefulness of other non-'A-list' film festivals (especially many smaller and not well-known ones) for *Call Me by Your Name*'s worldwide distribution. For example, there would be questions related to how we should gauge these festivals' actual contribution to it. And, if we cannot make the estimation due to a lack of data, further questions may also be raised regarding how we could be sure of the international film festival circuit being an 'alternative' to the Hollywood distribution and exhibition system. When generalizing from the case of *Call Me by Your Name* so as to understand the functions of the international film festival circuit, there would also be questions as to how we could possibly measure that circuit's alternative quality.

Hierarchy type 2: Film festivals' geographical locations and geopolitical reach

The indicated reputation hierarchies of the film festivals that screened *Call Me by Your Name* reveal the awkwardness of the notion of alternativeness; additional peculiarities can be found when we look closely at these festivals' geographical locations and geopolitical reach. The geopolitical hierarchies of the international film festival circuit determined the benefits and obstacles *Call Me by Your Name* would meet along that circuit.

Let me refer to Table 11.1 again. In terms of continental representativeness, the eight FIAPF-accredited film festivals that selected *Call Me by Your Name* are held in America (North), Asia (South), Europe and Oceania. Four of them are European. The geographical spread of the rest of the film festivals in Table 11.1 appears wider. These non-FIAPF-accredited film festivals are held in 32 countries/territories. I summarize the geographical spread of all the film festivals from Table 11.1

in the list below, with the numbers in parentheses next to the countries/territories indicating the number of film festivals in those regions at which *Call Me by Your Name* was screened. To be more specific, there are:

- Five countries in North and South America, namely Brazil (1), Canada (4), Mexico (1), United States (18), Uruguay (1).
- Five Asian countries/territories, namely India (2), Macao (1),[56] Singapore (1), Taiwan (1), The Philippines (1);
- Twenty European (and Eurasian) countries, namely Belgium (1), Croatia (1), Denmark (1), Finland (1), France (2), Georgia (1), Germany (2), Greece (1), Hungary (1), Norway (1), Poland (1), Russia (1), Serbia (1), Slovenia (1), Spain (1), Sweden (1), Switzerland (1), Turkey (1), Ukraine (1), United Kingdom (1);
- Two Oceanian countries, namely Australia (3), New Zealand (1).

The geographical variety of countries/territories paints a picture of the geopolitical hierarchies that could possibly be found along the international film festival circuit with regard to how *Call Me by Your Name* used the circuit as a major distribution platform. American and European film festivals evidently showed much greater interest in *Call Me by Your Name*, thereby assisting its circulation in the two Americas and Europe. In the USA alone, 18 film festivals took turns to screen *Call Me by Your Name* in one year; Canada is next in the ranking, with four festivals that included the film in their selections that same year. More interesting is *Call Me by Your Name*'s absence from many other film festivals, which are hence missing in Table 11.1. For instance, only two film festivals in East Asia (Macao and Taiwan), and no film festivals in Africa and the Middle East, selected *Call Me by Your Name* for their programmes. The film's absence from most film festivals in these geopolitical regions reflected certain political, social and cultural orientations determining how film festivals there would operate and curate films. I would argue that, due to these orientations, the film festivals in question, despite being important nodes of the international film festival circuit, might not be as free as their western (mainly Euro/American) counterparts in curating films. As for being part of a film distribution network alternative to that of Hollywood, it is arguable that these film festivals would have represented stumbling blocks to the distribution of *Call Me by Your Name*.

The experience of the film among the East Asian nodes of the international film festival circuit reveals such issues. These nodes include the IFFs of Beijing, Busan, Hong Kong, Shanghai and Tokyo, as well as the Taipei Golden Horse Film Festival (TGHFF). Of these six East Asian film festivals, which are the most important platforms for film circulation and film business activities in the region, only the TGHFF screened *Call Me by Your Name*. Since its establishment in 1962 (as the 'Golden Horse Awards'), the TGHFF has been one of the most prestigious film events in the Chinese-speaking world devoted to the achievements of Chinese-language film industries.[57] Currently, it has four parts: the 'Awards', the 'Film Festival', the 'Film Project Promotion' and the 'Film Academy'. The 'Film Project Promotion' offers a 'Chinese-language film project matching and co-production platform' where filmmakers can potentially raise funding for their new Chinese-language film projects. In terms of involvement in the current East Asian film business network, the TGHFF is not as active as the other five festivals because, contrary to the others, it does not have an official film market.[58] The other five IFFs, i.e. those in Beijing, Busan, Hong Kong, Shanghai and Tokyo, did not screen *Call Me by Your Name*, although the film was theatrically released in all the host countries/territories of these respective festivals except mainland China (i.e. in Hong Kong, Japan and South Korea).[59] Besides the TGHFF, the IFF & Awards Macao also showed *Call Me by Your Name*. Established in 2016, this new festival in Macao is of relatively unimportance in terms of East Asia's film business.

Among the host countries/territories of the said East Asian film festivals, the People's Republic of China (PRC) has been catching up with global film business activities since its accession to the World Trade Organization in 2001. Over the past two decades, the mainland Chinese film industry has seen a sea change in its infrastructure after a series of mergers, and the restructuring of state-owned film studios and other film industry facilities. Film conglomerates modelled on the Hollywood system were set up – understandably, with the blessings of the state authorities. Moreover, the two major international film festivals in Shanghai and Beijing were strategically launched in 1993 and 2011, respectively, for growing the national film industry based in mainland China. Their establishment also sent a clear and loud message to the world about the PRC's proactive involvement in the global film business. Hence, the widely reported news about *Call Me by Your Name* being pulled, suddenly and without official explanation, from the 2018 Beijing IFF's film programme came as a surprise, especially to those who expected the PRC's film industry to be accepting and adopting similar practices, cultures, values and interests to those of other parts of the world, particularly the West.[60] It was speculated widely in film trade press that *Call Me by Your Name* had been removed from the Beijing IFF's programme because of the Chinese film censorship disapproving LGBTQ+ themes in films and other media. While homosexuality is not illegal in present-day China, media content topics related to LGBTQ+ are still taboo there, and are therefore repressed by the authorities.[61] The Chinese censors would not allow the public screening of a film containing a strong gay element, no matter that the film illuminates universal themes, such as love, growing up, self-discovery, the father-and-son relationship, and regardless of its high artistic quality and multiple accolades received (including an Academy Award).[62] As Elena Pollacchi notes when studying the peculiar features of the Beijing IFF, the festival intends to model itself on the three most important film festivals in the world – Venice, Cannes and Berlin.[63] But the Beijing IFF has always been under the tight control of the Chinese authorities. Instead of contributing to the global film circulation, it has prioritized building its own 'reputational capital'.[64] This film withdrawal incident at the Beijing IFF thus became a very visible stumbling block to *Call Me by Your Name* on the film's festival journey in 2017–18. Simultaneously, the case of *Call Me by Your Name* exposed this festival's limited ability as a 'site of translation',[65] when it came to translating a part of foreign film cultures to the specific political, social and cultural contexts of the PRC.

Conclusion

Call Me by Your Name provides a case in point for exploring how the international film festival circuit is alternative to the Hollywood distribution and exhibition system. The film succeeded in many parts of the circuit while remaining inaccessible to others, many of which (for instance, the Beijing IFF) have specific agendas magnified by the concerns of governmental bodies and other stakeholders. Thanks to the film's artistic and commercial success, these stumbling blocks do not seem to have been a substantial problem, for *Call Me by Your Name* gained a strong foothold on the global audience market beyond the international film festival circuit mainly via other types of releases, most notably theatrical and online.

NOTES

1. See 'History', the Venice IFF's official website (English), labiennale.org/en/cinema (accessed 18 November 2023); 'Accredited Festivals', FIAPF's official website, www.fiapf.org (accessed 18 November 2023).
2. See Cindy Hing-Yuk Wong, *Film Festivals: Culture, People, and Power on the Global Screen* (New Brunswick and London: Rutgers University Press, 2011), 2.
3. See 'A Story Begins: History of Sundance Institute' in 'About Us', the Sundance Institute's official website, www.sundance.org (accessed 18 November 2023).
4. See Tom Grater, 'Luca Guadagnino on the 10-Year Journey Behind *Call Me by Your Name*', *Screen Daily*, 31 December 2017, accessed 18 November 2023, https://www.screendaily.com/features/luca-guadagnino-on-the-10-year-journey-behind-call-me-by-your-name/5125216.article.
5. See '*Call Me by Your Name*', Projects, the Sundance Institute's official website, www.sundance.org/projects/call-me-by-your-name [now defunct] (accessed 25 May 2022).
6. Fionnuala Halligan, '*Call Me by Your Name*: Sundance Review', *Screen Daily*, 23 January 2017, accessed 18 November 2023, https://www.screendaily.com/reviews/call-me-by-your-name-sundance-review/5114034.article.

7. Boyd Van Hoeij, '*Call Me by Your Name*: Film Review | Sundance 2017', *The Hollywood Reporter*, 23 January 2017, accessed 18 November 2023, https://www.hollywoodreporter.com/review/call-me-by-your-name-review-967150.

8. Peter Debruge, 'Film Review: *Call Me by Your Name*', *Variety*, 23 January 2017, accessed 18 November 2023, https://variety.com/2017/film/reviews/call-me-by-your-name-review-1201966646.

9. '*Call Me by Your Name* (2017)', Box Office Mojo, accessed 18 November 2023, www.boxofficemojo.com.

10. See Skadi Loist, 'The Film Festival Circuit: Networks, Hierarchies, and Circulation', in *Film Festivals: History, Theory, Method, Practice*, ed. Marijke de Valck, Brendan Kredell and Skadi Loist (Oxon: Routledge, 2016), 49.

11. Loist, 'Circuit', 50–52.

12. See Thomas Elsaesser, 'Film Festival Networks: The New Topographies of Cinema in Europe', in *European Cinema: Face to Face with Hollywood*, by Thomas Elsaesser (Amsterdam: Amsterdam University Press, 2005), 84; Marijke de Valck, *Film Festivals: From European Geopolitics to Global Cinephilia* (Amsterdam: Amsterdam University Press, 2007), 15.

13. See Melanie Goodfellow, 'Mystery Swirls around Future of Dubai International Film Festival', *Screen Daily*, 18 April 2018, accessed 18 November 2023, https://www.screendaily.com/news/mystery-swirls-around-future-of-dubai-international-film-festival/5128387.article; Nick Vivarelli, 'Dubai Film Festival Cancels Next Edition, Ends Existing Format', *Variety*, 19 April 2018, accessed 18 November 2023, https://variety.com/2018/film/festivals/dubai-international-film-festival-cancels-next-edition-ends-existing-format-1202758329.

14. Hybrid editions were especially useful in helping film festivals to maintain their presence in the global film business environment during the COVID-19 pandemic, when social distancing policy was widely enforced, and international travels were severely restricted. See Patrick Frater, 'Global Film Festivals Are Taking a Hybrid Route That's Here to Stay', *Variety*, 18 December 2020, accessed 18 November 2023, https://variety.com/2020/biz/global/global-film-festivals-hybrid-1234865457.

15. See Cathy Hackl, 'The Future of the Film Festival', *Forbes*, 17 November 2020, accessed 18 November 2023, https://www.forbes.com/sites/cathyhackl/2020/11/17/the-future-of-the-film-festival/?sh=45cdae974d8a; Zack Sharf, 'Cannes Announces 2020 Official Lineup: *French Dispatch*, *Ammonite*, New McQueen and Ghibli', *IndieWire*, 3 June 2020, accessed 18 November 2023, https://www.indiewire.com/2020/06/cannes-2020-lineup-films-competiton-1202235061.

16. See Ruby Cheung, 'Corporatising a Film Festival: Hong Kong', in *Film Festival Yearbook 1: The Festival Circuit*, ed. Dina Iordanova with Ragan Rhyne (St Andrews: St Andrews Film Studies with College Gate Press, 2009), 104; Ruby Cheung, 'East Asian Film Festivals: Film Markets', in *Film Festival Yearbook 3: Film Festivals and East Asia*, ed. Dina Iordanova and Ruby Cheung (St Andrews: St Andrews Film Studies, 2011), 47. See also

'EXPO 2006' in 'About the Expo', the Entertainment Expo Hong Kong's official website (English), www.eexpohk.com (accessed 18 November 2023).

17. See 'The Organisation', *La Biennale di Venezia*'s official website (English), www.labiennale. org (accessed 18 November 2023).

18. There were unprecedented collaborations between film festivals in 2020 when many of them were adversely affected by the COVID-19 pandemic. For example, the 2020 Cannes Film Festival, whose physical version was cancelled, reached an agreement with the San Sebastián IFF to allow the 2020 Cannes Official Selection titles to compete at the 2020 San Sebastián IFF – a step that the Cannes rules had up till then excluded. See Melanie Goodfellow, 'Cannes Film Festival to Unveil 56 Official Selection Titles', *Screen Daily*, 3 June 2020, accessed 18 November 2023, https://www.screendaily.com/ news/cannes-film-festival-to-unveil-56-official-selection-titles/5150294.article. The Venice IFF, the Telluride Film Festival, the Toronto IFF and the New York Film Festival, which usually compete with each other for films and festivalgoers in the autumn, released a joint statement stating their unprecedented collaboration in 2020. See Eric Kohn, 'How Venice, Telluride, NYFF, and TIFF's 2020 Collaboration Will Affect the Festival Circuit', *IndieWire*, 8 July 2020, accessed 18 November 2023, https://www.indiewire.com/ 2020/07/fall-film-festivals-working-together-1234572013.

19. Elsaesser, 'Film Festival Networks', 84.

20. De Valck, *Film Festivals*, 15.

21. See Bill Nichols, 'Discovering Form, Inferring Meaning: New Cinemas and the Film Festival Circuit', *Film Quarterly* 47, no. 3 (1994), 16–30.

22. Nichols, 'Discovering Form', 17.

23. Nichols, 'Discovering Form', 16, emphasis added.

24. See Elsaesser, 'Film Festival Networks', 83.

25. Elsaesser, 'Film Festival Networks', 88.

26. De Valck, *Film Festivals*, 15, emphasis added.

27. See De Valck, *Film Festivals*, 19.

28. Dina Iordanova, 'The Film Festival Circuit', in *Film Festival Yearbook 1: The Festival Circuit*, ed. Dina Iordanova with Ragan Rhyne (St Andrews: St Andrews Film Studies with College Gate Press, 2009), 24.

29. See Iordanova, 'Circuit', 29.

30. Jonathan Rosenbaum, *Movie Wars: How Hollywood and the Media Conspire to Limit What Films We Can See* (Chicago: A Cappella, 2002), 161.

31. Iordanova, 'Circuit', 25, original emphasis.

32. See Iordanova, 'Circuit', 26.

33. See Dina Iordanova, 'The Film Festival as an Industry Node', *Media Industries Journal* 1, no. 3 (2015), 7.

34. Iordanova, 'Industry Node', 7.

35. See Iordanova, 'Industry Node', 9.

36. See Wong, *Film Festivals*, 5.

37. See Wong, *Film Festivals*, 3–4.

38. See Wong, *Film Festivals*, 190–222.

39. Cheung, 'Film Markets', 54; see also Ruby Cheung, *New Hong Kong Cinema: Transitions to Becoming Chinese in 21st-Century East Asia* (New York and Oxford: Berghahn Books, 2016), 207–10.

40. Iordanova, 'Circuit', 31.

41. See Emanuel Levy, *Cinema of Outsiders: The Rise of American Independent Film* (New York and London: New York University Press, 1999), 1–11; Yannis Tzioumakis, *American Independent Cinema: An Introduction*, second edition (Edinburgh: Edinburgh University Press, 2017), 1–10.

42. See André Aciman, *Call Me by Your Name* (New York: Farrar, Straus and Giroux, 2007); Debruge, 'Film Review'.

43. Ashley Lee, 'Why Luca Guadagnino Didn't Include Gay Actors or Explicit Sex Scenes in *Call Me by Your Name* (Q&A)', *The Hollywood Reporter*, 8 February 2017, accessed 18 November 2023, https://www.hollywoodreporter.com/news/general-news/call-me-by-your-name-why-luca-guadagnino-left-gay-actors-explicit-sex-scenes-q-a-973256.

44. Quoted in Lee, 'Why Luca'.

45. The film's worldwide success arguably gave Aciman the drive to continue writing the characters' stories in the sequel *Find Me* (2019); the dramatic twists that occur in both their lives ultimately result in a sort of happy ending. See André Aciman, *Find Me* (London: Faber & Faber, 2019).

46. See Kate Erbland, 'Sundance 2017: Check Out the Full Lineup, Including Competition Titles, Premieres and Shorts', *IndieWire*, 6 December 2016, accessed 18 November 2023, https://www.indiewire.com/2016/12/sundance-2017-full-lineup-competition-premieres-shorts-1201752136; Matt Grobar, '*Call Me by Your Name* Director Luca Guadagnino on the "Wonderful Risk" Worth Taking – Sundance Studio', *Deadline Hollywood*, 1 February 2017, accessed 18 November 2023, https://deadline.com/2017/02/call-me-by-your-name-sundance-armie-hammer-luca-guadagnino-michael-stuhlbarg-video-interview-1201894437.

47. See Leo Barraclough, 'Armie Hammer's *Call Me by Your Name* Joins Berlinale's Panorama Lineup', *Variety*, 25 January 2017, accessed 18 November 2023, https://variety.com/2017/film/global/armie-hammer-call-me-by-your-name-berlinale-panorama-1201969419. See 'Archive', the Berlin IFF's official website, www.berlinale.de (accessed 18 November 2023).

48. Quoted in Lee, 'Why Luca'.

49. See 'Release Info', *Call Me by Your Name*'s entry on IMDb.com (accessed 18 November 2023).

50. See Minhae Shim, 'Top 14 Film Markets', *The Independent*, 25 October 2013, accessed 18 November 2023, https://independent-magazine.org/2013/10/25/top-12-film-markets_the-independents-guide-to-film-distribution.

51. See FIAPF, *FIAPF – Accredited Festival Directory | 2018 Edition* (Bern and Brussels: International Federation of Film Producers Associations, 2018), 15.

52. Wong, *Film Festivals*, 2.

53. See Rahul Hamid, 'From Urban Bohemia to Euro Glamour: The Establishment and Early Years of the New York Film Festival', in *Film Festival Yearbook 1: The Festival Circuit*, ed. Dina Iordanova with Ragan Rhyne (St Andrews: St Andrews Film Studies with College Gate Press, 2009), 67–81; Wong, *Film Festivals*, 12.

54. See Lee, 'Why Luca'.

55. See 'Distributors' in 'Company Credits', *Call Me by Your Name*'s entry on IMDb.com (accessed 18 November 2023).

56. Macao (a.k.a. Macau) is a former Portuguese colony. It is now one of the two special administrative regions (SAR) of the People's Republic of China (PRC). The other SAR of the PRC is Hong Kong.

57. See 'About Us', the TGHFF's official website (English), www.goldenhorse.org.tw (accessed 18 November 2023).

58. See Cheung, *New Hong Kong Cinema*, 193–94, 207–10; Ruby Cheung, 'East Asia's Film Business', in *The Palgrave Handbook of Asian Cinema*, ed. Aaron Han Joon Magnan-Park, Gina Marchetti and See Kam Tan (London: Palgrave Macmillan, 2018), 100.

59. See 'Release Info', *Call Me by Your Name*'s entry on IMDb.com (accessed 18 November 2023).

60. See Patrick Brzeski, 'Beijing Film Festival Drops *Call Me by Your Name* as China Tightens Grip on Media', *The Hollywood Reporter*, 26 March 2018, accessed 18 November 2023, https://www.hollywoodreporter.com/news/beijing-film-festival-drops-call-me-by-your-name-as-china-tightens-grip-media-1097204; Pei Li and Adam Jourdan, 'Beijing Festival Pulls Award-Winning Gay Film amid Content Squeeze', *Reuters*, 26 March 2018, accessed 18 November 2023, https://www.reuters.com/article/entertainment-News/idCAKBN1H20PK-OCAEN?edition-redirect=ca.

61. See Shen Lu and Katie Hunt, 'China Bans Same-Sex Romance from TV Screens', *CNN*, 3 March 2016, accessed 18 November 2023, https://edition.cnn.com/2016/03/03/asia/china-bans-same-sex-dramas/index.html; Ilaria Maria Sala, '"No Ghosts. No Gay Love Stories. No Nudity": Tales of Film-Making in China', *The Guardian*, 22 September 2016, accessed 18 November 2023, https://www.theguardian.com/film/2016/sep/22/tales-of-film-making-in-china-hollywood-hong-kong.

62. While the Film Industry Promotion Law of the PRC, with effect from 1 March 2017, does not stipulate specifically about any bans on LGBTQ+ topics in films, it does have vaguely worded provisions on 'penalties on foreign filmmakers for "damaging China's national dignity, honor and interests, or harming social stability or hurting national feelings"'. Mathew Scott, 'New Film Law Casts Shadow over Giant Chinese Market', *Variety*, 17 May 2017, accessed 18 November 2023, https://variety.com/2017/biz/news/new-film-law-casts-shadow-over-giant-chinese-market-feng-xiaogang-1202430869.

63. See Elena Pollacchi, '"Mature at Birth": The Beijing International Film Festival between the National Film Industry and the Global Film Festival Circuit', in *Chinese Film Festivals: Sites of Translation*, ed. Chris Berry and Luke Robinson (New York: Palgrave Macmillan, 2017), 37.

64. Pollacchi, '"Mature at Birth"', 46–50.

65. Chris Berry and Luke Robinson, 'Introduction', in *Chinese Film Festivals: Sites of Translation*, ed. Chris Berry and Luke Robinson (New York: Palgrave Macmillan, 2017), 1–10.

REFERENCES

Aciman, André. *Call Me by Your Name*. New York: Farrar, Straus and Giroux, 2007.

Aciman, André. *Find Me*. London: Faber & Faber, 2019.

Barraclough, Leo. 'Armie Hammer's *Call Me by Your Name* Joins Berlinale's Panorama Lineup.' *Variety*, 25 January 2017. Accessed 18 November 2023. https://variety.com/2017/film/global/armie-hammer-call-me-by-your-name-berlinale-panorama-1201969419.

Berry, Chris, and Luke Robinson. 'Introduction.' In *Chinese Film Festivals: Sites of Translation*, edited by Chris Berry and Luke Robinson, 1–11. New York: Palgrave Macmillan, 2017.

Box Office Mojo. '*Call Me by Your Name* (2017).' www.boxofficemojo.com. Accessed 18 November 2023.

Brzeski, Patrick. 'Beijing Film Festival Drops *Call Me by Your Name* as China Tightens Grip on Media.' *The Hollywood Reporter*, 26 March 2018. Accessed 18 November 2023. https://www.hollywoodreporter.com/news/general-news/beijing-film-festival-drops-call-me-by-your-name-as-china-tightens-grip-media-1097204/.

Cheung, Ruby. 'Corporatising a Film Festival: Hong Kong.' In *Film Festival Yearbook 1: The Festival Circuit*, edited by Dina Iordanova with Ragan Rhyne, 99–115. St Andrews: St Andrews Film Studies with College Gate Press, 2009.

Cheung, Ruby. 'East Asian Film Festivals: Film Markets.' In *Film Festival Yearbook 3: Film Festivals and East Asia*, edited by Dina Iordanova and Ruby Cheung, 40–61. St Andrews: St Andrews Film Studies, 2011.

Cheung, Ruby. *New Hong Kong Cinema: Transitions to Becoming Chinese in 21st-Century East Asia*. New York and Oxford: Berghahn Books, 2016.

Cheung, Ruby. 'East Asia's Film Business.' In *The Palgrave Handbook of Asian Cinema*, edited by Aaron Han Joon Magnan-Park, Gina Marchetti and See Kam Tan, 89–107. London: Palgrave Macmillan, 2018.

Debruge, Peter. 'Film Review: *Call Me by Your Name*.' *Variety*, 23 January 2017. Accessed 18 November 2023. https://variety.com/2017/film/reviews/call-me-by-your-name-review-1201966646.

De Valck, Marijke. *Film Festivals: From European Geopolitics to Global Cinephilia*. Amsterdam: Amsterdam University Press, 2007.

Elsaesser, Thomas. 'Film Festival Networks: The New Topographies of Cinema in Europe.' In *European Cinema: Face to Face with Hollywood*, by Thomas Elsaesser, 82–108. Amsterdam: Amsterdam University Press, 2005.

Erbland, Kate. 'Sundance 2017: Check Out the Full Lineup, Including Competition Titles, Premieres and Shorts.' *IndieWire*, 6 December 2016. Accessed 18 November 2023. https://www.indiewire.com/2016/12/sundance-2017-full-lineup-competition-premieres-shorts-1201752136.

FIAPF. *FIAPF – Accredited Festival Directory | 2018 Edition*. Bern and Brussels: International Federation of Film Producers Associations, 2018.

Frater, Patrick. 'Global Film Festivals Are Taking a Hybrid Route That's Here to Stay.' *Variety*, 18 December 2020. Accessed 18 November 2023. https://variety.com/2020/biz/global/global-film-festivals-hybrid-1234865457.

Goodfellow, Melanie. 'Mystery Swirls around Future of Dubai International Film Festival.' *Screen Daily*, 18 April 2018. Accessed 18 November 2023. https://www.screendaily.com/news/mystery-swirls-around-future-of-dubai-international-film-festival/5128387.article.

Goodfellow, Melanie. 'Cannes Film Festival to Unveil 56 Official Selection Titles.' *Screen Daily*, 3 June 2020. Accessed 18 November 2023. https://www.screendaily.com/news/cannes-film-festival-to-unveil-56-official-selection-titles/5150294.article.

Grater, Tom. 'Luca Guadagnino on the 10-Year Journey Behind *Call Me by Your Name*.' *Screen Daily*, 31 December 2017. Accessed 18 November 2023. https://www.screendaily.com/features/luca-guadagnino-on-the-10-year-journey-behind-call-me-by-your-name/5125216.article.

Grobar, Matt. '*Call Me by Your Name* Director Luca Guadagnino on the "Wonderful Risk" Worth Taking – Sundance Studio.' *Deadline Hollywood*, 1 February 2017. Accessed 18 November 2023. https://deadline.com/2017/02/call-me-by-your-name-sundance-armie-hammer-luca-guadagnino-michael-stuhlbarg-video-interview-1201894437.

Guadagnino, Luca, dir. *Io sono l'amore (I Am Love)*. First Sun, Mikado Film, Rai Cinema, 2009.

Guadagnino, Luca, dir. *A Bigger Splash*. Frenesy Film Company, Cota Film, 2015.

Guadagnino, Luca, dir. *Call Me by Your Name*. Frenesy Film Company, La Cinefacture, RT Features, 2017.

Hackl, Cathy. 'The Future of the Film Festival.' *Forbes*, 17 November 2020. Accessed 18 November 2023. https://www.forbes.com/sites/cathyhackl/2020/11/17/the-future-of-the-film-festival/?sh=45cdae974d8a.

Halligan, Fionnuala. '*Call Me by Your Name*: Sundance Review.' *Screen Daily*, 23 January 2017. Accessed 18 November 2023. https://www.screendaily.com/reviews/call-me-by-your-name-sundance-review/5114034.article.

Hamid, Rahul. 'From Urban Bohemia to Euro Glamour: The Establishment and Early Years of the New York Film Festival.' In *Film Festival Yearbook 1: The Festival Circuit*, edited by Dina Iordanova with Ragan Rhyne, 67–81. St Andrews: St Andrews Film Studies with College Gate Press, 2009.

Iordanova, Dina. 'The Film Festival Circuit.' In *Film Festival Yearbook 1: The Festival Circuit*, edited by Dina Iordanova with Ragan Rhyne, 23–39. St Andrews: St Andrews Film Studies with College Gate Press, 2009.

Iordanova, Dina. 'The Film Festival as an Industry Node.' *Media Industries Journal* 1, no. 3 (2015): 7–11.

Kohn, Eric. 'How Venice, Telluride, NYFF, and TIFF's 2020 Collaboration Will Affect the Festival Circuit.' *IndieWire*, 8 July 2020. Accessed 18 November 2023. https://www.indiewire.com/2020/07/fall-film-festivals-working-together-1234572013.

Lanzmann, Claude, dir. *Shoah*. Historia, Les Films Aleph, Ministère de la Culture de la République Française, 1985.

Lee, Ashley. 'Why Luca Guadagnino Didn't Include Gay Actors or Explicit Sex Scenes in *Call Me by Your Name* (Q&A).' *The Hollywood Reporter*, 8 February 2017. Accessed 18 November 2023. https://www.hollywoodreporter.com/news/general-news/call-me-by-your-name-why-luca-guadagnino-left-gay-actors-explicit-sex-scenes-q-a-973256.

Levy, Emanuel. *Cinema of Outsiders: The Rise of American Independent Film*. New York and London: New York University Press, 1999.

Li, Pei, and Adam Jourdan. 'Beijing Festival Pulls Award-Winning Gay Film amid Content Squeeze.' *Reuters*, 26 March 2018. Accessed 18 November 2023. https://www.reuters.com/article/entertainmentNews/idCAKBN1H20PK-OCAEN?edition-redirect=ca.

Loist, Skadi. 'The Film Festival Circuit: Networks, Hierarchies, and Circulation.' In *Film Festivals: History, Theory, Method, Practice*, edited by Marijke de Valck, Brendan Kredell and Skadi Loist, 49–64. Oxford: Routledge, 2016.

Lu, Shen, and Katie Hunt. 'China Bans Same-Sex Romance from TV Screens.' *CNN*, 3 March 2016. Accessed 18 November 2023. https://edition.cnn.com/2016/03/03/asia/china-bans-same-sex-dramas/index.html.

Nichols, Bill. 'Discovering Form, Inferring Meaning: New Cinemas and the Film Festival Circuit.' *Film Quarterly* 47, no. 3 (1994): 16–30.

Pollacchi, Elena. '"Mature at Birth": The Beijing International Film Festival between the National Film Industry and the Global Film Festival Circuit.' In *Chinese Film Festivals: Sites of Translation*, edited by Chris Berry and Luke Robinson, 35–55. New York: Palgrave Macmillan, 2017.

Rosenbaum, Jonathan. *Movie Wars: How Hollywood and the Media Conspire to Limit What Films We Can See*. Chicago: A Cappella, 2002.

Sala, Ilaria Maria. '"No Ghosts. No Gay Love Stories. No Nudity": Tales of Film-Making in China.' *The Guardian*, 22 September 2016. Accessed 18 November 2023. https://www.theguardian.com/film/2016/sep/22/tales-of-film-making-in-china-hollywood-hong-kong.

Scott, Mathew. 'New Film Law Casts Shadow over Giant Chinese Market.' *Variety*, 17 May 2017. Accessed 18 November 2023. https://variety.com/2017/biz/news/new-film-law-casts-shadow-over-giant-chinese-market-feng-xiaogang-1202430869.

Sharf, Zack. 'Cannes Announces 2020 Official Lineup: *French Dispatch*, *Ammonite*, New McQueen and Ghibli.' *IndieWire*, 3 June 2020. Accessed 18 November 2023. https://www. indiewire.com/2020/06/cannes-2020-lineup-films-competiton-1202235061.

Shim, Minhae. 'Top 14 Film Markets.' *The Independent*, 25 October 2013. Accessed 18 November 2023. https://independent-magazine.org/2013/10/25/top-12-film-markets_ the-independents-guide-to-film-distribution.

Tzioumakis, Yannis. *American Independent Cinema: An Introduction*. Second Edition. Edinburgh: Edinburgh University Press, 2017.

Van Hoeij, Boyd. '*Call Me by Your Name*: Film Review | Sundance 2017.' *The Hollywood Reporter*, 23 January 2017. Accessed 18 November 2023. https://www.hollywoodreporter. com/review/call-me-by-your-name-review-967150.

Vivarelli, Nick. 'Dubai Film Festival Cancels Next Edition, Ends Existing Format.' *Variety*, 19 April 2018. Accessed 18 November 2023. https://variety.com/2018/film/festivals/dubai-international-film-festival-cancels-next-edition-ends-existing-format-1202758329.

Wong, Cindy Hing-Yuk. *Film Festivals: Culture, People, and Power on the Global Screen*. New Brunswick and London: Rutgers University Press, 2011.

12

Tell Tim Chalamet to Tweet at Me: Situating Timothée Chalamet's Social Media Presence and Perceived (B)Romance with Armie Hammer

Francesca Sobande

Since his impactful role as 17-year-old Elio Perlman in *Call Me by Your Name* (Luca Guadagnino, 2017), Timothée Chalamet's global fame has intensified and his social media presence has attracted many – from piquing the interest of fans who fawn over him to being closely monitored by media reporters. Although they have not been a source of much scholarship, Chalamet's social media posts contribute to the construction of his hyper-visible, yet enigmatic, online presence and public image. Furthermore, Chalamet's social media use is part of the marketing that surrounds *Call Me by Your Name*, including digitally mediated documentation of his off-screen dynamic with Armie Hammer who plays his on-screen love interest (Oliver).

Alluding to the desirability of Chalamet, who has frequently been associated with digital culture and fandom when being referred to as 'the internet's boyfriend',[1] the 2018 song 'Okra' by Black American rapper and singer-songwriter Tyler, the Creator features lyrics which include a nod to 'Tim' Chalamet who is beckoned 'to get at me'. Inspired by this lyric, this chapter's title is a play on it to capture public demand for Chalamet's tweets and social media posts which are notoriously sporadic, and, sometimes, even cryptic. Analysis of Chalamet's social media presence, dynamic with Armie Hammer and press framing of such activity aids a nuanced understanding of how Chalamet's stardom, self-depiction and perceived (b)romance with Hammer shape the iconic nature of *Call Me by Your Name* and the film's connection to conversations concerning gender, sexuality and class.

Drawing on York's research regarding 'reluctant celebrity',[2] in addition to other celebrity, screen and digital studies, this chapter explores how Chalamet's social media presence is entangled with *Call Me by Your Name* marketing and commentaries, such as discourse regarding how Chalamet depicts and embodies particular (white) masculinities and perceived sexualities. Such analysis also accounts for how narratives related to *Call Me by Your Name* have been generatively jammed and remixed as a result of Lil Nas X's popular song 'MONTERO (Call Me by Your Name)' (2021),[3] which foregrounds Black queerness and creativity in a way that departs from a focus on white queerness that underpins Luca Guadagnino's 2017 film *Call Me by Your Name*.

The future of *Call Me by Your Name* is uncertain. Will a film sequel occur? Will future digital discussions that are anchored by the hashtag #CMBYN be more reflective of the richness of Lil Nas X fandom communities than the perspectives and postings of *Call Me by Your Name* film fans? Will statements in response to sexual assault and rape allegations against Hammer be issued by cast and production members whose public image is, arguably, entangled with his? This chapter does not present answers to these questions but ponders over related activity and unspoken words to consider how matters regarding star social media presence and the construction of an off-screen (b)romance are entwined with the image of *Call Me by Your Name*.

'Is it better to speak or die?': Timothée Chalamet's (un)seen life on social media

Timothée Chalamet's coveted Instagram presence is indicated by the 18.5 million followers that he currently has in December 2023 (having risen from 12.1 million in May 2021). The star's profile picture is now a photo of Guadagnino, having changed since the start of writing this chapter, when it was a close-up photograph of him wearing a very light pink or off-white cap that obscured his eyes and part of his face. Chalamet, like many people on social media, has been known to delete Instagram pictures, which has resulted in the emergence of Pinterest, Instagram and online accounts that document the fleeting social media posts of his that once were. In other words, and as his previous Instagram profile picture may point to, Chalamet's social media presence offers momentary glimpses into his life, but much remains actively and understandably obscured. Still, Chalamet's celebrity image is one that is shaped by his approachableness, as perceived by both fans and media commentators.

From being framed as the 'boy next door'[4] to 'the internet's boyfriend', Chalamet has become the object of much affection and adoration, at least partly due to perceptions of him as being affable, humble, grounded and open to interacting with fans. Thus, the star's sporadic social media activity should not be mistaken for reclusiveness. Instead, Chalamet's social media presence and self-representation illuminate some of the ways that celebrities are constructed as being both open and enigmatic, accessible yet unknowable, a public figure but a person with a private life that they are rightly protective of.

As Lam and Raphael assert in their study of 'X-Men Bromance: Film, Audience and Promotion',

> [c]elebrity culture is conceptualised as one that takes place between the private and the public. Within this concept, the focus of attention from both media and audience is equally directed to the public spheres of a celebrity figure's profession, and the private spheres of their 'ordinary' lives.[5]

Such observations are central to my analysis of Chalamet's stardom, particularly as his star image is one, arguably, both actively and aloofly cultivated on social media which followers may perceive as providing them with snapshots of both his private and public life – or, even, a blurring of them.

York's insightful book *Reluctant Celebrity: Affect and Privilege in Contemporary Stardom* offers a detailed explanation of differences between reluctance, reclusiveness and modesty. As York affirms, '[r]eluctant celebrity is not, first and foremost, a gesture of refusal'.[6] Expanding on this point, York asserts that 'reluctance marks an ambivalence rather than a rejection: a condition of sustaining positive and negative reactions while acting in a way that suggests apparent compliance'.[7] Although I do not perceive Chalamet to be a reluctant celebrity, York's theorizing of the detailed differences between reluctance, reclusiveness and modesty is highly relevant to the analysis that features in my chapter. The notion of modesty is particularly applicable to traits that have been attributed to Chalamet which contribute to his overall stardom and the tenderness and 'soft boy' image[8] that is sometimes regarded as being a part of that (see Figure 12.1).

In the words of Lam and Raphael, '[t]he private becomes a space where media and audiences speculate about the "real" celebrity, constructing narratives that either reinforce or subvert the established public image of celebrity figures'.[9] However, it could be argued that despite the social media presence of celebrities sometimes being associated with depictions of their so-called 'private lives', what they choose to make visible is far from being reflective of the intimate and interior moments of who they are. While it is difficult to determine exactly how Chalamet feels about his own use of social media, ambivalence is a term that may spring to mind. For example, the brevity and infrequency of Chalamet's posts on Instagram may be interpreted as indicating his simultaneous interest and disinterest in

FIGURE 12.1: Elio (Timothée Chalamet) and Oliver (Armie Hammer) lying down in the grass. Luca Guadagnino (dir.), *Call Me by Your Name*, 2017. Italy/France/USA/Brazil. © Frenesy, La Cinefacture.

engaging with the platform and sharing posts that provide a window into elements of his life.

Perhaps, in a way that somewhat resembles one of *Call Me by Your Name*'s themes (unspoken feelings which are alluded to via the line 'is it better to speak or die?'), Chalamet's use of Instagram is shrouded in ambiguity and unarticulated details of what various images and posts may be intended to communicate or obscure. However, his Instagram also features hyper-visible content. Therefore, in an article for *W Magazine*, Munzenrieder writes about 'Decoding the Mysteries of Timothée Chalamet's Weird Social Media'. In Munzenrieder's incisive words,

> Chalamet is of the generation to which social media is considered default. [...] Yet, Chalamet is far from a social media power user. His output remains infrequent, and often cryptic. Unless he has something to promote, a few posts a month seems to suffice for Timmée.[10]

Elaborating on Chalamet's use of social media, Munzenrieder states:

> It's tempting to attempt to assemble a grand theory of Chalamet social media, but while he lets us in on tiny, cryptic pinpoint [sic] of his life (okay, he likes Berlin disco mixes, who knew?), he still remains relatively guarded of his privacy.

While celebrities of older generations have the luxury of ignoring social media altogether if they want, Chalamet has perhaps found the answer for superstars his age: posting just enough to seem not stuck up and above it, but still not in a way that actually makes it seems [sic] like he cares too much. There's no need to chase social clout when you're already the king of Gen Z.[11]

Shaped by such words, this chapter is not meant to construct a grand theory of Chalamet's social media use. Rather than emphasizing Chalamet's potential intentions when using social media, and with an awareness of 'The Challenges of Theorizing Celebrity Agency',[12] this work is an account of some of the ways that the interconnectedness of Chalamet's star and social media image, as well as that of Armie Hammer, influence interpretations of *Call Me by Your Name* and the ongoing narratives and contestations that surround it. To explore this topic, it is helpful to focus on some of the social media content posted by Chalamet which directly relates to the film, while considering how the social media presence of Chalamet's co-star Armie Hammer is connected to this too.

'I remember everything': Constructing and deconstructing Chalamet and Hammer's (b)romance

When first embarking on writing this chapter, despite the public image of Chalamet and Hammer differing, both celebrities were often (but not always) framed in the media in ways that were celebratory and involved high praise of both their on-screen chemistry in *Call Me by Your Name* (see Figure 12.2) in addition to their entertaining off-screen interactions which left some people speculating about the nature of their relationship. Much has changed since then. A March 2021 *Vanity Fair* article title highlights some of this: 'The Fall of Armie Hammer: A Family Saga of Sex, Money, Drugs, and Betrayal'.[13]

Furthermore, other editorials and media pieces over the following year reflected how the 'All-American' sheen that Hammer was once ascribed had significantly shifted: 'Armie Hammer: A Timeline of Events Leading Up to the Sexual Assault',[14] 'The Rape Allegations against Armie Hammer, Explained',[15] 'A Breakdown of Armie Hammer's Cannibalism and Abuse Controversy',[16] 'The Memes and Internet Thirst about the Armie Hammer Story Aren't Funny'.[17] These articles, and others, illustrate how the so-called (b)romance between Chalamet and Hammer was once framed in relation to *Call Me by Your Name*, while also reflecting on how the film's public image, as a result of Hammer's, has changed in recent years.

As I have previously argued as part of research on Chalamet in *Call Me by Your Name* and the popular culture construct of 'the internet's boyfriend':

FIGURE 12.2: Elio (Timothée Chalamet) shaking a statue's hand which Oliver (Armie Hammer) is holding out to him. In the background is Lake Garda. Luca Guadagnino (dir.), *Call Me by Your Name*, 2017. Italy/France/USA/Brazil. © Frenesy, La Cinefacture.

> At times, Chalamet's on-screen portrayal of teenage Elio exploring his sexuality during a 1980s summer in Italy is misinterpreted as reason enough to suggest that he embodies a non-traditional and non-heteronormative form of masculinity. Chalamet's assumed similarities to his on-screen character, Elio, are perhaps heightened due to the fact they are both connected to France and America, but beyond that there is little to suggest their similarity.[18]

Claims and impressions of Chalamet's allegedly 'new', 'different' and 'soft boy' masculinity appear to contribute to the idea, or illusion, of potential romance between him and Hammer. In other words, how Chalamet's image and embodiment are often read or framed as 'non-traditional', and, even, 'androgynous', seems to be sutured into how his off-screen dynamic with Hammer is sometimes constructed and deconstructed.

To say that the *Call Me by Your Name* fandom is a strong and vibrant one would be an understatement. There are countless threads and assemblages of content that communicate the idea that Chalamet and Hammer's off-screen relationship is not one devoid of sexual chemistry. On many occasions, Hammer has publicly spoken about the intimacy that they depict in *Call Me by Your Name*, such as when reflecting on 'the challenges of the role – including conveying the erotic allure of a peach'.[19] However, the fact that Hammer and Chalamet have not shied away from speaking about such topics is far from being reason enough to assume that the two are more than friends. To borrow the words of Kooijman on the character of Will (played by Eric McCormack) in *Will & Grace*, both Chalamet and Hammer appear to be 'just gay in the fictional world'.[20] Also, as is highlighted in the work of Martin Jr. and Battles on 'The straight labor of playing gay':

> Given the highly erotic novel and relative instability of textual identities that served as *CMBYN*'s source material, the intense intimacy between the characters led to a great deal of interest in how the actors achieved such 'convincing' performances and the actors frequently resorted to humor to discuss their experiences filming.[21]

Furthermore, Martin Jr. and Battles observe that 'as universalizing discourses produce anxieties over the boundaries between straight and gay masculinities, humor is deployed as the actors work to maintain their own investments in straightness',[22] including when being interviewed together.

Blurred boundaries between fiction and reality[23] are a through line of much of celebrity culture. It is important to acknowledge that there can be distinct differences between how Chalamet and Hammer are portrayed in fan-fiction that remediates their filmic romance and how they are portrayed in work produced by the press and mainstream media that promotes the film. It is also crucial to consider different kinds of media as contributing to a megatextual media-verse that includes diverging depictions and discourses related to Chalamet and Hammer, while also pushing dominant narratives across a range of media texts. For example, the (b)romanticization of their dynamic that occurred around the time of the film's launch and during the immediate aftermath of it was not solely confined to fanfiction, meme culture or mainstream media. Rather, such a framing of their perceived dynamic and supposedly soft boy image took shape in ways impacted by different types and genres of media.

In January 2022, Chalamet's Instagram still featured several images of him and Hammer on the set of *Call Me by Your Name* or together during the key promotional period that surrounded the film. Accompanying captions included statements such as '#callmebyyourname is out in the UK [peach emoji] [union jack emoji] [peach emoji] [union jack emoji] [peach emoji] [union jack emoji]'[24] and 'one last one with armie [sic] from Berlin'.[25] The 1000+ comments that featured below each of these posts provided a glimpse of the glee that has sometimes been a part of fans' engagement with Chalamet's Instagram content that depicts both him and Hammer. Although media-captured interactions between the two stars have waned in the years since the film's release, online constructions of their perceived (b)romance persist. Such constructions vary from media discourse, fan edits and remixed depictions that focus on their imagined friendship to those that stress their so-called sexual chemistry. Furthermore, such constructions, I argue, are also shaped by Chalamet's identity, or, at least, normative ideas concerning it.

Chalamet is framed as being a comfortingly self-deprecating character who frequently makes time for fan photos, wherever he is, while also being positioned as alluringly 'different' – arguably, partly due to how his dual nationality is depicted and discussed in ways that allude to him being a coveted '(inter)national treasure' that is perceived as embodying authentic markers of French sophistication and Europeanness.[26]

YouTube videos such as 'Armie Hammer & Timothée Chalamet cute moments (Part 1)',[27] 'Armie Hammer & Timothee Chalamet | Lovers' eyes'[28] and 'timothee chalamet and armie hammer being soulmates for 12 minutes',[29] which have been viewed a collective total of more than 1.7 million times as of December 2023, are symbolic of the off-screen intimacy that some associate with the relationship between the two actors. Sometimes, the social media posts of the stars have played into such ideas about them which have aided the cementing of their somewhat celebrity couple status. That said, as is discussed in articles such as 'Armie Hammer Responds to Fan Who Wants Him to Be Gay With Timothée Chalamet',[30] there have also been moments when the actors have made clear the platonic nature of their friendship.

In their study of 'X-Men Bromance: Film, Audience and Promotion', Lam and Raphael note that '[a]lthough the use of the celebrity bromance was not confirmed as a promotional strategy, it provided a means to generate interest and discussion'.[31] Their research illuminates,

> [n]arratives of the public facets of the celebrity figure – their public personas – play out through dispersed media outlets, wherein construction takes place through an intertextual web of images. These images most often serve the creation of individual celebrity persona, but occasionally fashion celebrities in plural: the celebrity couple.[32]

Among such intertextual webs of images are memes, GIFs and fan edits which adoringly position different famous people as being partners of some sort. Hence, my prior work considered how elements of digital remix culture, namely memes, contributed to how the 44th US President Barack Obama and Joe Biden, who is now the 46th US President, have been portrayed as being involved in an interracial bromance – a platonic but intimate friendship.

When examining representations of Obama and Biden I argued that

> [t]he power dynamics signaled in Obama–Biden memes often position Obama as calm, collected, and self-assured, in contrast to the unbridled eagerness and goofiness projected onto Biden. Although such memes don't symbolize an end to racism,

they buck historic trends of portraying Black people in buffoonish ways. They are also consistent with media discourse regarding the allegedly post-racial nature of the US, claims of which became a hallmark of the perceived symbolism of Obama's presidency.[33]

Unlike the racial dynamics at the root of how Obama and Biden's relationship has sometimes been digitally remixed, the (b)romance between Chalamet and Hammer is one that is undoubtedly shaped by whiteness and its normative nature in celebrity culture – specifically, the dominant status of a 'class-coded' white masculinity[34].

Both Chalamet and Hammer embody white, slender or statuesque, and, at least at the time *Call Me by Your Name* was filmed, relatively youthful masculinities. While it is not possible to determine exactly what about the perceived Chalamet and Hammer (b)romance appeals to all who are attracted to the idea of them, it is reasonable to recognize that some of the many compliments that they are showered with are symptomatic of whiteness that bolsters the desirability politics that celebrity culture is ensconced in. Prior work on notions of the 'renaissance man' has highlighted celebrity culture's fascination with a 'brand of white and upper-class "Englishness"'[35] that is associated with the image of actors such as Hugh Grant. In a similar vein, representations of white middle-class American masculinity have attracted much cinematic and industry attention. This is evidenced by contemporary discourse regarding a so-called soft boy aesthetic – a term that typically frames very slim, young, pale and vaguely stylish white men as embodying a sensitive, safe and sometimes desexualized masculinity that is far from being associated with predatory behaviour. Accordingly, an image of Chalamet and Hammer, smiling and suited at an event, accompanies a 2018 *Vogue* article titled, 'Calling All Softboys: There's a Tender New Trend in Menswear'.[36]

Relatedly, even when the potentially, yet unestablished, sexual nature of their off-screen relationship is discussed and represented online, the dynamic between Chalamet and Hammer is often still framed in ways that allude to a wholesome cuteness that is a hallmark of the archetypal all-American 'boy next door' heart-throb, positioned as being one of the so-called 'good' ones who can do no wrong. However, notions of 'coming-of-age' innocence, self-actualizing sexual awakening, sweetness and a supposed sense of soft boy desire that have been attributed to *Call Me by Your Name* have been disrupted by the changed public perception of Hammer following news about rape allegations. Some may feel that it is too strong a statement to suggest that there has been an intentional *Call Me by Your Name* silence on this matter. But the relative absence of comments from the faces behind and in front of the film's camera may be interpreted as an uncomfortable silence that fails to distract from the shadow cast over *Call Me by Your Name* by Hammer. Here, it is helpful to revisit York's work on reluctant celebrity.

When considering the related work of Rojek on Johnny Depp, York notes that reluctance is not the same as reclusiveness, 'though often in discourses of celebrity, the two are taken to be equivalent, and a reluctant celebrity can count on being routinely described as reclusive in the media'.[37] A 'reluctant' celebrity may still choose to share aspects of their personal life in the public eye, yet tentatively or begrudgingly. Whereas a 'reclusive' celebrity may seek to entirely withdraw from such discourse and refuse to engage in commentary concerning their life. Armie Hammer, who has been known for his candour on social media and in interviews, now appears to have made the move towards being a reclusive celebrity, following the allegations against him, and as is evident by his social media break that stains the once effervescent, ethereal and marketable *Call Me by Your Name* image.

Still, despite any intention to fade into obscurity amid the rape allegations and their investigation (charges being dropped in mid 2023; Hammer was off social media between January 2021 and autumn 2023), Hammer's image continues to be a public one that is connected to ideas about *Call Me by Your Name* and, in turn, some impressions of Chalamet's stardom. In fact, in January 2021 it was reported that 'Timothée Chalamet and Luca Guadagnino Could Reunite for a Movie about Cannibalism' (*Bones and All*, 2022),[38] but online users were quick to point out the eeriness of this possibility, particularly when taking into consideration that allegations against Hammer include claims of his allegedly cannibalistic tendencies.[39]

The decoupling of Chalamet and Hammer's contemporary star images was always inevitable, but the accelerated speed at which this may now occur will likely be impacted by the assault and rape allegations that Hammer is now known for. It is too early to tell whether the social media presence of each actor may involve alterations to indicate their personal distance from the other (e.g. the deletion of posts featuring images of them both). However, it seems unlikely that some of the light-hearted and in-joke public interactions that once took place between both stars online will continue to be part of their social media approach.

'Cinema is a mirror of reality and it is a filter': The shifting star image of Call Me by Your Name

The star image of Chalamet and Hammer is constantly evolving, and consequently, so is that of *Call Me by Your Name*. An elusiveness, and reclusiveness, is now associated with Hammer, who seems to actively avoid the media since the assault allegations against him were made public. Contrastingly, the enigmatic and affable qualities often attributed to Chalamet continue to be strongly associated with *Call Me by Your Name*, in addition to a wide range of high-profile films he has featured in, such as *Lady Bird* (Greta Gerwig, 2017), *Beautiful Boy* (Felix Van Groeningen, 2018), *Little Women* (Greta Gerwig, 2019), *The French Dispatch* (Wes Anderson, 2021) and *Dune* (Denis Villeneuve, 2021). As articles such as 'The Making (and Remaking) of Timothée Chalamet'[40] suggest, Chalamet has become more globally established in ways that are not solely dependent on his connection to *Call Me by Your Name*. Nevertheless, his portrayal of wide-eyed Elio in *Call Me by Your Name* continues to commonly be construed as his 'breakthrough' role.

Media articles such as 'how a queer arthouse movie fueled the internet's most unlikely fandom'[41] have delved into the online waves created by Guadagnino's film. At the point that piece was written, *Call Me by Your Name* is framed as being somewhat subversive and different to who and what is typically at the centre of pop culture. In the words of Greenwood,

> [t]hought the stan-provoked slew of niche memes, love-heart-eye emojis, and hashtag campaigns was reserved for the pop cultural elite? Think again. There's an unlikely film – a queer arthouse love story – that's captured the hearts of the swooning, liberal, and social media savvy youth of today.[42]

Since then, *Call Me by Your Name* has come to be known, or, at least, treated as being part of the pop culture centre rather than adjacent to or outside of it. Acknowledging this does not deny the significance of the fact that the film still also is 'a queer arthouse love story'[43] but acknowledging the high-profile nature of *Call Me by Your Name* seems important, especially when critically accounting for how the whiteness that underpins it may partly propel some of its praise and appeal.

In March 2021, Black American rapper, singer and songwriter Lil Nas X released the song (and music video for it) 'MONTERO (Call Me by Your Name)'.[44] It is difficult to capture in words all that the song and artistry that surrounds it may symbolize, but one thing for sure is that unlike the film *Call Me by Your Name*, the much-anticipated creation by Lil Nas X distinctly connects to Black gay, queer and femme experiences and aesthetics. Media pieces such as 'Satanic Panic over Lil Nas X's "Montero" Proves That Black Queer Sexuality Is Still a Challenge for Some'[45] highlight the bigoted and stigmatizing backlash to the song that has been articulated, and which is reflective of the intersections of antiblackness and homophobia. Prior to the release of 'MONTERO (Call Me by Your Name)' by Lil Nas X, the hashtag #CMBYN mainly yielded comments about the film which foregrounded images of, and ideas about, white, cisgender, heterosexual actors. Now, although such content continues to appear alongside the hashtag, so too do posts about, and which feature images of, Lil Nas X. Among those that are most prominent at the moment (Spring 2021) are posts by Lil Nas X who has used the hashtag #CMBYN when promoting 'MONTERO (Call Me by Your Name)'.

Some of such posts feature an image of bare-chested Lil Nas X adorning black feather wings and a black cap with horns. The iconic music video plays with classical imagery, including Graeco-Roman aesthetics and imagery associated with theology, but as part of an impactful narrative that critiques oppressive and judgemental systems that may be associated with such classical motifs. The music video, and the Black queer creativity that it centres, seem a world away from all the digital media that was spawned by the film *Call Me by Your Name* which foregrounds whiteness. Although both the film and music draw on elements of Graeco-Roman imagery, there are far more differences between these media texts than there are similarities. Perhaps, posts by Lil Nas X and fans of 'MONTERO (Call Me by Your Name)' can be interpreted as constituting a remixing of digital *Call Me by Your Name* content, commentaries and communities. Make no mistake about it, the recent work of Lil Nas X should not be perceived as a mere reaction to *Call Me by Your Name*. Rather, 'MONTERO (Call Me by Your Name)' is art in its own right. Still, there is scope to see some of the digital activity surrounding the song as generatively jamming and disrupting the whiteness which much of prior online *Call Me by Your Name* activity appears to emerge within.

The film *Call Me by Your Name*'s centring of white and middle-class masculinities serves as a shield from certain types of oppressive backlash and moral panic (e.g. racist and classist) that have been directed at stars such as Lil Nas X when releasing 'MONTERO (Call Me by Your Name)'. In the years since the film *Call Me by Your Name* was released, there has been more discussion of how whiteness functions in and through it, but there remain questions worthy of further exploration such as the following: how do issues regarding race, class, sexuality and cultural difference combine in *Call Me by Your Name* and its fandom in ways that elucidate the relationship between the film and whiteness, queer culture and global media?

As the title of this chapter suggests, this work considers how digitally (re)presented dynamics between the two main actors in *Call Me by Your Name* (Timothée Chalamet and Armie Hammer), their star images, and social media depictions and discourses shape ideas about the film. There is a reflection on how expressions, or the appearance, of elusiveness and reclusiveness impact this (for example, Chalamet's sporadic/cryptic social media use and Hammer's online disengagement in the wake of assault allegations made against him). The star, or possibly *brand*, image of *Call Me by Your Name* is a constellation of images, interpretations and individuals. Perceptions and understandings of the component parts of such an image are constantly shifting in ways that may alter the overall pop culture position and legacy of *Call Me by Your Name*, which is a film that continues to be adored and digitally remixed by fans but is also one that may be viewed as being cloaked by a fraught silence concerning Hammer and the allegations that have been made.

NOTES

1. The 'internet's boyfriend' is 'a popular culture concept which symbolizes certain present-day issues to do with gender and sexuality, online experiences and fandom, the politics of how and why celebrities are admired, and the changing nature of how celebrity is constructed and functions'. Francesca Sobande, 'The Internet's "Transnational" Boyfriend: Digital (Re)Presentations of Celebrity Men', *Feminist Media Studies* 21, no. 4 (2021): 540, https://doi.org/10.1080/14680777.2021.1900312. Specifically, the term 'the internet's boyfriend' encompasses how famous men and celebrity expressions of masculinity are digitally depicted and remixed as part of discourse that frames certain individuals as desired and idealized (e.g. Timothée Chalamet, Oscar Isaac, Idris Elba, Keanu Reeves).

2. See Lorraine York, *Reluctant Celebrity: Affect and Privilege in Contemporary Stardom* (Cham: Palgrave Macmillan, 2018).

3. Lil Nas X, 'MONTERO (Call Me by Your Name)', Columbia, 2021.

4. Gabe Bergado quoted in Sobande, 'The Internet's "Transnational" Boyfriend', 546.

5. Celia Lam and Jackie Raphael, 'X-Men Bromance: Film, Audience and Promotion', *Celebrity Studies* 9, no. 3 (2018), 355.

6. York, *Reluctant Celebrity*, 4.

7. York, *Reluctant Celebrity*, 4.

8. See Natalie Frantz, 'Decoding the Soft Boy Aesthetic', *L'Officiel*, 11 May 2020, https://www.lofficielusa.com/pop-culture/what-is-soft-boy-aesthetic-harry-styles-timothee-chalamet.

9. Lam and Raphael, 'X-Men Bromance', 355.

10. See Kyle Munzenrieder, 'Decoding the Mysteries of Timothée Chalamet's Weird Social Media', *W Magazine*, 13 April 2020, https://www.wmagazine.com/story/timothee-chalamets-weird-social-media.

11. See Munzenrieder, 'Decoding'.

12. See Lorraine York, 'Star Turn: The Challenges of Theorizing Celebrity Agency', *The Journal of Popular Culture* 46, no. 6 (2013): 1330–47.

13. See Julie Miller, 'The Fall of Armie Hammer: A Family Saga of Sex, Money, Drugs, and Betrayal', *Vanity Fair*, 11 March 2021, https://www.vanityfair.com/hollywood/2021/03/the-fall-of-armie-hammer-a-family-saga-of-sex-money-drugs-and-betrayal.

14. See Rachel Brodsky, 'Armie Hammer: A Timeline of Events Leading Up to the Sexual Assault Investigation Against the Actor', *The Independent*, 30 March 2021, https://www.independent.co.uk/arts-entertainment/films/news/armie-hammer-sexual-assault-timeline-b1819793.html.

15. Constance Grady, 'The Rape Allegations against Armie Hammer, Explained', *Vox*, 19 March 2021, https://www.vox.com/culture/22338844/armie-hammer-rape-accusation-effie-cannibalism-explained.

16. Karla Rodriguez, 'A Breakdown of Armie Hammer's Cannibalism and Abuse Controversy', *Complex*, 18 March 2021, https://www.complex.com/pop-culture/armie-hammer-cannibalism-abuse-controversy/.

17. Bonnie McLaren, 'The Memes and Internet Thirst about the Armie Hammer Story Aren't Funny', *Grazia*, 10 February 2021, https://graziadaily.co.uk/celebrity/news/armie-hammer-twitter.

18. Sobande, 'The Internet's "Transnational" Boyfriend' 545–46.

19. Ryan Gilbey, 'Armie Hammer on Gay Romance *Call Me by Your Name*: "There Were Fetishes I Didn't Understand"', *The Guardian*, 28 September 2017, https://www.theguardian.com/film/2017/sep/28/armie-hammer-call-me-by-your-name-there-were-all-these-fetishes-i-didnt-understand.

20. Jaap Kooijman, 'After Will & Ellen: Uneventful Queer Television', *Critical Studies in Television* 14, no. 4 (2019), 452.

21. Alfred L. Martin Jr. and Kathleen Battles, 'The Straight Labor of Playing Gay', *Critical Studies in Media Communication* 38, no. 2 (2021), 134, https://doi.org/10.1080/15295036.2021.1876899.

22. Martin Jr. and Battles, 134.

23. Jason Mittell, *Complex TV: The Poetics of Contemporary Television Storytelling* (New York: New York University Press, 2015).

24. The Instagram post, at @tchalamet, is dated 28 October 2017.

25. The Instagram post is dated 17 February 2017.

26. Sobande, 'The Internet's "Transnational" Boyfriend' 546.

27. bowie28, 'Armie Hammer & Timothée Chalamet Cute Moments (Part 1)', YouTube, 23 October 2017, https://www.youtube.com/watch?v=HfU57MuT1Ww.

28. spaceyume, 'Armie Hammer & Timothee Chalamet | Lovers' Eyes', YouTube, 4 February 2018, https://www.youtube.com/watch?v=YLoI4DtZxAo.

29. -stranger, 'timothee chalamet and armie hammer being soulmates for 12 minutes', YouTube, 12 June 2020, https://www.youtube.com/watch?v=zcirRM9nWo0.

30. Sam Damshenas, 'Armie Hammer Responds to Fan Who Wants Him to be Gay with Timothée Chalamet', *Gay Times*, accessed 13 April 2023, https://www.gaytimes.co.uk/culture/armie-hammer-responds-to-fan-who-wants-him-to-be-gay-with-timothee-chalamet/.

31. Lam and Raphael, 'X-Men Bromance', 355.

32. Lam and Raphael, 355.

33. Francesca Sobande, 'Re-meme-bering, Romanticizing and Reframing the Obamas Online', in *Race/Gender/Class/Media: Considering Diversity across Audiences, Content, and Producers*, fourth edition, ed. Rebecca Ann Lind (New York and Abingdon: Routledge, 2019), 48.

34. Marion Hallet, 'Renaissance Man: Hugh Grant's Performance of Class, White Englishness, Joyfully Mature Masculinity', *Celebrity Studies*, volume 14, no. 1 (2023): 83–100, https://doi.org/10.1080/19392397.2022.2159675, 84.

35. Hallet, 83.

36. Steff Yotka, 'Calling All Softboys: There's a Tender New Trend in Menswear', *Vogue*, 29 March 2018, https://www.vogue.com/article/softboy-2018-menswear-trend?verso=true

37. York, *Reluctant Celebrity*, 4.

38. See Justin Curto, 'Timothée Chalamet and Luca Guadagnino Could Reunite for a Movie about Cannibalism', *Vulture*, 29 January 2021. https://www.vulture.com/2021/01/timothee-chalamet-luca-guadagnino-cannibalism-movie.html.

39. See Natalie Morin, 'Armie Hammer's Ex Can't Believe Timothée Chalamet Is Making a Cannibal Movie Either', *Refinery29*, 1 February 2021, https://www.refinery29.com/en-gb/2021/02/10287148/armie-hammer-wife-cannibal-movie-timothee-chalamet.

40. Daniel Riley, 'The Making (and Remaking) of Timothée Chalamet', *GQ*, 15 October 2020, https://www.gq.com/story/timothee-chalamet-november-2020-cover-profile.

41. Douglas Greenwood, 'How a Queer Arthouse Movie Fueled the Internet's Most Unlikely Fandom', *i-D*, 30 October 2017, https://i-d.vice.com/en_uk/article/gyjb94/how-a-queer-arthouse-movie-fueled-the-internets-most-unlikely-fandom.

42. Greenwood, 'Queer Arthouse Movie'.

43. See Greenwood, 'Queer Arthouse Movie'.

44. The music video is directed by Tanu Muino and Lil Nas X.

45. Jenessa Williams, 'Satanic Panic over Lil Nas X's "Montero" Proves That Black Queer Sexuality Is Still a Challenge for Some', *The Forty-Five*, 1 April 2021, https://thefortyfive.com/opinion/lil-nas-x-montero-backlash-black-queer-art/.

REFERENCES

Anderson, Wes, dir. *The French Dispatch*. American Empirical Pictures, Indian Paintbrush, Studio Babelsberg, 2021.

bowie28. 'Armie Hammer & Timothée Chalamet Cute Moments (Part 1).' YouTube, 23 October 2017. https://www.youtube.com/watch?v=HfU57MuT1Ww.

Brodsky, Rachel. 'Armie Hammer: A Timeline of Events Leading Up to the Sexual Assault Investigation Against the Actor.' *The Independent*, 30 March 2021. https://www.independent.co.uk/arts-entertainment/films/news/armie-hammer-sexual-assault-timeline-b1819793.html.

Curto, Justin. 'Timothée Chalamet and Luca Guadagnino Could Reunite for a Movie about Cannibalism.' *Vulture*, 29 January 2021. https://www.vulture.com/2021/01/timothee-chalamet-luca-guadagnino-cannibalism-movie.html.

Damshenas, Sam. 'Armie Hammer Responds to Fan Who Wants Him to be Gay with Timothée Chalamet.' *Gay Times*. Accessed 13 April 2023. https://www.gaytimes.co.uk/culture/armie-hammer-responds-to-fan-who-wants-him-to-be-gay-with-timothee-chalamet/.

Frantz, Natalie. 'Decoding the Soft Boy Aesthetic.' *L'Officiel*, 11 May 2020. https://www.lofficielusa.com/pop-culture/what-is-soft-boy-aesthetic-harry-styles-timothee-chalamet.

Gerwig, Greta, dir. *Lady Bird*. IAC Films, Scott Rudin Productions, Entertainment 360, 2017.

Gerwig, Greta, dir. *Little Women*. Columbia Pictures, New Regency Productions, Pascal Pictures, 2019.

Gilbey, Ryan. 'Armie Hammer on Gay Romance *Call Me by Your Name*: "There Were Fetishes I Didn't Understand".' *The Guardian*, 28 September 2017. https://www.theguardian.com/

film/2017/sep/28/armie-hammer-call-me-by-your-name-there-were-all-these-fetishes-i-didnt-understand.

Grady, Constance. 'The Rape Allegations against Armie Hammer, Explained.' *Vox*, 19 March 2021. https://www.vox.com/culture/22338844/armie-hammer-rape-accusation-effie-cannibalism-explained.

Greenwood, Douglas. 'How a Queer Arthouse Movie Fueled the Internet's Most Unlikely Fandom.' *i-D*, 30 October 2017. https://i-d.vice.com/en_uk/article/gyjb94/how-a-queer-arthouse-movie-fueled-the-internets-most-unlikely-fandom.

Guadagnino, Luca, dir. *Call Me by Your Name*. Frenesy Film Company, La Cinefacture, RT Features, 2017.

Guadagnino, Luca, dir. *Bones and All*. Frenesy Film Company, Per Capita Productions, 2022.

Hallet, Marion. 'Renaissance Man: Hugh Grant's Performance of Class, White Englishness, and Joyfully Mature Masculinity', *Celebrity Studies* 14, no. 1 (2023): 83–100, https://doi.org/10.1080/19392397.2022.2159675

Kooijman, Jaap. 'After Will & Ellen: Uneventful Queer Television.' *Critical Studies in Television*, 14, no. 4 (2019): 451–55.

Lam, Celia, and Jackie Raphael. 'X-Men Bromance: Film, Audience and Promotion.' *Celebrity Studies*, 9, no. 3 (2018): 355–74.

Lil Nas X. 'MONTERO (Call Me by Your Name).' Columbia, 2021.

Martin Jr., Alfred L., and Kathleen Battles. 'The Straight Labor of Playing Gay.' *Critical Studies in Media Communication*, 38, no. 2 (2021): 127–40. https://doi.org/10.1080/15295036.2021.1876899.

McLaren, Bonnie. 'The Memes and Internet Thirst about the Armie Hammer Story Aren't Funny.' *Grazia*, 10 February 2021. https://graziadaily.co.uk/celebrity/news/armie-hammer-twitter.

Miller, Julie. 'The Fall of Armie Hammer: A Family Saga of Sex, Money, Drugs, and Betrayal.' *Vanity Fair*, 11 March 2021. https://www.vanityfair.com/hollywood/2021/03/the-fall-of-armie-hammer-a-family-saga-of-sex-money-drugs-and-betrayal.

Morin, Natalie. 'Armie Hammer's Ex Can't Believe Timothée Chalamet Is Making a Cannibal Movie Either.' *Refinery29*, 1 February 2021. https://www.refinery29.com/en-gb/2021/02/10287148/armie-hammer-wife-cannibal-movie-timothee-chalamet

Muino, Tanu, and Lil Nas X. 'MONTERO (Call Me by Your Name).' Music video. Columbia, 2021.

Munzenrieder, Kyle. 'Decoding the Mysteries of Timothée Chalamet's Weird Social Media.' *W Magazine*, 13 April 2020. https://www.wmagazine.com/story/timothee-chalamets-weird-social-media.

Riley, Daniel. 'The Making (and Remaking) of Timothée Chalamet.' *GQ*, 15 October 2020. https://www.gq.com/story/timothee-chalamet-november-2020-cover-profile.

Rodriguez, Karla. 'A Breakdown of Armie Hammer's Cannibalism and Abuse Controversy.' *Complex*, 18 March 2021. https://www.complex.com/pop-culture/armie-hammer-cannibalism-abuse-controversy/.

Sobande, Francesca. 'Re-meme-bering, Romanticizing and Reframing the Obamas Online.' In *Race/Gender/Class/Media: Considering Diversity across Audiences, Content, and Producers*, edited by Rebecca Ann Lind, 47–50. Fourth Edition. New York and Abingdon: Routledge, 2019.

Sobande, Francesca. 'The Internet's "Transnational" Boyfriend: Digital (Re)Presentations of Celebrity Men.' *Feminist Media Studies*, 21, no. 4 (2021): 539–55. https://doi.org/10.1080/14680777.2021.1900312.

Spaceyume. 'Armie Hammer & Timothee Chalamet | Lovers' Eyes.' YouTube, 4 February 2018. https://www.youtube.com/watch?v=YLoI4DtZxAo.

stranger. 'timothee chalamet and armie hammer being soulmates for 12 minutes.' YouTube, 12 June 2020. https://www.youtube.com/watch?v=zcirRM9nWo0.

Van Groeningen, Felix, dir. *Beautiful Boy*. Amazon Studios, Big Indie Pictures, Plan B Entertainment, 2018.

Villeneuve, Denis, dir. *Dune*. Warner Bros., Legendary Entertainment, Villeneuve Films, 2021.

Williams, Jenessa. 'Satanic Panic over Lil Nas X's "Montero" Proves That Black Queer Sexuality Is Still a Challenge for Some.' *The Forty-Five*, 1 April 2021. https://thefortyfive.com/opinion/lil-nas-x-montero-backlash-black-queer-art/.

York, Lorraine. 'Star Turn: The Challenges of Theorizing Celebrity Agency.' *The Journal of Popular Culture*, 46, no. 6 (2013): 1330–47.

York, Lorraine. *Reluctant Celebrity: Affect and Privilege in Contemporary Stardom*. Cham: Palgrave Macmillan, 2018.

13

The Sexiest Risk-Taker?
Armie Hammer, White Masculinity and
Call Me by Your Name

Jonathan A. Cannon

Summer 1983. Somewhere in northern Italy. After the opening credits in *Call Me by Your Name* (Luca Guadagnino, 2017) – featuring photographic, fragmentary examples of Hellenistic and ancient Roman statuary finish – we cut to a scene in which Elio Perlman (Timothée Chalamet) and friend Marzia (Esther Garrel) are interrupted by the arrival of an outsider from America. Elio labels the male stranger as '*l'usurpateur*' (in English: 'the usurper'). Historically, the figure of the usurper was found in the ancient Greek and Roman worlds, taking power and land by force as a controversial, illegitimate tyrant. However, in regards to the newly arrived outlander, this reference made by Elio may be uttered out of jest as he glances and smirks back at Marzia lying down on the bed. They travel to the open window of the upstairs bedroom together; Elio and Marzia stare down at the approaching green car. Emerging out of the small Fiat 128 stands a tall American, who enthusiastically shakes the hand of Samuel Perlman (Michael Stuhlbarg), Elio's father and professor of archaeology. 'Oh my goodness, you're bigger than your picture', exclaims Mr Perlman motioning his hands upward at the young man. 'Well, I couldn't get all of me in the photo, that's the problem', he replies to Mr Perlman. This marks the entry of Oliver in *Call Me by Your Name*, played by Armie Hammer. The scene, moreover, signals our attention to how Armie Hammer embodies and performs the role of Oliver as a mainstream Hollywood star in an independent arthouse film.

However, a lot has changed for Hammer and his star image since his portrayal of Oliver in *Call Me by Your Name* and his films and personal life thereafter up to the present. The seeds of controversy for Hammer in the last year or so prior to writing this chapter have been sown, so to speak, through online posts, both in the visuals and language displayed. In the midst of the COVID-19 pandemic early in 2021, word circulated on the internet that, as Elizabeth Wagmeister details in her article for *Variety* titled 'Armie Hammer's Hollywood Career Is in Freefall as Sex Scandal Explodes on Social Media', Hammer was 'trending online for being a cannibal'.[1] Further in her article, Wagmeister details that the abrupt turn – or more bluntly put, complete nosedive for Hammer's film career – is evident in the visual proof of circulated imagery, apparently alluding not only to cannibalism but also to bondage and fantasies of rape:

> Unverified messages have been blasted across social media, reportedly showing Hammer chatting with several women in explicit conversations displaying his fetishes, where he allegedly expresses his sexual appetite to drink blood, cut toes and enslave sex partners. The messages, allegedly sent by Hammer, describe rape fantasies.[2]

Going beyond the realm of either edge or kink culture, what the above statement by Wagmeister communicates about Hammer is that the star's appeal has fallen dramatically in the contemporary Hollywood industry. Because of these serious allegations brought forth to Hammer in his personal life, it is important for me to address this controversial behaviour as a film scholar who critically studies the phenomenon of stardom across a variety of contexts. However, while no doubt still recognizing the shocking words and content casually circulated by Hammer across social media platforms, I feel as though it is equally important to present a wider picture of Hammer. Accordingly, two key questions form the crux of my investigation. First, how does this controversial or risky behaviour, for example, inform a viewer of previous filmic characterizations of Hammer and his post-*Call Me by Your Name* career? And second, how do corporeal fantasies of a film star – imagined, or allegedly acted upon – participate in an objective contextualization of the star's mechanics in and outside of the film's diegesis? In evaluating Hammer's star persona through the concept of risk, I seek to uncover reasons as to why *Call Me by Your Name* matters to our understanding of Hammer as a Hollywood star in an independent feature film of this nature.

Based on the Hammer dynasty, one might initially believe that Armie had both ingenuity and risk-taking – for movie roles, and courting scandal and controversy – in his blood. As the great-grandson of American oil tycoon Julian Armand Hammer (his own namesake) and the son of businessman Michael Armand Hammer, Armand 'Armie' Douglas Hammer has become one of the most recognizable A-list Hollywood names in the previous decade, especially from *The Social Network* (David Fincher, 2010) onward. Hammer has worked alongside some of the most popular Hollywood directors (such as Gore Verbinski, Guy Ritchie, Clint

Eastwood and David Fincher) and A-list stars (such as Johnny Depp, Henry Cavill and Felicity Jones) while also flirting with projects on the fringes of the industry, in independent, arthouse fare. Well-spoken – with an enunciation of boarding-school aplomb – and yet with a sassy *savoir faire* in his visage and cadence, Hammer is candidly aware of his work in television and film but also oddly mysterious in how this confidence is worked through and portrayed on screen. While sidestepping critical discussions of his acting process, Hammer prefers to interview via anecdotes about his childhood in Grand Cayman,[3] awkward teenage years upon moving to Los Angeles and being bullied for his British-like accent, being a progeny of the Hammer business empire, his collection of Adidas tracksuits, road trips and his frequent visits to New York City.[4]

Much of the popular discourse surrounding Hammer's aesthetic in the public eye, his personal life and his film and brief television oeuvre combine to make him, like many stars in Hollywood, subject to scrutiny regarding his choice of roles, the genres he commonly works in, patterns of preparation for roles and characters, and his testimonies of on-set work and relationships forged between the actors he plays alongside and the directors who helm each project. Hammer's body of cinematic work, while eclectic, needs to be filtered and winnowed, I believe, with a careful eye to parse out the philosophical strands and cultural meanings behind what Hammer is doing with a character, especially through the performance of white masculinity. For instance, does Hammer adhere to or play against type in *Call Me by Your Name*? Is he featuring familiar cues of hegemonic masculinity,[5] rendered 'white', in a way that is different, co-dependent on or directly congruent to previous performances? Is his role as Oliver in *Call Me by Your Name* unique in his overall filmography? And, did *Call Me by Your Name* usher in or help forge a new phase in Hammer's acting chops and trajectory as a bankable A-list Hollywood star? These questions, I feel, are important to further unpack.

Risk-taker

The calculus of difference for Hammer, in *Call Me by Your Name* and other roles, can perhaps be found in the various *risks* he is willing to take in terms of the range of masculinities he displays for film. On *The Ellen DeGeneres Show* in 2017 (Figure 13.1), Hammer and co-star Timothée Chalamet discussed their performances as Oliver (Hammer) and Elio (Chalamet) in *Call Me by Your Name* with DeGeneres. In the interview, both Hammer and Chalamet can be seen talking candidly about their preparation and execution of the roles and the multiple 'make-out' scenes they had, directed by Luca Guadagnino. DeGeneres, an openly lesbian host of her self-titled talk show – and former lead character Ellen

FIGURE 13.1: The sexiest risk-taker? Armie Hammer with Timothée Chalamet on *The Ellen DeGeneres Show*, 2017.

Morgan in the American sitcom *Ellen* (ABC, 1994–98) – praised Hammer and Chalamet for presenting gay characters and a queer romance in a genuine and sensitive light, even though both actors identify as heterosexual males in real life. However, at the end of the interview, DeGeneres cheekily embarrasses Hammer in front of Chalamet and her studio audience with a feature story in *People* with the magazine's claim of Hammer being the 'Sexiest Man Alive'. While this is not an uncommon labelling of celebrity in US popular culture broadly put, Hammer's co-star Chalamet's response to the photograph and feature story in *People* was: 'I knew he was sexy *and* took risks but I didn't know if he was the sexiest risk-taker'.[6]

With this cheeky albeit shrewd observation by Chalamet, it is interesting that Hammer neither wholeheartedly agrees nor vehemently disagrees with the tenor of his co-star's statement, as DeGeneres laughs and the crowd applauds simultaneously. Given this anecdote and Hammer's range of performances of white masculinity in Hollywood films, can Armie Hammer indeed be considered one of the sexiest risk-takers in the industry? In an effort to contextualize his work in Guadagnino's film within Hammer's wider career and screen image, I want to critically examine *Call Me by Your Name*, textually and extratextually, which builds upon but also evolves Hammer's screen persona and range. Indeed, Hammer's film roles – ranging from his first lead role as evangelist preacher Billy Graham in *Billy: The Early Years* (Robby Benson, 2008) to Cameron and Tyler Winklevoss (a.k.a. the Winklevoss twins) in *The Social Network* (David Fincher, 2010),[7] to Clyde Tolson in *J. Edgar* (Clint Eastwood, 2011) to John Reid (a.k.a. The Lone Ranger) in *The Lone Ranger* (Gore Verbinski, 2013) to Illya Kuryakin in *The Man from U.N.C.L.E.* (Guy Ritchie, 2015), to Ord in *Free Fire* (Ben Wheatley, 2016) to Martin Ginsburg in *On the Basis of Sex* (Mimi Leder, 2018) – display the rhetoric of risk-taking not only in terms of performance but also in terms of ideology. That is, Hammer challenges and provokes different audience expectations regarding topics involving race, gender, sexuality, class and age, while also showcasing, in turn, an impressive professional ability to work within and outside of the confines and restrictions of A-list Hollywood acting.

With such risk-taking evident in Hammer's acting and persona before *Call Me by Your Name*, it becomes clear that star discourse and conversations about masculinity presented in the film should be reconsidered on the basis of Hammer, and not primarily on Chalamet's performance. As such, repositioning the meaning of Hammer's performance as Oliver in terms of risk aids in a more balanced understanding of Hammer's star power in *Call Me by Your Name* as both reference and refracting point.

I, however, want to argue that risk-taking is by no means an anomaly of Hammer both as an individual and as an actor. In fact, elements of risk are peppered throughout Hammer's on-screen and off-screen presence – through filmic characterizations, late-night talk show chitchat, movie-plug interviews and magazine features. While this may denote a flippant attitude towards his occupation and craft, on the contrary this 'devil-may-care attitude' combined with consciousness may be the 'secret recipe', so to speak, of Hammer's ability to navigate both sexual ambiguity and human pathos in his character of Oliver in *Call Me by Your Name*.

Through critically contextualizing and surveying Hammer's work we can, therefore, notice several salient patterns that form the crux of his body of work in film. First, there are biopics, which include *Billy: The Early Years*, *On the Basis of Sex*, *J. Edgar* and *The Social Network*; second, there are action-packed adventures, which include *The Lone Ranger*, *Free Fire*, *The Man from U.N.C.L.E.*; and there are romances including *Call Me by Your Name*. These different films demonstrate Hammer's adeptness at covering a range of genres under similar guises as a white male, which some of his characters blur the boundaries between male heterosexuality and bi-curiosity.

However, what separates Hammer's performance in *Call Me by Your Name* from other films in his filmography is that it, I will show, represents the acme of his risk-taking in forms of pre-production preparation. This is evident in Hammer's research on the role of Oliver via Aciman's novel, learning Italian, the sensitivity of the role of a queer character/chemistry with Chalamet as the main protagonist of the novel and film, Elio, and his ability to renegotiate his acting process through the experience of an independent arthouse director in the form of Luca Guadagnino.

Acting risky

Through the course of my research on Hammer, I found that the majority of commentary in the trade press emphasized his charm rather than his actual acting ability, outside of *Call Me by Your Name* and his theatre stints in New York City. Harking back to Hammer's evangelical Christian roots on his Tulsan mother's side with *Billy: The Early Years* as the famed preacher, Hammer was able to break into the medium of film. However, the big break would be him playing both 'Winklevie' (as Mark Zuckerberg, CEO of Facebook, once affectionately called them) in Fincher's *The Social Network*, which used innovative split-screen technology to duplicate Hammer's form exactly into 'twin' beings performing simultaneously.

In *Billy: The Early Years*, Hammer delivers a performance that would build upon his stature and charismatic white aesthetic. In the role of Graham (Figure 13.2), Hammer affirms a tenant of whiteness illustrated by Richard Dyer in his text *White* (1997). According to Dyer, '[w]hiteness, really white whiteness is unattainable. Its ideal forms are impossible'.[8] Even in his first Hollywood role as the evangelical American preacher Billy Graham, Hammer's presentation of white masculinity participates within rather than goes against the grain of the typical Hollywood biopic, pointing to the convenience of the genre to simply show parts of and fully tell and contextualize the historical, social biographical story arc of Graham and the limits to his real-life whiteness as a celebrity preacher in postwar America.

Risk-taking is also evident in more subdued roles that Hammer has co-starred in with other A-list stars in the Hollywood industry, such as Leonardo DiCaprio. In Clint Eastwood's *J. Edgar*, for instance, there is a lingering homoerotic tension between J. Edgar Hoover (DiCaprio) and Hammer's portrayal of Clyde Tolson. What makes this queer desire even greater is that the Hoover–Tolson romance was not openly disclosed until Eastwood's biopic broached the topic.

The act of kissing is an age-old trope in cinema, not least in Hammer's oeuvre. There have been smooches with willing members of the opposite sex ever since the Thomas Edison-produced *The Kiss* (William Heise, 1896). There have also been awkward instances where the locking of lips presents more questions than answers about both the initiation and the reception of the kiss. Case in point is Eastwood's *J. Edgar*. After claiming he wants to marry Dorothy Lamour, Hoover refuses to commit to the relationship he and Tolson have cultivated. The scuffle on the floor

FIGURE 13.2: Armie Hammer as Billy Graham. Robby Benson (dir.), *Billy: The Early Years*, 2008. USA. © SOLEX/MATP Productions.

of the hotel room that ensues happens after Tolson tells Hoover that he is making a fool out of him. It is Tolson, Hammer's character, who in a moment of *amour fou* kisses Hoover, where Hoover reciprocates but pushes away and says that it must never happen again.[9] This 'friendship' is not so dissimilar to that posed by Oliver and Elio in *Call Me by Your Name*.

Although not disclosed officially as 'lovers', the queer romantic friendship that Hoover–Tolson have is beautifully conveyed through the *mise en scène*, including flashbacks to when they were young vs. the present moment in the diegesis of their ageing identities. Hammer has aged his face and body to suit the progression of time and the temporal passage of decades. Part of the queer subtext in *J. Edgar* should be credited to screenwriter Dustin Lance Black. Black is a recognized member of the LGBTQ+ community who wrote *The Journey of Jared Price* (Dustin Lance Black, 2000), *Milk* (Gus Van Sant, 2008) and *Pedro* (Nick Oceano, 2008) prior to his screenplay for Eastwood's biopic.

Harking back to his family's history once again, with a nod to his grandfather's links to communism and the Soviet Union in early twentieth-century American history, Hammer plays Illya Kuryakin in *The Man from U.N.C.L.E.* opposite Henry Cavill as Napoleon Solo, as Hammer's co-star. The premise of the film is based on the beloved TV programme of the same name, wherein the role of spy Illya Kuryakin was originally played in the 1960s by David McCallum. Hammer also played Ord in *Free Fire* opposite Brie Larson as Justine, and Martin 'Marty'

Ginsburg in *On the Basis of Sex* opposite Felicity Jones. What this points to is the ability of Hammer to usually work in tandem with another A-list Hollywood star, as seen with my example above in this section of Hammer with DiCaprio in *J. Edgar*. This ability would provide some essential grounding and negotiations towards his star status for Hammer as a Hollywood actor working with an international director like Luca Guadagnino and acting alongside Timothée Chalamet in *Call Me by Your Name*.

Hammer as Oliver in Call Me by Your Name

Oliver is a graduate student, bibliophile and snob. Elio has a penchant for growing up similarly cultured in the US-European jet-set academic culture. The two formally meet each other in Mr Perlman's home office at the family's rural villa (Figure 13.3). Both are young, eager and learned. Elio appears to approach a more casual yet clean mode of dress as a teenager amid dark curly hair. Conversely, Oliver conveys a mode of dress stereotypical of a wealthy New Englander with his tucked-in Ralph Lauren shirts and evenly coiffed blond hair. Given this, why was Hammer cast in the role of Oliver for *Call Me by Your Name*?

FIGURE 13.3: Elio (Timothée Chalamet) and Oliver (Armie Hammer) meet for the first time. Luca Guadagnino (dir.), *Call Me by Your Name*, 2017. Italy/France/USA/Brazil. © Frenesy, La Cinefacture.

Mutual attraction towards talent and craft can be observed in how Hammer and Guadagnino talk about each other and offer clues as to why each wanted to work with the other on *Call Me by Your Name*. Hammer, for example, is quoted saying of Guadagnino: 'I probably fell in love with Luca the same way Elio fell in love with [...] Oliver'.[10] Guadagnino, further, is quoted celebrating his admiration for Hammer: 'I fell in love with Armie when I saw him in *The Social Network*. And then I had the privilege of meeting him, and fell in love again. And I've never recovered from falling in love with him.'[11] What these statements from the popular press confirm about the professional relationship between Hammer and Guadagnino is teamwork. The Hammer–Guadagnino professional dynamic further legitimized Hammer's risk-taking ability as an actor by having a director who wanted to take artistic and moral risks with characters, in turn, for the purposes of authenticity and quality storytelling.

Since the narrative of *Call Me by Your Name* is rooted in a coming-of-age queer romance, it is fitting that Hammer, coming from a monied, conservative family, would get out of his comfort zone as both a person and actor for the role of Oliver. 'I've never been so intimately involved with a director before', states Hammer, 'Luca was able to look at me and completely undress me. He knew every single one of my insecurities, every time I needed to be pushed and when I needed to be protected'.[12] Hammer put his trust in Guadagnino, who identifies as gay, to channel the appropriate emotions, blocking, gestures and overall characterization of Oliver.

Of course, how the United States views and negotiates queer coming-of-age narratives can appear to be at polar opposites with European modes – whether literary, theatrical or filmic – of narrating adolescence, identity and romantic love. According to Miller,

[f]or Hammer, challenging himself with the part [of Oliver] was ultimately a freeing experience. 'So much of this movie is about stripping everything away and exposing yourself', he explained. 'I grew up in conservative white America, where you just don't talk about yourself, your desires, wanting to express your sensuality – it's taboo.'[13]

The charming risk of Armie Hammer

Hammer's appeal is no doubt due to his charm and physical attractiveness. To be sure, aesthetics are among the most prominent means by which an audience knows of a star, follows their work and derives pleasure from the film text. The white privilege that marks Hammer's elitist prowess is something that points to notions of class and potential snobbery. However, Hammer's role as Maxim de Winter in Netflix's *Rebecca* adaptation (Ben Wheatley, 2020) opposite Lily James as Mrs de Winter presents a dilemma for the viewer. While Hammer would typically look dapper in a well-fitted suit at a film festival or other gala event, the mustard yellow suit in *Rebecca* wears him. This sartorial misstep parodies potential charm. While there are cues towards potential mannerisms and utterances familiar to the way Hammer moves and speaks as an actor, these attempts fall flat. This is also because of the lack of charm in the character of Maxim de Winter, the unemotional, standoffish owner of Manderley. Therefore, charm wins most of the time for Hammer but with *Rebecca* the limitations of his presence in a film are glaringly evident.

It was Hammer's charm that was often quoted in the popular press as a reason for the casting choice by Guadagnino for *Call Me by Your Name*. According to Nick Vivarelli in *Variety*'s 13 February 2017 interview with Guadagnino, Hammer was the obvious choice because of his charming persona.

> I saw him in *The Social Network*, like everybody, and then cultivated my passion for Armie with the movies he made afterwards. I always found him a very sophisticated actor, with a great range. So when I came to think of Oliver [...] I thought we could use that quality, his incredible charm.[14]

However, how did Guadagnino convince Hammer? While Hammer was asked 'through his agent' and initially passed on *Call Me by Your Name*, Hammer claims in Vivarelli that 'Well, the conversation was too good. I couldn't pass'.[15] Therefore, the mutual risk – of Guadagnino thinking Hammer would be best for the role of Oliver and Hammer risking his heterosexual white man alpha status as an A-list Hollywood star – made for an aleatory experience for both director and one of the lead actors. Collectively, this aleatory risk through a white male Hollywood star such as Hammer illustrates the chance happenings at play in the selection and casting of the actors in *Call Me by Your Name*.

The naked truth of Hammer as Oliver in Call Me by Your Name

Another fascinating aspect of Oliver's queer romantic masculinity in *Call Me by Your Name* is the lack of male full-frontal nudity in Guadagnino's film. Interestingly, according to Zack Sharf's piece for *IndieWire* titled '*Call Me by Your Name* Screenwriter Is Disappointed There's No Male Full Frontal Nudity', '[t]here's a lot to see in Luca Guadagnino's sensual film, from the gorgeous Italian countryside to that deadline-making sex scene involving a peach, but one thing you absolutely won't see in *Call Me by Your Name* is a penis'.[16] While characters' bodies can be seen in different states of undress and semi-nudity (male torso with bathing trunks or jeans), the possible phallocentric imagery is replaced by other modes of sensuality such as talk and breath. This is evident towards the end of the movie when Oliver, telephoning the Perlman family from back in America sometime later, speaks in a repeated, whispery, breathy tone.

Sharf continues, however, that it was the documentation of star talent that lent itself to being written proof of there being no male frontal nudity under the stars' contracts. 'The contracts for Armie Hammer and Timothee [sic] Chalamet prohibited any full frontal nudity from being featured in the film, much to the dismay of the script's original writer James Ivory.'[17] Indeed, we recall that Ivory was the original writer/director of *Call Me by Your Name* and, in turn, Guadagnino was originally the film's location consultant. According to Sharf, Guadagnino 'revised Ivory's original script and apparently he took out a majority of the film's nudity'.[18]

However, for Ivory, the European perspective of male full-frontal nudity is much different than in the more conservative bent of American society. '[I]t's just this American attitude. Nobody seems to care that much, or be shocked, about a totally naked woman. It's the men. This is something that must be so deeply cultural that one should ask: Why?'[19] Indeed, as Sharf finally puts it: 'butts are on full display'.[20] The ironic display of male buttocks compared to that of the penis presents an ongoing paradox towards the heteronormative assumptions of realism towards the anxiety of representing the fully nude male body in film more generally.[21]

Although Hammer had played a gay character through Clyde Tolson in Eastwood's *J. Edgar*, the risk/fear antithesis was nevertheless present in *Call Me by Your Name*. According to Kyle Buchanan's article titled '*Call Me by Your Name* Director Luca Guadagnino on Armie Hammer Sequels, and Screen Intimacy' in *Vulture*, Guadagnino revealed Hammer's motivation as a heterosexual male in his private life playing a gay male involved in a queer romance: 'I don't think it was "Oh no, I don't want to play a gay character" because he had already done that twice'.[22] Guadagnino, furthermore, continues by stating that 'I think the mold of Armie is the mold of cinema with a capital C'.[23] Therefore, by Guadagnino's inference, it appears as though Hammer is defined as a Hollywood actor that takes risks for the benefit of creating performances of white masculinity that present sexual ambiguity as markers of character development and intrigue across Hammer's oeuvre.

Conclusion: The meta-risks of Armie Hammer

As one of the very first critical studies of Hammer's star persona contextualized within and beyond the filmic text of *Call Me by Your Name*, I accepted in the course of this chapter the challenge of providing both textual analysis and extrafilmic discourse on a figure increasingly defined through the trope of risk. While this angle initially seemed fruitful when I began the project, Hammer was met with scandal. Josh Duhamel replaced Hammer in the role of Tom Fowler in *Shotgun Wedding* (released 29 June 2022 and directed by Jason Moore [*Pitch Perfect*, 2012; *Sisters*, 2015]), opposite singer-cum-actor Jennifer Lopez in the role of Darcy Rivera. Despite appearing in Kenneth Branagh's *Death on the Nile* (2022) in the role of Simon Doyle, Hammer might have to wait a little while longer to make any significant comeback into the entertainment limelight.

With the swift action of his agency William Morris effectively removing Hammer from their company and subsequently Hammer temporarily withdrawing his social media presence on Twitter (now X) and Instagram, it appears as though Hammer's moment as an indie star after *Call Me by Your Name* has come and gone. Or has it? Hammer is certainly not the first film star to be impacted by public scandal nor the last, and hopefully more information about the accusations and acts claimed to have been done by Hammer will surface in the public press and with witness testimony. With the trope of risk overlapping now into Hammer's private life, albeit to an extreme, it should nevertheless act as a cause for pause to surmise the possibility of looking back to how Hammer performs white masculinity as a means of gendered hegemony towards risky acting, risky roles and risky behaviour. This, it would seem, is evident of a mode of self-reflexivity on the part of Hammer and his films; each suggests an explicit awareness of what it is doing with the image of Hammer to serve the purposes of narrative logic and actively capitalizing on Hammer's star persona as risk-taker.

This is why here I suggest the repeated risk-taking in character roles in tandem with his star persona render Hammer as a risk-taker to be known for meta-risks. Meta-risks are risks that collectively highlight the self-referential nature of their performer in the contexts of role selection and execution, as evident in *Call Me by Your Name* and the role of Oliver. Armie Hammer was not playing Armie Hammer to perform the role of Oliver. Instead, the role of Oliver allowed Hammer to explore avenues of character and sexuality previously explored in films such as *J. Edgar*. And like Elio longing for Oliver at the end of *Call Me by Your Name* staring into the living room fireplace of the Perlman family villa, we will have to wait and see if Hammer will rise out like a phoenix from the ashes of scandal.

NOTES

1. Elizabeth Wagmeister, 'Armie Hammer's Hollywood Career Is in Freefall as Sex Scandal Explodes on Social Media', *Variety*, 4 February 2021. https://variety.com/2021/film/news/armie-hammer-sex-cannibal-allegations-hollywood-career-1234901106/.

2. Wagmeister, 'Armie Hammer'.

3. See Seth Abramovitch, 'Armie Hammer on His Steamy New Movie, a Charmed Upbringing and Hollywood's "Double Standards"', *The Hollywood Reporter*, 20 November 2017, https://www.hollywoodreporter.com/features/armie-hammer-his-steamy-new-movie-a-charmed-upbringing-oscars-double-standards-1059752.

4. Team Coco, 'Armie Hammer Is Retiring His Tracksuits', YouTube, 28 March 2018, https://www.youtube.com/watch?v=d0NNHSo1Ads.

5. See R. W. Connell, *Masculinities* (Cambridge: Polity Press, 1995).

6. *TheEllenShow*, 'Armie Hammer and Timothée Chalamet Talk Passionate First Rehearsal', YouTube, 29 November 2017, https://www.youtube.com/watch?v=F0rX-PrnC_Ps.

7. See Monica Hesse, '*Social Network* Twins Played by Unrelated Men. The Solution? Use Only One Face', *Washington Post*, 1 October 2010, https://www.washingtonpost.com/wp-dyn/content/article/2010/09/30/AR2010093002654.html.

8. Richard Dyer, *White: Twentieth Anniversary Edition* (London and New York: Routledge, [1997] 2017), 78.

9. See David Denby, 'The Man in Charge', *New Yorker*, 7 November 2011, https://www.newyorker.com/magazine/2011/11/14/the-man-in-charge; David Keeps, 'J. Edgar Hoover's Trophy Boy', *New York Magazine*, 4 November 2011, https://nymag.com/movies/features/armie-hammer-2011-11/.

10. Mike Miller, 'Armie Hammer's *Call Me by Your Name* Director Breaks Down the Film's Intimate Peach Scene', *People*, 4 October 2017, https://people.com/movies/armie-hammers-call-me-by-your-name-director-breaks-down-the-films-intimate-peach-scene/.

11. Miller, 'Armie Hammer's Director'.

12. Quoted in Miller, 'Armie Hammer's Director'.

13. Quoted in Miller, 'Armie Hammer's Director'.

14. Quoted in Nick Vivarelli, 'Berlinale: Luca Guadagnino on Why *Call Me by Your Name* Strikes Such Deep Chords', *Variety*, 13 February 2017, https://variety.com/2017/film/global/berlinale-luca-guadagnino-call-me-by-your-name-1201986720/.

15. Quoted in Vivarelli, 'Berlinale'.

16. Zack Sharf, '*Call Me by Your Name* Screenwriter Is Disappointed There's No Male Full Frontal Nudity', *IndieWire*, 6 October 2017, https://www.indiewire.com/2017/10/call-me-by-your-name-full-frontal-nudity-armie-hammer-1201884646/.

17. Sharf, 'Screenwriter'.

18. Sharf, 'Screenwriter'.

19. Quoted in Sharf, 'Screenwriter'.

20. Sharf, 'Screenwriter'.

21. See Peter Lehman, *Running Scared: Masculinity and the Representation of the Male Body* (Detroit: Wayne State University Press, 2007).

22. Quoted in Kyle Buchanan, '*Call Me by Your Name* Director Luca Guadagnino on Armie Hammer Sequels, and Screen Intimacy', *Vulture*, 17 November 2017, https://www.vulture.com/2017/11/director-luca-guadagnino-talks-call-me-by-your-name-sequels.html.
23. Quoted in Buchanan, 'Director'.

REFERENCES

Abramovitch, Seth. 'Armie Hammer on His Steamy New Movie, a Charmed Upbringing and Hollywood's "Double Standards".' *The Hollywood Reporter*, 20 November 2017. https://www.hollywoodreporter.com/features/armie-hammer-his-steamy-new-movie-a-charmed-upbringing-oscars-double-standards-1059752.

Benson, Robby, dir. *Billy: The Early Years*. Solex Productions, American Trademark Pictures, 821 Entertainment Group, Momentum Releasing, 2008.

Black, Dustin Lance, dir. *The Journey of Jared Price*. 10% Productions, Sock Puppet Enterprises, 2000.

Branagh, Kenneth, dir. *Death on the Nile*. Kinberg Genre, 20th Century Studios, 2022.

Buchanan, Kyle. '*Call Me by Your Name* Director Luca Guadagnino on Armie Hammer Sequels, and Screen Intimacy.' *Vulture*, 17 November 2017. https://www.vulture.com/2017/11/director-luca-guadagnino-talks-call-me-by-your-name-sequels.html.

Connell, R. W. *Masculinities*. Cambridge: Polity Press, 1995.

Denby, David. 'The Man in Charge.' *New Yorker*, 7 November 2011. https://www.newyorker.com/magazine/2011/11/14/the-man-in-charge.

Dyer, Richard. *White: Twentieth Anniversary Edition*. London and New York: Routledge, [1997] 2017.

Eastwood, Clint, dir. *J. Edgar*. Imagine Entertainment, Malpaso Productions, Wintergreen Productions, 2011.

Fincher, David, dir. *The Social Network*. Columbia Pictures, Relativity Media, Scott Rudin Productions, 2010.

Guadagnino, Luca, dir. *Call Me by Your Name*. Frenesy Film Company, La Cinefacture, RT Features, 2017.

Heise, William, dir. *The Kiss*. Edison Manufacturing Company, 1896.

Hesse, Monica. '*Social Network* Twins Played by Unrelated Men. The Solution? Use Only One Face.' *Washington Post*, 1 October 2010. https://www.washingtonpost.com/wp-dyn/content/article/2010/09/30/AR2010093002654.html.

Keeps, David A. 'J. Edgar Hoover's Trophy Boy.' *New York Magazine*, 4 November 2011. https://nymag.com/movies/features/armie-hammer-2011-11/.

Leder, Mimi, dir. *On the Basis of Sex*. Focus Features, Participant Media, Robert Cort Productions, Alibaba Pictures, 2018.

Lehman, Peter. *Running Scared: Masculinity and the Representation of the Male Body*. Detroit: Wayne State University Press, 2007.

Miller, Mike. 'Armie Hammer's *Call Me by Your Name* Director Breaks Down the Film's Intimate Peach Scene.' *People*, 4 October 2017. https://people.com/movies/armie-hammers-call-me-by-your-name-director-breaks-down-the-films-intimate-peach-scene/.

Moore, Jason, dir. *Pitch Perfect*. Brownstone Productions, Gold Circle Films, 2012.

Moore, Jason, dir. *Sisters*. Little Stranger, 2015.

Moore, Jason, dir. *Shotgun Wedding*. Mandeville Films, Maximum Effort, Nuyorican Productions, 2022.

Oceano, Nick, dir. *Pedro*. BMP Films, 2008.

Ritchie, Guy, dir. *The Man from U.N.C.L.E.* Warner Bros., Wigram Productions, 2015.

Sharf, Zack. '*Call Me by Your Name* Screenwriter Is Disappointed There's No Male Full Frontal Nudity.' *IndieWire*, 6 October 2017. https://www.indiewire.com/2017/10/call-me-by-your-name-full-frontal-nudity-armie-hammer-1201884646/.

Team Coco. 'Armie Hammer Is Retiring His Tracksuits.' YouTube, 28 March 2018. https://www.youtube.com/watch?v=d0NNHSo1Ads.

TheEllenShow. 'Armie Hammer and Timothée Chalamet Talk Passionate First Rehearsal.' YouTube, 29 November 2017. https://www.youtube.com/watch?v=F0rXPrnC_Ps.

Van Sant, Gus, dir. *Milk*. Focus Features, Axon Films, Groundswell Productions, 2008.

Verbinski, Gore, dir. *The Lone Ranger*. Walt Disney Pictures, Jerry Bruckheimer Films, Blind Wink, Infinitum Nihil, 2013.

Vivarelli, Nick. 'Berlinale: Luca Guadagnino on Why *Call Me by Your Name* Strikes Such Deep Chords.' *Variety*, 13 February 2017. https://variety.com/2017/film/global/berlinale-luca-guadagnino-call-me-by-your-name-1201986720/.

Wagmeister, Elizabeth. 'Armie Hammer's Hollywood Career Is in Freefall as Sex Scandal Explodes on Social Media.' *Variety*, 4 February 2021. https://variety.com/2021/film/news/armie-hammer-sex-cannibal-allegations-hollywood-career-1234901106/.

Wheatley, Ben, dir. *Free Fire*. Film4, Protagonist Pictures, Rook Films, 2016.

Wheatley, Ben, dir. *Rebecca*. Netflix, Working Title, 2020.

14

'Finally, a Gay Movie without a Bad Vibe': Queer Nostalgia, Affection and Gender Identity in *Call Me by Your Name*

Vinicius Ferreira, Victor Schlude and Gêsa Cavalcanti

In recent years, growing numbers of researchers have been concerned with the multiple layers and aspects of nostalgia. This interest in nostalgia, in addition to the increased interest in gender and sexuality research, opens the field for studies of queer nostalgia. This segment of studies, marked by a plurality of perspectives, has sought, in general terms, to reflect on how cultural narratives, especially in the media, promote a temporal dynamic as a form of empowerment, a celebration of queer culture and also as an exercise in memory of queer heritage.

In this chapter, we understand queer nostalgia not as a romantic or conservative rescue of the past, but as a mnemonic practice marked by the desire for new roots and the defence of a common heritage that has the power to resignify personal and community memories by establishing a new grammar of similarity and difference.[1] As a result, queer nostalgia would be not only an economic phenomenon (which makes the consumer market more dynamic) but also cultural (related to our way of experiencing the world and connecting with the Other). Perhaps, we add, queer nostalgia is yet an essentially political phenomenon, considering that it talks about projects and desires for the future.[2]

In analyzing the nostalgic representation of *Call Me by Your Name* (Luca Guadagnino, 2017), especially regarding the operationalization of gender and sexuality roles, what moves us as analysts of representation is the attempt to demonstrate which effects of meaning are proposed and which power relations are established during the representational process. We start from the assumption that representation is never a neutral action, but rather a practice of discursive production permeated by power logic and constituting what we understand as reality.[3]

It is the repeated representations that we consume and share through the media that authenticate what is considered acceptable or unspeakable, normal or abnormal, punishable or plausible for gratification. In this way, the media would contribute to the promotion of permanences or ruptures in the notions of sex, gender identity, sexual orientation, and in the ways of experiencing affections. Therefore, analyzing audiovisual productions and their processes as social mechanisms responsible for regulating, applying and reinforcing the naturalization of the sex-gender system would be, for Teresa de Lauretis, one of the keys to understanding gender inequalities and prejudice against sexual orientations considered dissident.[4]

The complexity of the assemblages present in the contemporary notion of nostalgia is what makes the subject so fascinating and requires a multidimensional gaze. The analysis of the scenes of the film alone, with the identification of the nostalgic triggers present, would not be enough to identify the social, cultural and economic impacts produced by the queer nostalgia present in *Call Me by Your Name*. Therefore, we propose a work that overflows the scenes and the editing of the film and aims to understand how this product is received, signified and resignified by the viewers. In this perspective, the analysis of the film must be carried out in a movement that starts from the movie itself, involving its circulation and consumption in a given context.

In our analysis, we adopt Brazil as a context to understand how *Call Me by Your Name* is perceived by YouTube critics and in the comments of viewers. The title of this chapter is based on one of the comments of our corpus[5] since it synthesizes a common idea that Brazilian viewers had regarding the movie. Our analysis goes beyond the representation of queer nostalgia in the film. Through the analysis of the repercussion in three Brazilian review videos by YouTubers, we seek to demonstrate the uses of queer nostalgia as an operator of gender and sexuality identities. As a result, we believe this work contributes to the understanding of how the movie *Call Me by Your Name* is inserted into the contemporary phenomenon of nostalgia and specifically in the queer nostalgia boom.[6]

Evaluative horizons and queer nostalgia

In this chapter, we will think of film through a theoretical/methodological architecture based on the dialogue between contemporary studies on nostalgia and the conceptual categories elaborated by the Circle of Bakhtin.[7] Throughout his work, Robert Stam has called attention to the critical value that Bakhtinian concepts can offer to a cinematic analysis.[8] Even though the Circle of Bakhtin has not directly reflected on cinema, their politicized view of language makes it possible to perceive media culture as an ideological battlefield, permeated by power relations and impregnated with dialogism (that is, a trans-individual production of meaning).

This theoretical framework allows us to perceive cinema as an integral part of the process of construction of social reality. Films, as communication and socio-ideological practices, are constantly collaborating with the production of the social world. In this perspective, there is no world already given; reality is being elaborated and transformed continuously from the uses we make of language.[9]

The Circle of Bakhtin defines a philosophy of life, marked by concepts such as alterity and answerability. Bakhtin argues that the act cannot be separated from its concrete realization. Such realization involves the subjects, objects and values subscribed to one's act.[10] Thus, whenever a subject speaks, one relates to something (an object, a person, an event) at a certain time, space and with a given axiology. Every act is an answer developed by one's life experiences and values. Therefore, according to a Bakhtinian philosophy of life, we cannot understand identity if not through the lens of alterity. In other words, I am nothing without the Other. In truth, the Other lives fully through me. In this sense, Bakhtin assumes three moments for the realization of the act: I-for-myself, the Other-for-me and I-for-the-Other. The three are in a constant dialogical exchange, meaning that an act is a necessary entanglement of one's values with the Other's values and the Other's views of ourselves and our values.

The Circle of Bakhtin sees the reader as an active subject. When we read, we assume certain assumptions and interpretations about the Other (a person, an event, an object). These assumptions and interpretations are necessarily connected to our life experiences and values. Hence, by watching a movie, we have an idea of what to expect or interpret (the genre of the movie; the cast and crew; the theme or narrative; and other elements) and what we take from it, given our values and ideas on everything we experience with and understand of the movie.

Online comments are a contemporary example that fully exemplifies this view. Users may comment in many different spaces online: blogs, social media posts and cyberspaces in general. By commenting, people can express various reactions to what is available online. Considering the context of this research, users can comment on YouTube videos. The comments may vary greatly, going from punctual reactions (such as indications of like and dislike of the video) to more elaborate texts (such as disagreement with the video; agreement supported by personal statement). Regardless of the reaction expressed in the comment, considering the Bakhtinian perspective of answerability, we understand that whenever a user comments on a YouTube video, one is actively connecting their personal views on the topic (I-to-myself), the video itself (other-for-me) and what one says to/about the video (I-for-the-other).

For this reason, the analysis of comments on YouTube videos about a specific product (the movie *Call Me by Your Name*) and a specific audience (the LGBT-QIA+ community) allows us to map a group of different values regarding the movie. Of course, the analysis does not comprehend what people *in general* think of the movie. Our analysis deals with a qualitative extract of Brazilian users who access LGBTQIA+ YouTube channels. The purpose of this analysis is to evaluate how these users express their feelings and reactions towards critical videos about *Call Me by Your Name*.

Furthermore, according to the Circle of Bakhtin, to evaluate a group of common or similar reactions constitutes what Valentin N. Voloshinov calls an 'evaluative horizon'.[11] Such a concept deals with the understanding that social groups of certain patterns or similarities (class, gender, race, generation, territoriality)[12] have common values about a topic or idea, which is always materialized in social interaction. Thus, by analyzing the comments of Brazilian users on YouTube videos about *Call Me by Your Name* posted on LGBTQIA+ channels, we have already established a potential social group.[13] Our analysis deals with the evaluation of the reactions to the videos through YouTube comments. Our interest is in identifying these different reactions to understand how the users respond to the videos, having their *evaluative horizons* regarding an LGBTQIA+ romantic narrative expressed.

The comments of the video reviews posted on YouTube about *Call Me by Your Name* would be, thus, fundamental to understand holistically the effects of meaning produced about homosexuality in the statements put into circulation by Luca Guadagnino's film. Although the comments do not allow us to state that the users belong to the LGBTQIA+ community, we have selected LGBTQIA+ YouTube channels which comment on the movie, not general cinema channels, defining a certain niche – therefore, a potential collective evaluative horizon – one in respect to the LGBTQIA+ community common topics or interests. What we try to perceive in these comments is how the affective tones and gestures, as well as the nostalgic triggers present in the film, contribute to the understanding of the ways of inhabiting the LGBTQIA+ world.

In the reflection about the metaphorical 'dialogue' between the film and its spectator, responsible for producing the circulating meanings, Bakhtinian theory directs us to pay attention to the discourse of the 'other'. The treatment given to the other, the word of others, has always been central in Bakhtin's work. This perception, according to Stam, leads to an ethical and political concern with film-making.[14] We begin to question, then, how does dominant cinema treat the other's discourse? How does cinema dominated by heterosexual men treat the discourse and voice of the homosexual?[15]

The answers to these questions, although provisional and always incomplete, demonstrate how a society of a given time always adds meaning to the discourses of the other, especially of those who find themselves in relatively powerless positions. To better understand the questions posed, we need to emphasize the circulation of the meanings about the subjects considered abject before culture.

What draws attention is that *Call Me by Your Name* was produced during an explosion of TV series and movies focused on characters with dissident sexuality; some examples of films are *Hoje Eu Quero Voltar Sozinho* (*The Way He Looks*, Daniel Ribeiro, 2014), *God's Own Country* (Francis Lee, 2017), *Love, Simon* (Greg Berlanti, 2018); while TV shows include *Looking* (2014–16), *Sense8* (2015–18) and *Pose* (2018–21). Plots involving queer stories have been gaining more and more popularity[16] and support from specialized critics. The relative prominence of the discourses of a group that has historically been constituted as other seems, at first sight, to represent a rupture in the operating logic of the media industry. This new scenario would add new questions to be thought about, such as, for example, what has led popular media to so eagerly want to represent stories about queer people? For whom are these stories being told?

The boom of this new thematic approach in audiovisual productions is, in most cases, also in line with the contemporary phenomenon of nostalgia. Kies and West III, when reflecting on the queer nostalgia present in these new media stories, raise two critical hypotheses, which seem pertinent to us, to try to explain these questions.[17] For the authors, this new media culture scene may signify a wave of the hetero-mainstream media industry that is seeking to meet the demands of a liberal audience newly sympathetic to issues of gender and sexuality, which they had previously neglected. Or, perhaps, it means that the dominance of white, cisgender identities present in these films and series is what allows historical fiction to depoliticize queer identities of the past by reaffirming a homonormative subject.[18]

The elaborate points Kies and West III make, however thought-provoking, cannot be adopted as automatic answers to the questions of representation and sense-making operated by *Call Me by Your Name*. Only the crossing of the analysis of the representation of the film added to its repercussion with the public will allow us to gauge concrete answers. What we can assume as a starting point is that the film is part of a market of nostalgia, characterized by the commercialization of narratives that, emotionally and affectively, refer to the past, either as a historical and cultural reference, as a space of experience or as an aesthetic model.[19] What remains to be answered is whether the nostalgic gesture present in the film triggers a romantic and depoliticizing apprehension or a critical intention of the uses of the past and what remains of it in the present.[20]

Such expectations meet the understanding of *Call Me by Your Name* as an idyllic romance. These interpretations connect the LGBTQIA+ community's sexual-romantic experiences to a necessary fantasy of the experienced/inexperienced. The love idyll is marked by passionate and/or romantic love,[21] having the romantic narrative expressed together with the passing of time and the transition of nature. According to Bakhtin, these romantic narratives may be present in the *Bildungs-roman*, which can be contemporarily understood as coming-of-age stories.[22] Thus, the experience of love is entangled with first sexual experiences and one's process of becoming an adult. Marked either by happy endings, tragic closures or heart-warming summer fantasies, these stories usually express an experience that is part of cis heterosexual white characters' sexual-affective trajectory.

However, queer characters may speak from a different place. Given the very present restrictions and repressions regarding gender and sexuality in our contemporary society, one's gender identity is not easily developed or assumed. Thus, sexual or affectionate experiences may not be commonly part of the early lives of queer people. These subjects are sometimes targets of late sexual-affectionate experiences or even traumatic and violent or premature sexual encounters in their youths. Therefore, romantic fantasy could function as a nostalgic resource to elaborate traumas and heartbreaks of queer people's lives. On the other hand, these fantasies may also function as triggers of social inequality, working as a reminder that *certain* queer people (i.e. cis white heteronormative gay men)[23] have more access to these experiences, whereas others will never.

Hence, the LGBTQIA+ idyllic romance is a representation of how romantic narratives can be interpreted by the LGBTQIA+ community. Of course, this is not just a contemporary issue. Flaubert's *Madame Bovary* (1856) is about a woman who faces the limitations of romantic experiences because of her gender.[24] The marriage condition back then certainly determines the conflict between the romantic novels the character reads and the experience she has. The limitations of her fantasies – and the fantasies themselves – are an experience grounded in gender. In contemporary society, as much as white women still suffer the same issues,[25] white heterosexuality may be considered a social pass in comparison to non-conforming queer identities. Therefore, LGBTQIA+ idyllic romances may work as both a fantasy and a social critique, which asks the heartbreaking question: who has the right to love and be loved back?

Queer representations in the media

Nostalgia is often related to utopian or despotic imaginings of social or political issues. It would be reductive to claim that it is merely a desire to return to a past place or time since nostalgia is a complex cultural phenomenon, a creative way of experiencing time that says much about who we are, how we live, how we understand ourselves and the world around us.[26]

The attachment to and appreciation of the past are not necessarily new trends; what gives prominence to the current nostalgia boom is that it brings unique elements that are key to understanding how we energize our identities and identifications. One dimension that seems to be consensual in the understanding of contemporary nostalgia is its relationship with our difficulty in dealing with time. The proliferation of nostalgic products seems to express our 'discontents' of being in time, our difficulty to imagine 'possible futures'.[27] The contemporary phenomenon of nostalgia maintains numerous links with media texts and technologies. Media culture, for Katharina Niemeyer, would offer the space and temporalities necessary for 'nostalgizing'. We would be referring to a 'media nostalgia', that is, an operationalization of time expressed by media texts that would allow us to alleviate the anguish of the present time, both individually and collectively.[28]

Queer nostalgia, for example, would be like a therapeutic process elaborated by the imagination in which individual and collective fantasies operate a kind of existential caress, a 'cure' for the ailments experienced both in the past and in the present. With this, dissident bodies and identities, as well as the LGBTQIA+ community itself, have managed to project a future in which they would reframe the notions of who they are, what they can be and what they want to be.[29] However, the eventual curative possibilities of media nostalgia, as thought by Niemeyer and Padva,[30] can only be attested to if we seek to bring the study of representation closer to its repercussions by the audience. Only by promoting this dialogue can we, as researchers, get closer to the sense effects produced by the film. We must be attentive to the different responses that nostalgic forms are capable of producing.

In December 2020, the website of the magazine *Epoca* had the following sentence as a headline: 'A Couple Is Arrested in Rio after Paying for Five-Star Hotels with Cloned Credit Cards'.[31] The news story is about a cis white homosexual male couple who paid several elite hotels with fake credit cards. The news became a popular meme in the LGBTQIA+ community because a user commented: 'Finally stories of trickster gay people. Nobody can take any more stories of gay people suffering. We want more gay people like that, gay people popping a wheeling on a motorcycle, gay people shooting, etc.'[32]

Both the headline and the Facebook post comment were screenshot and shared on different social media. On the Twitter (now X) thread cited above, a user commented: 'Enough of Timothée Chalamet crying on his little bicycle'. This comment had an enormous repercussion on social media, becoming a popular meme. Here, we have different evaluative horizons on queer identities, indicating two movements of the I-for-the-Other. The first is the positive evaluation of a criminal queer couple, who would bring diversity to queer representations. The second is a negative evaluation with the undermining of queer experiences as mostly formed by 'gay people suffering' and the description of Chalamet's character in *Call Me by Your Name* as someone who 'cries on his little bicycle'. Both negative assumptions on queer experiences emphasize tragic queer stories, which are certainly common due to the adverse conditions of queer people in society. However, we must consider how the second comment produces an ambiguous meaning. At the same time as it is mocking the Facebook comment, which criticizes tragic queer stories by celebrating queer criminals, it also undermines the tragic experience present in *Call Me by Your Name*. Even though this undermining of the movie plot may not be intentional – or even part of the joke – it associates the phrase 'gay people suffering' with the movie.

From the ambiguity present above, we ask: are tragic queer stories sensible memories or annoying realities? Is *Call Me by Your Name* the representation of a tragic queer story? If not, is it a gay fairy tale? What is the possibility of a white young gay person in the '80s to fully live a love story and not be ashamed of it? If this gay romance ends well, is it a desirable fantasy or a deceitful lie? If it ends badly, is it a sensible memory or an annoying reality? As seen above, the exercise of investigating evaluative horizons is not to answer these questions ourselves but to understand how people respond to them, given their experiences, values and trajectories. In other words, the purpose is to investigate the common movements materialized in the I-for-the-Other which are constructed on the YouTube comments we will further analyze. In this sense, we consider that the I-for-the-Other necessarily involves the other two: I-for-myself and the-Other-for-me. Therefore, to speak of a movie's couple is not only to speak about a relationship disconnected from my own life; to speak of a movie's couple is essential to speak of how I see romantic relationships in general and how they (or the lack of them) constitute my individual experience.

Call Me by Your Name *and queer nostalgia*

Call Me by Your Name is a 2017 movie directed by Luca Guadagnino that landed four Oscar nominations[33] and was widely acclaimed by critics. The film is based on the eponymous novel written by André Aciman and grossed at the box office approximately twelve times its modest budget of $3.5 million.[34] The film portrays a narrative of love and sexual exploration through the affair between Elio (Timothée Chalamet) and Oliver (Armie Hammer). Set in an Italian summer in 1983, the narrative begins with the arrival of Oliver, an American graduate student who will spend a few months in field research with Elio's father, Mr Perlman (Michael Stuhlbarg).

The film narrates the idyllic romance lived by Oliver and Elio. According to Bakhtin, this narrative form deals mainly with (everyday) life themes, using nature as a resource to build atmosphere and a sentimental aura. Another important aspect we may highlight from Bakhtin's discussion is regarding time. While discussing the idyllic, the author describes its chronotope, a Bakhtinian concept used to relate the forms of space and time in a dialogical relationship to the thematic and stylistic choices made in a novel/artwork. In the idyllic chronotope, space is described as sentimentally aligned to the characters or story, which means that nature sets the tone for smooth, tragic or joyful events in the narrative. Time has a different rhythm in this narrative, since one of the peculiarities of the idyll is how things grow, pass, die and flow over the course of the days. Therefore, the idea of time suspension is related to a day-by-day chronology, in which time may seem to be slow because it is passing as characters routinely live it. The sense of routine and repetition is quintessential to set this tone in the idyllic narrative.[35]

Hence, the love affair between the main characters is displayed in a hot, slow day-by-day narrative where nature plays an important role. The landscape is frequently shown depicting calm green portraits of bushes, trees and other plants, through which sunbeams often escape, always reminding us of the summer. The soundtrack is also mainly composed of the sound of nature, developing a calm and easy atmosphere. Consequently, in a way, the movie embodies the experience of a slow and tranquil summer, sharing the characters' sensations with the viewers shot by shot. Furthermore, the atmosphere of the movie enables viewers to perceive *Call Me by Your Name* as both a coming-of-age story and a romantic story. We see Elio exploring his sexual desire through the object of his affection: Oliver. In the first days, there is a distance that also helps to create the tension of this love story. First, Elio seems to be having difficulty understanding the nature of his feelings towards Oliver. When he acknowledges that it is love/desire, he cannot tell if the North American reciprocates his feelings.

This summer is yet, as we argued, a form of time suspension that allows for a representation of a past without the regular obstacles imposed on same-sex couples. The social constructions of gender, masculinity, homophobia and the stigma of HIV/AIDS, as exemplifications of those possible hindrances, are limited not only by the time suspension but also by this supportive context that surrounds Oliver's life. At the same time that we may understand the movie's 'LGBTQIA+-friendly' atmosphere as a fantasy, it may also relate to the context of progressive families/social groups, in which gender oppression would be less present.

The moment when Oliver and Elio's relationship stops being potential and becomes real, we, as viewers, know, just as the characters know, that it has a very specific timestamp: the duration of the summer. However, the summer advances as slowly and calmly as the couple's romance, giving us – and the characters – an unreal sensation of time. This mismatch between time and experience is what makes desire linger. In the narrative, the desire for the summer not to end, which seems possible for its slow rhythm, also becomes the desire for the couple's romance not to end, which may give the viewers hope, even when the end of their love story is unavoidable.

Another relevant aspect is how the love between those two men is displayed: there's more touch than dialogue, which is a welcome subversion of the logic of LGBTQIA+ movies and TV shows, where the physical affection expressions are placed in the second plane, or even totally erased.[36] This point allows us to highlight the influence of James Ivory's *Maurice* (1987). Although the two films are different in terms of the intensity of the conflicts and the duration of the time suspension, which alters the intensity with which the external conflicts reach the characters, both privilege gesture above dialogue; we argue, again, that the temporal suspension and an early nostalgia is improved by the choices made by Guadagnino and Ivory.[37] The images below exemplify not only an aesthetic similarity but also this materialization of affection through touch (Figure 14.1).

Moving to the end of *Call Me by Your Name*, there is a sense of closure that is approaching the couple, especially by the repetition of the first night that Elio sees Oliver dancing with another partner, a woman. However, this time, they are both on a trip together, by themselves, before Oliver goes back to his home country. At this point, they are closer than in the beginning, but a certain rupture is announced with the repetition of the same event: they listen to the same song that played when Oliver kissed a young French woman earlier in the movie. Oliver starts dancing with an Italian woman, non-sexually, while Elio watches and suddenly throws up, which makes him feel childish in contrast to the other adults. After that, the end finally comes, which is marked by a sad farewell in a train station.

Elio is mourning his loss and the weather follows his heart. A summer rain sets the atmosphere for Elio to deal with his pain. At the very end of the movie, winter

FIGURE 14.1: Lovers in the grass: James Wilby and Hugh Grant. James Ivory (dir.), *Maurice*, 1987. UK. © Maurice Productions Limited; Timothée Chalamet and Armie Hammer. Luca Guadagnino (dir.), *Call Me by Your Name*, 2017. Italy/France/USA/Brazil. © Frenesy, La Cinefacture.

has come and Elio cries looking at the fireplace right after speaking to Oliver on the phone. The boy feels sad about the distance that has grown between them and the fact that Oliver is getting married sometime soon. However, he smiles briefly while crying, probably remembering the conversation with his father, who told Elio he must embrace sorrow to hold the love he has so fully lived. This necessary pain to the sensible preservation of a young passion connects to the discussion Sigmund Freud develops about the First World War:

> When it has renounced everything that has been lost, then it has consumed itself, and our libido is once more free (in so far as we are still young and active) to replace the lost objects by fresh ones equally or still more precious. It is to be hoped that the same will be true of the losses caused by this war. When the mourning is over, it will be found that our high opinion of the riches of civilization has lost nothing from our discovery of their fragility. We shall build up again all that war has destroyed, and perhaps on firmer ground and more lasting than before.[38]

The act of living and dealing with loss, although concretely more serious in war than in love, speaks to the *works of mourning*. To feel pain and sorrow after losing someone we have deeply loved is a type of death that speaks for the *I-to-myself*. Inside our heads, we may believe love will cease to exist and happiness has come to an end. Regardless of what others say, there is this belief that our feelings and hearts are over, together with our relationship. To recover from that, and especially loving someone new, involves being open for *the-Other-for-me*. It is about understanding the importance of alterity in one's life and experience. We must not live by the sole and individual thoughts in our heads, but by sharing them with the world and the ones around us. Going through this process is probably the closest form of preparation for love that life has been able to give us. Only by elaborating on the role of the Other in our lives may we be open to saying *I love you* not for ourselves but *I-for-the-Other*.

We believe that the love lost is a key aspect of the romantic narrative of the film, frequently brought up by the spectators in their comments, which we will further analyze. Therefore, in each category, we will be discussing how the love lost appears in the comments and produces different interpretations of love experiences.

Analyzing the repercussions

The second phase of this research uses descriptive analysis, a research conception that, as the name suggests, aims to describe a certain phenomenon or population. Here, the phenomenon in question is the reception of *Call Me by Your Name* by Brazilian viewers on YouTube.

Considering this, we are analyzing videos made by Brazilian YouTubers. For the definition of the analysis universe, we searched for critics of the movie and the YouTube algorithm returned 31 videos about *Call Me by Your Name*. Considering that we aim here to analyze queer nostalgia, we chose to filter for channels that have LGBTQIA+ themes, selecting the three most viewed. These are presented in Table 14.1.

Each of these videos presents a different approach to *Call Me by Your Name*. The first two talk more from a place of affection that manifests itself both in the way that YouTubers present themselves as fans (videos 1 and 2) and mainly in the ways in which they are deeply involved with the characters and the atmosphere of the movie. Although charged with affection, they try to work with tangible aspects such as photography, narrative and other technical audiovisual elements. The same cannot be said about video 3.

Video 1 begins by talking about how, above all, 'regardless of having a gay theme, […] it is a film about love, it is a film about affection, about coming-of-age'. This video is less of a review and more of a summary of the film. However,

TABLE 14.1: Analysis universe.

Video	YouTube channel and video title	Information
1	Federico Devito, 'Assista: CALL ME BY YOUR NAME!' ['Watch: *Call Me by Your Name*!'][39] (see Figure 14.2)	Posted on 24 January 2018, the video has, at the time of collection, 53,331 views and 352 comments.
2	Caio Braz, 'CALL ME BY YOUR NAME É O FILME MAIS LINDO QUE EXISTE' ['*Call Me by Your Name* is the most beautiful movie'][40] (see Figure 14.2)	Posted on 28 January 2018, the video has, at the time of collection, 30,106 views and 391 comments.
3	Pink Popcorn, 'ME CHAME PELO SEU NOME / O que achei / Pink Popcorn' ['*Call Me by Your Name* | What I thought | Pink Popcorn'][41] (see Figure 14.3)	Posted on 15 February 2018, the video has, at the time of collection, 6152 views and 99 comments.

FIGURE 14.2: Video 1: Screen grab from Federico Devito's YouTube video 'Assista: CALL ME BY YOUR NAME!', 2018.

FIGURE 14.3: Video 2: Screen grab from Caio Braz's YouTube video 'CALL ME BY YOUR NAME É O FILME MAIS LINDO QUE EXISTE', 2018.

FIGURE 14.4: Video 3: Screen grab from Pink Popcorn's YouTube video 'ME CHAME PELO SEU NOME / O que achei / Pink Popcorn', 2018.

there is an emphasis on how the relationship initiative comes from Elio and also an emphasis on quality. In addition, the film is also said to be an important representation of LGBTQIA+ relations. Part of this video is an interview conducted by the channel with the director of the film. At this point, there is a highlight on the idea of the utopia of a world without prejudice in *Call Me by Your Name*. Luca Guadagnino agrees with the idea that the film may seem utopian, but he cites the philosopher Slavoj Žižek saying that 'utopia is the only way for you to build our future'.[42]

On Caio Braz's channel (video 2), the YouTuber classifies the film as an LGBT production and is very positive about the film's importance to the community and its representation path. Caio Braz opens the video by comparing *Call Me by Your Name* with *Moonlight* (Barry Jenkins, 2016) and stating that the first one is more powerful for the LGBT community, because 'since *Brokeback Mountain* [he] didn't cry as much in a movie'. A highlight of the movie for the YouTuber is the character Elio who, according to him, is the character that best allows the identification of gay people. Another point mentioned is the non-problematization of Oliver's sexual orientation, which may be considered to be bisexual.

Video 3 maintains more distance from the work since the YouTuber does not assume himself to be a fan. Besides, he argues that the movie touched him very little, and he also sees the plotless as romantic and more sensual. However, this criticism is more opinionated and less technical, since little is said about the construction of the narrative and representation and much is said about how the YouTuber felt by watching.

Aiming to understand the repercussions of these videos, we choose to work with three categories to analyze user comments on YouTube channels. They are plot relevance, LGBTQIA+ approach and self-representation.[43]

First of all, before we present our findings, we made a quantitative analysis of the content of the comments collected. The majority are positive, since they talk, generally, about the fierce love between the characters, the aesthetics, the summer, the sex and the feeling of being enchanted that the movie brings. The negative comments are about how overrated the film is, the slowness of the narrative and some comments that evaluate the actors negatively. In addition, many considered the film positive but were not satisfied with the ending. It is also important to highlight that although there is an LGBTQIA+ target audience on these YouTube channels, we cannot rule out the possibility that part of the comments were made by heterosexual people.

Plot relevance

In our first category, we looked at how interacting viewers talked about the relevance of the story told in *Call Me by Your Name* to the LGBTQIA+ community. At this point, we realized that many of the comments prefer to treat the film by dissociating it from the idea of being an LGBTQIA+ movie.

Even though these are niche channels, being aimed at the LGBTQIA+ community, the analysis of the comments allowed us to realize that many of the people who commented disassociate the film from the idea of a necessarily LGBTQIA+ narrative or, for that matter, of an LGBTQIA+ identification. Many say that this is a film 'about love' and about how that story could be happening to anyone, of any sexual orientation, and that this is the appeal of the film. See Table 14.2. We perceive a similar movement in the analysis of the LGBTQIA+ representation category, aimed at the analysis of the characters Elio and Oliver, as we will see later.

We also noticed comments that place the film in the LGBTQIA+ audiovisual production scene, establishing comparisons with productions such as *Moonlight*, *Brokeback Mountain* (Ang Lee, 2005) and *The Way He Looks*. In this sense, we can quote the comment of a YouTube user in video 2:

> *Moonlight* is just as good, if not better than *Call Me by Your Name* in many aspects. The difference between them is that in your case, you can identify much more with the story of the white European teenager, who discovers his first great love,

than with the black boy in the ghetto who has his sexuality devastated by racism and homophobia. It is just a matter of projection because the two stories are very powerful and can, calmly, be placed on the level of masterpieces of contemporary cinema.

The comment highlights important aspects that reappear at other times, the idea of reinforcing the construction of the white body as a visible and desired body. We consider here that there is a kind of visibility/invisibility pyramid that allows a certain type of people covered by the acronym LGBTQIA+ to be better represented: these people are those who come closest to the heteronormative standard.[45] The story of *Call Me by Your Name* would be at the top of this pyramid by representing white men, who meet the current aesthetic standard. Following this discussion, we emphasize, in Table 14.3, some other comments which illustrate the same perspective:

TABLE 14.2: Examples of comments expressing the category Plot relevance.

Reference	Comment
Video 3	I liked the movie! It's a summer romance. It will have worked with those who believe in love.
Video 1	Everybody should watch this movie regardless of their sex, sexual orientation, and religion.
Video 2	I am a straight trans man, and I watched this movie today, and coincidentally I watched the movie last week, and yes this movie made me believe in love, an unforgettable film that makes me want to watch it over and over again.
Video 2	the thing is ... The film does not literally raise a gay flag you know, it is just about love at first sight, about love, he could have fallen in love with an alien, a dog, a peach kkk understand it ...[44]
Video 1	I just believe that a film that talks about love at this level of intensity, should not be classified as LGBT. It is just a film, which, like no other, has managed to move viewers so much.

TABLE 14.3: Further examples of comments expressing the category Plot relevance.

Reference	Comment
Video 2	*Call Me by Your Name* evokes the desire for the male figure of a middle-class white man, the standard and normative gay type.
Video 2	*Moonlight* is superior in all aspects to me, both plot, script, and performances!
Video 1	The best LGBTQ-themed film is *The Way He Looks* without a doubt
Video 2	How embarrassing, the movie is much of the very same, movies about white bourgeois gay men are always popping up.

Besides the emphasis on different representations of gay people in various productions, that is a specific criticism of the identity privileged by *Call Me by Your Name* and, in a certain way, a direct conclusion for its success: the representation of normative identities. It is interesting to notice how movies with very different plots, tones and even audiences, in a certain way, are being compared basically with the standard of 'gay people in love'. Therefore, it could be said that the dispute or discontent expressed in the comments is much more related to how people value these identities and their trajectories and experiences with love/sexual stories than to the movie productions themselves.

It is also noteworthy how heartbreak and love loss are interpreted through different identity prisms, relating them to skin colour (white and Black) or sexual orientation (homosexual or heterosexual). In truth, we could argue the movie recognizes both perspectives – the universal and the specific ones. It is a romantic narrative about heartbreak and loss, as we have illustrated in the previous discussion on mourning in love experiences. However, it certainly defines this major narrative in the trajectory of two white queer characters and bodies, having a potential opposition to white heterosexual bodies – in the sense it is a queer story – but also to queer bodies of colour. These oppositions seem to mean different things to different users, considering their comments either praise or criticize one of these perspectives on the movie, amplifying ('it is just about love at first sight') or restricting ('movies about white bourgeois gay men') the love experience narrated in the film.

LGBTQIA+ approach

In this category, what interests us is to analyze specifically the representativeness of the main characters, Elio and Oliver, as LGBTQIA+ characters. As we have already commented, we find a disfellowshipping that can be related both to the temporal suspension proposed by the film and to the desire to erase conflicts that come from viewers. This last option seems possible when we consider that the comments point to the fact that the characters' not defining themselves as gay or bisexual is something positive. Still, we also find comments that argue that, although there is no discussion about sexual orientation, the film does advocate for the bisexual flag. See Table 14.4.

Once more, there is a dispute between a more universal narrative and a specific one, which evokes different interpretations of the movie. In the scope of these comments, it seems that the romantic aspect of the movie is more highlighted when the story is defined as universal, not LGBTQIA+; whereas, when the story is defined as LGBTQIA+, problems with some aspects of its representation are emphasized. Therefore, it seems that the discussion of love loss is more acceptable if the movie is interpreted as a general love story, not an LGBTQIA+ one. As much as this interpretation makes sense, giving love loss can be understood as a universal

TABLE 14.4: Examples of comments expressing the category LGBTQIA+ approach.

Reference	Comment
Video 3	For those who are just used to commercial films, it will be difficult to appreciate this film, which is very poetic. Elio is 17 years old and Oliver is 24 years old, both allow themselves to love, without closing themselves to gay or straight logos.
Video 1	It's [sic] has a bisexual 'theme'! Very important to delimit this space.
Video 1	Yes, it is a wonderful film and one that brings a great deal of representation to Bisexuals who are very dimmed in the LGBTQ community.

experience, the comments following this train of thought end up erasing identity traits that are key and specific to the narrative of the film, which is still a queer story.

Self-representation

In this category, we try to understand if and how *Call Me by Your Name* operates the notion of otherness, considering the idea of man as an unfinished subject who 'is always and always on the border, looking inside himself, he looks the other in the eyes or with the eyes of the other'.[46]

Even though the *Call Me by Your Name* plot has representational problems, such as the fact that both characters are white, are within the social standards of beauty and come from a good financial situation – aspects which were already mentioned in comments previously analyzed – the film generates a desire for belonging. This desire is manifested not only by the idea of finding love but by the desire for a different future: a future that expands this temporary time suspension in which Elio and Oliver had their love affair. This desire is connected to the discussion being carried out on love loss and its connection to a universal love story. Comments in Table 14.5 are examples of this effect.

TABLE 14.5: Examples of comments expressing the category Self-representation.

Reference	Comment
Video 1	The history shows that the teenager's parents are an erudite couple, who are always reading, gaining knowledge. They are smart people. A clear message that prejudice is a characteristic of people with less knowledge. Something that I see as a great slap in the face of our prejudiced society. Another big slap that the film gives and that serves as a moral lesson is the dialogue between the father and the son, showing how a real father SHOULD be.
Video 1	I don't like a romance movie or a gay movie but this movie made me change my mind
Video 2	This movie is beautiful because it shows how good it is to be in love, how good it is to be able to give yourself to those you love and also, how important it is to have a family that knows how to deal with feelings (Elio has a dream family, right?)

In fact, in many of the previous comments, the users associate their personal experiences and identify themselves, individually, with their interpretations of the movie. Of course, as we have considered, the evaluation of film by the spectators is inseparable from the emotional impact the work has caused them. Here, we associate this movement not only with interpretative movements themselves but also with nostalgia. For Keightley and Pickering, nostalgia works with the mnemonic imagination as a way to make sense of the pain experienced, facilitating the creative reformulation of painful pasts so that these re-signified memories can be positively inserted in the present and future projections.[47]

The 'curative' power played by nostalgic media productions can be seen in numerous comments. The film provokes in part of its audience a true catharsis:

> I cried more watching this movie than when I was born. Just to remember crying again, also to remember his father's monologue. I wish all LGBT people were lucky enough to have a father and mother like his. (*While I'm typing, remembering and crying again kkk.*)[48]

Thus, in more than one comment, the speech of Elio's father is brought up, emphasizing the relation of the spectator's reception with the discussion on love lost previously approached.

Conclusions

We argued that the celebration in this chapter's title is valid: *Call Me by Your Name* is an LGBTQIA+ film that does not touch on the main problems usually explored in narratives about non-heterosexual people, in the sense that the process of coming out of the closet, the pain of not being accepted by the family, homophobia in general, the stigma of HIV/AIDS, are not questions for Oliver and Elio.

Hollywood cinema traditionally (re)produces the reiterative discourse about the naturalization of the sex–gender–desire triad by assuming heterosexuality as self-evident. The plots of many major film productions start from the prerogative of a heterosexual narrator who will tell the stories of presumably heterosexual characters seeking love, marriage, family and children. The characters' sexual orientation is only problematized when some conduct is deemed inappropriate, and their sexuality (for example, homosexuality) is then questioned or assessed. In this way, the original heteroglossia of the world in all its noisy diversity would be reduced in Hollywood films to what Stam calls a monotonous murmur of monoglossia.[49]

Criticisms of Hollywood cinema due to its fixed formulas, stereotyped characters and an attempt to 'Americanize' the world are not recent. What has drawn attention in recent years is the critical emphasis on issues related to the diversity of the cultural industry as a whole, and especially on aspects that concern issues of gender, race and sexuality. This new reflective scenario appears to be causing changes in the functioning of the system's machinery. Big names in the industry are being removed and punished for allegations of harassment, women are starting to earn a salary closer to their fellow male actors, awards have sought to diversify their nominees, casting choices have adopted representation, and a greater plurality of stories and characters has occupied the scene. *Call Me by Your Name* was produced and launched during this scenario in which the audiovisual industry and a part of its audience demonstrate to be more attentive to the discourse of diversity.

Works such as *Call Me by Your Name* can then be read as part of this movement of inclusion and celebration of people and social groups that had hitherto been neglected by the media culture and society as a whole. The film's success with the specialized critics and the public indicates that the film was able to capture and transmit, through its history, the yearnings of its time.

By privileging the romance between two men in its plot, the movie demonstrates an effort to break with the 'monotonous murmur of monoglossia' which dominates Hollywood cinema. The visibility given to another way of experiencing sexuality and affection, beyond heterosexual moulds, has the potential to produce multiple positive effects on its audience. The film's exercise of setting this love story in the past causes its audience to distance themselves from the present and re-imagine their history.

Call Me by Your Name has the power to bring heterosexuals closer to their 'others', but their actions go beyond, they also empower and give the notion of belonging to non-normative bodies. The queer body can project itself onto the screen because before it a world is represented where the subject seen as deviant can escape, can learn, can exist and resist.[50]

Many of the comments posted on YouTube by Brazilian users in the context of the film's reception attest that *Call Me by Your Name* triggers a 'therapeutic process' in the LGBTQIA+ audience that helps in the re-elaboration of their identity and in the positivization of the space to be socially occupied by dissident subjects.

The dialogue between Elio and his father is one of the most highlighted scenes among the comments as a trigger for nostalgic emotions. Nostalgia is then evoked in its reflexive dimension,[51] it is not about a desire to rescue or return home, or return to the family, as a mythical place of happiness and welcome. On the contrary, according to one of the comments highlighted, '[a]nother big slap that the film gives and that serves as a moral lesson is a dialogue between the father and the son, showing how a real father SHOULD be'. What reflexive nostalgia awakens is the capacity for multiple planes of consciousness creatively operated by the mnemonic imagination. The perception of the passage of time, with the realization that those children or teenagers may no longer be misunderstood by their relatives, makes it possible not only to elaborate on their pain but also to wish for another type of future.

NOTES

1. See Gilad Padva, *Queer Nostalgia in Cinema and Pop Culture* (New York: Palgrave Macmillan, 2014), 11.

2. See Vinicius Ferreira and Ana Paula Goulart Ribeiro, 'O passado e o tempo da vida: Cinema e nostalgia "queer"', in *Tempo e memória: Interfaces entre os campos da comunicação e da história*, ed. Ana Regina Rêgo, Teresinha Queiroz and António Hohldfeldt (Porto Alegre: EDIPUCRS, 2020), 495.

3. See Stuart Hall, *Cultura e Representação*, trans. Daniel Miranda and William Oliveira (Rio de Janeiro: PUC-Rio: Apicuri, 2016), 26.

4. See Teresa de Lauretis, 'Eccentric Subjects: Feminist Theory and Historical Consciousness', *Feminist Studies* 16, no. 1 (1990): 123, http://www.jstor.org/stable/3177959.

5. A YouTube user's comment retrieved from the comment section of 'AUTODESCOBERTA DO AMOR (Me Chame pelo Seu Nome | Crítica)', accessed 13 April 2023, https://www.youtube.com/watch?v=WPPX2SljjoQ.

6. See Andreas Huyssen, *Seduzidos pela Memória: Arquitetura, monumento, mídia* (Rio de Janeiro: Aeroplano Editora, 2000), 14.

7. The Circle of Bakhtin is a group of Russian thinkers and researchers who gathered regularly between 1919 and 1929. Their studies were related to the Marxist theory, literature and the philosophy of language. Among the many intellectuals who composed the group, our work will establish a closer dialogue with Valentin N. Voloshinov and Mikhail M. Bakhtin.

8. See Robert Stam, *Bakhtin: Da Teoria Literária à Cultura de Massa*, trans. Heloísa Jahn (São Paulo: Editora Ática, 1992), 53.

9. See V. N. Voloshinov, *Marxism and the Philosophy of Language*, trans. Ladislav Matejka and I. R. Titunik (Cambridge, Mass. and London: Harvard University Press, [1929] 1986), 17.

10. See especially M. M. Bakhtin, *Toward a Philosophy of the Act*, ed. Vadim Liapunov and Michael Holquist, trans. Vadim Liapunov (Austin: Texas University Press, 1993). In this work, we understand the act as any enunciative positioning, verbal or non-verbal.

11. We are using *evaluative horizon*, a term used in Voloshinov's *Marxism and the Philosophy of Language*, to express the ideas developed in Voloshinov's 'Discourse in Life and Discourse in Art (Concerning Sociological Poetics)' towards *spatial and semantical horizon, social evaluation* and *intonational metaphor*. See V. N. Voloshinov, 'Discourse in Life and Discourse in Art (Concerning Sociological Poetics)', in V. N. Voloshinov, *Freudianism: A Marxist Critique*, trans. I. R. Titunik (New York: Academic Press, 1976), 93–116.

12. The Circle of Bakhtin does not define any of these common elements. The definition of Voloshinov is solely focused on the idea of 'social groups' (see 'Discourse in Life and

Discourse in Art'). However, for the context of this work and considering contemporary discussion on the matter, we understand that social groups can be defined by different layers and patterns of unity, such as the ones described – emphasis given to class, gender and race – but also many other possible elements and factors.

13. By selecting LGBTQIA+ YouTube channels as part of our scope, we have attempted to define a corpus of comments that belong to a certain niche. However, since people do not declare their gender and sexuality identity when posting a comment nor is this information somehow public in their profile, it is not possible to affirm that any of the users belong to the LGBTQIA+ community or not – unless they declare so in their own comments. Therefore, we merely defined a scope of LGBTQIA+ channels – rather than generic cinema or video analysis channels, understanding these users could belong or relate to the LGBTQIA+ community/common topics in general, creating some kind of collective evaluative horizon.

14. See Stam, *Bakhtin*.

15. Even though many mainstream productions highlight and privilege LGBTQIA+ stories, a contradiction between a cinema dominated by heterosexual men and an authentic homosexual voice may be visible in different gestures and aspects of its production. In the case of *Call Me by Your Name*, both the screenwriter and the director belong to the LGBTQIA+ community, which does not exempt the film from the same contradictions of the industry. In this case, it has mostly been highlighted by the sexual identity of the cast, mostly heterosexual.

16. GLAAD has been analyzing the presence of LGBTQ characters for 26 years. In the first report were counted 12 total LGBTQ regular characters in TV shows; in the 2021–22 report there was a total of 637 LGBTQ regular characters. In films released by major studios, in 2020, for instance, ten of the 44 theatrical releases (23 per cent) featured 20 LGBTQ characters; according to GLAAD, the following year the percentage is down slightly but 16 of the 77 films released by those studios (20.8 per cent) featured 28 LGBTQ characters. See GLAAD, *Where We Are on TV 2021–2022* (Report), available at https://www.glaad.org/whereweareontv21, accessed 13 April 2023.

17. See Bridget Kies and Thomas J. West III, 'Queer Nostalgia and Queer Histories in Uncertain Times', *Queer Studies in Media & Popular Culture* 2, no. 1 (2017): 161.

18. See Kies and West III, 162.

19. See Ana Paula Goulart Ribeiro, *Mercado da nostalgia e narrativas audiovisuais*, E-Compós (Brasília) 21, no. 3 (2018): 1, https://doi.org/10.30962/ec.1491.

20. See Fredric Jameson, *Postmodernism, or, the Cultural Logic of Late Capitalism* (Durham: Duke University Press, 1991); Svetlana Boym, *The Future of Nostalgia* (Nova York: Basic Books, 2001).

21. See Anthony Giddens, *The Transformation of Intimacy: Sexuality, Love and Eroticism in Modern Societies* (Cambridge: Polity Press, 1992), especially Chapter 3, 'Romantic Love and Other Attachments', 37–48.

22. See M. M. Bakhtin, *The Dialogic Imagination: Four Essays by M. M. Bakhtin*, ed. Michael Holquist, trans. Caryl Emerson and Michael Holquist (Austin: University of Texas Press, 1981). We do not assume that coming-of-age stories and the *Bildungsroman* are the same genres. We believe that, nowadays, coming-of-age stories are a group of contemporary narratives which can be associated with the typical themes and issues present in the *Bildungsroman*.

23. The conception of heteronormativity we mention here follows the thought of Judith Butler, who considers the heterosexual matrix as a hegemonic production of sexuality and identity of different genders (heterosexuals, homosexuals, transsexuals and others). See Judith Butler, *Gender Trouble: Feminism and the Subversion of Identity* (New York: Routledge, [1990] 2006).

24. Gustave Flaubert, *Madame Bovary: Mœurs de province* (Paris: *Revue de Paris*, 1856 [serialized form]; Paris: Michel Lévy Frères, 1957 [novel in two parts]).

25. Women's independence is not a reality fully achieved throughout the world. Even in countries where women have achieved more rights, gender violence rates are extremely high, which makes us question the overcoming of issues clearly established two or even three centuries ago.

26. See Katharina Niemeyer, *Media and Nostalgia: Yearning for the Past, Present and Future* (London: Palgrave Macmillan, 2014), 2; Katharina Niemeyer, 'The Power of Nostalgia', *Nostalgia e mídia*, ed. Lucia Santa Cruz and Talitha Ferraz (Rio de Janeiro: E-Papers, 2018), 29; Ana Paula Goulart Ribeiro, *Mercado da nostalgia e narrativas audiovisuais*, *E-Compós* (Brasília) 21, no. 3 (2018): 10, https://doi.org/10.30962/ec.1491.

27. Ribeiro, *Mercado*, 11. Translated from the Portuguese, 'futuros possíveis', by the authors.

28. See Niemeyer, 'Power'; Niemeyer, *Media*.

29. See Padva, *Queer Nostalgia*, 91.

30. See Niemeyer, 'Power', 39; Padva, *Queer Nostalgia*, 11.

31. See Paolla Serra, 'Casal é preso no Rio após pagar hotéis cinco estrelas com cartões clonados', *Epoca*, 11 December 2020, https://epoca.globo.com/rio/casal-preso-no-rio-apos-pagar-hoteis-cinco-estrelas-com-cartoes-clonados-24792206. Headline translated into English by the authors.

32. Comment on 5gu account, Twitter, 11 December 2020. English translation by the authors.

33. Best Picture, Best Adapted Screenplay, Best Original Song and Best Actor for Timothée Chalamet as the protagonist, Elio.

34. See '*Call Me by Your Name* (2017)', Box Office Mojo, accessed 13 April 2023, www.boxofficemojo.com.

35. See M. M. Bakhtin, 'Forms of Time and of the Chronotope in the Novel', in *The Dialogic Imagination: Four Essays by M. M. Bakhtin*, ed. Michael Holquist, trans. Caryl Emerson and Michael Holquist (Austin: University of Texas Press, 1981), 84-258.

36. See Gêsa Cavalcanti, Vinicius Ferreira and Daiane Sigliano, 'Liberdade, Liberdade: Repercussão da cena de sexo gay na telenovela', *Cambiassu: Estudos em Comunicação* (Online) 13 (2017), 107.

37. By supporting this argument, we perceive that Ivory's and Guadagnino's movies work with 'temporary suspension' and 'early nostalgia': the viewers know that the romance will come to an end, but the moments between the couples are dilated. This mismatch between expectation and reality may be associated both with the affective exploration romantic movies usually invest in and mainstream romantic love conceptions.

38. Sigmund Freud, 'On Transience', in *The Standard Edition of the Complete Psychological Works of Sigmund Freud, Volume XIV*, by Sigmund Freud, trans. James Strachey (London: The Hogarth Press and the Institute of Psycho-Analysis, [1915] 1916), 307.

39. Federico Devito, 'Assista: CALL ME BY YOUR NAME' [Watch: *Call Me by Your Name!*], YouTube, 24 January 2018, https://youtu.be/0gJM5F8CK-8.

40. Caio Braz, 'CALL ME BY YOUR NAME É O FILME MAIS LINDO QUE EXISTE' ['*Call Me by Your Name* is the most beautiful movie'], YouTube, 28 January 2018, https://youtu.be/MWGe31SoI1Q.

41. Pink Popcorn, 'ME CHAME PELO SEU NOME | O que achei | Pink Popcorn' ['*Call Me by Your Name* / What I thought / Pink Popcorn'], YouTube, 15 February 2018, https://youtu.be/1GU-DsUpmVI.

42. Guadagnino is making in the moment an indirect citation of a Žižek lecture entitled *Slavoj Žižek: The Reality of the Virtual* (Ben Wright, 2004) in which the author argues that we need to reinvent utopia – not in a classic sense – so that we can build our future.

43. All the comments that are presented in the tables or quoted in the body of the text were originally written in Brazilian Portuguese and translated to English by the authors.

44. 'kkk' is one of the ways Brazilians express laughter in instant messages, such as 'haha' in English.

45. See Gayle Rubin, 'Reflexionando sobre el sexo: Notas para una teoría radical de la sexualidad', *Placer y peligro: Explorando la sexualidad femenina*, trans. Julio Velscao and María Angeles Toda, ed. Carole S. Vance (Madrid: Revolución, 1989), 136.

46. Mikhail Bakhtin, 'Toward a Reworking of the Dostoevsky Book', in *Problems of Dostoevsky's Poetics*, trans. and ed. Caryl Emerson (Minneapolis & London: University of Minnesota Press, 1984), 287.

47. See Emily Keightley and Michael Pickering, *The Mnemonic Imagination: Remembering as Creative Practice* (London: Palgrave Macmillan, 2012).

48. Emphasis added.

49. See Stam, *Bakhtin*, 65.

50. See Ferreira and Ribeiro, 'O passado e o tempo da vida', 491.

51. See Boym, *Future of Nostalgia*.

REFERENCES

Bakhtin, M. M. *The Dialogic Imagination: Four Essays by M. M. Bakhtin*. Translated by Caryl Emerson and Michael Holquist and edited by Michael Holquist. Austin: University of Texas Press, 1981.

Bakhtin, M. M. *Toward a Philosophy of the Act*. Translated by Vadim Liapunov and edited by Vadim Liapunov and Michael Holquist. Austin: Texas University Press, 1993.

Berlanti, Greg, dir. *Love, Simon*. Fox 2000 Pictures, Temple Hill Productions, TSG Entertainment, 2018.

Box Office Mojo. 'Call Me by Your Name (2017).' Accessed 13 April 2023. www.boxoffice-mojo.com.

Boym, Svetlana. *The Future of Nostalgia*. Nova York: Basic Books, 2001.

Braz, Caio. 'CALL ME BY YOUR NAME É O FILME MAIS LINDO QUE EXISTE' ['*Call Me by Your Name* is the most beautiful movie']. YouTube, 28 January 2018. https://youtu.be/MWGe31SoI1Q.

Butler, Judith. *Gender Trouble: Feminism and the Subversion of Identity*. New York: Routledge, [1990] 2006.

Cavalcanti, Gêsa, Vinicius Ferreira and Daiane Sigliano. 'Liberdade, Liberdade: Repercussão da cena de sexo gay na telenovela.' *Cambiassu: Estudos em Comunicação (Online)* 13 (2017): 101–20.

de Lauretis, Teresa. 'Eccentric Subjects: Feminist Theory and Historical Consciousness.' *Feminist Studies* 16, no. 1 (1990): 115–50. http://www.jstor.org/stable/3177959.

Devito, Federico. 'Assista: CALL ME BY YOUR NAME!' ['Watch: *Call Me by Your Name!*] YouTube, 24 January 2018. https://youtu.be/0gJM5F8CK-8.

Ferreira, Vinicius, and Ana Paula Goulart Ribeiro. 'O passado e o tempo da vida: Cinema e nostalgia "queer".' In *Tempo e memória: Interfaces entre os campos da comunicação e da história*, edited by Ana Regina Rêgo, Teresinha Queiroz and António Hohldfeldt, 489–502. Porto Alegre: EDIPUCRS, 2020.

Flaubert, Gustave. *Madame Bovary: Mœurs de province*. Paris: *Revue de Paris*, 1856 (serialized form). Paris: Michel Lévy Frères, 1957 (novel in two parts).

Freud, Sigmund. 'On Transience.' In *The Standard Edition of the Complete Psychological Works of Sigmund Freud*. Translated by James Strachey. Volume XIV, by Sigmund Freud, 303–08. London: The Hogarth Press and the Institute of Psycho-Analysis, [1915] 1916.

Giddens, Anthony. *The Transformation of Intimacy: Sexuality, Love and Eroticism in Modern Societies*. Cambridge: Polity Press, 1992.

GLAAD, *Where We are on TV 2021–2022* (Report). Accessed 13 April 2023. https://www.glaad.org/whereweareontv21.

Guadagnino, Luca, dir. *Call Me by Your Name*. Frenesy Film Company, La Cinefacture, RT Features, 2017.

Hall, Stuart. *Cultura e Representação*. Translated by Daniel Miranda and William Oliveira. Rio de Janeiro: PUC-Rio: Apicuri, 2016.

Huyssen, Andreas. *Seduzidos pela Memória: Arquitetura, monumento, mídia*. Rio de Janeiro: Aeroplano Editora, 2000.

Ivory, James, dir. *Maurice*. Merchant Ivory Productions, Cinecom Pictures, Channel 4, 1987.

Jenkins, Barry, dir. *Moonlight*. A24, PASTEL, Plan B Entertainment, 2016.

Keightley, Emily, and Michael Pickering. *The Mnemonic Imagination: Remembering as Creative Practice*. London: Palgrave Macmillan, 2012.

Kies, Bridget, and Thomas J. West III. 'Queer Nostalgia and Queer Histories in Uncertain Times.' *Queer Studies in Media & Popular Culture* 2, no. 1 (2017): 161–65.

Lannan, Michael, creator. *Looking* (TV). Fair Harbor Productions, HBO, 2014–16.

Lee, Ang, dir. *Brokeback Mountain*. River Road Entertainment, Focus Features, 2005.

Lee, Francis, dir. *God's Own Country*. BFI, Creative England, Shudder Films, Inflammable Films, 2017.

Murphy, Ryan, Brad Falchuk and Steven Canals, creators. *Pose* (TV). Color Force, Brad Falchuk Teley-Vision, Ryan Murphy Television, 2018-21.

Niemeyer, Katharina. *Media and Nostalgia: Yearning for the Past, Present and Future*. London: Palgrave Macmillan, 2014.

Niemeyer, Katharina. 'The Power of Nostalgia.' In *Nostalgia e mídia*, edited by Lucia Santa Cruz and Talitha Ferraz, 29–47. Rio de Janeiro: E-Papers, 2018.

Padva, Gilad. *Queer Nostalgia in Cinema and Pop Culture*. New York: Palgrave Macmillan, 2014.

Pink Popcorn. 'ME CHAME PELO SEU NOME / O que achei / Pink Popcorn' ['*Call Me by Your Name* / What I thought / Pink Popcorn']. YouTube, 15 February 2018. https://youtu.be/1GU-DsUpmVI.

Ribeiro, Ana Paula Goulart. *Mercado da nostalgia e narrativas audiovisuais*. *E-Compós (Brasília)* 21, no. 3 (2018). https://doi.org/10.30962/ec.1491.

Ribeiro, Daniel, dir. *Hoje Eu Quero Voltar Sozinho* (*The Way He Looks*). Lacuna Filmes, Polana Filmes, 2014.

Rubin, Gayle. 'Reflexionando sobre el sexo: Notas para una teoría radical de la sexualidad.' In *Placer y peligro: Explorando la sexualidad femenina*, translated by Julio Velscao and María Angeles Toda and edited by Carole S. Vance, 113–90. Madrid: Revolución, 1989.

Serra, Paolla. 'Casal é preso no Rio após pagar hotéis cinco estrelas com cartões clonados.' *Epoca*, 11 December 2020. https://epoca.globo.com/rio/casal-preso-no-rio-apos-pagar-hoteis-cinco-estrelas-com-cartoes-clonados-24792206.

Stam, Robert. *Bakhtin: Da Teoria Literária à Cultura de Massa*. Translated by Heloísa Jahn. São Paulo: Editora Ática, 1992.

Voloshinov, V. N. 'Discourse in Life and Discourse in Art (Concerning Sociological Poetics).' In *Freudianism: A Marxist Critique*, by V. N. Voloshinov. Translated by I. R. Titunik, 93–116. New York: Academic Press, 1976.

Voloshinov, V. N. *Marxism and the Philosophy of Language*. Translated by Ladislav Matejka and I. R. Titunik. Cambridge and London: Harvard University Press, [1929] 1986.

Wachowskis, The, and J. Michael Straczynski, creators. *Sense8* (TV). Anarchos Productions (Season 1), Venus Castina Productions (Season 2), Studio JMS, Georgeville Television, Unpronounceable Productions, 2015-18.

Contributors

Sarah Artt is Lecturer in Film and Literature at Edinburgh Napier University. She writes widely about film, television and literature for general and scholarly audiences. Her academic work has been published in the journals *Science Fiction Film and Television*, *Scope: An Online Journal of Film and Television Studies* and in edited collections by BrillRodopi, WinterVerlag and Bloomsbury. Her public work has appeared in *The Conversation*. She is the author of *Quiet Pictures: Women and Silence in Contemporary British and French Cinema* (Bloomsbury, 2024).

* * * * *

Jonathan A. Cannon is an independent researcher from Vancouver, Canada. Jonathan holds a BA and an MA in Film Studies from the University of British Columbia. His research interests include star/celebrity studies, representations of masculinity in film and popular culture.

* * * * *

Gêsa Cavalcanti has a PhD in Communication from the Federal University of Pernambuco, with a major in Publicity and Advertising. Gêsa is currently a Professor in the Department of Communication at the Federal University of Rio Grande do Norte. Gêsa is also a researcher at the OBITEL Network (Ibero-American Observatory of Television Fiction).

* * * * *

Ruby Cheung is Associate Professor in Film Studies at the University of Southampton. She is an internationally recognized specialist in the study of contemporary Hong Kong cinema, Chinese-language film industries and film festivals. Ruby is the author of *New Hong Kong Cinema: Transitions to Becoming Chinese in 21st-Century East Asia* (Berghahn Books, 2015) and *Hong Kong's New Indie Cinema* (Palgrave Macmillan, 2023; winner of Best Monograph at the 2024 British Association of Film, Television and Screen Studies Awards). She is the main editor of *Cinemas, Identities and Beyond* (Cambridge Scholars Publishing, 2009) and co-editor of *Film Festival Yearbook 2: Film Festivals and Imagined Communities* (St Andrews Film Studies, 2010) and *Film Festival Yearbook 3: Film Festivals and East Asia* (St Andrews Film Studies, 2011).

* * * * *

NIKOLAI ENDRES received his PhD in Comparative Literature from the University of North Carolina-Chapel Hill in 2000. As Professor of World Literature and Film at Western Kentucky University, he teaches Great Books, British literature, classics, mythology, critical theory, queer cinema and gay and lesbian studies. He has published on Plato, Petronius, Gustave Flaubert, Richard Wagner, Oscar Wilde, F. Scott Fitzgerald, Mary Renault, Gore Vidal and others. He just completed a first book about the late American novelist Patricia Nell Warren, author of the famous gay novel *The Front Runner*. His next projects are the Romosexuality of E. M. Forster's *Maurice* and classics beyond whiteness in the photographs of the Baron von Gloeden.

* * * * *

JACOB ENGELBERG is Assistant Professor of Film, Media, and Culture at the University of Amsterdam. He has published work in the *Journal of Bisexuality* and *Porn Studies*, where he has also edited a special issue on bisexuality and pornographic film. Jacob has published chapters in the following edited collections: Screening Adult Cinema (Routledge, 2025), A Companion to Ingmar Bergman (Wiley-Blackwell, 2024) and Transnational Horror: Folklore, Genre, and Cultural Politics (Liverpool University Press, 2024). Jacob's forthcoming monograph, entitled Cinemas of Bisexual Transgression, is under contract with Duke University Press.

* * * * *

VINICIUS FERREIRA is a Professor in the Department of Communication at Salgado de Oliveira University, a doctoral student in Communication and Culture at the Federal University of Rio de Janeiro (UFRJ), an Executive Board member of the Brazilian Association of Media History Researchers and Vice Chair of the Communication Interfaces section of the Brazilian Society of Interdisciplinary Communication Studies.

* * * * *

EDWARD LAMBERTI is the author of *Performing Ethics through Film Style: Levinas with the Dardenne Brothers, Barbet Schroeder and Paul Schrader* (Edinburgh University Press, 2019) and the editor of *Behind the Scenes at the BBFC: Film Classification from the Silver Screen to the Digital Age* (BFI/Palgrave, 2012; longlisted for the 2013 Kraszna-Krausz Award for Best Moving Image Book). He has a PhD in Film Studies Research from King's College London and is Policy Manager at the BBFC.

* * * * *

KINGSLEY MARSHALL is an academic, composer, film producer, and Head of the School of Film & Television at Falmouth University. His academic research focuses on the use of music and sound design in film and television, cultures of film and television production, and the representation and deployment of artificial intelligence in film and television. He has published widely and speaks regularly at international conferences. He is co-editor of Philosophical Reflections on Black Mirror (Bloomsbury, 2021).

* * * * *

CLAIRE MONK is Professor of Film & Film Culture at De Montfort University. She is a specialist in heritage cinema, reception and the films of Merchant Ivory Productions, known for her work to bring gender and sexuality into the heritage-film debates and on audiences and participatory practices around the films, beginning with *Heritage Film Audiences* (Edinburgh University Press, 2011). The BFI's 2019 UK Blu-ray premiere release of James Ivory's 1987 *Maurice* features her audio commentary, acclaimed by *The Arts Desk* as 'revelatory'. Her current projects include a production study of Ivory's *Maurice* situated in the text's cultural history and adaptations across time and media and the re-evaluation of Ivory's wider oeuvre.

* * * * *

DANIEL PAUL is Assistant Professor of Italian at Brigham Young University, where he is also affiliated faculty for Global Women's Studies and International Cinema Studies. His primary research focuses on representations of masculinity in Italian cinema and his scholarly interests include disability studies, trauma theory and Black Italy. His work has appeared in The Italianist, The Journal of Italian Cinema and Media Studies, and Italian Culture.

* * * * *

STUART RICHARDS is a Senior Lecturer in Screen Studies at the University of South Australia. He is author of the books *The Queer Film Festival: Popcorn and Politics* (Palgrave Macmillan, 2017) and *Agatha Christie and Gothic Horror: Adaptations and Televisuality* (Amsterdam University Press, 2024). He has previously worked with both the Melbourne Queer Film Festival and the San Francisco Frameline International LGBTQ Film Festival.

* * * * *

VICTOR SCHLUDE is a PhD student in Applied Linguistics at the State University of Campinas. He holds a Master's degree in the same field and institution. His main research interests are critical theories, language and neoliberalism studies, language and education, masculinities and affection.

* * * * *

FRANCESCA SOBANDE is a Senior Lecturer in Digital Media Studies at the School of Journalism, Media and Culture, Cardiff University. She is the author of *Big Brands Are Watching You: Marketing Social Justice and Digital Culture* (University of California Press, 2024), *The Digital Lives of Black Women in Britain* (Palgrave Macmillan, 2020) and *Consuming Crisis: Commodifying Care and COVID-19* (SAGE, 2022). Francesca is also co-editor, with Akwugo Emejulu, of *To Exist Is to Resist: Black Feminism in Europe* (Pluto Press, 2019) and co-author, with layla-roxanne hill, of *Black Oot Here: Black Lives in Scotland* (Bloomsbury, 2022).

* * * * *

ADAM VAUGHAN is a Lecturer in the Department of Film and Media at Solent University and teaches across their Film and Television and Film Production courses. His research interests include the performance of identity in documentary film, queer cinema and the political implications of personal identity in LGBTQ+ cinema. He is currently working on the monograph from his PhD thesis, entitled *Doing Documentary, Becoming Subjects: Performance and Performativity in Documentary Cinema*. He has contributed chapters to edited collections on twenty-first-century European documentary and the historical biopics of Derek Jarman. He is also Online Editor for the *Screening Sex* network.

* * * * *

MICHAEL WILLIAMS is Professor in Film Studies at the University of Southampton. He is the author of *Film Stardom and the Ancient Past: Idols, Artefacts and Epics* (Palgrave Macmillan, 2018) and *Film Stardom, Myth and Classicism: The Rise of the Hollywood Gods* (Palgrave Macmillan, 2013). He has published on stardom and representations of the past, with a particular focus on queer imagery and reception, and is also the author of *Ivor Novello: Screen Idol* (BFI, 2003) and co-editor of *British Silent Cinema and the Great War* (Palgrave Macmillan, 2011).

Index

Italicized titles with just a family name in brackets indicate literary works.
All other italicized titles indicate films, except where noted as TV or otherwise.
Italicized numbers indicate figures.

1980s, the 18, 22, 23, 24, 26–30, 35,
37, 44, 45, 47–48, 51n24, 58, 77, 81,
84, 103, 117, 140, 141, 142, 153,
156, 157, 159–61, 182, 227, 258, 270,
292

A

Abramovitch, Seth 282n3
Academy Awards 5, 6, 34, 36–37, 41,
48–49n1, 52n33, 76, 93, 155, 185, 188,
234, 243, 292, 308n33
Achilles 152
Aciman, André 1, 2, 6, 10, 17, 27, 34, 58,
59, 60, 61, 62, 63, 64, 65, 69, 71–72,
76, 83, 86, 94, 101, 117, 131, 155,
156, 159, 164, 166n20, 166n23, 175,
179, 199, 217n19, 234, 247n42, 274,
292
    as actor in film of *Call Me by Your*
       Name 21, *138*, 158
    Find Me (novel) 104, 247n45
    input into film of *Call Me by Your*
       Name 27–28, 66
    on bisexuality 199
    on Elio's interiority 63, 64
    on the peach sequence 70
Adams, John 1, 77, 78, 79, 82, 136–37,
142
Adonis 60, 160, 185

AIDS 5, 18, 26–30, 31n15, 32n26, 37, 39,
48, 140, 141, 143, 159–61, 162, 163, 165,
184, 217n13, 293, 304
Akomfrah, John 209
Aldrich, Robert 172
Alexander, Jonathan 107n14, 183
Alexander (Oliver Stone, 2004) 156
Alexander the Great 156, 164, 173
Althusser, Louis 204, 217–18n28
Altman, Rick 218n30
Amato, Andrea 143
Amherst, Michael 205
amica geniale, L' (*My Brilliant Friend*,
    Saverio Costanzo, creator,
    2018–23) 4
Amin, Kadji 165n4
Ancient Greece *see* Graeco-Roman
    culture
Ancient Rome *see* Graeco-Roman culture;
    Rome
Anderson, Wes 83, 263
Angelides, Steven 214
Angel, Katherine 105
Antinous 153, 173, 180
Arcadia 5, 17, 18–26, 28, 30, 177
Argentina 39, 47
Argento, Dario 3
Aristogeiton 152
Aronczyk, Melissa 146n13

Arroyo, Eduardo 199

Artt, Sarah 6–7, 8, 122

Athlete of Ephesos, the (sculpture) 173–75, *174*

B

Baby (TV, 2018–20) 145n8

Bach, Johann Sebastian 78, 82, 153

bacio, Un (*One Kiss*, Ivan Cotroneo, 2016) 143, 144

Badlands (Terrence Malick, 1973) 61

Bakhtin, Mikhail 23, 286–87, 288, 290, 292–93, 306n7, 306n10, 306n12, 308n22, 308n35 *see also* Circle of Bakhtin

Bandolero 81

Baron, Cynthia 95

Barraclough, Leo 247n47

Basile, Giambattista 3

Battles, Kathleen 259

Bazin, André 59, 63, 65, 74n20

Beard, Mary 189

Beautiful Boy (Felix Van Groeningen, 2018) 185, 263

Beautiful Thing (Hettie MacDonald, 1996) 20

Ben-Hur: A Tale of the Christ (Fred Niblo, 1925) 175

Benson, Robby 273

Benzina (*Gasoline*, Monica Stambrini, 2001) 132

Bergado, Gabe 265n4

Bergamo 5, 17, 19, *20*, 22, 23–24, 85, 120, 124, 139, 142, 157, 158, 164

Bergman, Ingmar 204

Berlanti, Greg 289

Bersani, Leo 219n45

Bertolucci, Bernardo 3

Bessegato, Ludovico 145n8

Biden, Joe 260–61

Bigger Splash, A (Luca Guadagnino, 2015) 3, 77, 97, 98, 106n3, 227

Billy: The Early Years (Robby Benson, 2008) 273, 274, 275, 276

Birkin, Jane 45

Black, Dustin Lance 276

Black, Shane 61

Bloomer, Jeffrey 152, 157

Bombay Talkie (James Ivory, 1970) 35

Bones and All (Luca Guadagnino, 2022) 3, 107n16, 262

Bonham Carter, Helena 51n19

Bono, Sonny 154

Book of Joshua 72

Bordwell, David 64

Borowczyk, Walerian 107n16

Boy Erased (Joel Edgerton, 2018) 157

Boy George 45

Boym, Svetlana 307n20, 307n51

Bradford, Jesse 45

Braga, Alice 115

Branagh, Kenneth 9, 281

Braudy, Leo 61, 64

Braz, Caio 296, 297, 298

Brodsky, Rachel 265n14

Brody, Richard 99, 106n1, 111, 115–16

Brokeback Mountain (Ang Lee, 2005) 144, 162, 164, 204, 298, 299

Brzeski, Patrick 248n60

Buchanan, Kyle 280

Buijsrogge, Bert 193n65

Bull, Clarence Sinclair 187

Busoni, Ferruccio 82, 153

Butler, Judith 217–18n28, 308n23

Butler, Rhett 188

C

Caillard, Leo 185

Cameron, Peter 44, 46

Caravaggio, Michelangelo Merisi da 25

Call Me by Your Name (film)

    Battle of Piave/confession scene 19, 24, 29, 64–67, 68–69, 96, 112–13, 119, *123*, 125, 140, 153

    cinematography 19, 22, 26, 28, 30, 44, 62, 65–69, 70, 72, 85, 91, 97–99, 110–13, 115–16, 119–22, 123–25, 137, 143, 157, 161, 162, 173, 176, 178, 181–84, 199–200, 203, 261

    digital fan art 8, 171, 181–82, 184–89

    end of relationship/final shot 20, 22–23, 28, 58, 66, 71–73, 85, *123*, 124–25, 135, 141–43, 182–84, *183*, 235, 280, 281, 294–95 *see also* Stevens, Sufjan – 'Visions of Gideon'

    ethics/the Other 7, 110–27, 204, 285, 287, 288–89, 291, 292, 295, 303, 305

    Isaac and Mounir 21–22, 25, 137, *138*, 153–54, 158, 163

    Italian politics 21, 22, 24–25, 27, 161

    Lake Garda sequence 5, 17, 19, 78, 99, 119, 160, 174, 176, 178, 179, 180–81, 182, 188, *258*

    Marzia 2, 8, 20, 21, 25, 62, 63, 69, 79, 95, 121–23, 131, 134, 137, 138, 140, 142–43, 145, 153, 159, 162, 179, 205, 206, 208–09, 212, 214, 270

    Monet's Berm/Elio and Oliver's first kiss 19, 20, 22, 24, *29*, 41, 42, 64–65, 67–69, *68*, 73, 79, 81, 95, 96–97, 105, *181*, *256*, *294*

    Mr Perlman 7, 17, 19, 22, 23, 25, 28, 72, 76, 78, 85, 99, 118, 119, 121, 131, 137, 140, 141, 144, 147n31, 153, 154, 158, 159, 163, 164, 173, 174, 176, 177, 179, 180, 188, 210, 243, 270, 277, 292

    Mrs Perlman 21, 58, 63, 65, 68, 80, 85, 119, 123, 125, 161, 164, 210, 304

    music 6, 19, 24–25, 28, 44–45, 46, 49n2, 64, 66, 74n29, 76–88, 92–93, 94, 95, 97, 110, 112, 120, 124, 125, 135–37, 142, 145n6, 153, 156, 163, 177, 180, 182–84, 231, 253, 254, 263–64 *see also* Adams, John; Lil Nas X; The Psychedelic Furs; Sakamoto, Ryuichi; Stevens, Sufjan

    opening titles 1, 8, 17, 35, 77, 124, 137, 160, 171, 173–76, *174*, 180, 270

    peach sequence 20, 21, 29, 42, 62, 69–71, *71*, 73, 99–102, *100*, 104, 156, 159, *160*, 165, 180, 201, 203, 210, 214, 259, 279, 300

    Perlmans' villa 17, 18–19, 20, 21–22, 23, 28, 35, 78, 79, 82, 84, 85, 94, 110, 121, 180, 183, 206, 214, 235, 277, 281

    representation of sex 6–8, 20–22, 25, 28, 29, 30, 43, 70, 91–109, 121–23, 131, 134, 138, 153, 156–57, 161, 162, 163, 178, 198–220, 279–80 *see also* peach sequence

    sound 5, 6, 7, 62, 64, 66, 70, 76–88, 91–109, 120, 125, 132, 135–37, 142, 180, 200, 293

    transnationalism 2, 7, 35, 132, 133, 210

Call Me by Your Name (novel) 1, 2, 6, 10, 17, 27, 34, 58, 59–74, 76, 77, 79–80, 83–84, 85, 86, 94, 101, 113, 117, 152, 153, 155, 156, 161, 164–65, 166n20, 166n23, 175, 179, 217n19, 234, 259, 274–75, 292

Canals, Steven 311

Cannon, Jonathan A. 9, 10

Canova, Antonio 178

Capotondi, Giuseppe 145n8

Capriolo, Vanda 58, *59*, 177

Carnicke, Sharon Marie 95

Carol (Todd Haynes, 2015) 144

Casar, Amira 21, *58*, 80, 119, *138*, 161, 177, 210, *277*

Cassel, Vincent 3

Catinari, Arnaldo 145n8

Cavalcanti, Gêsa 10, 308n36

Cavill, Henry 272, 276

Chalamet, Timothée 1, 3, *5*, 9, 17, *20*, *29*, 41, *42*, *46*, 49n2, *71*, 76, 91, *96*, *98*, *100*, *103*, 107n16, 110, *116*, *120*, *123*, 125, 131, *134*, *138*, 151, *160*, 171, 173, 174, 180, *181*, 182, 184, 185, *186*, 187, 188, 189, 199, *207*, *208*, *209*, 227, 253–64, *256*, *258*, 270, *277*, 280, 291, 292, *294*
    chemistry with Armie Hammer 253, 257–62, 272–73, *273*, 274
    on *Call Me by Your Name* 77, 176, 179, 180
    performance in *Call Me by Your Name* 6, 8, 58, *59*, *60*, 61, *63*, 64, 66, 68, 69, 70, 72, *78*, 85, 102, 106, 111, 113, 274
    physicality 153, 179, 181, *183*, 186, 187, 258
    physicality compared with that of Armie Hammer 25, 102, 152, *177*, 261
    social media 4, 9, 253–64

Champagne, John 25

Charioteer, The (Renault) 165

Cher 154

Cheung, Ruby 8–9, 245n16, 248n58

Children of Men (Alfonso Cuarón, 2006) 66

Christianity 155, 159, 163–64, 275

chrononormativity 7, 27, 118, 135–39, 141, 144

Circle of Bakhtin 286–288, 306n7, 306–07n12 *see also* Bakhtin, Mikhail

City of Your Final Destination, The (James Ivory, 2009) 40, 43–44, 46–47, 52n33

class 5, 10, 18, 37–39, 42, 43, 46, 53n44, 157, 162, 253, 261, 264, 274, 279, 288, 301, 307n12

classical antiquity *see* Graeco-Roman culture

Clueless (Amy Heckerling, 1995) 61

Columbia University 153

Conlon, Luisa 45

Connell, R.W. 282n5

Cooke, Paul 53n40

Costanzo, Anthony Roth 5, 45, *46*

Costanzo, Saverio 4

Corri, Nick 44

Cotroneo, Ivan 143, 144

Couët, Geoffrey 106n9

Craxi, Benedetto 'Bettino' 24, 161

Crema 17, 131

Cuarón, Alfonso 66, 209

Curto, Justin 267n38

D

Damshenas, Sam 266n30

Dardenne brothers, the 113–14

Dargis, Manohla 163

David and Jonathan 152, 164, 165

David, F. R. 206

Davis, Colin 114

Davis, Whitney 172

Dean, Tim 27

Death in Venice (*Der Tod in Venedig*, Mann) 151, 158, 165

Death on the Nile (Kenneth Branagh, 2022) 9, 281

Debruge, Peter 140–41, 245n8

DeGeneres, Ellen 10, 272–73, *273*

de la Iglesia, Eloy 209

de Laurentiis, Giada 133

de Lauretis, Teresa 286, 306n4

De, Madhubanti 40, 50n12, 50n13

de Navarre, Marguerite 80

Denby, David 282n9

Denis, Claire 114

Depp, Johnny 262, 272

Deschamps, Catherine 209

De Sica, Andrea 145n8

Desmas, Anne–Lise 192n54

De Valck, Marijke 232, 245n10–12

Devito, Federico 296, 297

DiCaprio, Leonardo 275, 277

Di Mattia, Joanna 58, 67, 94, 96, 157, 163

Diocles 31n3

Diodorus 156

Diputado, El (*Confessions of a Congressman*, Eloy de la Iglesia, 1978) 209

divo, Il (Paolo Sorrentino, 2008) 3

Dogman (Matteo Garrone, 2018) 3

Dolan, Xavier 102

Donne, John 160

Dover, Kenneth J. 165n5

Downing, Lisa 203

Downton Abbey 39

Driscoll, Catherine 133–34

du Bois, Victoire 79, 179, *208*

Duhamel, Josh 281

Duncan, Derek 145n7

Dune (Denis Villeneuve, 2021) 263

du Plessis, Michael 203

Dyer, Richard 61, 70, 172, 184, 192n48, 275

E

Eadie, Jo 211–12, 220n67

Eastwood, Clint 271–72, 274, 275, 276, 280

Edelman, Lee 147n36

Edgerton, Joel 157

Edison, Thomas 275

Eisner, Shiri 203, 216n8, 217n27

Ellen DeGeneres Show, The (TV) 10, 272–73, *273*

Ellen (TV, ABC, 1994–98) 272–73

Ellis, Brett Easton 163

Elsaesser, Thomas 145n6, 231–32, 245n12, 246n24

Endres, Nikolai 7–8, 26, 168n62, 175

Engelberg, Jacob 8

Erbland, Kate 247n46

Esposito, Joe 81

È stata la mano di Dio (*The Hand of God*, Paolo Sorrentino, 2021) 3

età di Cosimo de' Medici, L' (*The Age of the Medici*, Roberto Rossellini, 1973) 3

Europeans, The (James Ivory, 1979) 49n2

Everyday Italian (TV) 133

Ezra, Elizabeth 146n14

F

Facebook *see* social media

Fair Haven (Kertin Karlhuber, 2016) 157

Falchuk, Brad 311

Fallon, Jimmy 185–86, *186*

Fasano, Walter 112, 234

Fathom, Joey 185, 192n56

Ferrante, Elena 4

Ferreira, Vinicius 10, 306n2, 308n36, 309n50

Fife Donaldson, Lucy 92, 94

film festivals 8–9, 41, 45, 46, 48, 106n8, 180, 182, 185, 199, 227–49, 279

Fincher, David 271, 272, 274, 275

Finch, Mark 40

Find Me (Aciman) *see* Aciman, André

Fire from Heaven (Renault) 156

Flaubert, Gustave 290

Fone, Byrne R. S. 20, 31n5

Forster, E.M. 5, 37, 40, 42, 43, 48, 50n16, 51n24, 53n43, 165n1, 180

Foucault, Michel 164

Frantz, Natalie 265n8

Frater, Patrick 245n14

Free Fire (Ben Wheatley, 2016) 274, 276

Freeman, Elizabeth 27, 135–36, 137, 140

French Dispatch, The (Wes Anderson, 2021) 263

Freud, Sigmund 214, 220n64, 295

Fullmer, Chelsea 50n6

G

Gabbriellini, Edoardo 98

Gainsbourg, Charlotte 47

Galt, Rosalind 2–3, 118, 146n15, 180, 184, 200–01, 203, 217n13

Ganymede 152, 154

Garber, Marjorie 209

Garbo, Greta 187

Garrel, Esther 20, 62, 79, 95, 121, 131, *138*, 153, 179, 205, *207*, *209*, 270

Garrett, Stephen 32n23, 147n31

Garrone, Matteo 3

Gaudreault, André 201, 217n16

Gay Men's Health Crisis (GMHC) 26, 161

Genette, Gérard 60

Georges, Emilie 2

Gerwig, Greta 263

Gianelle, Zachary J. 156, 167n32

Giddens, Anthony 307n21

Gideon 72, 163

Gifford, Terry 18, 22, 24, 30

Gilbey, Ryan 266n19

Ginsburg, Martin 274, 276–77

Giordana, Marco Tullio 3

Giovannini, Joseph 49n5, 50n8

Girard, René 208, 218n40

Girodet de Roussy-Trioson, Anne-Louis 178

Godfrey, Patrick 51n27

God's Own Country (Francis Lee, 2017) 189, 289

Go Fish (Rose Troche, 1994) 91, 106

Gomorra (*Gomorrah*, Matteo Garrone, 2008) 3

Goodfellow, Melanie 245n13, 246n18

Grady, Constance 265n15

Graeco-Roman culture 17–18, 19–20, 25, 60, 151, 164, 172, 211, 264, 270
    sculpture 1, 8, 18, 19, 24–25, 119, 160, 171–82, *174*, *181*, 185–89, *186*, 258, 270
    sexuality 7–8, 25–26, 30, 60, 151–68, 175, 178

Graham, Billy 273, 275, 276

grande bellezza, La (*The Great Beauty*, Paolo Sorrentino, 2013) 3

Grant, Catherine 60

Grant, Hugh 37, *38*, *42*, 45, 53n43, 53n44, 180, 261, *294*

Grater, Tom 244n4

Graves, Rupert 37, *38*, 51n19, 51n22, 53n44

Gray, Billy 167n48

Gray, Tim 132, 144, 147n38

Grazer, Jack Dylan 115, 210

Greenwood, Douglas 263, 267n43

Greven, David 200, 202–03, 206

Greydanus, Steven D. 155

Grimaldi, Aurelio 25

Grindr 159

Grobar, Matt 247n46

Grønstad, Asbjørn 112, 115, 116, 120

Gruen, Samuel 45

Guadagnino, Luca 1, 2, 3–4, 5, 9, 17, 28, 34, 35, 36, 58, 86, 91, 106n3, 131, 133, 135, 137, 151, 152, 155, 156, 158, 159, 161, 162, 163–64, 171, 172, 179, 186, 198, 210, 227–28, 234, 235, 253, 254, 262, 263, 270, 272, 273, 275, 277, 279, 280, 285, 288, 292, 294, 309n37, 309n42
    'desire trilogy' 77, 81, 131, 227
    directorial style 7, 64, 72, 94, 97–98, 107n16, 110–12, 115, 116, 124, 157
    on bisexuality 199
    on *Call Me by Your Name* 27, 28, 77, 84, 110–11, 132, 156–57, 159, 234, 298

on working with Armie Hammer 278, 279, 280

use of music 66, 72, 76, 80–81, 83, 84, 85

Guru, The (James Ivory 1969) 52n33

H

Hackl, Cathy 245n15

Hadrian (Roman Emperor) 153, 173, 180

Haigh, Andrew 201

Halberstam, Jack 27, 92, 93, 136

Hallet, Marion 266n34

Halligan, Fionnuala 244n6

Hall, Stuart 306n3

Halperin, David M. 25, 168n57, 213, 220n58

Halpern Smith, Laurie 54n57

Hamid, Rahul 248n53

Hammer, Armie 1, 17, 20, 29, 41, 42, 58, 63, 71, 76, 78, 91, 98, 100, 102, 103, 110, 116, 120, 123, 131, 134, 151, 160, 171, 173, 174, 179, 181, 184–85, 199, 208, 209, 227, 256, 258, 264, 270–83, 276, 277, 292, 294

    chemistry with Timothée Chalamet 253, 257–62, 272–73, 273, 274

    controversy 9, 10, 254, 257, 261, 262, 264, 270–71, 280–81

    masculinity 10, 185, 275

    performance in *Call Me by Your Name* 8, 66, 69, 106

    physicality compared with that of Timothée Chalamet 25, 102, 152, 177, 261

    social media 9, 262, 264

Hammer, Julian Armand 271

Hammer, Michael Armand 271

Hanukkah 23, 72, 85, 124, 159

Haring, Keith 161

Harmodius 152

Harrod, Mary 2

Harvard University 153

Harvey, Stephen 50n11

Haskell, Molly 112, 115, 117, 160, 185

Haydn, Joseph 153

Hayek, Salma 3

Haynes, Todd 52n33, 144

Healy, Claire Marie 52n38, 53n41

Heckerling, Amy 61

Hedwig and the Angry Inch (musical) 69, 74n29

Heise, William 275

Hemmings, Clare 209, 212, 218n29

Henderson, John 189

Hephaestion 156, 164

Heptaméron (de Navarre) 80

Heraclitus 151, 153, 160, 165

Herring, Scott 31n6

Hershey, Barbara 45

Hesketh-Harvey, Kit 51n24

Hesse, Monica 282

HIV *see* AIDS

Hoje Eu Quero Voltar Sozinho (*The Way He Looks*, Daniel Ribeiro, 2014) 289, 299, 301

Holdaway, Dom 145–46n8, 146n17

Hole, Kristin Lené 114, 124, 125–26

Hollinghurst, Alan 213

homophobia 22, 37, 46, 153–54, 165, 184, 200, 201, 202, 263, 293, 300, 304

Hoover, J. Edgar 275–76

Hopkins, Anthony 47

Horowitz, Jake 107n16

Householder, The (James Ivory, 1963) 49n2

Howard, Adam Coleman 44

Howards End (James Ivory, 1992) 40, 49n1

Hunt, Katie 248n61

Hutchinson, Pamela 88n24, 161, 166n27, 167n37

Huyssen, Andreas 306n6

I

In & Out (Frank Oz, 1997) 204
Inconnu du lac, L' (*Stranger by the Lake*,
    Alain Guiraudie, 2013) 93, 106n8
Incredibly True Adventure of Two Girls in
    Love, The (Maria Maggenti, 1995) 204
India 34, 40, 49n2
Instagram *see* social media
Iordanova, Dina 232, 233, 246n29, 246n32,
    246n33, 246n35
Io sono l'amore (*I Am Love*, Luca Guadag-
    nino, 2009) 3, 77, 97–98, 227
Irigaray, Luce 209
Ishiguro, Kazuo 40
Isolde 152
Ivory, James 1, 2, 5, 34–54, 64, 76, 83,
    155, 162, 179, 180, 188, 234, 280, 294,
    309n37

J

J'ai pas sommeil (*I Can't Sleep*, Claire Denis,
    1994) 114, 126
James, Lily 279
Jameson, Fredric 307n20
Janowitz, Tama 44
J. Edgar (Clint Eastwood, 2011) 274,
    275–76, 277, 280, 281
Jenkins, Barry 144, 178, 189, 298
Jenkins, Henry 185, 192n56
Jhabvala, Cyrus 49n2
Jhabvala, Ruth Prawer 34, 37, 40, 44, 46,
    49n1, 49n2, 51n27
Jones, Felicity 272, 277
Jones, James 44, 45
Jones, Kaylie 44
Jones, Toby 3
Jourdan, Adam 248n60
Journey of Jared Price, The (Dustin Lance
    Black, 2000) 276
Judaism 2, 47, 49n2, 124, 163–64, 227

K

Karlhuber, Kerstion 157
Kapoor, Shashi 49n2
Keats, Amanda 165
Keightley, Emily 304, 309n47
Kempley, Rita 50n11
Kerbrat-Orecchioni, Catherine 217n16
Kiarostami, Abbas 115
Kies, Bridget 289, 307n17, 307n18
Kill Your Darlings (John Krokidas, 2013) 201
Kilpatrick, Emily 80
Kiss Kiss Bang Bang (Shane Black, 2005) 61
Kiss, The (William Heise, 1896) 275
Kline, Kevin 204
Kohn, Eric 246n18
Kooijman, Jaap 259
Kornhaber, Spencer 32n26, 147n31, 167n44
Kramer, Larry 161
Kristofferson, Kris 45
Krokidas, John 201
Kwietniowski, Richard 40

L

Lady Bird (Greta Gerwig, 2017) 263
Lamartire, Letizia 145n8
Lamberti, Edward 7
Lam, Celia 255, 260
Lamour, Dorothy 275
Lane, Anthony 207–08
Lannan, Michael 311
Lanzmann, Claude 229
Laplante, André 66, 67
Lara, Alexandra Maria 47
Larson, Brie 276
Larson, Sarah 50n15, 51n22, 52n30
Law, Jude 4
Leder, Mimi 274
Lee, Ang 144, 204, 299
Lee, Ashley 145n4, 247n43
Lee, Francis 189, 289

Le Fanu, Mark 65

Lehman, Peter 282n21

Levi, Carlo 153

Levinas, Emmanuel 7, 113–15, 118, 124, 127n33

Levy, Emanuel 247n41

Lewis, Jon 216n10

LGBTQ+/queer cinema 1–2, 4, 5, 9, 36, 40, 41, 47–48, 131, 144, 157, 159, 162, 228, 235, 243, 248n62, 276, 294, 299–304, 307n16

Li, Chen 173

Life Aquatic with Steve Zissou, The (Wes Anderson, 2004) 83

Lil Nas X 9, 254, 263–64, 267n44

Linney, Laura 47

Li, Pei 248n60

Liszt, Franz 82, 153

Little Women (Greta Gerwig, 2019) 263

Liz, Mariana 2

Lodge, Guy 106n1, 200

Loist, Skadi 245n10

London 39, 49n2, 163

Lone Ranger, The (Gore Verbinski, 2013) 274

Long, Robert Emmet 44, 50n8

Looking (TV, Michael Lannan, creator, 2014–16) 289

Lopez, Jennifer 281

Los Angeles 272

Losh, Elizabeth 183

Lovelock, Michael 182

Love, Simon (Greg Berlanti, 2018) 289

Lowenthal, David 174

Luchetti, Daniele 4

Lu, Shen 248n61

Lynch, David 204

M

Madame Bovary (Flaubert) 290

Madsen, Krista 50n8

Maggenti, Maria 204

Magnan-Park, Aaron Han Joon 248n58

Malick, Terrence 61

Malparte 176

Malraux, André 174

Man from U.N.C.L.E., The (Guy Ritchie, 2015) 274, 276

Mann, Thomas 165n1

Mapplethorpe, Robert 30

Marchetti, Gina 248n58

Marcus, Laura 179

Marshall, Kingsley 6, 180

Mars-Jones, Adam 99

Martin Jr., Alfred L. 259

Marx, Leo 30

Matthias & Maxime (Xavier Dolan, 2019) 102

Maurice (James Ivory, 1987) 5, 35, 36–48, *38*, 41, 42, 49n2, 51n19–27, 52n29, 52–53n40, 53n42–44, 180, 181, 188, *294*
    comparison to *Call Me by Your Name* 41–43, *42*, 47–48, 294
    novel (Forster) 5, 37, 43, 48, 50n16, 51n24, 151, 165

McCallum, David 276

McCaughan, Charles 44

McCormack, Eric 259

McFarling, Tina 54n55

McLaren, Bonnie 266n17

Medhurst, Andy 92, 101–02

meglio gioventù, La (*The Best of Youth*, Marco Tullio Giordana, 2003) 3

Melissa P. (Luca Guadagnino, 2005) 3

Melnikova, Irina 81–82, 88n19

Merchant, Ismail 5, 34–54, 162

Merchant Ivory Productions 34–48, 162, 180
    as queer filmmakers 36–41, 44, 45, 48n1

Messina, Piero 145n8

Metwally, Omar 47

Metzger, Radley 107n16

Michelangelo 152, 185, 186, 187

Mieli, Mario 214–16, 220n64

Milk (Gus Van Sant, 2008) 276

Miller, D. A. 8, 131, 143, 158–59, 198, 200, 201–02, 206, 213, 214

Miller, Julie 265n13

Miller, Mike 278

Mirell, Barb 4, 167n46, 193n68

Mitchell, John Cameron 74n29

Mitchell, Ty 104

Mittel, Jason 266n23

Miz Cracker 106n1, 131, 132, 144, 198

Molaioli, Andrea 145n8

Monk, Claire 5, 50n12, 50n17, 51n22, 52n28, 52–53n40, 53n46, 162, 181, 188

Moonlight (Barry Jenkins, 2016) 144, 178, 189, 298, 299–300, 301

Moore, Jason 281

Morabito, Marco 2

Morin, Natalie 267n39

Mowlabocus, Sharif 92, 101–02

Mozart, Wolfgang Amadeus 45

Mr. & Mrs. Bridge (James Ivory, 1990) 46, 52n33

Muino, Tanu 267n44

Mukdeeprom, Sayombhu 110–11, 112

Mulholland Drive (David Lynch, 2001) 204

Mumbai 35

Munzenrieder, Kyle 256–57, 265n10, 265n11

Murphy, Ryan 311

Mussolini, Benito 21

N

Nambot, François 106n9

Nancy, Jean-Luc 115

Naples 164

Narcissus and Echo 156

Nautiyal, Jaishikha 210

Neale, Steve 146n20

Né Giulietta né Romeo (*A Little Lust*, Veronica Pivetti, 2015) 132, 143, 144

Negri, Anna 145n8

Newman, Michael Z. 132–33

Newman, Paul 52n33

New Pope, The (TV, Paolo Sorrentino, 2020) 4

New York 26, 34, 36, 39, 44, 45, 48, 49n2, 157, 272, 275

Nicholls, Phoebe 37

Nichols, Bill 231, 246n21

Niemeyer, Katharina 291, 308n26, 308n28, 308n30

Nightingale, Benedict 48

Nissinen, Martti 168n55

Norton, Rictor 31n3

nostalgia 17, 24–25, 26, 81, 137, 139–41, 142, 143, 161–63, 164, 178, 285–86, 289, 290–91, 304, 305, 309n37 *see also* queer nostalgia

Novarro, Ramón 173, 175

O

Obama, Barack 260–61

Oceano, Nick 276

Omnes, Yves-Marie 106n3

On the Basis of Sex (Mimi Leder, 2018) 274, 277

Oscars *see* Academy Awards

Ovid 69, 156

Oz, Frank 204

Özpetek, Fernan 132

Ozu, Yasujirô 111–12

P

Padva, Gilad 139, 291, 306n1, 308n29, 308n30

paiderastia 152–53, 155, 157–59, 164, 165n4

Paoletti, John T. 186, 187

Paris 39, 44, 45, 93, 163, 164

Parker, Nicole Ari 204

Pasolini, Pier Paolo 147n33

pastoral 5, 17–32, 178

Patroclus 152

Paul, Daniel 7, 118, 147n39

Paul, Nildeep 40, 50n12, 50n13

Pazzagli, Leonardo 143

Pear, Robert 167n41

Pedro (Nick Oceano, 2008) 276

Persian Boy, The (Renault) 156

Persona (Ingmar Bergman, 1966) 204

Peters, Bernadette 44

Petrey, Sandy 127n31

Petronius Arbiter, Gaius 211, 219n49

Phaedrus (Plato) 151, 154–55, 158, 161,
    163, 164, 165

philosophy 19, 111–12, 125–26, 152, 154,
    154–57, 160, 165 *see also Call Me by
    Your Name*
        (film) – ethics/the Other; Levinas,
        Emmanuel

Pickering, Michael 304, 309n47

Picture of Dorian Gray, The (Wilde) 151,
    160, 165

Pierce-Roberts, Tony 45

Pink Popcorn 296, 298–99, *298*

Pinocchio (Matteo Garrone, 2019) 3

Pinterest *see* social media

Pitch Perfect (Jason Moore, 2012) 281

Pivetti, Veronica 132

Placido, Michele 145n8

Plato 7, 69, 151, 152, 154–55, 156–59, 161,
    163, 164, 165, 174, 179

Podolsky, Robin 114, 115, 127n22

Pollacchi, Elena 243–44, 249n63

Pose (TV, 2018–21) 289

Pourquoi pas! (*Why Not!*, Coline Serreau,
    1977) 209

Poussin, Nicolas 18

Pramaggiore, Maria 209

Praxiteles 160, 176, 180

Promesse, La (*The Promise*, Luc and Jean-
    Pierre Dardenne, 1996) 113–14

Psychedelic Furs, The 23, 81, 85, 124

Puccini, Giacomo 25

Pym, John 52n34

Q

queer nostalgia 10, 139, 285–309 *see also*
    nostalgia

Quick, Tyler 167n46, 191n37

R

race 10, 186, 260–61, 263–64, 272, 274,
    275, 279, 288, 305, 306–07n12

Radin, Victoria 54n56

Ramsey, Carol 45

Raphael, Jackie 255, 260

Ratskoff, Ben 198, 200

Ravel, Maurice 66, 80

Rawle, Steven 133

Raykoff, Ivan 78

Reagan, Ronald 27, 159

Reality (Matteo Garrone, 2012) 3

Rebecca (Ben Wheatley, 2020) 279

Reilly, John C. 3

Remains of the Day, The (James Ivory,
    1993) 40, 48–49n1, 52n33

Renault, Mary 151, 156, 165

Renoir, Jean 111

Rhyne, Ragan 245n16, 246n28, 248n53

Ribeiro, Ana Paula Goulart 306n2, 307n19,
    308n26, 309n50

Ribeiro, Daniel 289

Richards, Stuart 6

Rich, B. Ruby 4–5, 10, 159

Richlin, Amy 164–65

Rigoletto, Sergio 145n7

Riley, Daniel 267n40

Ritchie, Guy 271, 274
Ritzberger Grillo, Rimau 143
Rivaroli, Anita 145n8
Robbins, Richard 34, 45, 49n2
Roberts, Beth Carol 205, 206–07
Robinson, Luke 249n65
Rocky Horror Picture Show, The (Jim Sharman, 1975) 39
Roden, Frederick S 163
Rodriguez, Karla 265n16
Rogers, Nathaniel 41, 49n3, 52n36
Rohmer, Éric 111
Rohrwacher, Alice 4
romance 1, 3, 4–5, 7, 8, 10, 17, 28, 36, 37, 48, 58, 72, 93, 110, 117, 118, 119–21, 125, 131, 132, 134, 135, 151, 164, 171, 178, 198, 235, 273, 274, 275, 278, 278, 279, 280, 289, 290, 292–94, 300, 303, 305, 309n37
Romani, Valentina 143
Rome 17, 69, 156, 157, 164–65, 172, 175, 177, 180, 187, 234 *see also* Ancient Rome
Romney, Jonathan 2
Ronan, Joseph 213, 218n31
Room with a View, A (James Ivory, 1985) 36–37, 40, 45, 48–49n1, 51n19, 52n33, 180
Rosenbaum, Jonathan 232
Rosenman, Howard 2, 34
Rossellini, Roberto 3
Rowden, Terry 146n14
Rubin, Gayle 309n45
Russell, Taylor 107n16
Rutherford, Emily 155, 156

S

Sakamoto, Ryuichi 64, 77
Saketopoulou, Avgi 104
Sala, Ilaria Maria 248n61
Sanada, Hiroyuki 47
Sands, Julian 51n19

San Filippo, Maria 204, 209, 212
San Francisco 161, 163
Sappho 151, 159, 165
Sarris, Andrew 50n11
Satie, Erik 82
Saturno contro (*Saturn in Opposition,* Ferzan Özpetek, 2007) 132
Satyricon, The (Petronius) 211, 219n49
Savages (James Ivory, 1972) 36
Schlichte, Garrett 198
Schlude, Victor 10
Schoenaerts, Matthias 98
Schoonover, Karl 2–3, 118, 146n15, 180, 184, 200–01, 203, 217n13
Scott, Mathew 248n62
Seamón, Jordan Kristine 210
Section 28, 39
Sedgwick, Eve Kosofsky 212
Seifert, Steve 39, 52n29
Sense8 (TV, 2015–18) 289
Serra, Paolla 308n31
Serreau, Coline 209
Sevigny, Chloë 115
sexuality 4, 7, 8, 21, 23–24, 25–26, 30, 36, 45, 79, 81, 104, 105, 132, 135, 140, 155, 159, 162, 198, 200, 202, 203, 204, 208, 209, 210, 213, 215, 218n32, 219n45, 219n49, 253, 258, 264, 265n1, 274, 281, 285, 289, 290, 304, 305, 307n13
    bisexual 8, 25, 146n17, 156, 158, 159, 163, 198–220, 274, 298, 302
    heterosexual/straight 1, 8, 10, 25, 36, 37, 38–39, 44, 51n19, 51n24, 121, 122, 123, 131, 132, 134, 135, 136, 138, 140, 142, 143, 144–45, 147n35, 153, 156, 176, 183, 185, 198–99, 201, 202, 203–08, 212–16, 216n5, 259, 263, 273, 274, 279, 280, 288, 290, 299, 300, 301, 302, 304–05, 307n15, 308n23

heteronormativity 7, 36, 118, 122, 132, 135, 136, 138, 139, 141, 144, 147n33, 214, 258, 280, 290, 300, 308n23

sexual identity 1, 18, 25, 134, 135, 163, 214, 286, 307n15

lesbian 36, 91, 218n29, 272

masturbation 8, 28, 29, 153, 178

see also Graeco-Roman culture; queer nostalgia

Shakespeare, William 152, 160

Sharf, Zack 245n15, 279–80, 282n19

Sharman, Jim 56

Shelley, Mary 66

Shelley, Percy Bysse 66

Sherman, John 190n13, 192n53

Shilts, Randy 26, 31n14, 31n18, 31n19

Shim, Minhae 247n50

Shoah (Claude Lanzmann, 1985) 229

Shotgun Wedding (Jason Moore, 2022) 281

Shuttleton, David 20, 31n4

Sigliano, Daiane 308n36

Sinnerbrink, Robert 113–14

Sisters (Jason Moore, 2015) 281

Sisygambis (Persian Queen) 156

Sivan, Troye 182–84, *183*, 186

SKAM Italia (TV, 2018–present) 145n8

Slaves of New York (James Ivory, 1989) 5, 43–45, 52n33

slow cinema 112, 115, 116

Smith, Dinitia 49n2

Sobande, Francesca 9–10, 179, 257–58, 260–61, 265n1, 265n4

Sobchack, Vivian 103

Sobieski, Leelee 45

social media 4, 9, 41, 43, 48, 49n2, 171, 181–89, 253–67, 271, 281, 287, 291

Facebook 188, 193n68, 193n72, 275, 291, 292

Instagram 49n2, 182, 185, 186, 187, 192n56, 254, 255–56, 259, 266n24, 266n25, 281

Pinterest 187, 188, 254

Twitter/X 152, 187, 188, 253, 281, 291, 308n32

YouTube 10, 43, 171, 182, 183, 184, 185, 186, 260, 286, 287–88, 292, 295–304, 305, 306n5, 307

Social Network, The (David Fincher, 2010) 271, 273–74, 275, 278, 279

Socrates 153, 154–55, 158, 160, 163, 164

Sodom and Gomorrah 163–64, 165

Soldier's Daughter Never Cries, A (James Ivory, 1998) 5, 43, 44, 45–46, *46*, 52n33

Sontag, Susan 104

Sorrentino, Paolo 3, 4

Sorrentino, Renee 156, 157

Soucy, Stephen 49n2

Speak Like a Child (John Akomfrah, 1998) 209

Spears, Peter 2, 34, *138*, 158

Speidel, Suzanne 37

Spenser, Edmund 31n3

Sprouse, Stephen 45

Stambrini, Monica 132

Stam, Robert 60, 286, 288, 304, 306n8, 307n14, 309n49

stardom and celebrity 4, 6, 8, 9, 10, 60, 93, 171–73, 175, 177, 179, 181–89, 232, 234, 253–64, 270–81

Stark, John 50n10

Star of David 151, 164

Stevens, Benjamin Eldon 153, 175, 178

Stevens, Sufjan 2, 6, 66, 72, 80, 83–86, 95, 175, 178

'Futile Devices' 79–80, 86

'Mystery of Love' 2, 76, 85, 120, 156, 184, 188

'Visions of Gideon' 72, 85, 125, 142, 163, 182

Stone, Oliver 156

Stone, Rob 53n40

Straczynski, J. Michael 311

Stranger's Child, The (Hollinghurst) 213

Strategia del ragno (*The Spider's Stratagem*, Bernardo Bertolucci, 1970) 3

Stuhlbarg, Michael 7, 17, 19, 76, 99, 118, 131, 153, 173, 174, 210, 270, 292

Suburra: Blood on Rome (TV, 2017–20) 145n8

Supremes, The 44

Suspiria (Dario Argento, 1977) 3

Suspiria (Luca Guadagnino, 2018) 3, 106n3

Sutton, Emma 50n17

Swanson, Gloria 173, 187

Swinton, Tilda 77, 97–98

Symposium (Plato) 69, 151, 158, 167n32

T

Talking Heads 76, 185

Tan See Kam 248n58

Teixeira, Rodrigo 2

Thatcher, Margaret 27, 39

Theocritus 18, 31n3

Théo et Hugo dans le même bateau (*Theo and Hugo*, Olivier Ducastel and Jacques Martineau, 2016) 93, 106n9

This Must Be the Place (Paolo Sorrentino, 2011) 3

Thompson, Anne 76, 86n1

Timoshkina, Alissa 2

Tolson, Clyde 274, 275–76, 280

Tonight Show Starring Jimmy Fallon, The (TV) 185–86

Tramontana, Mary Katharine 216n6

Trask, Stephen 74n29

Travolta, John 179

Tristan 153

Troche, Rose 91

Tsai, Tsung-Han 50n17

Turban, Jack 156, 157

Turk, Tisha 189

Turner, Kyle 111, 119

Twitter/X *see* social media

Tyler, the Creator 253

Tzioumakis, Yannis 247n41

U

Udden, James 66

Ultra Violet 36

Urdang, Robin 76, 78

Uruguay 47

V

Van Groeningen, Felix 185, 263

van Harten, Zora 80, 87n14

Van Hoeij, Boyd 245n7

Van Sant, Gus 276

Vaughan, Adam 5

Venice 164

Venus 19, 160, 180, 187

Verbinski, Gore 271, 274

Vernallis, Carol 187, 193n63

Vidal, Gore 151, 165

Villeneuve, Denis 263

Virgil 18

Vivarelli, Nick 245n13, 279, 282n14, 282n15

Voloshinov, Valentin N. 288, 306n7, 306n9, 306n11, 306–07n12

W

Wachowskis, the 311

Wagmeister, Elizabeth 271

Walker, Alexander 53n43, 53n44

Warhol, Andy 36, 44, 45

Watteau, Jean-Antoine 18

Waugh, Thomas 50n11, 53n43, 53n44

We Are Who We Are (TV, Luca Guadagnino, 2020) 3–4, 115, 210

Weaver, Hilary 193n70

Weekend (Andrew Haigh, 2001) 201

Wei, John 182, 191n38

Wenning, Katherine 44, 45

West III, Thomas J. 289, 307n17, 307n18

Weston, Hillary 110, 111

Wheatley, Ben 274, 279

White, Armond 162

White Countess, The (James Ivory 2005) 40,
    49n2

White, Edmund 161

Wilby, James 37, *38*, 42, 45, 51n19, 51n22,
    180, *294*

Wilde, Oscar 151, 152, 164, 165

Wild Party, The (James Ivory, 1975) 52n33

Will and Grace 259

Williams, Craig A. 168n58

Williams, Jenessa 267n45

Williams, Linda 93, 94, 102

Williams, Michael 8, 19, 190n5, 190n6,
    190n7, 191n34

Williams, Raymond 24

Winklevoss twins (Cameron and Tyler)
    273–74, 275

Wong, Cindy Hing-Yuk 233, 244n2,
    247n36, 247n37, 247n38

Wong, Curtis M. 191n39

Woods, James 152

Woodward, Joanne 52n33

Wright Wexman, Virginia 218n30

X

Ximénez, Mario 32n25

X/Twitter *see* social media

Y

Yahweh 163

York, Lorraine 254, 265n2

Yoshino, Kenji 212

Yotka, Steff 266n36

Young Pope, The (TV, Paolo Sorrentino,
    2016) 4

Youth (Paolo Sorrentino, 2015) 3

YouTube *see* social media

Y tu mamá también (*And Your Mother Too*,
    Alfonso Cuarón, 2001) 209

Z

Zeus 69, 152, 154

Žižek, Slavoj 298, 309n42

Zuckerberg, Mark 275